From the Reviews

"Thompson brings just the right mix of strengths: historian, biblical scholar, essayist of international breadth, and keen observer of current events. He seems equally at home in the 11th and the 20th centuries, equally comfortable in America, Europe, and Asia, and equally conversant with the arcana of Catholic theology and the menace of the American militia movement . . . [This] superb overview of the nature of apocalyptic thinking and its importance to human behavior provides insight into and context for the disturbing millennial events of recent vintage, and helps us prepare for the next two years, when even crazier events may take place."

—James Reston, Jr., *Wilson Quarterly*

A "fascinating, unsettling yet sympathetic study of millenarianism."

—*New York Times Book Review*

"As a recent religious affairs correspondent for *The Daily Telegraph,* Thompson is close to the pulse of contemporary End of Time movements: Waco, Heaven's Gate, New Age, the Tokyo Aum Shinrikyo sect. This fine history now furnishes both a thoughtful look at earlier millenarian upswellings and a fascinating worldscape of contemporary phenomena as they intensify with the approach of the year 2000. What were people's responses to the coming and passing of the year 1000, when no one wore watches and few people were even aware of what year it was? Why have movements which herald the end of time and the birth of a new age occurred in relation to some natural and economic disasters and not to others? How have people responded to the disappointment of the many unfulfilled millenarian prophecies and what will happen when current prophecies do not unfold as expected? Informative and engrossing."

—*NAPRA ReView*

"Well written, well researched, and entertaining, this is highly recommended for all libraries."

—*Library Journal*

"In the bodies of the Heaven's Gate suicides and in the rubble of the Oklahoma City federal building, Thompson detects the destructive work of men impassioned by an ancient yet perilously potent vision of a calamitous apocalypse followed by a heavenly millennium of peace and enlightenment. This cultural history informed by rare theological understanding first identifies the Zoroastrian, Hebrew, and Christian origins of millennarian and apocalyptic beliefs, then explores the repeated sociopolitical eruptions caused by these volatile beliefs. It may surprise many to learn that the Branch Davidians killed in Waco were acting out a tragic script that cost hundreds of peasants their lives in sixteenth-century Europe. Similarly, Thompson shows that Nazism and Marxism both drew much of their power from secularized versions of millennarian beliefs. And despite the defeat of both those ideologies, such beliefs continue to haunt Japan, Korea, and most of all, the U.S., where Baptist preachers and New Age gurus alike anticipate the year 2000 with a strange combination of foreboding and hope. An insightful book of compelling timeliness."

—*Booklist*

"Thompson's extraordinary book is literally a revelation, a detailed map of the battle-plan of Armageddon that serves as a guidebook to the Heavens and the Hells . . . a superb and often breathtaking account."

—J. G. Ballard, *Daily Telegraph*

The End of Time

DAMIAN THOMPSON

The End of Time

*Faith and Fear in
the Shadow of the Millennium*

UNIVERSITY PRESS OF NEW ENGLAND
Hanover and London

To my mother
and in memory of
my father

UNIVERSITY PRESS OF NEW ENGLAND,
Hanover, NH 03755

Copyright © 1996 by Damian Thompson

Originally published in 1996 by Sinclair-Stevenson, London.
University Press of New England edition 1997.
First University Press of New England paperback edition 1998.

Printed in the United States of America   5   4   3   2

CIP data appear at the end of the book

Contents

Acknowledgements

Many people have shown me extraordinary kindness during the course of the year I spent writing this book. Perhaps my greatest debt is to two distinguished millennial scholars: Stephen O'Leary, who gave me a free run of his remarkable library in Los Angeles; and Richard Landes, who allowed me to plunder his ground-breaking research into the year 1000 before it was published. Neither Stephen nor Richard had anything to gain by welcoming an amateur who was effectively trespassing on their territory; I was deeply touched by their unselfishness and hospitality, and also that of Stephen's wife, Mary Rose.

I have almost lost count of the academics, fellow journalists and friends who offered me help and advice. They include Eileen Barker and the staff of INFORM, Brenda Brasher, Andrew Brown, Clive Calver and Keith Ewing of the Evangelical Alliance, Susannah Herbert, Peter Jones, Koko Kawanami, Rosamond McKitterick, John Martin, J. Gordon Melton, David Orton, Josh Parr, Michael Walsh, Richard West, Robert Whelan, Dennis Whyte, and Alexandra Wyke (who first encouraged me to write about the millennium). In South Korea, I was offered splendid hospitality by Brothers Bernardin and Patrick of the Franciscan Capuchin Friars of Seoul, whose undemonstrative Christian witness is in such refreshing contrast to the activities of the local Pentecostalists. In Japan, I was lucky enough to stay with one of the most original essayists of our time, Murray Sayle; he and his wife, Jenny, provided many fascinating insights into life in their adopted country.

My closest friends have acceded patiently to my insistent requests that they read and comment on the manuscript. Tim Wong and Cristina

Acknowledgements

Odone offered unflagging moral support; Brian Brindley ruthlessly excised stylistic howlers; Tony Trowbridge came to the rescue many times with his encyclopaedic knowledge and candid advice.

I would also like to thank my agent Simon Trewin, without whose enthusiasm this book would not have been written; Benita Edzard, William Miller, Junzo Sawa and Katsuyuki Isoo; and finally my editor at Sinclair-Stevenson, Neil Taylor. Working with him has been one of the great pleasures of the past year.

Introduction

An Anglo-Saxon monk called Byrhtferth once observed that one thousand, or rather M, should be regarded as a 'perfect number'. Writing soon after the year 1000, he based his argument on the theory that the history of the world had been divided by God into consecutive periods of a thousand years each. But, he added helpfully, 'these ages did not consist of perfect numbers of years'. Some were longer than others.[1]

Confusion about the meaning of the millennium is an enduring feature of Western civilisation, and the predictable reawakening of interest in the subject during the 1990s has done little to clear it up. Most people are aware that there is more to the millennium than the mere passing of 1,000 years. They do not need to be told that the crossing of such a barrier has psychological ramifications, and they may already feel mild twinges of that anxiety and excitement which the media has dubbed 'Pre-Millennial Tension'. They also know that it is associated with outlandish behaviour on the part of groups labelled 'millenarian'. But they are often surprised to learn that the Millennium (with a capital M) is used as a technical term by theologians and social scientists, and that it has nothing to do with the date. Furthermore, very few of those movements which history calls millenarian have been inspired by the years 1000 or 2000.

So what, precisely, is a millenarian? Used in its strictest sense, the word applies to people who live in daily anticipation of the dawn of the 'Millennium' described in the Book of Revelation, the last book of the New Testament. This text, otherwise known as the Book of the Apocalypse, is the last and most controversial book of the New

Testament: it consists of a series of fantastic visions of the End of Time in which the forces of Christ and Satan do battle amid scenes of stomach-churning violence and cruelty. Towards the end of the book, the battle ceases for a period of a thousand years, during which Satan is caged and Christ and his saints reign on earth. This is the Millennium, and those believers who expect this thousand-year paradise to dawn at any moment are therefore millenarians.

As the study of human behaviour evolved, it became clear that, although belief in an imminent new world seems to result in specific patterns of behaviour, the phenomenon is not confined to literal belief in the Millennium of Revelation. Some social scientists prefer to use the term 'chiliasm' (from the Greek word for thousand) to describe Christian millenarianism which is inspired directly by the Book of Revelation. We need not worry too much about this distinction; but we should take on board the general point that millenarianism can incorporate the ideas of almost any religion and, indeed, those of secular ideology. Modern sociologists cheerfully apply the word millenarian to groups ranging from Islamic Mahdist movements to Melanesian cargo cults. There is also widespread support for Norman Cohn's suggestion that both Marxism and Nazism represent forms of secular millenarianism. They certainly appear to fit the definition of the phenomenon in the *American Encyclopaedia of Religion* as 'a belief that the end of the world is at hand and that in its wake will appear a New World, inexhaustibly fertile, harmonious, sanctified, and just'. (Millenarian conceptions of justice, it need hardly be said, are not those of the International Court of Human Rights.)

The history of the past 2,000 years suggests that people who believe that their world is moving inexorably towards a total and miraculous transformation, in which old scores will be settled and the Elect rewarded, will react along broadly similar lines. All millenarian movements are distinguished by the abnormal behaviour of their adherents, which can range from retreat to the wilderness to await the End to acts of unimaginable violence designed to bring it about. Either way, there is a tremendous release of emotional energy which gives these movements a sense of mission. The same patterns crop up in movements separated by vast stretches of space and time. There is a pronounced tendency, for example, for millenarian groups to veer towards extreme attitudes to sexual behaviour, in which sex is either forbidden or to be enjoyed indiscriminately. The millenarian sense of identity, too, is distinctive. It invariably possesses a narcissistic, self-righteous quality – and small wonder, since these groups believe that only they will witness, and *survive*, the End. It is also paranoid. As the American historian Richard Landes argues: 'Anyone or any group so instrumental in the final battle must expect the ubiquitous forces of evil to target them particularly.'[2]

The fanatical behaviour of millenarians, therefore, is intimately connected to their distinctive beliefs. But sociologists and historians are often far more interested in why such movements arise than in the (to them) distasteful details of their eschatological fantasies. And this is where they cannot agree. There have been attempts to cast all millenarians in the role of proto-revolutionaries. The phrase 'relative deprivation' is employed to describe the economic imbalance leading the dispossessed to develop uncontrollable resentments against the established order which are then channelled not into political activism but into fantasies of invulnerability and escape. There is a school of thought which insists that millenarianism always springs from the clash of cultures, one technologically superior to the other. Another theory focusses on natural and economic disasters, which it maintains are the only phenomena sufficiently disorientating to produce millenarianism.

All these theories marshal evidence from widely differing cultures. The disaster school, for example, points to the reappearance of processions of revolutionary flagellants immediately after the outbreak of the Black Death, and to the military defeat and forced migration which preceded the American Indian Ghost Dance. The latter, though, fits equally easily into the theory based on the clash of cultures. The point is that these supposedly rival theories of millenarianism are not always mutually exclusive. And nor, it should be said, are any of them entirely satisfactory. Why were millenarian movements thrown up by drought in late-nineteenth-century Brazil, but not by the infinitely more severe Irish potato famine? By the Tokyo earthquake of 1923 but not by the Second World War? Perhaps the notion of a unified theory of millenarianism is as illusory, and as outdated, as the comprehensive theory of historical development.

Yet it would be ludicrous to deny that political and economic change cannot be the major factor in producing this strange mind-set. Psychological studies of people caught up in millenarian movements suggest that they do not attract a significantly higher proportion of the mentally ill than conventional religions or political parties. We can therefore hardly escape the conclusion that millenarianism often arises from feelings of deprivation in matters of status, wealth, security or self-esteem. Furthermore, it will tend to spring up during periods of crisis, which, in the words of one commentator, can be 'as blatant and acute as the sack of a city or as subtle and prolonged as the passage from isolated agrarian community to industrial megopolis'.[3] In other words, it can occur at almost any time, anywhere.

The real problem with theories of millenarianism is the narrowness of the concept itself. It is not quite the same thing as apocalyptic belief, which maintains that mankind is nearing the End of the World as we know it but does not necessarily imagine a violent or sudden change. All millenarianism is apocalyptic (from the Greek word meaning 'to unveil'), but all apocalyptic belief is not millenarian: far from it. Classic millenarians, from self-flagellating medieval peasants to Sioux Ghost Dancers, are often people who, if not clinically mad, have reached what George Rosen has called 'the wilder shores of sanity'. They are relatively easy to distinguish from the population at large, and never more so than at the moment. We see this in the disturbing phenomenon of doomsday cults and sects, which is assuming greater prominence as we approach the end of the second Christian millennium. The world is still trying to make sense of the gas attack on the Tokyo underground by the unquestionably millenarian Aum Shinrikyo cult. The terrifying prospect of cult members releasing poison gas into the nerve centre of our cities reinforces our image of millenarians as outsiders, alien invaders. It reinforces the comforting and misleading impression that there is no common ground between fanatical millenarians and the rest of society.

Yet the reality is that as we near the year 2000 there is mounting evidence of the persistence and growth of apocalyptic belief. It is flourishing among people who are not by any stretch of the imagination suffering from 'relative deprivation'. We can be sure that of the 5,000 people injured in the Tokyo subway, more than a few held End-time beliefs themselves: many of the most successful new religious movements in Japan are strongly apocalyptic. Indeed, all around the world apocalyptic religion is enjoying unprecedented success in attracting recruits. Every year, millions of people in the Third World are converted to a fundamentalist Christianity which teaches that the Second Coming is at hand. In traditionalist Catholic circles from Argentina to Japan, there is mounting excitement over worldwide apparitions of the Virgin which foretell the 'collapse of evil' and the triumph of the papacy before the year 2000. And there are signs that the New Age preoccupation with catastrophic 'earth changes' and extra-terrestrial messages is beginning to filter through into the general population. Books which prophesy imminent catastrophe are regularly near the top of the best-seller lists; moreover, nearly all of them forecast that the changes will reach their climax in the years immediately surrounding the millennial anniversary.

What is it about the advent of the year 2000 which propels millions of people in the direction of apocalyptic belief? Why should Christians who know perfectly well that Christ was not born in AD 1 attach such importance to the calendar change? Even more strangely, why should the prospect of a new millennium quicken the pulse of millions of non-Christians? This book is an attempt to answer these questions by examining a series of profound changes which are occurring across the globe in the last decade of the old millennium. But before we can do that, it is first necessary to examine the often unrecognised role played by apocalypticism in the development of Western civilisation. Belief in the approaching End of Time, we shall discover, is not the exclusive preserve of placard-waving prophets of doom. It is one of the great driving forces of history.

PART ONE

A Brief History of End-Time

The Roots of Apocalypse

The measurement of time is inextricably bound up with belief in the supernatural. We need look no further for proof of this than the currents of revival and anxiety which are flowing through the world's religious communities as the year 2000 approaches. The American evangelicals whose frenzied scriptural arithmetic points to the Second Coming of Christ 2,000 years after his birth are engaged in an activity which has been threatening the stability of the Christian Church since the second century: they are trying to align God's calendar with man's. Liberal commentators who write them off as fundamentalist crazies are puzzled and sometimes frightened by the insidious appeal of their ideas. This is because they do not understand them.

The process of decoding scripture to unveil the date of the Second Coming, which invariably strikes Western cynics as deeply comic, is an expression of an urge far older than Christianity. The existence of a divine plan for humanity which can be glimpsed by arranging man's experience into epochs has been taken for granted in every society which has recorded history. Indeed, it explains why they recorded it in the first place. But the connection between time and belief goes deeper than that. In prehistoric times, and in primitive societies until well into this century, the supernatural and the passage of time as represented by the yearly cycle were so closely linked that they were virtually indistinguishable. And this fact, which modern man finds so difficult to grasp, is the proper starting point for a study of the millennium.

Almost everywhere, priests were the first specialists in timing. Freed from the necessity of growing their own food, they were able to keep a close watch on the sky's changing lights, and find the 'right time' for food planting, for lifting the taboo on the new harvest and for ceremonies associated with the agricultural year. But it would be wrong to imagine that this primitive liturgy consisted of no more than a string of harvest festivals. In every such society, ceremonial also registered the effect of the passing year on the human psyche: there was invariably a point on the annual cycle at which demons, diseases and sins were expelled through fasting, purifications, ritual expulsions or the extinguishing and rekindling of fire. In many cases these ceremonies coincided with the celebration with the New Year, thus establishing a link between the regeneration of time and of the human spirit. And, even when they did not coincide, the fact that the purification occurred on an annual basis illustrates a vital point: that a vast range of cultures naturally reserved certain intense spiritual experiences to a specific moment in the year. The point of these experiences, however, was perhaps not so much to celebrate time as to escape from it. Mircea Eliade, this century's most influential anthropologist of religion, saw in the confessional ceremonies 'primitive man's need to free himself from the recollection of sin, of a succession of personal events that, taken together, constitute history'.[1]

If religion offered an escape from time, it also performed the very necessary function of moving it on. In the absence of a written calendar, the source of the priest's authority was often his right to identify the new moon, without which the agricultural year could not proceed and the people would starve. Just such a situation is described in Chinua Achebe's novel *Arrow of God*, set in a Nigerian Ibo village in the early colonial era. In the book, it is the special responsibility of the

Chief Priest, Ezeulu, to spot the new moon in the sky – not easy during the rainy season – and to announce the time for such feasts as the pumpkin festival, at which his ritual dance cleanses the people from their sins. It is also his privilege, after hearing the voice of his god, to initiate the yam harvest, the equivalent of the New Year. But the story is set at a time when the old way of life is beginning to disintegrate. Ezeulu's authority is under threat from rivals, and he responds by failing to hear his god, Ulu, telling him that the time for the harvest has come; as a result, food stocks run low and the community suffers a time of great stress. It is 'locked in the old year'.[2]

Achebe's novel describes a society in which the coming of the moon is not yet seen as a natural, mechanical event but as a something that requires the intervention of a priest. Even in more sophisticated societies which had some knowledge of astronomy, and whose calendar had become one of the state's most powerful instruments of social control, the art of timing was still the preserve of the priesthood. This is not surprising: calendars were closely connected with people's religious beliefs and with the collective psyche. Wherever they appeared, they had the ability to change people's moods. The Maya of Central America, for example, felt an overwhelming sense of dread at the end of every twenty-day month, the last five days of which were believed to be a time of bad luck; and these feelings were magnified at the end of longer calendar periods. Calendars and time had to be treated with respect and great caution. In Assyria, priests in observatories informed the king of the sighting of the new moon; Julius Caesar had to consult the Pontifex Maximus when he wanted to improve the calendar. The word itself comes from the Latin verb *calendare*, meaning to call out, and is a memento of the Roman practice of sending officials through the streets to proclaim the start of the month after the priests had identified the new moon. To this day, in the Catholic Church, the dates of the movable feasts for the coming year are proclaimed from the pulpit, to a special chant on the feast of the Epiphany.

It is hard to exaggerate the importance of the cycle of the year in determining the structure, and to a large extent the theology, of all the ancient Near Eastern religions. The idea that Hebrew religion was sharply distinguished from neighbouring beliefs by its unwavering monotheism and a 'linear' rather than cyclical view of history is no longer universally accepted. Anthropologists have even disposed of the notion that the Hebrews had a unique self-image as the 'chosen people': there is a school of thought which says it was no different from other neighbouring peoples' sense of destiny. According to one recent authority, the Hebrew, Babylonians and Assyrians 'shared a perspective concerning time and history that was so close as to be almost identical'.[3] All three states were closely organised round the ritual observance of the cycles of the sun and moon. The division of the Hebrew state into twelve tribes, for example, is now thought to have been a deliberate replication of the months of the year.

Furthermore, all were strongly influenced by the Chaldean concept of the Great Year, which takes the movement of the sun as a model for the whole of human history and which spread throughout the entire Hellenised world. In the third century BC, the Babylonian astrologer Berossus popularised a version of the doctrine in which the universe is eternal but periodically destroyed and recreated every Great Year. He taught that when the seven planets assemble in Cancer, or the Great Winter, there will be a deluge; when they meet in Capricorn, at the Great Summer solstice, the entire cosmos will be consumed by fire.

The Babylonians and the Greeks, in common with many civilisations throughout history, believed that historical cycles would be endlessly repeated. The Hebrews were unusual (though again not unique) in believing in a single cycle. But they shared the assumption of the vast majority of societies that history moves through a predetermined process of birth and decay, with a flood taking place towards the beginning of the cycle and fire towards the end. Quite why flood and fire should occur in this order is a mystery; but the fact that they occur at all is evidence of the powerful effect of catastrophe upon the collective memory. Disaster, whether in the form of war, flood, exile or total cosmic destruction, appears to perform a vital function for societies which believe in a divine sequence of world history, repeatable or otherwise. These catastrophes are markers which help them to divide that sequence into phases, and to discover their own place in the eternal scheme. The concept of successive epochs punctuated by disaster is not, however, incompatible with the notion of world history as an infinitely expanded year. The division of history into four eras is found in apparently unrelated civilisations in Greece, Mesopotamia and India and includes both the classical series of 'metallic' ages (the age of gold, silver, bronze and iron) and the Hindu system of four yugas. All are probably inspired by the four seasons of the year, and may have a common origin in a neolithic creation ceremony: we can never know for sure.

There is no mystery, however, about the inspiration for the Great Week, a hugely influential theory which divided history into seven phases based on the seven-day week. This was Jewish in origin, but was taken up by the classical world and accepted by both the early Christian millenarians and their opponents; its influence can still be felt today in the activities of some born-again Christians who are expecting Christ to initiate the final 'day' in human history. The Great Week is, of course, based on a man-made unit of time rather than naturally observed phenomena such as the movement of the sun or the moon. But one should not read too much into this: the roots of the Jewish obsession with the number seven lie in Sumer, often considered to be the first civilised society, where seven became the number of days in the week precisely because it was divinely inspired. Divide a lunar month of twenty-eight days by the sacred number four, and one arrives at seven, which for the Sumerians was the number of the known planets, of the gates between the overworld and the underworld, and of the winds which represent time rushing by.[4]

Although, as far as we know, the Sumerians thought in terms of a fourfold division of history and had no concept of a Great Week, they were entirely familiar with the notion that history progresses in phases consisting of a specific number of years. Their most important unit of time was the *sar* of 3,600 years, which was used as early as the third millennium BC in the

Sumerian king list. No fewer than six of its eight monarchs are said to have ruled for multiples of 3,600 years, a record which is preposterous even by the generous standards of biblical longevity; but it is important to bear in mind that such calculations were central to Sumerian theology. The notion that one could date historical events with reference to a king's reign lay far in the future. The *sar* was the ultimate expression of the number six, whose connection with time in ancient Mesopotamia has given us our sixty seconds and sixty minutes; 3,600, being six squared times one hundred, seems to have been the number of the universe itself. It was also ten times 360, the number of days in an ideal year, a fact which has been described as 'the first evidence we have that the Sumerian city-states of the third millennium BC, the very beginning of the literate period, were organised according to a cosmic law of recurrent seasonal cycles'.[5]

The ornate number-mysticism which gave birth to the *sar* survived well into medieval times through the influence of Plato, for whom its components – the solar number twelve and the lunar number thirty – were proof of its compatibility with the dimensions of the ideal society. The medieval world believed that Plato had proposed a literal Great Year of 36,000 years, and for centuries a belief in historical cycles of this length coexisted uneasily with Great Week mythology. It still figures prominently in Islamic tradition and modern astrology: the New Age belief that the world is moving inexorably through a precession of the equinoxes towards the Age of Aquarius is built on the concept of the Platonic year.

In fact, it is unlikely that Plato believed in the literal truth of his numerology: such calculations expressed an ideal which reflected a higher level of truth than historical reality. We need to remember this when considering the maze of historiographical theories devised by the ancient world. Virtually every numerical figure possesses a hidden significance which subverts any attempt to take it at face value. The purpose of these historical schemes is to align human behaviour with the divine plan, not the other way round. This is the context in which we should see the ancient world's periodic anniversary celebrations, such as the Hebrew jubilees. Held after seven sets of seven-year 'weeks', these were a response to a law set out in Leviticus which allowed anyone forced to sell ancestral lands to reclaim them every fiftieth year. This, in principle, would have restored the structure as it had been divinely ordained in ancient days. In practice, historians are not sure that this was ever put into effect; the point is, however, that the jubilee – a concept with which we are still familiar, and which was arguably a forerunner of our system of centuries – was designed to bring society back into line with the just cosmic order. In our own day, it has become the inspiration for the Roman Catholic Church's celebration of the year 2000.

The fact that this sort of realignment was regarded as urgently necessary by all the ancient Near Eastern societies brings us to the question of where, exactly, they placed themselves in their respective cycles of birth and decay. For the Babylonians, Hebrews, Greeks and early Christians, as well as for the main Indian religions, the answer was roughly the same. Mankind had, through failure to observe divine law, reached a late stage in a sequence which would culminate in the destruction of the world, usually by fire. It is true, of course, that in some of these cultures an endless succession of repetitive cycles means that there is no true eschatology (concept of the end): in Hinduism and Buddhistm, there is only an individual escape from the wheel of death and rebirth. But their belief in a downward spiral of world epochs, often separated from each other by individual catastrophes, to be followed by fire and a new beginning, is strikingly similar to Babylonian, Iranian and some Greek theories (to which some authorities believe they may be related). And if we overlook for the moment the distinction between single and multiple cycles, the theme of epochs brought to an end by human wickedness, and of closeness to the End, emerges as the common denominator of the world's historic religions.

Belief in moral decline is an inevitable accompaniment to the nearly universal belief in an original paradise. The primordial

9

paradise, characterised by perfection, abundance and purity, appears in all religions originating in the Middle East and in most of the world's tribal mythologies. Often this happy state has been lost through some tragic aberration on the part of mankind. The oldest surviving description of paradise comes from the Sumerians, who around 4000 BC described a magical land of Dilmun: 'That place was pure, that place was clean. In Dilmun the raven croaked not. The kite shrieked not kite-like. The lion mangled not. The wolf ravaged not the lambs... None caused the doves to fly away.' All this happened a long time ago, 'when there was no fear, no terror' and 'man had no rival'.[6] According to linguists, the Sumerians gave the Hebrews the name for their paradise, the Garden of Eden. But no other connection between the two myths has been discovered; indeed, all the ancient paradise stories are apparently independent of each other, despite such recurring themes as the primordial garden. If they have a common ancestor, it may well lie so far back in prehistory that it also gave birth to African, Aboriginal Australian and American Indian myths. These conceive of paradise as a time before a moral fall, in which man did not need to work and lived in harmony with the animals. The primitive belief in the moral superiority of ancestors may have its roots in a single preliterate tradition; or it may be an intrinsic feature of human psychology. As with the fourfold division of history, we shall never know for sure.

Nor is it ·clear why so many civilisations believed in a *progressive* decline. But having developed that concept it is not surprising that they should have placed themselves towards the end of the process. It might seem an obvious point to make, but it is easier to imagine the past than the future. A detailed scheme of future phases in world history can never hope to carry the weight of a retrospective analysis which explains the dire state of the world. And, in any case, a theory which envisages moral deterioration over a long period starting from now, as it were, devalues the images of current depravity on which religious belief inevitably feeds. Even Indian traditions which present the grim possibility that the present wickedness will endure for thousands of years emphasise that this age, the

Kali yuga, is the final one before the renewal of creation. At any rate, the sense of debasement, of accumulated moral failure which can be remedied, if at all, only by correct behaviour, is a poignant feature of many ancient texts.

'I wish I were not of this race, that I had died before or had not yet been born,' wrote Hesiod, a Greek farmer from the eighth century BC whose epic *Works and Days* is our earliest account of successive races of gold, silver, bronze and iron. 'This is the age of iron,' he lamented. 'Now, by day, men work and grieve unceasingly; by night they waste away and die. The gods will give harsh burdens, but will mingle in some good; Zeus will destroy this mortal race of men.' Hesiod's historical scheme is either four- or five-fold, depending on whether one counts the age of gold as history or paradise. According to Hesiod, the gods on Olympus made a golden race of men who lived when Zeus' predecessor Cronos was king in heaven. 'Like gods they lived with hearts free from sorrow and remote from toil and grief; nor was miserable age their lot but always unwearied in feet and hands they made merry in feasting, beyond the reach of all evils. And when they died, it was as if they were given over to sleep.'[7] The golden race disappeared when Zeus came to power in heaven, and were succeeded by a silver race who, while heroic, were morally flawed. From then on, each epoch ends in disaster. The silver race's violent behaviour and neglect of their religious duties led Zeus to replace them with men of the bronze race, who soon exterminated each other. They were succeeded by the heroes of antiquity, who represented an improvement in the quality of human stock. But they perished in war and adventures and were succeeded by the age of iron.

The metallic metaphor also crops up in Iran, in a Mazdean book, the *Sudar-nask*, which refers to ages of gold, silver, steel and iron. Here the theme is also moral deterioration, but leading to a final cleansing fire. Hesiod, in contrast, seems to offer the possibility of some sort of salvation through correct behaviour. *Works and Days* can be read as a manual for surviving the misery of the iron age by acting in conformity with the divine will. It contains advice on such mundane matters as when to plant and harvest, when to set sail and when to urinate. ('Do not make water standing towards the Sun, unless he has risen or set,' advises Hesiod.) The implication is that, if enough people live in harmony with the cosmic order, mankind may yet succeed in breaking out of the cycle of decline. This possibility is also present in later Greek and Roman treatments of the myth and may help to explain its enduring appeal. Plato, for example, was profoundly depressed by the thought that he had been born into the latter stages of the iron age, but did not rule out the prospect of escape. 'We must do all we can to imitate the life which is said to have existed in the days of Cronos; and, in so far as the immortal element dwells within us, to that we must hearken, both in public and private life.'[8]

In its wish to recapture the golden age, Greek thought is not unlike the Hindu and Buddhist vision of an impending return to the first age. This may be no coincidence, since Indian and Greek religions also share a belief in a four-fold historical division. The Hindu epic the *Mahābhārata* describes the Krita yuga, the perfect first age, in which men were so saintly that they were not required to perform religious ceremonies: 'The Krita Yuga was without disease; there was no lessening of the years; there was no hatred, or vanity, or evil thought whatsoever; no sorrow, no fear.' This is followed by the Treta, Dvapara and Kali yugas, the last being the current age of decadence. As in other traditions, the end of each age is hastened by individual catastrophes. In Hinduism and Buddhism, however, there is a distinctive understanding of moral decline as a process of forgetting one's true identity and purpose as a result of distraction by the physical world.

The similarities between classical and Eastern visions of the historical cycle have been seized on eagerly by proponents of the theory that the Judaeo-Christian 'linear' conception of time is unrelated to other time-systems. The fact that this claim is often made by those who believe that only Judaism and Christianity are divinely inspired is, in a way, a perfect illustration of the intertwining of religious belief and systems of measuring time. But the linear/cyclical distinction is a crude one, to say the least. It often makes more sense to talk of single and repeatable cycles, though even here Judaism and Christianity do not stand on their own. The Persian Zoroastrian religion also envisages a final end to history after a cosmic struggle between good and evil souls.

The Hebrews' sense of history has more in common with cyclical pagan religions than Jewish and Christian propagandists would have us believe. Nicholas Campion, in his monumental study of historical schemes, *The Great Year* (1994), sees the Hebrew conception of history as a wave alternating between successive renewals of God's covenant (with Adam, Noah, Abraham, Jacob, Moses and David) and divine punishments for disobedience (the Flood, destruction of Sodom and Gomorrah, exile in Egypt, Philistine oppression and Babylonian exile).[9] This is not a history of progressive moral decay, it is true; but for the Hebrews, as much as for any other ancient people, the driving force behind history was catastrophe brought about by immoral behaviour.

Yet by the second century BC there was something new in the air. Put very simply, the Jews started thinking in terms of a glorious new world rather than a return to their ancient ideal, the Kingdom of David. It was a shift of emphasis which was to change the course of human history. Christianity would not have been possible without it.

As we have seen, the early religion of the Hebrews saw moral behaviour – that is, obedience to God – as the key to the restoration of the Kingdom. In this, it strongly resembled the Greek faith in rules of behaviour which would bring about a return to the golden age. There is even a parallel with Eastern writers who proposed ways in which the end of the Kali yuga could be hastened, bringing about the return of the Krita yuga – return being the operative word. But the radical Judaism of the last centuries BC, and subsequently Christianity, offered a more exciting prospect. If we think in terms of Eliade's idea of a universal longing to escape from time itself, we can say that they opened up a new escape route, leading forwards rather than backwards. It was mapped out in a new literary genre

13

called apocalypse, from the Greek *Apo-calyptein*, meaning 'to un-veil'. Apocalyptic literature takes the form of a revelation of the end of history. Violent and grotesque images are juxtaposed with glimpses of a world transformed; the underlying theme is usually a titanic struggle between good and evil, though the narrative tends to be obscured by complex allegories rooted in number-mysticism. Apocalypticism has been described as a genre born out of crisis, designed to stiffen the resolve of an embattled community by dangling in front of it the vision of a sudden and permanent release from its captivity. It is underground literature, the consolation of the persecuted.

This certainly applied to the Jews, whose history up to the destruction of the temple in AD 69 was one of a series of trials and disappointments: collapse of the Davidic kingdom, Babylonian exile, Seleucid oppression and Roman invasion. And it was in response to this sense of repeated failure that the vision of the future in the Hebrew scriptures gradually shifted from prophecy to apocalypse. Apocalypticism differed in vital respects from the earlier Jewish prophetic tradition. The old Hebrew prophets were chiefly concerned with the triumph of the Jewish people over their enemies. The apocalyptic texts put the struggle firmly in the context of good versus evil, light versus dark. Furthermore, they carry this battle into the realm of the supernatural. The Book of Daniel, the only full-scale apocalypse in the Hebrew bible, was written around 168 BC, during the Greek Seleucid occupation of Jerusalem. It includes the revolutionary concept of resurrection of the dead: this must have been a powerful inducement to continued resistance at a time when Jews were being martyred for their faith. And, crucially, it even hints at the date of the final establishment of God's kingdom. (This feature explains both its dubious standing in rabbinic Jewish tradition, which tends to be anti-apocalyptic, and its hold over generations of literal-minded Christians.)

What lay behind this astonishing shift in approach? It is important to know the answer to this question, for what we are effectively talking about is the origin of the modern notion of the End of the World. The answer, according to an influential school of thought led by Professor Norman Cohn, is that apocalyptic faith – that is, belief in a new world occupied by the just after a period of crisis and judgement – was not invented by the Jews, but borrowed by them from the Persians. In Cohn's view, apocalypticism was first manifested in the teachings of Zoroaster, a prophet from Central Asia who probably lived around 1400 BC, whose teachings of a coming battle between good and evil became the official religion of the Persian Empire. Zoroaster, originally a priest of the traditional religion, spoke of a coming transformation known as 'the making wonderful', in which there would be a universal bodily resurrection. This would be followed by a great assembly, in which all people would be judged. The wicked would be destroyed, while the righteous would become immortal. In the new world, young people are forever fifteen years old, and the mature remain at the age of forty. But this is not a reversion to the original paradise; nothing in the past approaches its perfection. It is the End of Time.[10]

Since we know so little about Zoroaster, we cannot know exactly why he developed the world's first eschatological faith. It may well have been a response to profound change in the world in which he lived, from one of peaceful herdsmen to a restless and warlike society in which military prowess was valued above all. Zoroaster, says Cohn,

> is the earliest known example of a particular type of prophet – the kind commonly called millenarian – and the experiences that determined the content of his teaching seem also to have been typical. Prophets who promise a total transformation of existence, a total perfecting of the world, often draw their original inspiration from the spectacle not simply of suffering, but of one particular type of suffering: that engendered by the destruction of an ancient way of life, with its familiar certainties and safeguards.[11]

The End of Time, in other words, appeals most to people who are disorientated, whose identity is under threat: people such as the Jews. Zoroastrian visions of resurrection, judgement and reward, with which the Jews would certainly have been familiar, must have offered a thrilling prospect to a nation whose self-image was at once so strong and so frequently challenged. It is little wonder that these visions were slowly appropriated, to emerge in dramatic form during a period of unique stress and excitement.

The Book of Daniel was written at a time of terrible humiliation for the Jewish people. The Greek Seleucid monarch Antiochus Epiphanes had brutally suppressed the traditional worship of the temple, stripping it of its gold and setting up a statue of Baal. Observance of the sabbath and circumcision were forbidden. Such persecution strongly reminded the Jews of the Babylonian captivity; so much so, in fact, that the Book of Daniel purports to have been written during that period, that is, 400 years before the actual date of its composition. Its 'prophecies' are therefore history – a cheap trick, perhaps, but an effective one, for it is employed by most apocalyptic writers. In the first section of the book, Daniel, a Jewish youth, is called to decipher a dream, which has been troubling King Nebuchadnezzar. The dream is of a great statue whose head is made of fine gold, breast and arms of silver, belly and thighs of bronze and feet of mixed iron and clay. The feet of this statue shatter when it is struck by a stone, and the iron, clay, bronze, silver and gold become 'like the chaff of the summer threshing floors, and the wind carried them away'. The stone, meanwhile, becomes a great mountain and fills the whole earth. The statue's gold, silver, bronze and iron are reminiscent of Hesiod, and Daniel's explanation of the dream makes this explicit. The gold, silver, bronze and mixed iron and clay are four kingdoms, the first being Nebuchadnezzar's, the next an 'inferior' kingdom, the third a bronze kingdom and the last a kingdom which is initially as strong as iron but, because it is mixed with clay, is divided against itself and is vanquished by the final, eternal kingdom represented by the stone. Later, the transient kingdoms are identified as those of Babylon, the Medes, the Persians and the Greeks, which gets them in the wrong historical order. The point is, however, that Daniel has borrowed the Babylonian concept of four successive kingdoms and turned them into 'evil empires'; when Ronald Reagan used this phrase to describe the Soviet Union, the audience of born-again Christians for whom it was intended would immediately have thought of Daniel. But there is nothing evil about the fifth empire, which is the kingdom of God on earth. Eighteen hundred years later, this vision inspired the radical English millenarians of the Commonwealth, who called themselves 'Fifth Monarchy Men'.

It is easy to see why Daniel's vision of the events leading up to the establishment of God's kingdom should appeal to political radicals. After a complex series of dynastic struggles, an evil 'King of the North' emerges who pollutes the temple and sets up 'the abomination that makes desolate'. But his fate is sealed: at 'the time of the end', there is a cataclysmic battle in which the tyrant is destroyed. Then a great prince called Michael appears on the scene, ushering in 'a time of trouble such as never has been since there was a nation till that time: but at that time your people shall be delivered, every one whose name shall be found written in the book. And many of those who sleep in the dust of the earth shall awake, some to everlasting life and some to shame and everlasting contempt. And those who are wise shall shine like the brightness of the firmament; and those who turn many to righteousness, like the stars for ever and ever' (Dan. 12: 1–3).

For Daniel's first audiences, and subsequently for biblical scholars, there was no mystery about the true identity of the King of the North: he was Antiochus Epiphanes. The 'abomination of desolation' was the statue of Zeus which he set up in the temple. We can date the composition of this section of Daniel to within a year or two, since it was clearly written in the interval between the start of the Maccabean revolt against Greek rule and its successful conclusion. But it is far more than propaganda. The extraordinary passage which holds out the hope of eternal life to faithful Jews overturns the grim doctrine of Sheol, a shadowy place where all the dead gather irrespective of their behaviour. The new order will be ruled by Jews but entirely transcends the restored kingdom envisaged by the prophets. It covers the whole world, and is peopled by the resurrected dead as well as the living.

And it is *imminent*. It is crucial to the book's morale-boosting function that it should present the destruction of Greek power as something which lies just around the corner. But, not content with this, its author or authors throw in a number of teasing and apparently contradictory indications of when this will occur. The period from 'the going forth of the commandment to restore and to build Jerusalem' until the time of everlasting righteousness will last seventy weeks. However, a text from Jeremiah is also recalled in which 'seventy days' means seventy years, which means that seventy weeks (490 days) must mean 490 years. And to further complicate matters, at the end of the book Daniel asks how long it will be until 'the end of these wonders' and receives the cryptic reply 'a time, two times, and half a time'. There will be 1,290 days after the desecration of the temple; but 'blessed is he who waits' for the end of 1,395 days.

These clues have kept Christian believers in the End-time busy for over 2,000 years, and as the year 2000 approaches the Book of Daniel is being scrutinised more closely than ever. But this need not detain us for the moment. Seen in the context of its own time, Daniel is highly innovative. It is evidence that by the second century BC Judaism had been transformed by its contact with the mystical dualism of Persian religion, and by the dynamics of oppression and revolt. The ancient, perhaps neolithic, rhythm of four-fold history can still be detected, but the beat has quickened: an age is fast approaching which will pluck the righteous from present captivity and even from their graves. 'Blessed is he who waits' for such a day, but he may not have to wait long. And, as if this mixture were not explosive enough, Daniel provides some mysterious numerical clues which, if applied correctly, will part the veil and reveal that which is hidden, the apocalypse.

Daniel's preoccupation with a new order was not confined to Jewish activists. By the first century BC the Roman republic was torn between feelings of apprehension and confidence. Belief in the imperishability of Rome could be found alongside the Stoic doctrine of recurring historical cycles, which dictated that the city must perish. According to Mircea Eliade, during every crisis Rome became obsessed with the idea that the life of the city was limited to a certain number of years, a 'mystic number' revealed to Romulus by twelve eagles, and that this had now been reached; it was even possible that the Great Year itself was over. So when Rome was 120 years old, there were fears that the eagles had each represented a decade in the city's life, and when it was 365 years old the worry was that Rome had reached the end of its own Great Year, in which every year was equivalent to a day.[12]

If all this is true (which is by no means certain), then these are the first examples of mass anxiety triggered by the approach of a specific date. There is certainly no denying the surge of prophetic activity in Roman and Jewish circles in the centuries before and after the birth of Christ, all of it conjuring up images of transformation through destruction and/or the birth of a new world. The eruption of Pompeii was widely thought to herald the fire that would consume the world. Virgil's so-called Messianic Eclogue, composed in 42 BC, startled later Christian readers with its prediction that with the 'birth of a child' a golden race would spring up throughout the earth. In fact, Virgil was not so much predicting the coming of a Messiah as demonstrating that the time in which he lived was unusually receptive to new religious ideas. This was particularly true of the Jewish world, in which apocalyptic theology was fast developing the messianic and millenarian features with which it has been associated ever since. The prospect of a new world of peace and justice is usually inseparable from the charismatic leader who promises to deliver it; which comes first is not always clear, but in first-century Judaism we catch glimpses of a familiar sequence of events. In around AD 55 an Egyptian Jew led a crowd of up to 30,000 into the desert, intending to march on Jerusalem; he claimed that at his command the walls of the city would collapse. We do not know what happened to them, but according to Josephus it was quite common for 'imposters and deceivers' to lead mobs into the desert under the pretence that God would deliver them.[13] These were classic millenarian movements whose understanding of history was apocalyptic and eschatological. They lived in daily expectation of a divine

19

intervention, as did the desert community at Qumran who assembled the Dead Sea Scrolls, and the preacher known as John the Baptist. Rarely, if ever, had so many Jews sensed that they were living in the Last Days.

This preoccupation with the approaching End was fully shared by the followers of Jesus of Nazareth. There is little doubt that the early Christians – and possibly Jesus himself – lived in daily expectation of the End of the World. Before Jesus' death, many of his supporters expected history to be brought to a conclusion by his glorious coming to power in Jerusalem. After his execution, when stories of his mysterious reappearance were circulating, their attention shifted to the 'second coming' which Jesus himself had frequently hinted would occur within their lifetimes. Conventional translations of the Lord's Prayer obscure its eschatological character. Most modern Christians have no idea that when they say it they are praying for the End of the World. The plea to be delivered from 'temptation', many scholars believe, should read 'and keep us from the Ordeal'. It is evidence of the Christian community's fear of the final world crisis, but also reflects its belief that it can be spared this terrible experience. Seen in this light, early Christianity presents a radical new twist to the belief in the imminence of the End of the World which permeated the first-century Middle East. It is the first religion to offer its adherents the possibility of escaping the flames in which the rest of the world will perish. And, since initially this Second Coming of Christ was to happen during the lifetime of the believer, the new faith established a highly ambiguous relationship with the secular state. St Paul's writings often emphasise the importance of living within the worldly order; yet, as Nicholas Campion has pointed out, their implications were not always conservative. 'If the individual could, by an act of loyalty to God rather than emperor, advance to the next stage of history, the consequences were profound, for normal political authority then became irrelevant.'[14]

This ambiguity is typical of early Christianity. The internal contradictions of New Testament texts frustrate any attempt to arrive at a coherent vision of the end of history. We cannot, for example, define the relationship between the new age ushered in by Christ and his Second Coming. Which comes first? Is release from what Paul calls the 'present evil age' immediately attainable by Christians, or must they wait for the returning Christ? The failure of the Gospels and epistles to clarify this point eventually created tensions within the Christian community which continue to this day. Yet for Paul the question would have been rendered almost irrelevant by the certainty that Christ would return very soon. The repeated injunction in the Gospels not to try to calculate the time and the hour of this event testifies to the intense curiosity this naturally aroused among the first Christians. Before long, however, it seems that this curiosity was replaced by disappointment and the need for an explanation for Christ's non-appearance.

It has been suggested that the Book of Revelation, written by one John on the Isle of Patmos towards the end of the first century, is an attempt to fill this gap. At first glance, there is something ludicrous about the notion that this surrealistic text is designed to make anything clearer. Its visions of creatures with many wings and eyes, of angels, dragons, glass seas and 'foul spirits like frogs', have an authentically psychedelic quality in that they are by turns breathtaking, tedious and frightening. Even as allegory, they verge on the incomprehensible. As with the Book of Daniel, Revelation's clues to the time of the End really leave us none the wiser; yet it clearly suggests that the End-time sequence has already begun, and subtly invites its readers to interpret its images in the light of their own times. One wonders whether the author intended to keep successive generations of Christians in a state of apocalyptic expectation, and therefore created images with a certain reusable quality. If so, he succeeded brilliantly, as the history of his most enduring creation, 'the Beast whose number is 666', demonstrates. The Beast, a devil in human form who will rule the world just before Armageddon and the Second Coming, has had an astonishing career, being identified at various times as Nero, George III, Napoleon, Hitler and Henry Kissinger. Comic as this seems, we should not underestimate the enduring power of Revelation's depiction of the Antichrist (as the Beast became known). Its message is that the personification of evil will arise in our midst as a commanding figure with an international following. Millions will yield to his persuasive charm, only to discover that they have thereby condemned themselves to an agonising death and everlasting punishment.

The Book of Revelation was excluded from the bible by the Eastern Church for several centuries, and one can understand why: no other scriptural text has its potential for turning a political drama into an End-time crisis by revealing the hand of the Antichrist in everyday events. But in the second century AD it was a far more important Christian text than the Gospels. To Christians undergoing Roman persecution it offered a stunning vision of the reward that awaited them in the heavenly city, where 'God shall wipe away all tears from their eyes; and there shall be no more death, neither sorrow, nor crying, neither shall there be any more pain; for the former things are passed away' (Rev. 21: 4). At the same time, it went some way to explaining the delay in Christ's Second Coming by revealing the full horror of the confrontation between good and evil that must precede it. In doing so, however, it introduced an inherently unstable, even dangerous, element into the life of the Christian community.

The key passage in Revelation comes after the destruction of Babylon when Christ appears on horseback, with eyes like flames of fire and wearing a robe dipped in blood. Behind him are the armies of heaven 'arrayed in fine linen, white and pure' to make war with the Beast and his army. Satan's earthly followers are put to the sword, while he is cast alive into a lake of fire and brimstone and falls into a bottomless pit. He stays there *for a thousand years* while Christ and his saints reign on earth. Then he is released for a final battle with the forces of God, after which, in one of the most beautiful passages in the bible, history yields to eternity. A new heaven and a new earth replace the old order, and a new Jerusalem comes down from heaven, 'prepared as a bride adorned for her husband'.

The thousand-year reign of Christ and his saints, the Millennium, is one of the most difficult concepts in Christianity. For

2,000 years, millenarians named after it have invoked it in support of their own visions of the imminent kingdom of God on earth. In the process, they have had to display great ingenuity. The sequence of events in Revelation is convoluted enough in itself, but it must also be reconciled with apocalyptic passages in Daniel, the Gospels and St Paul, who in the letter to the Thessalonians suggests that right at the start of the End-time all believing Christians will be carried up to heaven in what has become known as the Rapture. But we need not worry for the moment about the intricacies of rival timetables such as pre- and postmilleniarian dispensationialism: it is most useful to focus on the origins of the thousand-year reign, and the way in which it has affected the Western conception of history.

For a start, why a thousand years? The obvious answer is that the author of Revelation was thinking of Psalm 90: 'For a thousand years in thy sight are but as yesterday when it is past.' But Revelation was not written in a vacuum: it is a product of an empire in which other Eastern religions were competing with Christianity and indeed Judaism for converts. It has been suggested that John may well have been aware of the Zoroastrian belief (developed long after Zoroaster) that Zurvan, the god of time, reigned for a thousand years before the creation. This Persian eschatology is in places reminiscent of Revelation: at one stage the evil spirit Ahriman lies prostrate for 3,000 years. It is, however, part of a much more tightly organised overarching structure, in which each successive historical epoch lasts either 1,000 or 3,000 years. We are back in the realm of numerology, in which certain numbers of years, such as the Mesopotamian *sar* of 3,600, are revealed as the components of a divinely sanctioned pattern of history. In the case of the *sar*, part of the explanation is that the Sumerians observed a 360-day year. The figure of a thousand, in contrast, is a straightforward product of the decimal system of counting. But of course the origins of that system also lie in a naturally occurring phenomenon – the ten fingers and thumbs of the human hands, which are actually pictured in Roman numerals. If we had been born with twelve digits instead of ten, we would not think in terms of centuries or millennia.

That is not to say that civilisations up to and including the Roman Empire automatically divided history into consecutive eras of a hundred years each. We must beware of imposing an anachronistic interpretation of decades, centuries or millennia on societies which, although familiar with the concepts of ten, a hundred or a thousand years, did not use them to measure time in the way that we do. In the Hebrew bible, for example, the figure of a thousand is wielded mostly for effect: there are references in Daniel and Enoch to a thousand thousand, ten thousand thousands and even ten thousand times ten thousand, but it seems unlikely that they were meant to be taken literally. By the time of the Jewish apocalypses which followed Daniel, however, the figure of a thousand or its multiples had acquired a strongly eschatological flavour: the coming messianic age was variously calculated by scribes at 2,000 and 7,000 years, but the most common figure was 1,000.[15] This is a point which should perhaps be borne in mind by modern commentators who refer incredulously to the illogical way in which 'the mere presence of three noughts in a date', as they often put it, concentrates men's minds on the End. Illogical it may be, but the association of thousands and the Last Things goes back a long way.

There is no way of telling whether the thousand-year reign of the saints in Revelation is intended purely as allegory; but we can be sure that the author could not have envisaged the techniques employed in subsequent attempts to work out the date at which it was due to begin. Apart from anything else, he might not have recognised the concept of the 'date' as we understand it. We must step back for a moment from the overheated visions of apocalyptic writers to consider the way early societies used the calendar to define chronology. The Babylonians, Hebrews, Greeks and Iranians constructed elaborate successions of world epochs; they even assigned symbolic numbers of years to these stages. But if at any stage one had asked two inhabitants of neighbouring cities what year it was, the chances of obtaining the same answer would have been slim indeed. Throughout the ancient world, there was a tendency for individual communities to date years from a great event in their own history, such as their liberation from an oppressor (or, alternatively, the beginning of an occupation). Even within a community, there was often no agreement about when the historical year began, or even about how long it lasted: historical years (that is, units of time which were strung together to date a specific event) were not the same as seasonal years. The truth is that the ancient world was not greatly concerned with establishing the timing of one historical event vis-à-vis another. On the occasions when historians needed to do so, the absence of a universally accepted system is often glaringly obvious: the Greek chronicler Polybius, recording the sack of Rome by Gauls in 387 BC, notes laboriously that it was contemporaneous with the peace of Antalcidas and the siege of Rhegium by Dionysius, and that it happened nineteen years after the battle of Aegospotami and sixteen years before the battle of Leuctra.[16]

Even the Romans, who invented the system of dating *ab urbe condita* (from the founding of their city), used it only for the narrow purpose of measuring time from that event to some subsequent event; and in any case they could not agree on precisely when Rome was founded, estimates varying from 759 to 729 BC. But it is safe to assume that no one lost any sleep over it. The practice of dating by consulships, or imperial regnal years, seems to have served the empire perfectly well. Calendrical innovations are invariably a response to pressing need, and there was no real need for a universal dating system; compare this, however, with the eternal problem of adjusting the calendar to the solar year, which did have major ramifications for Roman life and was therefore one of Julius Caesar's highest priorities.

The lack of an agreed starting point for a chronological system means, of course, that there is no consensus about which decade or century has been reached; indeed, the whole concept of living 'in' a period of ten or a hundred years belongs to a much later era. But in a society which uses a decimal system of counting it is inevitable that groups of ten, a hundred or a thousand years should possess a certain abstract force. In the case of a hundred years, furthermore, the fact that this approaches the upper limit of human life expectancy adds an extra nuance. The Romans appear to have borrowed the concept of centuries from the Etruscans, who thought in terms of eras which came to an end on the death of the oldest living member of a generation. At the end of each generation – that is, roughly every century – diviners would create its epitaph, and these eras may have been linked to form a world week. In 44 BC, an Etruscan diviner in Rome announced a ninth era, which he predicted would be succeeded by a tenth era, and this final era would witness the disappearance of all Etruscans except the diviners themselves.[17]

The Etruscan era could well have been the inspiration for the Roman *saecula*, an era in the life of Rome which lasted, depending on the whim of the emperor, either 100 or 110 years. The *saecula* gave its name to the Secular Games, the first events in history which regularly summoned up the conflicting emotions we associate with the end of a century: sorrow or relief at the end of one era, optimism and apprehension at the beginning of another. There is something familiar about the way in which the Roman authorities used the games to bolster their own image, though they had the added luxury of being able to bring an era to a premature conclusion. The first large-scale Secular Games were held in 17 BC by Augustus, who had consulted the sibylline books to ascertain that a *saecula* lasted 110 years and that his were the fifth since Rome was founded. This did not, however, stop Claudius from staging the next games in AD 47, thus making a nonsense of the stipulation that the preceding games should not have taken place within living memory. But Claudius was playing by different rules: invoking the concept of 100-year eras, his Secular Games commemorated the 800th anniversary of Rome.

The Secular Games of AD 248 were held to celebrate the thousandth anniversary of Rome. Like the Claudian games, they accepted Varro's date of 753 BC for the founding of Rome, though as we have seen there were other candidates. (So it is possible that the games took place to the accompaniment of grumbling from the sort of pedant who, in our own time, delights in pointing out that Christ was not born in AD 1, and that, in any case, the millennium begins in 2001.) In fact, the festivities were a year late, because in 247 the emperor had not yet returned from fighting off the barbarians, which gives us a clue to the rather desperate tone of the event. The games had always been used by emperors as a way of renewing the confidence of the Roman people in the future of their city. By 248, this was no mean task. For many years, Romans had viewed the past with a nostalgia born out of an acute awareness of decline. The empire, weakened by the massing of enemy armies on most of its borders and by spectacular inflation, was at the mercy of the ever-growing army needed to protect it. Roman citizenship had become as debased as the currency: it was now available to any free man of the empire. The emperor himself was an Arab, Philip, chosen by the army rather than the senate. Even the Roman gods were out of fashion, sidelined by the passion for Near Eastern 'mystery' religions.

Yet an observer at the Secular Games might not have guessed any of this. They seem to have been a brilliantly stage-managed exercise in restoring the self-esteem not only of the city but of its traditional religion. Rome's sacred college, keeper of the sibylline books, presided over ceremonies lasting several days and nights. The emperor, vested as high priest, carried out age-old rituals at the altars:

> Along the Tiber he burned lambs and black she-goats to the Fates, who caused men to prosper or fail. He sacrificed white bulls to Jupiter the Best and the Greatest, king of gods and patron of Rome; a pregnant sow to Mother Earth, who gave the empire food in abundance or held it back and made men starve. He offered cakes and burned incense to Ilithyia, goddess of childbirth, without whose assistance the empire's population dropped. Matrons knelt to Juno in supplication for blessings. Twenty-seven aristocratic youths and twenty-seven highborn young virgins, their lives unpolluted by the death of either parent, chanted ancient hymns to Apollo and his chaste sister Diana.[18]

For a few days at least, the population of Rome seem to have responded appropriately. Wheat, barley and beans were handed out, and the crowd danced and drank. Thousands held torches as pageants were performed on the Campius Martius. There may well have been a sense, however transitory, of 'pure thrill at being alive for the thousandth year of the greatest city on earth'.[19] There was certainly a longing in some quarters for a new age of stability and devotion to old gods, and for these traditionalists the millennial celebrations were an obvious focal point. We might argue that the nostalgic tone of the festivities seems to signify the end, rather than the beginning, of an era: but this is to judge them with the benefit of hindsight. Perhaps the millennium triggered a certain anxiety that, with the passage of a thousand years, the city had reached the end of its allotted span; but, if so, there is no record of it. What we do know is that, within a year or two of the celebrations, Philip's successor Decius launched the first empire-wide persecution of Christians, in which those who refused to sacrifice to the Roman gods were 'whipped till their skin hung down like rags, clubbed into senselessness, or stretched slowly on the rack until their joints came apart'.[20] This campaign was of a different order to the local persecutions in which the first Christian martyrs perished. Its comprehensiveness and intensity point to a new sense of resolution on the part of the authorities: one that may well be influenced by the experience of passing into a new millennium.

The Christians, by this stage, had evolved into a Church with sufficient resources to survive even an intense campaign of persecution. There was still curiosity about the timing of Christ's reappearance, but there was also a network of bishops intent on maintaining uniformity of belief. For a long time these two things were not incompatible, since no one in the Church, from the Pope downwards, believed that the Second Coming would be long delayed. But by the second century the disruptive potential of End-time speculation was already painfully evident. A heresy called Montanism, which taught that the new Jerusalem was about to descend, literally, on to an obscure region of Phrygia, briefly threatened to supplant orthodox Christianity. Montanism was millenarian and led to the frenzied behaviour we associate today with End-time cults. Its founder, Montanus, and a priestess called Maximilla may have undergone voluntary martyrdom when the Millennium did not materialise; thereafter, apocalyptic disappointment and suicide became linked in the public mind, as they are today. And apocalypticism itself, which had been a vital resource for the first Christians, began to be regarded by the Church authorities with understandable mistrust.

The basic framework of Christian End-time belief was brilliantly simple. Some Jewish radicals of the first century AD believed in a Great Week which would be brought to an end by the arrival of the Messiah 5,000 or 6,000 years after the Creation. The early Christians slotted the Millennium of Revelation neatly into a seven-day Great Week. The Epistle of Barnabas, written around AD 120, puts it succinctly. 'Listen carefully, my children, to these words: "God finished his work in six days . . ." That means that in 6000 years God will bring all things to completion, because for Him "a day of the Lord is as 1000 years . . ." Therefore, my children, in six days, that is in 6000 years, the universe will be brought to its end. "And on the seventh day he rested . . ." '[21] Here, in a nutshell, is the idea that over the centuries was to launch a thousand different theories about the date of the Second Coming. Note that the Epistle leaves out one crucial ingredient. Although it is the first Christian document to mention the age of the world, it does not say what that age might be. For once that detail is known, so is the date of Christ's return and the dawn of the seventh and final millennium.

A curious feature of the Christian Great Week theory is that it could be invoked by supporters and opponents of apocalypticism alike. For millenarians, the world was perpetually on the verge of its 6,000th birthday; for conservatives, that anniversary was always beyond the life expectancy of the current generation. The most conservative perspective of all was that of St Augustine of Hippo, who ridiculed attempts to calculate the time of the End. 'In vain therefore do we try to reckon and set limits to the years that remain to this world, when we hear from the Mouth of Truth that it is not ours to know this. Yet some have said that 400, some 500, others even a thousand years must be reached between the Lord's ascension and his last coming.' He reserved his most withering tone, however, for those who were for ever discerning an End-time significance in current affairs. He warned against falling into a panic over present happenings 'as if they were the ultimate and extreme of all things, so that we may not be laughed at by those who have read of more and worse things in the history of the world'.[22]

The Bishop of Hippo's advice to End-time mathematicians, echoed by Church authorities ever since, was to relax their busy fingers. But there is little sign that this advice was heeded. Augustine recorded an outbreak of panic in Constantinople in AD 398, a year which he believed marked the completion of 365 years from the Crucifixion. But this scare had nothing to do with the Second Coming: on the contrary, said Augustine, there was a wicked pagan legend circulating which claimed that St Peter had done a deal with the devil that Christianity would last only 365 years. Then an earthquake struck, sending people fleeing to church. 'Everyone, almost with violence, demanded baptism from whom he could,' reports Augustine. 'Not only in church, but also in their homes and through the streets and squares there was a cry for the saving sacrament, that they might escape wrath . . .'[23] A more conventional panic arose from the sack of Rome in 410, when Augustine reported that some exclaimed: 'Behold, from Adam all the years have passed, and behold, the 6,000 years are completed.' This linking of the sack of Rome to the fateful year must have been a purely instinctive reaction to events. And it is, for this reason, a useful insight into the way people at the time responded to violence and devastation. They did not just conclude, as anyone might have, that the End of the World had come. With the aid of an old-established tradition, they created an instant chronology which explained why it was ending. They were exhibiting a basic human urge to align great events – even terrible ones – with the numerical configuration of a divine plan.

Although the End-time significance of the sixth millennium was well established, there was no widely accepted calendar which placed the year 410 at the end of it. There was, however, already an important Christian chronology which maintained that the world had been created 5,500 years before the birth of

Christ. The end of the world was therefore scheduled for around the year we know as AD 500. Hippolytus of Rome, a third-century theologian, supported this claim with a mass of scriptural evidence beginning with the dimensions of the ark of the covenant (five and a half cubits). Known to historians as AM I, this *era mundi* was not generally used to record the date: the Roman system of dating by consulships survived well into the Christian era. It was, however, widely accepted, though few writers were as bold as Hippolytus in spelling out its implications: 'From the birth of the Christ one must count another 500 years, and only then the end will come.'[24] But the mere fact of acknowledging this does not make Hippolytus an apocalyptic writer. On the contrary, he was pointing out that the End lay nearly 200 years in the future. AM I, in other words, was a weapon that could be used against millenarians who expected the year 6000 to occur in their lifetimes. But it was a weapon with built-in obsolescence. By the fifth century – the 5900s AM I – a delay tactic had become a millennial countdown.

As it turned out, AM I did not survive to celebrate its 6,000th year, in Western Europe at any rate. For as the American medieval historian Richard Landes has demonstrated, just before that date arrived it was mysteriously replaced by a new *era mundi*, AM II, which placed the Incarnation 5,200 years after the Creation and thus rejuvenated the world by 300 years. [25] By the year 500 there is no document recognising the arrival of the year 6000 and no history dating by AM I. There is also no evidence of apocalyptic panic, though there are intriguing traces of unusual activity. According to one text, the 490s were twice disturbed by 'ignorant' and 'delirious' prophets announcing the arrival of the Antichrist: that is all we know. Landes has suggested that the earlier, dangerous chronology was suppressed by a Church which was determined not to suffer the consequences of millennial panic. This may sound like a conspiracy theory, but there is no other way to explain the disappearance of AM I at such a convenient moment. And Landes produces one piece of evidence which cannot be dismissed as coincidence: when AM II reached its 5900s, it met an identical fate.

The question of the age of the world has been described as an 'over-riding concern' of historians in the early medieval period. It was undoubtedly risky territory to explore, in that every time a chronicler invoked one of the many available variants of AM II he was effectively dating the Second Coming for anyone who believed in the millennial week. In fact, most writers were at pains to distance themselves from the year-6000 theory, while acknowledging the extent of popular interest in it. Some condemned eschatological calculations while obligingly providing a total of the number of years left until the year 6000. The Venerable Bede complained that he was forever being asked by *rustici* how many years were left in the millennium. He was not amused. In *De temporum ratione* he condemned those who believed that 'the Advent should be most anticipated at the end of the sixth millennium' as well as the belief that the Millennium of Revelation would be an earthly one.[26]

As the clock of AM II ticked away, the Church found itself in a quandary. Try as it might to promote the sensible Augustinian line, it had centuries ago endorsed a calendar which lent implicit support to the dubious (but not officially heretical) notion of the millennial week. It is true that, even by the 700s, the *era mundi* was far from being what the modern world considers as 'the date': most dating was by regnal years. But, with various estimates of the world's age heading towards the magic figure of 6,000, there was an urgent need for an alternative. The answer was provided by Bede, who during his lifetime was known throughout Europe and whose reputation grew hugely during the eighth century. His tables for reckoning the date of Easter resurrected an old, and little-used, system which defused the calendrical time-bomb by ignoring the age of the world and timing from the birth of Christ: Anno Domini.

Anno Domini was actually the creation of a Scythian monk, Dionysius Exiguous ('Dennis the Small'), who in 525 was asked by Pope John I to compile a new Easter cycle. He used the calendar of Diocletian, which began the year on 1 January, but was reluctant to date years from the reign 'of an impious persecutor'. So he dated *ab incarnatione*, assigning the birth of Christ to 25 December immediately preceding 1 January in the year AD 1, which coincided with the year 754 *ab urbe condita*. In the process, he laid the foundations for the first universal dating system. But he was also responsible for two anomalies, both of which are certain to give rise to much pedantic point-scoring in the run-up to the year 2000.

In the first place, Dionysius, following an existing tradition, probably postdated the birth of the historical Jesus by between four and seven years. The true second millennium of Christ's birth therefore falls at some stage during the 1990s. Secondly, there is no gap between 1 BC and AD 1. Modern suggestions that there should have been a year 0 would have meant nothing to Dionysius, who was working at a time when the concept of zero had not yet arrived from the Arab world. Given that we begin the year in January rather than on Christmas day, BC now stands back to back with AD at a point seven days after the traditional date of Christ's birth. Accordingly, Jesus would not have celebrated his first birthday until just before the start of AD 2. This means that a period of 2,000 years since his traditional date of birth will not have elapsed until the end, not the beginning, of the year 2000.

It is not clear why Anno Domini failed to catch on at first. It appeared from time to time in the sixth and seventh centuries – the Synod of Whitby of 664 is an example – but it was not until the Carolingians adopted Bede's Easter tables that it became the norm. The now apocalyptic AM II, meanwhile, all but disappeared from documents in the fifty years before its sixth millennium in or around AD 800. Whether this means that the idea of the year 6000 had relaxed its grip on the popular imagination is another question. There is a suspicious intensification of signs and prodigies in the last years of the 5900s. In the year 786 (5985 AM), 'the sign of the cross appeared in the clothing of men, and blood poured forth from the skies and the earth, and other signs appeared whence an enormous dread and salubrious fear invaded the populace so that many corrected their ways'.[27] Three years later, Charlemagne issued a document arguing for better clerical training 'since we know that in the last days false teachers will come . . .'[28]

Was the dawn of the millennial year 6000 AM II a non-event

or an open secret? We shall encounter a similar problem with the year 1000. In the meantime, it is worth noting that no contemporary document even hints that Charlemagne's own coronation on Christmas Day 800 coincided with the opening of the final chapter in human history. Yet the dating system which would have established this 'magnificent coincidence'[29] had only just faded from view. The word conspiracy is too strong, but it does look as if both secular and religious authorities deliberately sought refuge in a dating system which laid to rest the spectre of apocalypticism.

The shift to the AD dating system is one of the defining events in human historiography. Apocalypticism did not, at this stage, carry the connotations of radical millenarian revolt which it acquired during the later middle ages. Our ignorance of the vast majority of the population is so great that we cannot predict their reaction if a universally accepted year 6000 had been allowed to dawn. But since apocalyptic expectations involve, by definition, the transformation or destruction of secular and religious institutions, both Church and state in Western Europe had reason to promote the apparently innocuous system of Anno Domini. And, of the two, the Church had more at stake. We come back to the entanglement of religious belief and the measurement of time. If the Church had lost control of chronology – and therefore, in a way, of the structure of history – it would have found itself in the situation of Ezeulu, the Nigerian priest who forfeited his authority because he could not spot the new moon. Anno Domini was crucially important because, in the short term, it consigned apocalyptic belief to the sidelines. The problem of what would happen when it produced its own millennium could safely be left to a future generation.

2

The Mystery of the Year 1000

In the spring of the year 1000, a community of monks in Lotharingia were celebrating the passion and resurrection of the Lord when they felt the whole earth 'shake with a vast and general tremor'. Soon afterwards, a comet appeared in the millennial sky and hung there for three months. 'It shone so brightly that its light seemed to fill the greater part of the sky, then it vanished at cock's crow,' wrote one contemporary.

> But whether it is a new star which God launches into space, or whether He merely increases the normal brightness of another star, only He can decide who in the mysterious secrecy of his wisdom prepares all things. What appears established with the greatest degree of certainty is that this phenomenon never appears in the sky to men without being the sure sign of some mysterious and terrible event. And indeed a fire soon consumed the church of St Michael the Archangel, built on a promontory in the ocean, which had always been the object of special veneration throughout the whole world.[1]

Fire in the heavens and on earth: no wonder people believed the Last Judgement was at hand. For centuries, well-attested natural phenomena such as the comet were cited by historians in support of their theory that the population of Christendom lived through the year 999 in a state of mortal fear, convinced that, with the completion of a thousand years since the birth of Christ, history had run its course. 'The Terrors of the Year 1000', as they became known, were believed to have inspired thousands of people to abandon their friends and families and hurry to Jerusalem to witness the Second Coming. 'The number of pilgrims was so great that they were compared to a desolating army,' wrote one nineteenth-century historian. 'Buildings of every sort were suffered to fall into ruins. It was thought useless to repair them, when the end of the world was so near . . . Knights, citizens and serfs travelled eastwards in company, taking with them their wives and children, singing psalms as they went, and looking with fearful eyes upon the sky, which they expected each moment to open, to let the Son of God descend in his glory.'[2] Back home, meanwhile, lords and peasants fled to church on 31 December, or gathered round crucifixes under the open sky. Rich men surrendered wagon-loads of jewels in the hope that Christ would find them in a state of grace. Debts were revoked; convicts were let out of prison. According to one modern popular author, there was even a wave of suicides by those who could not stand the pressure of waiting for the Last Judgement.[3]

The great nineteenth-century French historian Michelet found evidence of terror and longing in statues of the period. 'See how they implore, with clasped hands, that desired but dreaded moment . . . which is to redeem them from their unspeakable sorrows,' he wrote. Michelet recorded a 'universal belief' that the thousandth year from the Nativity would be the End of the World. But as a good socialist he believed that it was awaited with as much excitement as fear, especially among the miserable and oppressed (categories into which he placed most of the population). 'The captive expected it in his gloomy dungeon . . . The serf expected it whilst tracing the furrow under the shadow of his lord's hated tower. The monk expected it amidst the privations of the cloister, amidst the solitary tumults of his heart, amidst temptations and backslidings, repentances and strange visions . . .' Warming to his theme,

Michelet speculated that for all these folk, even 'a bed of fire' in the afterlife was preferable to their lot on earth. 'Nor could that moment be without its charm, when the shrill and withering trump of the archangel should peal in the ear of their tyrants,' he wrote. 'For then, from dungeon, cloister and from furrow, one tremendous shriek of laughter would burst forth from the stricken and oppressed.'[4]

In the event, however, the only shrieks of laughter have been the derisive ones of twentieth-century historians. For there were no Terrors of the Year 1000, it seems. It is a romantic invention, dating back no further than the sixteenth century. Indeed, some modern historians – especially the French Marxists who once dominated the field – feel it is beneath their dignity even to mention the millennium, except perhaps in a contemptuous footnote. In their lofty view, it demeans the men and women of the late tenth century to suggest that they expected the End of Time at the millennium of Christ's birth: they had far more important matters on their mind, such as the evolution of feudal structures. Other historians do address the subject of the Terrors at some length, but only so that they may demonstrate how utterly without foundation is the notion of an apocalyptic year 1000. In the words of one French historian, 'it is necessary to wring the neck of this legend'.[5]

In theory, at least, this should not be difficult: the anti-apocalyptic school, as it is known, has some powerful evidence at its disposal. It is an undeniable fact that, among the limited range of documents which survives from the late tenth century and early eleventh, not one makes a reference to widespread fear of the world ending in the year 1000. On the contrary, many make it clear that men did envisage a second Christian millennium. There is no shortage of deeds and wills, made shortly before 1000, the provisions of which look many years ahead. In 998 the Council of Rome imposed on the French king, Robert, a penance of seven years; in the following year the Pope granted the Archbishop of Rheims the privilege of crowning future kings of France, proof of his assumption that others would be crowned.

The only tenth-century writer who links the Second Coming

to the year 1000 does so only to dismiss the notion. The theologian Abbo of Fleury, writing in 995, recalls that he heard a sermon preached in Paris around the year 960 in which the preacher announced that 'as soon as the number of a thousand years was completed, the Antichrist would come and the Last Judgement would follow soon', an argument which the impeccably orthodox Abbo was easily able to demolish by quoting scripture.[6] For the truth is that nowhere in the Gospels or Revelation is it stated, or even implied, that the Second Coming will occur a thousand years after the Nativity. Throughout Christian history, the most commonly accepted view among apocalyptic believers has been that the Millennium, the thousand-year reign of the saints described in Revelation, will begin after the Second Coming; this is known as premillennialism, because Christ will come *before* the Millennium. Admittedly, this was not the teaching of the Catholic Church at the end of the tenth century; but nor did the Church teach the opposite view, known as postmillennialism, in which Christ comes at the end of the thousand years. Catholic teaching was, and still is, based on that of St Augustine, who taught that, although the reign of the saints had in some respects already begun, the reference to a thousand years was purely figurative. According to many historians, therefore, the absence of millennial terrors should not surprise us: the Catholic Church, the sole religious authority in the West, never taught that the world would end in the year 1000, and indeed explicitly opposed any attempt to unveil the time of the End. The peasant or nobleman who cowered in church on 31 December 999 would therefore have been advertising his own lack of faith in the teaching of the Church.

But, even if there were a scriptural foundation for believing that Christ would return on 1 January 1000, most modern authorities are convinced that the date would have passed without incident, for the simple reason that the vast majority of people did not know what year it was. This argument is frequently made by historians of the anti-apocalyptic school. The AD dating system was far from universal at the time, they say; most educated people still dated current events by regnal years. In any case, it was all a matter of supreme unconcern to the tenth-century peasant, whose existence was governed entirely by the unalterable progression of the seasons. He, poor fellow, was effectively still stuck in the cyclical time of primitive societies. For him, and for most historians, the year 1000 was – and one often encounters the phrase – 'a year like any other'.

And yet, as the third Christian millennium approaches, the neck of the Legend of the Year 1000 remains unwrung. Indeed, the creature has taken on a new lease of life. The shelves of bookshops are overflowing with popular books of millennial prophecy, many of which describe peasants and their masters trembling in churches on the fateful day. Stephen Skinner's *Millennium Prophecies*, a lavishly illustrated paperback published by Virgin in 1994, waxes eloquent on the subject. 'December [999] saw fanaticism reach new heights as communities attempted to rid their area of the ungodly so that the Angel of Judgement would not need to call,' it says. 'Bands of flagellants roamed the countryside; mobs called for the execution of supposed sorcerers or unpopular burghers, and even some farm animals were freed to roam through the towns, giving a slightly surrealistic air to the proceedings.'[7] Although Skinner appears not to realise it, these are the historical equivalent of urban myths; and, like the legends of the vanishing hitchhiker and the poodle in the microwave, have developed a momentum of their own. No dinner-party conversation about the millennium is complete without a prediction that the world is about to experience mass popular convulsions 'just like it did last time'.

Historians opposed to an apocalyptic reading of the year 1000 can, of course, afford to dismiss these claims; indeed, they enjoy setting the record straight. But what they do not enjoy, and even seem to resent, is any attempt by their fellow academics to challenge the orthodox view of 1000 as 'a year like any other'. Nevertheless, as the millennial anniversary of that date draws closer, that is what is happening. Since the late 1980s, a small group of younger historians of the period, working quite independently, have floated the possibility of a year 1000 which was highly charged with apocalyptic significance. While accepting that the romantic picture of the terrors is essentially a myth, these historians argue that the millennia of Christ's birth in 1000 and resurrection in 1033 were the defining moments in the history of the period. For them, the strange events of those years, such as the vast Peace rallies in the fields of southern France and the German Emperor's reinterment of Charlemagne's bones on the feast of Pentecost 1000, can be understood only if they are seen in an apocalyptic light. As for the absence of contemporary references to the significance of the date, that can be compared to the dog which did not bark in the night: it is a curious incident which may point to a conspiracy of silence.

On one point, however, everyone can agree, and that is the crucial importance of the period in determining the shape of the world we know today. Yet at the same time we know relatively little about it. The dispute about the importance of the year 1000 is a function, first and foremost, of sheer obscurity. Guy Bois calls the era 'one of the most mysterious in our history', ruled by kings who come across as pale shadows of their Carolingian predecessors.[8] Felipe Fernández-Armesto considers the Latin West to be 'perhaps the least civilized civilization of a thousand years ago' in comparison with China, Japan, Islam, India, South-east Asia and eastern Christendom.[9] Was Europe still in the Dark Ages? The documents of the time send out conflicting signals, pointing sometimes to late antiquity and at other times to the middle ages. *Servi* and *ancillae* straight out of a Latin primer work alongside that quintessential medieval figure, the villein. There is a disorientating quality to the landscape: Viking emissaries wander through Byzantium, like extras who have strayed on to the wrong set; Russian Christians are auctioned off as slaves in Muslim Spain.

Western Europe was in many ways the poor relation of Byzantium. Grand and squalid, the court at Constantinople still banqueted on couches and regarded Frankish and Saxon claims to the Roman legacy with amused contempt. Western visitors to Constantinople, meanwhile, were overawed by the city's size –

with its shops, factories and palaces it was the only place in the world which bore any resemblance to a modern city – but were also repelled by its oriental decadence. One of the most revealing documents of the entire period is an account of a visit to Byzantium in 969 by Liudprand, an envoy of Otto the Great. Liudprand described the eastern Emperor Nicephorus ('the king of the Greeks') as a pig-like creature with mole's eyes who was coloured like an Ethiopian; he was lying, crafty and merciless, ate garlic and leeks and, worst of all, drank bathwater. Nicephorus, for his part, taunted Liudprand with the line 'you are not Romans but Lombards', to which his visitor replied that Lombards, Saxons, Franks all felt that the word Roman was synonymous with luxury and vice.[10]

In retrospect, Europe was clearly on the verge of what we call the middle ages. The modern linguistic frontier between France and Germany was taking shape: when the Emperor Otto II met Hugh Capet, Duke of the Franks, they needed an interpreter. In northern France, the feudal system was as well established as it was two centuries later. A monastic revival was under way in France and England. In the north of Europe, Christianity was chasing the religion of Thor and Wodin from its last strongholds: the year 1000 saw the conversion of Iceland, while Denmark and Norway were in the hands of their first Christian kings, and Christianity was making headway among the Swedes. In the east, the rulers of the Ukraine and Hungary had just been baptised; in the south, the collapse of the caliphate in 1002 was welcomed by Christians embarking on what was to be a 500-year campaign to banish the Moors from Spain. Underlying these events, meanwhile, was a steady growth in population which would form the basis of medieval economic growth and which partly explains why, seen from our perspective, early medieval man had so much time on his hands. Only a huge surplus of labour can explain why cathedrals and public buildings sprang up in such numbers, and on such a scale; or why, for that matter, so many people were able to take two or three years out of their life to go on pilgrimage.

But the inhabitants of Europe in the year 1000 would not, of course, have been able to foresee the economic boom of the twelfth century, or the flowering of culture in the Age of Chivalry; nor would they have been able to discern the trend towards urbanisation and a society based on money. On the contrary – and this is where the concept of 'a year like any other' begins to look dubious – there was a widespread feeling that the world was sliding irrevocably into chaos. The last years of the tenth century saw a terrifying and unexpected series of Danish raids on England and a combination of anarchy and famine in France. And, this being the tenth century, one obvious explanation presented itself – an explanation which since New Testament times had been eagerly seized on by Christian believers who were suffering persecution or whose sense of reality was in some way dislocated: the world had entered the reign of the Antichrist prophesied in the Book of Revelation.

The Terrors of the Year 1000 might be a myth, but there can be no denying the sense of doom which permeates so many documents of the period. Throughout the tenth and early eleventh centuries, preachers and chroniclers regularly assured their audiences that their misfortunes were fulfilments of biblical prophecies about the Last Days. It is true that in doing so they were invoking a tradition as old as Christianity itself. But the frequency with which contemporary sources refer to the End of the World, and their obsession with manifestations of the devil, suggest that the end of the millennium coincided with a sense of eschatological crisis. In England, for example, the sermons of Wulfstan, Archbishop of York, refer frequently to the Antichrist in their exhortations to repentance before the fast-approaching Day of Judgement. Wulfstan assures his listeners that England's calamities are punishment for their sins, and identifies the Danish wars with the warning of the End in Chapter 24 of Matthew's Gospel: 'For nation will rise against nation, and kingdom against kingdom, and there will be famines and earthquakes in various places.'

In France, meanwhile, the collapse of the Carolingian dynasty created a vacuum in which the lesser nobility were able to assert their independence – a crucial shift in the power-structure which was to have profound and positive consequences for European society. To the monks who recorded these events, however, it seemed as if society had entered a terminal crisis. 'With the world coming to an end, since men are driven by a briefer life, so does a more atrocious cupidity burn in them,' wrote a monk at St Hilaire of Poitiers in a document dating from around 995. 'Whence it occurs that they take away the possessions of the holy church, now by force, now by extortion, now by the claims of unjust ministers, so that only the name of the holy church remains.'[11] A similar observation was made by Ralph Glaber, the gossipy Burgundian monk whose five-volume *Histories* is one of the most important sources for events in Western Europe at the millennium. Describing the events of the 990s, Glaber reminds his readers that 'Holy Gospel reveals as an evident fact that, as the last days go by, charity will be chilled and iniquity will blossom amongst men.' At such a time, a lust for wantonness and incontinence among the laity and irreligious laxity among the clergy go hand in hand: 'When the piety of bishops wanes, and the austerity of abbots softens, when the rigour of the monastic discipline grows cold, and by their example the rest of the people break God's commands, does it not seem as if the whole of mankind is sliding back of its own free will into the old abyss of perdition?'[12] (Glaber's remark about bishops sounds oddly like the hand-wringing of a modern fundamentalist: nearly a thousand years later, delegates at an evangelical conference in London argued that the 'apostasy' of the former Bishop of Durham, David Jenkins, was a sign of the End.)[13]

It is one thing, however, to show that apocalyptic feelings were running high in Western Europe at the end of the tenth century, much as they did at any time of rapid change; quite another to prove that this was *because* the millennium was about to end. But this is exactly what the revisionist school of historians mentioned earlier has set out to do. The chief advocate of this point of view is Professor Richard Landes of Boston University, who, as we saw in the first chapter, has demonstrated that two versions of the AM dating system mysteriously disappeared from the West just before they were

43

due to reach the long-awaited apocalyptic year 6000 – once in AD 500, and once in AD 800. The Catholic Church, says Landes, was anxious to ensure that its calendar could not be used to trigger an apocalyptic panic. We know from Abbo that decades earlier there were people who believed that the world would end in 1000; but the Church was determined to suppress any such speculation, which verged on the heretical and could have terrible consequences for the stability of society. Hence the complete absence of contemporary sources explicitly linking the apocalypse and the year 1000. This does not mean that the clergy could not invoke the figure of the Antichrist, and even hint that the Last Days had arrived, in order to persuade people to repent. But there could be no question of fixing people's attention on a date in the near future. For a cleric to have dwelt on the eschatological significance of the date 1000 would have been foolhardy and even dangerous. And yet, argues Landes, if we read between the lines of contemporary accounts, a powerful subliminal message emerges. Despite everything the Church could do to play down their significance, both the millennium of Christ's birth and that of his death thirty-three years later possessed resonances for people at all levels of society; so much so, in fact, that at times the political and social events surrounding those two dates were seen as part of an unfolding apocalyptic drama.[14]

The lovable but infuriating figure of Ralph Glaber is central to the apocalyptic interpretation of the year 1000. Anti-apocalyptic historians tend to regard Glaber as 'unreliable', and there is evidence that his fellow monks thought so too: he worked in at least ten monasteries during his career and was thrown out of more than one of them for unruly behaviour. In the words of the late Henri Focillon, the only major French historian this century to challenge the orthodox view of 1000 as a non-event, Glaber was a 'crude apocalyptic genius' who 'has no principle of order or critical sense. But he does possess – and this in the eyes of modern historians is a more serious failing – the artist's gifts.'[15] Glaber records, for example, a magnificently creepy encounter with the devil, who appears when the bell rings for

Matins. He stands at the foot of the monk's bed, a black figure with flattened nose, enormous mouth, goat's beard, dog's teeth and humped back, and plants subversive thoughts in the mind of the sleeper. 'Why do you monks bother with vigils, fasts and humiliations . . . when countless laymen, steeped in disgraceful deeds, will earn the same rest as you? One day, one hour of repentance could suffice to earn eternal bliss . . . So why do you trouble to rise at the sound of the bell when you might go on sleeping?'[16] Fanciful passages like this have made it easy for some historians to dismiss Glaber, though this does not stop them citing the absence of apocalyptic 'terrors' in his work as evidence that nothing much happened in the year 1000. This strikes the revisionists as a case of wanting to have one's cake and eat it: they suspect the real reason for Glaber's unpopularity is precisely that his work undermines the orthodox view that the millennium is of little significance.

Glaber describes his *Histories*, written in the 1030s, as 'the story of the events and prodigies which happened around and after the millennial year of the Incarnation of the Saviour'. When, in Book II, he comes to describe the various disasters which occurred in the decade before the year 1000 he dates them with reference to that year. 'In the seventh year from the millennium . . . almost all the cities of Italy and Gaul were devastated by violent conflagrations, and Rome itself largely razed by fire . . . as one man, [the people] gave out a terrible scream and turned to rush to confess to the Prince of the Apostles.' Later, he records that many eminent men died around this time. The impression that these calamities are connected to the approach of the millennium is reinforced when Glaber refers briefly to an outbreak of heresy in Sardinia. 'All this accords with the prophecy of St John, who said that the devil would be freed after a thousand years,' he says.[17] This is a fascinating comment which, taken in conjunction with Abbo's report of the sermon in Paris, seems to confirm the existence of a popular belief in the End of the World at the millennium. But Glaber does not elaborate, and never returns to the point. His gloomy tone continues, however. As the 'millennium of the birth of the all-vivifying word' approached, he recalls, 'almost the whole world suffered the loss of great men, noble laymen and clerics'.

After describing the comet, Glaber moves to the year 1003, when something miraculous happens:

> Just before the third year after the millennium, throughout the whole world, but especially in Italy and Gaul, men began to reconstruct churches, although for the most part the existing ones were properly built and not in the least unworthy. But it seemed as if each Christian community were aiming to surpass all others in the splendour of construction. It was as if the whole world were shaking itself, shrugging off the burden of the past, and cladding itself everywhere in a white mantle of churches. Almost all the episcopal churches and those of the monasteries dedicated to various saints, and little village chapels, were rebuilt better than before by the faithful.[18]

There is something very distinctive about the chain of events described by Glaber: disasters, mysterious portents, and then a sense of all things made new. Its shape is not unlike that of the ultimate apocalyptic drama, in which the world falls into chaos before the Second Coming. It also mirrors the sequence of events which all millenarians believe will be played out in the near future – except, of course, that they look forward to a completely new heaven and earth. But what are we to make of it? Is the passion for rebuilding churches a simple sign of people's relief that the world has not ended – or is it an expression of a more profound faith in the future? Richard Landes, for one, is not prepared to accept that the dawn of the new Christian millennium in the middle of these events is a coincidence, any more than the disappearance of the AM I calendar just before the fateful year 6000 was a coincidence. For in both cases, a suspicious event, or sequence of events, occurs again when the conditions are replicated. Like its elder brother, AM II disappears just before its 6,000th birthday; and, in the same way, when a new millennium occurs – that of Christ's death in 1033 – the drama of the year 1000 seems to repeat itself.

Furthermore, Glaber suggests that, as the second millennium approached, some people were actually prepared for a sense of *déjà vu.* 'After the many prophecies which had broken upon the world, before, after and around the millennium of the Lord Christ,' he says, 'there were plenty of able men of penetrating intellect who foretold others, just as great, at the approach of the millennium of the Lord's Passion, and such wonders were soon manifest.' This time around, the disasters are truly terrifying. A famine forces men to eat potters' clay and wolves gorge on the dead. 'Men feared that the orderly procession of the seasons and the laws of nature . . . had relapsed into eternal chaos; and they feared that mankind would end,' says Glaber, who now uses the year 1033 to set the date. Heresy breaks out among the Lombards: 'Like the pagans, [the heretics] worshipped idols, and like the Jews, they made vain sacrifices.' In 1033, the roads to Jerusalem fill up with an unprecedented number of pilgrims. Asked why this is happening, the 'more truthful of that time . . . cautiously responded that it presaged nothing else but the coming of the Lost One, the Antichrist, who according to divine authority stands ready to come at the End of the Age. Then the road to the eastern region from which he was to come was opened to all nations, so that all might go forth to meet him without delay.'[19] This appears to be unambiguous evidence of millenarian sentiment occurring at *and produced by* the millennium of Christ's death. It is so clear-cut that one begins to wonder whether the legend of the Terrors of the Year 1000 is not, after all, based on fact. There is no record of crowds fleeing to Jerusalem in 1000, but if they did so in 1033 it is tempting to speculate that there may be something after all in the spectre of the 'desolating army', its eyes fixed on the skies for the sight of the descending Christ. Or could it be that popular legend has somehow transplanted the events of 1033 to the earlier and more famous millennium?

Finally, Glaber's description of the dawning of the 1033 millennium conjures up a picture of a relieved population offering thanks for the renewal of creation. 'At the millennial anniversary of the passion of the Lord, the clouds cleared in obedience to divine mercy and goodness, and the smiling sky began to shine and blow gentle breezes,' he says.

At that point, in the region of Aquitaine, bishops, abbots and other men devoted to holy religion first began to gather councils of the whole people . . . When the news of these assemblies was heard, the entire populace joyfully came, unanimously prepared to follow whatever should be commanded them by the pastors of the church. A voice descending from heaven could not have done more. For everyone was still under the effects of the previous calamities and feared the future loss of abundance.[20]

Glaber is describing something called the 'Peace of God': a movement of popular revulsion against warring noblemen which was initiated by the clergy and lasted in one form or another for several decades. This movement, which began in the 990s, is regarded by pro-apocalyptic scholars as vital to their case. But, before looking at their ideas on the subject, it is worth noting that Glaber is not the only contemporary source whose references to the year 1000 can be used to undermine the thesis that it was a date like any other. Another chronicler, Thietmar of Merseburg, describes it as 'the best year since the immaculate Virgin brought forth our Salvation', when 'a radiant dawn was seen to shine upon the world'. Meanwhile, the author of the *Annales Hildesheimenses*, writing in the late 1030s, says: 'With Otto III ruling, the thousandth year passing the number of established reckoning according to that which is written: The thousandth surpasses and transcends all years.' And the monk from St Amand of Lobbes in Lotharingia who painstakingly recorded the earthquake 'in the year of the incarnation 1000, indiction 13, epacts 12, concurrents 1, paschal term 9, the 4th of the kalends of April, the sixth day' adds these cryptic words: 'For these, and other signs which were foretold as necessary, having been fulfilled, from here already our hope grows more certain of those things which remain to be completed in order.'[21] In the words of Richard Landes: 'Only by insisting that we have no right to speculate on the meaning of "these and other signs" and "our hope" on the one hand, and by overlooking the unusual attention to detailing the date, can one claim this provides no evidence of apocalyptic concerns in the year 1000.'[22]

*

Landes believes that the Peace of God movement, whose early phase lasted from the 990s until the 1030s, bears the stamp of an authentic millenarian movement. His theory draws on new research into documents of the period and on sociological analysis of millenarian beliefs in general. The latter have interested him since his student days in the late 1960s and early 1970s – a period when he watched many contemporaries work themselves up into a state of feverish excitement in anticipation of the collapse of the existing order, only to face a period of painful readjustment when it survived. Could something similar have happened in France around the year 1000?

The Peace of God provides some of the most memorable tableaux in medieval history. Huge throngs gather in open fields to venerate relics and witness their miraculous power: when the remains of St Martial are raised up at a gathering in Limoges in 994, the entire crowd is healed of its ailments. Holy banners flutter in the wind as the lesser nobility – the newly powerful warrior elite – swear oaths of peace. This is not spontaneous: they are responding to a public opinion skilfully manipulated by clerical magnates worried about the security of their estates. That is why the bishops called the councils in the first place. But, in doing so, they clearly tapped a vein of intense religious enthusiasm in the population which several scholars working in this area believe is linked to the advent of the millennium. Daniel Callahan, in his study of the cult of the saints in Aquitaine, finds that charters of the period refer to fear of the proximity of the Last Judgement more often than in the past or the future;[23] Bernhard Töpfer has examined the extraordinary growth of relic cults shortly before the year 1000.[24] To understand the Peace councils, says Landes, medieval historians need to grasp the dynamics of apocalyptic behaviour and learn to identify its traces. His study of events in Limoges in 994, when in response to an outbreak of 'fire plague' the bishop, abbot and duke called a three-day fast followed by a council, suggests a classic millenarian sequence. First, there was that essential ingredient of most millenarian scenarios, a disaster. The plague was possibly an outbreak of ergotism, a hallucinogenic poison which appeared with the spread of rye cultivation;

it can affect whole communities, producing visions 'from atrocious visions of hell to ecstatic ones of heaven', and indeed did so in France as recently as the 1950s. This was followed by a mass religious response of terror and guilt, public acts of repentance, a miracle producing euphoria and, finally, an alliance of peace and justice mutually sworn by all the lords present. This course of events, like those described by Glaber, corresponds closely to the millenarian scenario evoked in the bible: 'from divinely sent terror and destruction, to repentance and turning to God, to collective salvation, to a new society on earth'.[25]

Now compare this to Ralph Glaber's vivid description of a council in 1033, at which miracles 'aroused such enthusiasm that the bishops raised their staffs towards heaven and all present stretched their palms to God, shouting with one voice "Peace! Peace!" '[26] This passage sounds suspiciously like a description of millennial fervour. There is no sense of apocalyptic terror, but then millenarian movements are not exclusively motivated by fear: the very name Peace of God suggests messianic hopes of a transformation of this world into a realm of peace and justice. People who expect an immediate apocalypse are not always paralysed by terror but often act constructively and energetically. And, when their initial prophecies have been proven false, they adjust rather than discard their millenarian beliefs. It is a strange fact that apocalyptic disappointment can produce a great surge of energy – enough, perhaps, to produce a 'white mantle of churches' in recognition of the fact that mankind has passed its moment of greatest danger and has entered a new millennium. Some people, at least, may have thought in these terms; others may well have transferred their fears and hopes, and those of their children, to the year 1033. At any rate, we must not assume that there was a standard response to the year 1000. The millennial fever of the Peace of God – if that is what it was – is closely bound up with far-reaching social changes which were, at that stage, peculiar to France. We should not be surprised, therefore, that there is no hint of similar excitement in England, Italy or Germany. But there are other clues to an apocalyptic year 1000.

The sudden reappearance of heresy in the West, after a gap of several centuries, may indeed be connected to the millennium, as Glaber suggests. Certainly, popular fear of heretics seems to be bound up with it, in the form of a belief that the devil would be loosed after a thousand years. One contemporary source tells us that the heretics:

> met on certain nights in an appointed house, each one carrying a light, and chanted, in the form of a litany, the Devil's names, until suddenly they saw the Devil come down among them in the guise of a beast. All lights were immediately extinguished, and they gave themselves up to a nameless debauch. Each man seized the nearest woman, not inquiring whether she were his mother, his sister, or a religious. The child born of this impure union was brought in on the eighth day after its birth; a great fire was lit and the baby passed through the flames in the pagan manner. The ashes of the poor creature were gathered up and preserved with the same veneration wherewith Christians preserved the body of Christ.[27]

What is extraordinary about this report is its resemblance to scare stories of ritual satanic abuse which circulated in the West at the end of the twentieth century, in which 'brood mares' were supposed to give birth to babies which were abused and then eaten. It has been suggested that the modern stories, circulated by evangelical Christians, are an unconscious response to the approach of the year 2000. We do not know for sure whether tenth-century reports of infanticidal heretics owe their currency to the proximity of the millennium, though Glaber implies as much. But we are on firm ground in suggesting that both types of story are apocalyptic: that is, they are informed by a belief that Satan will inspire terrible atrocities in the years before the final conflict between good and evil.

Another striking clue to an apocalyptic year 1000 can be found in the unlikely setting of the German imperial court. Indeed, the mysterious behaviour of the young Emperor Otto III in and around the millennial year is hard to understand except as role-playing in an imagined End-time drama. The Ottonians, despite or perhaps because of their barbarian ancestry, were obsessed with the idea of ruling a reincarnated Roman Empire.

Otto, who was half Saxon and half Greek by birth, succeeded to the throne at the age of three and took over the reins of power in 994 at the age of fourteen. He had been brought up among clerics who were fascinated by the apocalyptic imagery of the Book of Revelation, and in a court which took very seriously the tradition of Rome as the last and greatest world empire. Otto was determined to present himself as a true Roman, even to the extent of reinstituting the ancient custom of the emperor dining alone.

Just before the millennium, Otto did in fact manage to seize control of Rome and to install his mentor Gerbert as pope; his intention was that the spiritual hegemony of the Roman Church would spread in tandem with the temporal power of the Emperor, to encompass Hungary, Russia and Scandinavia. He adopted a seal which included the words *Renovatio imperii Romanorum*; the implication was that, under him, the history of the world had reached its glorious apogee. In the year 1000, Otto visited Charlemagne's capital of Aachen. 'He was in doubt where the bones of Charlemagne lay,' records Thietmar. 'So he had the floor [of the basilica] secretly breached, and ordered workmen to dig where he thought they were. In due course the bones were found seated on the royal throne. Otto removed the golden cross which hung on Charles's neck, and such of the clothes as had not crumbled to dust, and the rest were reinterred with great devotion.'[28] This reburial, which took place on the feast of Pentecost, is clearly a symbolic event; and it becomes even more so when we remember that Charlemagne was crowned in a year, 800, which at the time was believed to mark the beginning of the seventh and final thousand-year period in history. For the Emperor of the year 1000 to have paid tribute to the Emperor of the year 6000 at such a juncture draws attention to a powerful symmetry. But, given the hostility of the Church to any suggestion of date-setting, it could not be officially acknowledged or explained, and the precise meaning of Otto's gesture remains elusive.

Any doubts about the young Emperor's sense of apocalyptic drama are dispelled, however, by his reaction to being driven out of Rome by a rebellion just after the millennium. His dreams of an eternal empire seem to have been immediately replaced by a belief, also hallowed by tradition, that the dissolution of the Roman Empire would be followed by the rule of Antichrist. According to Adso of Montier-en-Der, a celebrated tenth-century apocalyptic writer, a Frankish emperor of Rome who was 'the last and greatest of rulers' would, after governing his empire, go to Jerusalem and put off his sceptre and crown at the Mount of Olives; this would be the end and consummation of the Christian empire and the beginning of the reign of Antichrist. This legend of the Last World Emperor was already centuries old in Otto's day and was to reappear at frequent intervals until the end of the middle ages. But few rulers took it as seriously as Otto, who, on losing control of Rome, ostentatiously resolved to renounce his titles, travel to Rome and become a monk – actions that, if one believed the legend, would hasten the end not just of the empire but of history itself. Otto, in other words, had changed his position from attempting to postpone the End by ruling over an eternal empire, to attempting to bring it about. As it turned out, he died in 1002, before he could do either. But the crucial point is that in the years surrounding the millennium we find the most powerful ruler in the West compulsively measuring his actions against an eschatological yardstick, totally preoccupied by the End of Time.

The Emperor Otto, of course, would have been well aware of the approach of the fateful year 1000. There remains, though, the awkward question of how many people in Western Europe would have had access to this information – and, if so, whether they would have cared. Inevitably, the apocalyptic and anti-apocalyptic schools differ on this point. The former admit that the Anno Domini calendar was not universal, but insist that it was extremely well established in the monasteries of western Europe. Anyone who came into contact with monks, either by working on monastic estates or by encountering them on their frequent travels, would have been in a position to establish the AD date; all they had to do was ask. But the anti-apocalyptic scholars point out, quite correctly, that the whole notion of 'date' had not fully developed by this stage. The vast majority of people in Europe had no need to know what year it was; and, in any case, there was no consensus about when the year began and ended. New Year's Day fell on 1 January in many places, but in Rome at Christmas, in Florence on 25 March, in Venice on 1 March and in France at Easter.[29]

But was it necessary to think in terms of calendars and dates to be aware of the onset of the millennium? We are in danger once again of imposing an anachronistic understanding of time on an earlier society. The millennium was not synonymous with 'entering a new century', a meaningless concept at the time. And the fact that there would be an overnight shift in the calendar year from CMXCIX to M, albeit at different times all over Europe, does not seem to have impressed anyone. From reading Glaber, it seems clear that what mattered to him above all was the simple fact that a thousand years had elapsed since the Saviour's birth. From this it followed that the next thirty-three years would witness the millennium of the life of Christ, culminating in the glorious anniversary of his death and resurrection. For the crowds shouting 'Peace! Peace!' in the fields of France, the beginning and end of this period seem to have aroused intense millennial expectations of a new heaven and a new earth; and the same may be true of the pilgrims who rushed to Jerusalem in 1033. In contrast, there must have been many people – in areas where the Anno Domini calendar was not established, such as the fringes of the West and most of Eastern Christendom – for whom the year 1000 really was a year like any other.

It seems likely, though, that the millennial experiences of most people lay somewhere in between these extremes. On the first page of his *Histories*, Glaber talks about 'many events [deaths, disasters, church building] which occurred with unusual frequency about the millennium of the Incarnation of Christ our Saviour', without explaining *why* they happened more often at this time. This is probably because he did not know why; although he implies that there was a connection between these interesting times and the millennium, he does not presume to understand God's purpose. Other documents of the period hint at popular feelings of anxiety or fear before both millennial anniversaries, and celebration or relief after them; but these are neither explained nor described in any detail. This may be because the authors, who were almost all monks, were forbidden to speculate on such matters. But it may also be because they could not fully account for such feelings. And if that is the case, then the gap between our perceptions of the millennium and those of the men and women of a thousand years ago is perhaps not so great after all.

3

Pursuing the Millennium

The medieval world's mental picture of the End of Time, and of the supernatural forces that will bring it about, often seems utterly remote from our own understanding of time and evil. We normally encounter the medieval apocalypse only in the form of art from the end of the period: paintings, statues and woodcuts of terrified mortals cowering before the Last Judgement, or of the Four Horsemen of the Apocalypse. So dramatic are these images that we can easily persuade ourselves that they belong to the realm of artistic inspiration rather than to that of simple, stark belief. But the truth is that no one during the middle ages doubted that the world would end after a terrible earthly confrontation between the forces of good and evil. The details of this drama, and the order of the acts, varied according to country and century: it might be indefinitely delayed, it might begin tomorrow, or it might have already been set in motion. But to deny its inevitability was unthinkable, tantamount to denying the truth of the Christian religion.

If it is hard to understand the literal belief of the most intelligent men of the middle ages in the doctrines and folklore of the End, it is also easy to dismiss these beliefs as long-dead superstitions with no relevance outside their own era. Yet the explosion of fundamentalist Christianity since the Second World War is testimony to the power of End-time beliefs which, in the role they assign to the Antichrist, have strong affinities with medieval apocalypticism. In the opinion of liberal Christians and secular commentators, this merely confirms the primitive and fear-filled character of fundamentalism. But these critics are mistaken if they imagine that the legacy of medieval eschatology is confined to the world of televangelists and charismatic healers. Ironically, many of the ideas we consider to be the very opposite of 'medieval', such as faith in progress and the promise of utopia, have roots in the religious beliefs of the middle ages – and End-time beliefs at that. The role played by apocalyptic belief in the development of Western society is complex, subtle and pervasive; and, once it is fully appreciated, the ungovernable passions that lie behind the twentieth century's most destructive conflicts become easier to understand.

We are entering a strange and frightening world in which nothing is predictable except the final triumph of good over evil after a battle of cosmic proportions. Christian apocalyptic belief has, down the centuries, always made great play of its fidelity to biblical prophecy. In practice, though, scripture is often little more than a ground bass for wild improvisations on the theme of the End. Even the most scrupulous Christian scholars have had to display great ingenuity in their quest for a coherent scenario of the Last Days which takes in Ezekiel, Daniel, the Gospels, St Paul and, of course, Revelation. The less inhibited authors of interpretative prophecies, meanwhile, have tended to allow their imaginations full rein. We possess literally thousands of texts, dating from the second century to the present day, in which not only are current affairs presented as the fulfilment of prophecy, but prophecy is used to reveal the nature, order and timing of the events leading up to the Last Judgement. Biblical apocalypse, which is itself highly rhetorical and allegorical, acquires an extra layer of complexity as prophecy authors invent new characters and allegorical images.

This is especially true of the middle ages, when End-time prophecies were a vital frame of reference for people of all walks of life. Their content and style vary enormously: many prophecies are pseudonymous, like the Book of Daniel, and play the old trick of predicting events which have already happened; others are the work of visionaries, whose glimpses of the End were for some reason often afforded them when they were lying in bed. But the theme which predominates is that of conflict. True to the roots of the genre in Persian dualism, these texts see all earthly dramas in terms of a battle between the forces of light and darkness. Evil is represented by the Antichrist, the human incarnation of Satan and one of the most powerful icons in history. According to one persistent tradition, no human agency would ever vanquish him: not even the Last Emperor, a mighty figure who, as we saw in the last chapter, was expected by some authorities to lay down his crown and sceptre on the Mount of Olives in order to allow Antichrist to begin the reign of evil foretold in scripture. Yet nearly all the prophecies also envisage a period of peace on earth; this is either a glorious lull before Antichrist appears or the Millennium established after his defeat.

This juxtaposition of terror and bliss is one of the most important features of apocalyptic belief, in the middle ages and in our own day. Many prophecies manage to fit both into a sequence of events; but we should not therefore assume that every believer has managed to sort out the two in his or her mind. The coexistence of visions of destruction and peace is a fundamental source of instability. Individual expectations have a habit of lurching from one to the other in a manner that points to the psychological turmoil associated with the End-time. In extreme cases, it is necessary for the faithful to engage in a life-and-death conflict with a satanic enemy before they can enjoy their glorious reward.

The middle ages provide us with unforgettable and gruesome examples of this sort of movement: self-contained groups which are not only apocalyptic, believing in an End-time, but truly millenarian. Curiously, these had been largely absent from the first millennium of Christianity. We have already encountered the second-century Montanists, who were classically millenarian in that they lived in daily expectation of the dawn of the

Millennium of the Book of Revelation: they were convinced that the New Jerusalem was about to come crashing down from the heavens at any moment. There are reports of ecstatic, cult-like behaviour among the Montanists, and even of suicide when the apocalypse failed to arrive, but on the whole we know little about the movement and its relation to society in general. And, after its disappearance, the millenarian trail goes cold for nearly a thousand years, thanks partly to the Catholic Church's resolute opposition to anything which smacked of apocalyptic fervour. It does not start up again until the Peace of God movement, which as we have seen almost certainly possessed millenarian features, and is not clearly visible until the People's Crusade at the end of the eleventh century.

This movement was a popular and unplanned response to Pope Urban II's call for an army to liberate Jerusalem from the Saracens. His Holiness had in mind a well-disciplined force of knights who, he hinted, would be rewarded with splendid new estates in the Middle East. But, in addition, his call was heard by thousands of peasants in the West who, significantly, had just endured a succession of natural disasters including drought, failed harvests and a particularly virulent form of plague which wiped out whole villages at a stroke. These peasants formed their own army of crusaders and began to wander eastwards. Gradually, their image of the real Jerusalem became confused with the perfect New Jerusalem of scripture; rumours circulated of a miraculous realm where the common people lived like princes. This is classic millenarianism, unmistakably the product of the 'relative deprivation' caused by famine and plague. And now the darker side of the millennial vision is also present: the peasants and vagabonds accompanying the crusade were responsible for the massacre of between 4,000 and 8,000 Jews, the first such mass slaughter in European history. The link between genocide and the millenarian imagination was to prove an enduring feature of the next few centuries, up to and including the twentieth. Indeed, the systematic killing of millions of people is probably only explicable in terms of an apocalyptic ideology which casts the victims, however defenceless, in the role of a demonic enemy: one whose removal is an

59

essential precondition for the establishment of the millennial kingdom, be it New Jerusalem, Thousand-Year Reich or Dictatorship of the Proletariat.

By the thirteenth century, outbreaks of millenarianism had become an unpleasantly familiar feature of life in the West. They are the subject of the most influential book ever written about apocalyptic belief, Norman Cohn's *The Pursuit of the Millennium*, whose processions of half-starved shepherds, unfrocked monks and bandits have weaved their way through nearly every academic discussion of millenarianism since it appeared forty years ago. This is partly because the book brilliantly conveys the full horror of its subject: it is not easy to banish from the mind the picture of crazed peasants whipping themselves into a frenzy before plunging into towns to slaughter Jews and merchants. But is is also because it firmly establishes the link between millenarian belief and popular anxiety, especially that inspired by social and economic dislocation. The climax of *The Pursuit of the Millennium* is provided by the revolutionary millenarian movements of fifteenth-century Bohemia and sixteenth-century Germany, in which whole communities erected barricades against the forces of the Antichrist. Although these uprisings were inspired by the Book of Revelation, whose scenes of barbaric cruelty they seemed determined to reproduce, there is an intoxicating whiff of class conflict in the air. Cohn does not suggest, however, that economic change is always the driving force behind millenarian movements. He believes that the common denominator of most of them is psychological disorientation, which can be produced by market forces but also by something as intangible as loss of faith in the Catholic Church; this, he argues, was the motivating factor for the radical apocalyptic movements of the late thirteenth and early fourteenth century, such as the Franciscan Spirituals.

Irrespective of their underlying motivation, the groups described by Cohn have much in common: they have set themselves apart from mainstream society in the belief that the world as they know it is about to be torn apart in an earth-shattering cataclysm. Yet their beliefs are not as far removed from those of medieval society at large as one might imagine. Cohn did not set out to survey the whole corpus of medieval apocalypticism: he was well aware that his homicidal mystical anarchists emerged from a society which was deeply preoccupied with questions of the End. One of the most remarkable features of the middle ages in Catholic Europe is the way in which apocalyptic belief, which was always part of Church teaching but had been sidelined for centuries, slowly worked its way towards the centre of power and civilisation.

This process of rehabilitation, which occurred between about 1000 and 1400, is evidence of the ability of End-time belief to insinuate itself into circles where one would not expect it to be welcomed or taken seriously. But perhaps we should not be surprised. In the first place, we should not underestimate the susceptibility of the human mind to apocalyptic ideas, especially at a time of rapid change. Apocalypticism, which developed as a genre at a time of acute stress for the Jews, feeds on uncertainty and disorientation – states of mind which are not confined to any one class or educational background, and which were never in short supply during the later middle ages. Secondly, apocalypticism is astonishingly versatile. End-time scenarios have the ability to adapt to their surroundings through a process of rapid mutation: from learned and solemn prophecy into rabid millenarian fantasy and back again. At any rate, apocalyptic belief did not fade away with the passing of the millennia of Christ's birth and death. Instead, it took on a new dynamism as the West attempted to come to terms with such momentous developments as the Crusades, the Reform of the papacy, the struggle between Pope and Holy Emperor, and the Great Schism, all of which seemed to presage the End. Augustine's attempts to replace lurid scenarios with a purely spiritual interpretation of biblical eschatology were all but forgotten, even in Rome.

Throughout the middle ages the terrifying spectre of the Antichrist intruded itself into the nightmares of pope and peasant alike. Historians often took prophetic tradition as seriously as scripture. A typical example of apocalyptic reasoning can be found in the writings of Guibert of Nogent (1064–

1125), who informed would-be Crusaders that they should seize Jerusalem as a necessary prelude to its eventual capture by Antichrist. 'The End of the world is already near,' he explained. 'According to prophecy, it is first necessary that the Christian empire be renewed in these parts, so that the head of all evil [Antichrist] who will have his imperial throne there may find some nourishment of faith against which he may fight.'[1] That an orthodox French abbot should offer such a starkly apocalyptic interpretation of events in the Middle East is evidence of the new respectability of End-time speculation. Guibert had little in common with the bands of excitable peasants who sewed crosses on their tunics and flocked towards Jerusalem. He was a highly educated priest who used apocalypticism to analyse current events much as a modern commentator might use political or economic theory. We should note in passing the contrast between Guibert's confident and explicit use of End-time imagery and the hesitant way in which, a generation earlier, Ralph Glaber had invoked the figure of the Antichrist in explaining the pilgrimages to Jerusalem in 1033. By the twelfth century, apocalyptic belief was no longer thought to be intrinsically dangerous. Most prophecies, despite their assumption that the End was near, had no connection with popular revolutionary movements. As Bernard McGinn puts it, they were 'attempts of the educated clerks to make sense of major changes in society within the universal scheme of history provided by apocalypticism'.[2]

This is an important point. Obsession with the Last Days often goes hand in hand with the division of history into ages, and since medieval authors believed that the terrible events unfolding on the world stage marked the beginning of the End there was a strong urge to relate them to a divine overview. With the adoption of the AD system, however, there was no longer a fascination with the year 6000. The emphasis shifted from the Great Week to the period of history beginning with the Incarnation, which historians sought to break down into divinely ordained ages. A classic example is the pattern of seven states in the life of the Church devised by Anselm of Havelberg (c. 1100–58), who based them on the seven seals in the Book of

Revelation. Anselm's states begin with the white horse of Revelation, 'the first state of the Church, gleaming and very beautiful in the brightness of miracles'; they end with Revelation's earthquake, which is the 'very strong persecution in the age of the Antichrist', followed by a seventh state of utter silence and finally the glory of the Second Coming. But even more striking is what happens in the middle: the states overlap, so that it is not clear which stage has been reached. And amid warnings of the deadly danger posed by false brethren, 'of whom there is now an innumerable multitude', there is a sudden change of tone. 'Religious men' and lovers of truth appear on the scene, and 'the youth of the Church is renewed like that of the eagle. By this it is both able to fly higher in contemplation and with almost unblinded eyes can behold the rays of the true sun more clearly.'[3]

Anselm believed that, however many religious men appeared, the triumph of Antichrist was assured; yet this awful foreknowledge does not seem to have dampened his spirits. Throughout the medieval and early modern period, one encounters a longing for the appearance of Antichrist which is entirely logical, given his pivotal role in bringing about the eventual triumph of Christ. It is rather like the thrill with which Jehovah's Witnesses greeted the outbreak of war in 1914: these terrible things must come to pass. With Anselm, however, there is an unmistakable note of optimism which relates not to the infinite beatitude of Christ's rule after the defeat of Antichrist, but to the forthcoming achievements of the Church. We are on the verge of something which, to the twentieth-century mind, ought to be the polar opposite of doom-laden apocalypticism: the future golden age *within history*.

The development of this concept is almost entirely due to one man: Joachim of Fiore (c. 1135–1202), a Calabrian abbot and semi-hermit who had visions of intricate patterns drawing together all the threads of revelation and history. Joachim was an apocalyptic thinker who was convinced that Saracen onslaughts on the Crusaders corresponded to the opening of the sixth seal of Revelation; he could therefore offer Richard the

Lionheart little comfort when the English King, *en route* to the Third Crusade, summoned him down from his mountain retreat and asked for a glimpse of the future. 'What black tidings lie beneath that cowl!' a contemporary is supposed to have exclaimed – a comment which, with hindsight, could hardly be more wide of the mark. For although Joachim believed that he lived in an age of unique crisis, and that the Antichrist would soon appear, he saw his defeat as ushering in a new age of history in which a reformed Church would form the perfect society: the Age of the Spirit.

When Abbot Joachim meditated on history he saw kaleidoscopic patterns of numbers, similar to but even more ornate than those of ancient numerology. He took to an extreme the principle, so characteristic of the medieval world but in fact as old as civilisation, that each event in history corresponds to an event in another dimension of time or space. According to Joachim, the Old and New Testaments were divided into seven parallel periods, and each numerical pattern in the Old had its counterpart in the New. The three chief patriarchs, Abraham, Isaac and Joseph, were therefore in harmony with Zacharias, John the Baptist and Christ, and with the three persons of the Trinity. The leading authority on Joachim, Marjorie Reeves, has summed up beautifully this way of looking at history, which appears so contrived to the modern observer: 'It is as if each happening had a vertical point of reference, a "thread" in the hand of God who combined threads into patterns on the inner side of history, whereas we look only for the horizontal connections and the pattern of visible cause and effect spun out along the time span.'[4]

We should bear in mind the incredible sophistication of Joachim's thinking when we consider his most celebrated inspiration, the Ages of the Father, Son and Spirit. Joachim believed that all of history would be encompassed by these three overlapping ages, or 'states', which involved a progressive revelation of divine wisdom. Inspired by the Trinity, he used three-part analogies to describe the relationship between the ages: it would be like that of winter, spring and summer; starlight, dawn and the perfect day; grass, corn and wheat;

nettles, roses and lilies. The Age of the Son was coming to an end; but it would not suddenly yield to that of the Spirit. Joachim calculated that since there had been forty-two generations from Adam to Christ, there would be forty-two from Christ to the new age. The year 1200 coincided with forty generations, he reckoned; the implication was that the Third Age would have arrived by 1260. It would not, however, manifest itself all at once: there would be a difficult period of transition, of battle with the Antichrist, in which a new breed of 'spiritual men', hermits and preachers, would come to the rescue of the forces of good. Then, at last, the new age would begin.

Joachim envisaged this Age of the Spirit as a sublimely happy era in which a renewed Church would regulate every aspect of life; it was, therefore, an exclusively Catholic vision. But this is not how it has gone down in history. For, although Joachim thought of himself as entirely orthodox, his glorious new era was to occur within history and was therefore more utopia than Millennium. And it also involved the creation of fresh social structures. These may have been Catholic orders and communities, but the fact remains that they were new. This has led to Joachim being blamed for every failed utopian experiment from Savonarola's Florence to Soviet Communism. Although this is unfair, there is a grain of truth in the charge. Joachim's tripartite scheme does seem to have influenced later revolutionaries, a number of whom conceived of their earthly paradise as a *third* stage in human history: the Third Reich is an obvious example. Joachim was not, of course, the first thinker to invest spiritual significance in the number three: the very earliest literate societies were overawed by its symbolic power as the sum of one and two. In a more general sense, however, the Abbot of Fiore did help to bring about an irreversible shift in human ideas. Without necessarily meaning to, he had made the crucial connection between apocalyptic change and political reconstruction. From the thirteenth century onwards, the two could never be entirely separated.

From the moment of his death, Joachim's ideas became public

property. They were amplified and distorted by his followers, alternately condemned and adopted by the Church hierarchy, and combined with the legend of the Last Emperor to justify the dynastic ambitions of European rulers. The traces of Joachimite thinking in the writings of popes, anti-papal polemicists, doomsday sects, Jesuits, English millenarian Protestants and French socialists are testimony not only to the power of his vision of a reformed godly society; they also illustrate the capacity of End-time ideas to mutate, so that different versions of an apocalyptic vision can be used simultaneously to bolster a political elite, to bring about measured reform and to justify bloody revolution.

Joachim's elegant formulations struck an immediate chord with supporters of peaceful and progressive change. Reform of the Church, a topic which began to loom large from the beginning of the thirteenth century, was also one of Joachim's central preoccupations. He ascribed great importance to the 'spiritual men' who would work towards the transformation of the Church in the Third Age. They would be thoroughly learned, yet their conversation would be 'light and spiritual as a cloud'. In emphasising their role, Joachim was making a point about ecclesiastical worldliness through the medium of prophecy, always a safer bet than voicing specific criticisms: a useful feature of the apocalyptic genre was that it could convey dissatisfaction with the status quo in a more subtle and, for the author, less dangerous way than outright polemic. But the essentially conservative Joachim would have been horrified to think that his vision of *reformatio* would exacerbate bitter divisions within the body of Christ and would even lead to heresy. Yet it was bound to happen, precisely because Joachim thought entirely in terms of apocalyptic. However much we stress the complex role of apocalypticism in European history – its usefulness as an analytical tool for the educated elite and as a surreptitious means of proposing reform – there is no denying its sheer volatility. Indeed, by offering the wonderful prospect of a golden age following the defeat of Antichrist, Joachim may have made it more unstable. The vision of the Third Age was so blindingly intense that it proved impossible for some would-be reformers to keep within the boundaries imposed by Catholic doctrine and the social order.

The image of an order of spiritual men, living a life of spartan holiness in the Last Days, proved irresistible to the radical wing of the Franciscans, who used it in support of their campaign for a return to the pristine simplicity of their founder's vision. Invoking Joachim gave this struggle a sense of urgency: for this purification was to be not a nostalgic return to the past, but a move towards the fulfilment of God's plan for the end of an age, in which St Francis took on a Christ-like role. Peter Olivi, leader of the Franciscan purists, gave a new twist to the Joachimite idea that the seven ages of the world corresponded to the seven ages of the Church: 'Just as in the sixth age [of the world], when carnal Judaism and the old age of the former era were rejected, so the carnal Church and the old age of this era will be rejected in the sixth status [age of the Church], for which reason Francis appeared at its outset marked with the wounds of Christ, totally conformed to Christ and crucified with him.'[5] It would be hard to come up with one sentence which combines so many features of apocalypticism: in it, we see a contemporary (though recently dead) figure assuming eschatological significance; the hope of a Joachimite golden age within history, brought about by reform; the 'thread' linking Christ to Francis; and, underlying everything, the Great Week and the ubiquitous human assumption that mankind is in the penultimate act of the cosmic drama.

For all its radical implications, Olivi's analysis uses Joachimite imagery to promote the cause of reform rather than revolution. But by the time he was writing, at the end of the thirteenth century, it was already clear that these images had the potential to inspire a far more extreme vision of the future, one which can without hesitation be described as millenarian. The Apostolic Brethren, founded in 1260, were the first group in European history to take the fatal step from preaching apocalyptic ideas to armed resistance to the forces of Church and state. Led by Fra Dolcino, the son of a priest from Parma, its members believed that authority had passed from the Roman Church to themselves, and that the Pope, cardinals, bishops and all the clergy would soon be exterminated by the forces of the Last Emperor in a tremendous battle leading to the Age of the Spirit. In 1304 Dolcino and his followers retreated to the Alpine valleys to await the coming conflagration. Three years later, after attracting local peasant support, they took up arms themselves and were slain in a battle at Monte Rebello.

The Apostolic Brethren undoubtedly represent a stage in the development of the revolutionary millenarian ideology which was to appear a century later among the Bohemian Taborites, and which was itself a precursor of the radical political millenarianism which flourished during the English Commonwealth. This, in its turn, contributed to the emergence of phenomena as varied as nineteenth-century anarchism and the American millennial vision. But it is a mistake to see the Apostolic Brethren only in terms of a revolutionary lineage. They are important in their own right, as one of the first 'doomsday cults'. Of all the apocalyptic mutations, none has appeared with such tragic regularity as the small group which hides behind fortifications in expectation of glorious deliverance from a cataclysmic onslaught by the forces of evil. All too often, the prophecy is self-fulfilling – or, at least, part of it is. The believers jump the gun by taking up arms themselves, and the onslaught materialises. If there is any truth in the notion of historical correspondence, then there is surely a thread leading from Monte Rebello in 1307 to Waco in 1993.

What led the Apostolic Brethren to the brink? As with the Montanists, we know frustratingly little about them, but there are some useful clues, not least the date of their foundation. The year 1260 is the first since 1033 which can unequivocally be described as an apocalyptic milestone. This was thanks to disciples of Joachim of Fiore, who in the 1240s produced a commentary on scripture supposedly written by him which announced that 1260 would witness the fruition of the divine plan. (The real Joachim had been much more cautious, merely hinting that this was when the new age would dawn.) This calculation gained wide acceptance among followers of Joachim, who included an ultra-radical Franciscan element which actually expected the Abbot's writings to replace the bible in the Third Age. But a sense of an approaching deadline was not confined to dissident clerics. This was a time of acute social tension in Italy: in 1258 there had been a famine, in 1259 a plague; warfare between the Guelph and Ghibelline had reduced the country to a state of misery and insecurity. Norman Cohn argues that these afflictions were felt to be 'a prelude to a final and overwhelming catastrophe'. Bands of flagellants appeared, desperately trying to atone for their sins by whipping themselves senseless. 'Amidst famine, plague and war multitudes of Italians were impatiently awaiting the dawning of the Age of the Holy Spirit, the age in which all men would live in peace, observing voluntary poverty, rapt in contemplative bliss. As month after month passed by, these millenarian expectations became ever more tense until, towards the end of the year, they took on a desperate and hysterical quality and men began to clutch at straws.'[6]

The ferment surrounding the year 1260 is hugely revealing. In contrast to the years 1000 and 1033, for which we have to piece together the evidence of millenarian excitement, we can see clearly the explosive effect of a deadline on apocalyptic expectations. The role of social and economic collapse in this millenarian eruption is not in question; but it is a revelation of the *date* of the dawn of the new age which produces the state of frenzy. One might point out that the flagellants behave not as if they are on the verge of a glorious new dispensation, but as if the world is about to end; but this is a distinction which, in practice, was often blurred. People who believe that the society in which they have lived their entire lives will fall apart at a specific moment are likely to exhibit signs of psychological disturbance even if their theology assures them that they will emerge unscathed.

It is also worth noting that millenarian movements which set deadlines do not immediately collapse once the moment has passed. The sense of overwhelming disappointment known as 'cognitive dissonance' often has the paradoxical effect of increasing the resilience of a hard core of believers. A new deadline is set and, when that passes, another is spotted on the horizon. This is the real story of the Apostolic Brethren, who were founded in 1260, the year of great disappointment, and who fixed their hopes on the end of the century. In a letter of 1300 Fra Dolcino predicts the immediate transfer of authority from the Roman Church, *illa Babylon meretrix magna*, to the Brethren, to be followed by a holocaust of the clergy. A second letter revises this time-scale, predicting great events for 1305; it was apparently in readiness for this date that the Brethren retreated to the Alps. Undaunted by the passing of this new deadline, they were ready to fight to the death in 1307.

The consequences of setting a deadline can be so far reaching that one wonders whether it is all that is needed to turn an apocalyptic world-view into millenarianism. It would depend, of course, on the closeness of the deadline: as we have seen, in an earlier era the redating of the apocalyptic *anno mundi* 6000 to a far distant point neatly defused the time-bomb. Could it be that the nearer the fateful moment, the more extreme the reaction of believers? Unfortunately, this is an over-simplification. Millenarianism has taken root in societies which have not yet taken on board the notion of a universally accepted date; the belief in 'imminent' transformation often means no more than that people expect it to happen at any moment, but it still produces a sense of living in 'apocalyptic time' which can result in shifts in identity and personality. Conversely, prophecies which set a date in the near future for terrible events exerted a powerful hold over the medieval imagination – but without producing the more colourful symptoms of End-time belief.

This did not mean, however, that people were not profoundly unnerved by the approach of a prophetic deadline. In the 1180s, for example, an anti-Muslim apocalyptic text known as the Toledo Letter began to circulate in Western Europe. Its use of astrology, which was quickly gaining influence at this time, coupled with the nightmarish quality of its prophecies, thrilled its audience. According to its pseudonymous author, 'the astrologer Corumphiza', the higher and lower planets will come together in Libra in September 1186.

A strong and very powerful wind will arise in the western regions, blackening the air and corrupting it with a poisonous stench. Then death and infirmity will seize many, and clanging and cries will be heard in the sky, terrifying the hearts of listeners. A wind will lift sand and dust from the face of the earth and will cover the cities located on the plain, especially in desert areas . . . Mecca, Barsara, Baghdad and Babylonia will be utterly destroyed . . . In the West discord will also arise and insurrections will occur among the people. There will be one among them who will gather innumerable armies and will make war along the seashore; in this war such a massacre will take place that the force of the spilled blood will be equal to the rising waves. It is held for certain that the future conjunction signifies the change of kingdoms, the pre-eminence of the Franks, the destruction of the Saracen nation, greater charity and the greatest exaltation of the law of Christ, and a longer life for those who will be born afterwards.[7]

When the Toledo Letter reached England, in 1186, the Archbishop of Canterbury ordered a three-day fast throughout his province. Then the deadline passed, and it might be thought that the resulting humiliation would ensure the disappearance of the Letter. On the contrary, it circulated throughout Europe for centuries, with changed dates and alterations but the same essential message. This was, in fact, par for the course. As the historian Robert Lerner puts it: 'Isolating a medieval prophetic text is often like trying to pull up a stubborn root in one's garden: no sooner do you think you have it all removed than you find it really ramifies far more deeply and widely.'[8]

There is a simple reason for the constant presence in the Christian medieval world of a 'millennial undertow' in the form of rapidly mutating End-time scenarios. Apocalyptic belief offered the ideal framework for integrating political realities – and in particular the experience of disorientating change – with religious belief. Indeed, for many centuries it was the only available framework, and it remained in place long after the growing complexity of the European world began to diminish the appeal of the cruder forms of prophecy belief among the educated classes. New factors came into play, such as the development of national aspirations, scientific advance and a more sophisticated historical understanding which could envisage without difficulty the passage of future centuries.

At first glance these appear to eat away at the very basis of apocalypticism: the inexorable approach of the End. But it is emphatically not the case that traditional belief in an unfolding End-time drama was swept away on a rising tide of reason. Its marginalisation in the circles of the European elite was a gradual process which did not preclude its re-emergence in new forms. The cherished liberal notion that faith in 'progress' was a rational alternative to apocalypticism does not bear close examination. On the contrary, apocalypticism's role in the evolution of our understanding of progress is vitally important. It is powerfully demonstrated by the theories of Joachim of Fiore and, to jump ahead, in the history of the country whose outlook is at the same time the most optimistic and the most millennial in the modern world – the United States.

Apocalypticism, as the communications scholar Stephen O'Leary has argued, can be seen as a form of rhetoric. The earliest surviving apocalyptic texts served as the propaganda of a Jewish resistance movement: Daniel's awe-inspiring vision of the dead plucked from their graves accompanied an off-stage call to arms. The fact that it was addressed to an oppressed minority, and describes with relish the tearing down of the mighty from their thrones, helps explain apocalypticism's perennial assaults on the social order. But we should not forget that it was originally directed against a foreign enemy, the Greek occupying power. So it is hardly surprising that prophecies of a titanic battle between the agents of God and Satan should come to play as important a role in the cause of Pope versus Emperor and French versus Germans as they did in conflicts where theological principle was at stake, such as the Wars of Religion or the English Civil War. The increasing use of apocalyptic rhetoric against a nation's enemies is not only a sign of the emergence of nationalism but a contributing factor to it. The identification of a foreign ruler as the Antichrist justified the national struggle; Joachim's promise of a golden age within history provided the incentive. Religious and political aspirations were seamlessly woven together in a cosmic tapestry.

We can chart the development of national consciousness simply by examining changes in the way prophecy was tailored to political ends. The tone was set by the most bitter of all medieval struggles between *sacerdotium* and *imperium*, that involving the Emperor Frederick II (1194–1250). For the first time we find Pope and Emperor gleefully identifying each other as foul apparitions from Revelation. 'The beast filled with the names of blasphemy has arisen from the sea,' wrote Pope Gregory VII. 'With the feet of a bear, a mouth like a lion, and the rest of his limbs like a leopard, in his rage he has opened his mouth to blaspheme the divine name. He even hurls like darts against God's tabernacle and against the saints who dwell in heaven.'[9]

Frederick, not to be outdone, replied: 'He, who is pope in name alone, has said that we are the beast rising from the sea full of the names of blasphemy and spotted like a leopard. We maintain that he is the monster of whom we read: "Another horse arose from the sea, a red one, and he who sat thereon took away peace from the earth so that the living slaughtered one another" [Rev. 6: 4].' The debate continued along similar lines well into the papacy of Innocent IV, when one of the Emperor's propagandists produced the apocalyptic trump card. According to a well-established system of computation, he wrote, 'the letter I equals 1, N equals 50 and 50 again, o is 70, C a 100 . . .' and INNOCENTIUS PAPA, we are somehow not too surprised to learn, adds up to 666.[10]

Frederick and his successors had no qualms about invoking the apocalyptic stereotype of the Last Emperor in support of their dynastic ambitions. During the fourteenth and fifteenth centuries this mythical figure, already venerable in the year 1000, became a focus of nationalist aspirations. The figure of a resurrected Frederick II played an important part in the fantasies of radical peasant movements which sprang up in Germany from time to time; a prophecy called *Gamaleon*, dating from the early fifteenth century, tells of a future German emperor who will end the Great Schism by transferring the seat of St Peter to Mainz. The new Church will be subject to the Emperor – Caesar – who will rule over a Europe in which the priests have been killed, the French, Hungarians and Slavs are subject peoples – and in which Jewry has been eliminated. The pre-echoes of Nazism are almost too obvious to need pointing out; but this combination of popular nationalism with atavistic savagery is not exclusively Teutonic, as we shall see when we come to consider the extraordinary happenings in fifteenth-century Bohemia.

It is, however, uncharacteristic of the 'political' prophecy of the period, which expressed what one might call mainstream national sentiment. Most prophecies were the work of educated clerks and courtiers anxious to promote a view of the future which exalted the role of their compatriots and literally demonised foreign rivals. Thus the German Last Emperor was a Third Frederick; the French a Second Charlemagne. As for the monarchs of the day, they were flattered (though not necessarily taken in) by the suggestion that they might turn out to be the Last Emperor who would initiate an indefinite period of earthly bliss. They did not, on the whole, allow apocalyptic rhetoric to interfere with the day-to-day business of government. But it undoubtedly lent a certain *frisson* to the conduct of foreign policy. To the medieval mind, as to present-day Christian fundamentalists, the concept of one world power invariably suggested an End-time scenario. Indeed, this connection may have been partly responsible for determining the political geography of the modern world: the imperial ventures of some sixteenth-century powers may have been rooted psychologically in prophecies which ascribed the role of Last World Emperor to their monarchs.

But at no stage in the history of medieval or early modern Europe was apocalypticism so sanitised that it became nothing more than political rhetoric. It remained a dangerously unstable element. In the sixteenth century, mainstream Protestant reformers who invoked the End-time in their battle against the Catholic Church did so cautiously, well aware that the use of such images could spin out of control. The terrible example of the Taborite experiment in Bohemia showed how easy it was to inflame millenarian expectations of the Second Coming.

Bohemia at the beginning of the fifteenth century was fertile territory for anti-papal reformers with a nationalist outlook. One half of all land belonged to the Church. The higher clergy tended to be German-speaking and unusually corrupt even by the standards of the day. The University of Prague, in contrast, was both strongly Czech and pro-reform. Its Rector, John Hus, argued that when papal decrees ran counter to the teaching of Christ they should be ignored. This struck a chord with the Czech nobility, and even earned him an audience at the court of King Wenceslas, who enjoyed an uneasy relationship with the Emperor. So when, in 1414, Hus travelled to the Council of Constance to argue the case for reform, and was burned as a heretic despite an imperial guarantee of safe conduct, Wenceslas and his barons felt a sense of national affront. The secular powers of Bohemia took control of the Church hierarchy. The stage appeared to be set for the establishment of a theologically conservative national Church along roughly the lines adopted by Henry VIII of England a century later.

Before long, however, the moderate Hussite reformers found themselves being dragged in the direction of outright heresy by an immensely strong millennial undertow. The end of the fourteenth century in Bohemia had been an unsettling time: Prague was overpopulated, while the feudal structure of rents and dues in the countryside had begun to crumble. Popular preachers, who for years had intruded apocalyptic themes into their sermons, were able to point to the Hussite reform as the fulfilment of prophecy. But it was an attempt to suppress the reform which turned their audience of artisans, slum-dwellers and landless labourers into millenarians. In 1419, when Wenceslas bowed to pressure from the Pope and attempted to remove Hussites from the government of Prague, there was an open revolt in which conservative councillors were thrown out of windows. The King promptly died of shock. From then on the radicals were swept up in an apocalyptic whirlwind. Huge open-air rallies were held on hilltops which represented Mount

Tabor, the place of the transfiguration of Jesus. An abandoned fortress was turned into a citadel which was renamed Tabor; a number of small towns became communes where brotherly love was intended to replace the rule of law. The Catholic doctrine of the priesthood was abandoned.

The Taborites, as historians know them, began to believe that only they would survive the Second Coming of Christ. The defrocked priests who led the movement prophesied that this would take place between 10 and 14 February 1420, when every town and village would be destroyed by fire with the exception of the five Taborite towns known as the mountains. In the words of a contemporary report of their beliefs: 'Christ will descend from heaven and live with them [the Taborites] in the body. Every eye will see him. He will make a great banquet in the real mountains and entering to see the guests will cast the evil into the darkness outside. All who were outside the mountains, like those who were once outside Noah's Ark in the Flood, will be consumed by fire in a moment.'[11] Peasants sold their belongings, rushed to the towns and threw their money at the feet of the Taborite priests.

When the deadline passed, the experiment merely moved into a new and more aggressive phase. A fresh doctrine appeared: that Christ had *secretly* returned at the time of the founding of Tabor. (This was to become a classic solution to the problem of cognitive dissonance, being adopted by, among others, the Jehovah's Witnesses with reference to 1914.) The Taborites' original pacifism was replaced by an incredible bloodthirstiness which enabled them to band together into an efficient military unit; in 1420 they came to the rescue of the moderate Hussites when they defeated the Emperor's troops outside Prague, though the alliance was short-lived. From then until 1434, when they were virtually annihilated by a Bohemian army, Taborite troops rampaged throughout central Europe. According to the official Catholic document condemning them, they saw themselves as 'the army sent by God into the whole world to execute all the plagues of the time of vengeance . . . Each of the faithful ought to wash his hands in blood of Christ's enemies.'

Yet there were limits beyond which even the Taborites would not go. Although they lived in the absolute certainty that Christ was about to return to usher in the Millennium, which was also the Age of the Spirit, something approaching a normal social hierarchy began to reappear in the Taborite towns. The abolition of feudal dues which marked the early, euphoric stage of the experiment was hastily revoked. Taborites set about collecting rent from local peasants with a vengeance; and when they found themselves confronted by an ultra-radical apocalyptic group within their own ranks they brutally suppressed it. These were the Adamites, or Pikarts, who were expelled from the Taborite stronghold after preaching that they were Saints of the Last Days and therefore incapable of sin. The Adamites embraced free love and danced naked around camp fires. They captured an island in the River Nezarka, from where they made night-time raids to local villages. Their slogan, from the scriptures, was 'And at midnight there was a cry made – Behold, the bridegroom cometh'; this, they believed, gave them licence to kill every man, woman and child they encountered. In October 1421, 400 trained Taborite troops were sent against them. Barricaded on their island, the Adamites believed that the enemy would be stricken blind. They fought courageously, until only one of them was left alive; and he was deliberately spared, so that he could give an account of Adamite doctrines before being burned at the stake.

The Taborite episode, which dragged on until the destruction of Mount Tabor by Bohemians in 1452, is more than simply a textbook example of millenarianism. This is the only large-scale millenarian movement before the Reformation which successfully defied the authority of the state to create an apocalyptic community with its own social hierarchy. And there is something about the *Animal Farm*-like progression from egalitarian euphoria to bitter retrenchment and eradication of dissidents which puts one in mind of other failed experiments. It does seem that extreme apocalyptic movements share an inescapable dynamic with those inspired by secular visions of revolution. Indeed, there is a school of thought which sees the development of a revolutionary mind-set among millenarians as

77

an important landmark on a road leading all the way from Montanus to Marx, in which the vision of a perfect society becomes steadily more secular, all-embracing and terrestrial.

There are certainly grounds for believing that revolutionary socialism is fundamentally a form of secular millenarianism. But it is not necessarily the most significant legacy of the apocalyptic tradition; and nor, for that matter, is the gruesome Taborite episode the most important manifestation of apocalyptic ferment during the fifteenth century. We can learn equally important lessons by considering the effect of prophecy belief on a complex, wealthy and sophisticated urban society: Florence during the Renaissance.

The notion of Renaissance – of rebirth leading to a golden age – appears to owe more to classical thinking than to medieval doom-merchants. Petrarch (1304–74), who is credited with inventing the distinction between ancient and modern, saw history in terms of eras brought about by human endeavour rather than the divine will. His golden age was to be a return to classical splendour made possible by the freeing of the human spirit from the shackles of control by the Church. This idea was taken up by the neo-Platonists of fifteenth-century Florence, whose dreams of escape from an age of ignorance through education mark a conscious return to the cyclical theories which had been supplanted by apocalypticism more than a thousand years earlier. Yet the millennial undertow was never far below the surface. On closer examination, the Renaissance golden age often turns out to be the Joachimite Third Age in classical fancy dress. The conventional picture of Renaissance Italy, in which a cultivated elite turns away from superstition and towards the study of art, architecture, music and astronomy, is highly selective. We do not see the prophets wandering through Rome and Florence proclaiming the End of an Age; nor do we spot the figure of the Antichrist lurking behind the doric columns of the *renovatio*.

The end of the fourteenth century in Italy was a period in which great hopes existed side by side with equally great fears. The exponents of the humanist golden age often thought in terms of a dreadful conflict which would precede it. Though they might call themselves Platonists, they were mesmerised by prophecies of the Antichrist. Prophecy, along with astrology and the occult, was a means by which God revealed the fundamental secrets of existence. If the heavenly bodies were about to move into a configuration which would bring about a new age on earth, that should be regarded as the fulfilment of biblical prophecy. The rediscovery of the classical Age of Gold would be the clearest possible indication that the Christian world sabbath had arrived. But who could tell what terrible drama might have to unfold before this glorious era could dawn? Nervous and highly strung, Renaissance Man scanned the horizon as intently as his medieval predecessor for signs of the End-time.

Those signs were never more ominous than in the autumn of 1494, when the young King Charles VIII of France was crossing the Alps in pursuit of his own fantasy of an apocalyptic world empire. Charles, like Otto III exactly five centuries before him, was a rare example of a monarch who took seriously prophecies which assigned him the role of Last Emperor. Convinced that he was a Second Charlemagne, he set off on an expedition to capture Naples which was intended as the first step on a crusade to recapture Jerusalem and restore a Christian empire under the King of France. 'There has seldom been in western European history a series of events so widely viewed within the framework of prophetic drama as the Italian expedition of Charles VIII,' writes Marjorie Reeves.[12] On the French side, it needed only the return of the magic name of Charles to revive dreams of Charlemagne; on the Italian side, meanwhile, Florence had fallen under the spell of an extraordinary preacher who told the city to accept the invasion as a divine chastisement opening the door to the Age of Gold.

The career of Girolamo Savonarola (1452–98) is a perfect illustration of the way in which rational hopes of a classical revival could become mixed up with a sense of End-time. From 1490, this Dominican visionary attracted large crowds in Florence with his prophecies of Antichrist. There was nothing unusual in this: Italy at the end of the quattrocento was extremely susceptible to eschatological anxiety. According to the Sienese chronicler Tizio, this was a time of 'presages, phantoms and astrological conjunctions of dreadful import'; wandering prophets preaching destruction found a ready audience. At first, Savonarola stuck to familiar themes of punishment and tribulation: he prophesied that 'the sword of the Lord will descend on the earth swiftly and soon', and that Florence would be destroyed unless there was an immediate moral reformation. But there was something about the approach of a Second Charlemagne at the head of a crusading army which strangely lifted Savonarola's spirits. He became convinced that, if Florence submitted to the invaders, its people would take on the mantle of God's elect, saved from destruction to play a glorious new role. 'You, O Florence, will be the reformation of all Italy and from here the renewal will begin to spread everywhere,' he said. The Turkish infidel would convert to Christianity, the sun would illuminate the world and the Church would be so full of love that angels would converse with men.[13]

It was thanks to Savonarola that Florence peacefully submitted to Charles, cast out its Medici rulers and became, for a short time, what McGinn has called a 'proto-Messianic republic'. Savonarola's teaching that Florence had become the chosen centre of divine illumination built on older traditions that the city was the head and heart of Italy, the favoured child of Rome who was destined to succeed her. It also reinforced the Joachimite image of *viri spirituales* leading a moral revolution, with the role played this time by the people of Florence. But the elevation of Florence to the status of New Jerusalem was to prove Savonarola's downfall; for it implied that Rome was the Antichrist, and that Florence would be the seat of a reformed papacy. This played into the hands of the notoriously corrupt Pope Alexander VI, who interrogated and then excommunicated Savonarola. His Florentine support eroded by papal opposition and the collapse of Charles VIII's army, Savonarola was publicly executed in May 1498.

The messianic republic lasted only three years, a far shorter time than the apocalyptic stronghold of Tabor. In terms of the fanatical behaviour of the protagonists, or the intensity of End-time belief, Savonarola's Florence is obviously not in the same league as Tabor. But it is, perhaps, more significant. This is the first time we see a whole society promised wealth, international influence and moral superiority if it is prepared to assume its apocalyptic function of bringing about the golden age. Quite what this entails is not always clear: there must be 'reformation of morals', and it is necessary that Antichrist should appear and be defeated. But, for disciples of Savonarola, what mattered was Florence's coming glory:

> All peoples and religions will conform to Florence's true religion, and there will be one sheepfold and one pastor. Florence will extend her hegemony in a benevolent *imperium*. The odour of her sanctity will extend throughout the world and people, seeing her felicity, will want to share her government and laws.[14]

It is this last claim which makes the modern reader sit up. It would be hard to come up with a more straightforward statement of belief in 'manifest destiny'. The British and American imperial spirit seems so closely bound up with Protestant enterprise that it is disconcerting to find it so clearly foreshadowed in Renaissance Italy. Yet the civilised values which Britain and America attempted to export to other peoples were often underpinned by a conception of history which was surprisingly close to that of Savonarola's Florence. They were intended to usher in a period of unprecedented human achievement which represented the apotheosis of history – an age which would resemble, and might even turn out to be, the thousand-year reign of Christ and his saints.

This is not millenarianism, as such, but it is certainly what historians and social scientists call a millennial vision, one that is inspired by the notion of a glorious End-time. A society which is gripped by a sense of manifest destiny is too busy to spend its time looking to the skies; on the contrary, it may believe that Christ will not return until after the Millennium has been brought about by its own efforts. The millennial vision may even become so secularised that the Second Coming, or the final conflagration, is viewed as a remote event or as pure mythology. But, once the idea of the climax of history has been invoked, the prospect of the End can never be banished from the imagination.

4

A New Jerusalem

It is hard to overestimate the impact of the Reformation on hopes and fears of the End. In the space of a couple of decades, the vernacular bible became available to millions of people in northern Europe. To the untutored layman, reading the text for the first time, it was impossible not to muse on the End of the World: the apocalypse casts a threatening shadow over most sections of the New Testament, and, although modern Christians shy away from this fact, it would have been glaringly obvious to its first lay readers. The floodgates of amateur prophecy were opened.

This was not quite what Martin Luther had intended when he broke the spiritual monopoly of the Catholic Church. The spread of Protestantism was not meant to be associated with turning the social order on its head or calculating the time of the End. Augustine's advice about relaxing busy fingers still held good. When Luther called the Pope Antichrist, he was employing apocalyptic imagery in time-honoured fashion, as political rhetoric. The biblical End-time sequences were, at most, a framework within which to analyse the immense political and theological upheavals of the Reformation. Indeed, Luther would have been happy to banish the Book of

Revelation from the bible altogether. He was well aware of its role in tearing apart the fabric of life in Bohemia at the beginning of the fifteenth century. He suspected that this drama could easily be played out again in the turmoil of political disintegration, and he did not have to wait long to be proved right.

There is no space here to describe in detail the events of the Peasants' Revolt in 1525, in which ill-equipped millenarian believers were led into a hopeless battle against the forces of the state by a half-mad intellectual called Thomas Müntzer. The revolt as a whole was not millenarian in character: it was a classic peasants' uprising. But in Thuringia, the rebels fell under the sway of Müntzer, a man obsessed by the blood-soaked imagery of Revelation, who promised them that their struggles would bring about the earthly bliss of the Millennium. The parallels with the Taborite episode are inescapable. Both tragedies arose out of what might be called theological disorientation: like the moderate Hussites a century earlier, once the conservative German reformers removed the cornerstone of the Church's authority – its exclusive right to interpret the bible – they found it impossible to maintain control of speculation about the End-time. But in both cases the initial theological protest against Rome was also bound up with the sort of political and social dislocation on which classic millenarian movements thrive. Essentially, they are parasitical: they have a habit of latching on to wider movements, such as peasant uprisings. Given the extreme nature of millenarian belief, which appeals to unstable personality types or to the acutely marginalised, and is difficult to sustain, these movements can produce intense and short-lived dramas in which true believers shut themselves off from society at large. They may even succeed in seizing control of a geographical area, thus dragging non-believers into a tragedy which to the Elect is the long-delayed fulfilment of prophecy.

This drama has never been played out in a more desperate fashion than in the city of Münster in 1534–5. It is a grotesque illustration of the uncontrollable and yet predictable dynamic of millenarian belief. The background is the situation of confusion and barely suppressed violence in Germany at the time, as large numbers of the dispossessed rejected both Catholicism and Lutheranism and opted instead for Anabaptism, a loose collection of apocalyptic sects, each with its own prophet. Münster in Westphalia became a centre for the most radical Anabaptists, who drove Catholics and Lutherans out of the town and announced that it was to become the New Jerusalem. As the forces of the local Catholic bishop laid siege to the town, Jan Matthys, the Anabaptist leader, instituted a reign of terror inside its walls: all books except the bible were banned and the cathedral was sacked. Then Matthys ventured outside and was hacked to pieces, whereupon Münster fell into the hands of someone even more brutal and fanatical: Jan Bockelson, a charismatic former tailor who began his rule by running naked through the town in a state of ecstasy. He then announced the institution of a new godly order, in which any misdemeanour, especially sex outside marriage, was punishable by death.[1]

Within a short space of time, however, Bockelson had shifted from puritanism to sexual licence. He was by no means the first millenarian leader to do so: a sudden lurch from one extreme to the other distinguished a number of earlier sects, possibly including Montanism, and it has since become a familiar feature of millenarian belief. Although it is hard to explain, there is perhaps a parallel to be drawn between contrasting extremes of sexual behaviour and the coexistence of nightmare and visions of bliss in the apocalyptic genre itself. At any rate, the inhabitants of Münster were informed that God had reinstituted polygamy. Fifty dissidents who opposed the move and took up arms were put to death. Bockelson's control of the town was impressive; a collection of ordinary citizens and mercenaries was turned into a well-disciplined fighting force, and a major assault by the episcopal army was repulsed.

Before long, however, the drama of Münster degenerated into Gothic horror. Towards the end of 1534, Bockelson turned himself from divinely appointed leader into King and Messiah of the Last Days – a wild inflation of spiritual claims which brings to mind the behaviour of David Koresh during the siege of Waco four and a half centuries later. The new King of Münster dressed in magnificent robes, surrounded by his teenage wives and a court of fawning admirers. But ordinary citizens were forced to live in squalid poverty until the Second Coming, which according to Bockelson would materialise only when all the world's priests, monks and rulers had been slaughtered. Meanwhile, mass beheadings of townsfolk were staged in the main square, many of them carried out personally by the King. The siege intensified; famine forced people to eat dogs, cats and rats; by the late spring the population was too feeble to resist the invaders, and in June Münster fell to a surprise attack. All the Anabaptist leaders were killed immediately except Bockelson, who was led about on a chain like a bear before being tortured to death.

The siege of Münster perfectly illustrates the combustible qualities of millenarianism when the paranoid fantasies of a messianic leader appear to be fulfilled: there is nothing like a siege to intensify the self-destructive impulses of apocalyptic belief (though this point, as we shall see, seems to have been lost on the authorities at Waco). Public opinion in the sixteenth century was almost as horrified by the episode as it would be today. But, as with certain millenarian outbreaks in the middle ages, it is not entirely divorced from the spirit of its times. The millennial kingdom of Jan Bockelson was a grossly distorted reflection of a desire among ordinary Protestants to build a New Jerusalem, a society sanctified by God which would represent the summit of human achievement. This was an ambition which was beginning to emerge in Renaissance Florence but which could only really develop in a non-Catholic environment.

The mere fact of breaking away from papal control did not, admittedly, produce a single, coherent Protestant vision of a New Jerusalem; on the contrary, it ensured that there would always be competing visions of millennial destiny, ranging from Joachimite dreams of a perfect society within history to terrified expectations of the Second Coming, and usually incorporating elements of both. The replacement of tradition by the plain biblical word as interpreted by the individual conscience led inevitably to idiosyncratic readings of Daniel and Revelation. A new generation of would-be prophets, whose late medieval predecessors relied on apocalyptic folklore for inspiration, could pore over the cryptic verses about 1,250 days and 'a time, times and half a time' and reach their own conclusions about the fulfilment of ancient Hebrew prophecies in their own society. Furthermore, they could mostly do so without fear of censure and, if they had access to a printing press, could explain their ideas to an audience several hundred times larger than any they could have attracted a century earlier. Inevitably, crisis of any sort sent amateur exegetes scurrying to their bibles for enlightenment. In the words of a young Welshman living in London during the shocking events of the 1640s: 'Afore I looked at the Scripture as a history of things that passed in other countries, pertaining to other persons; but now I looked upon it as a mystery to be opened at this time, belonging also to us.'[2]

But, if Protestantism heightened consciousness of the End, it often did so in subtle ways. As Ruth Bloch has argued, it gave rise to millennial aspirations by intensifying the ambiguity towards the world that had always been a source of tension within Christianity.[3] The abolition of devotional works, monasteries and the priesthood made the world the only possible arena for the expression of grace. Protestants were called to righteous and productive work in the world, and this encouraged a millennial view of history. The work of transforming the world from the province of Satan to the Kingdom of Christ was a preparation for his return. Instead of passively longing for the End, like Michelet's peasants of the year 1000, many Protestants believed it to be their duty to propel the world towards it by their own unceasing efforts to build a prosperous and God-fearing society.

The development of this ethic can be seen most clearly in seventeenth-century England up to the Restoration, after which the millennial torch was passed to Puritan America. Indeed, the different extent to which End-time ideas filtered into the mainstream of national life in the two countries was to become a crucial factor in the evolution of a distinctive American personality; it accounts for much of the contrast between British and American national psychology. But the millennial elements in American culture have their roots in England: they could not have taken shape without a bizarre flowering of English apocalyptic thought which is a direct consequence of the Reformation.

Early in the reign of Elizabeth, the identification of the Pope as Antichrist became a feature of the Englishman's mental landscape, where it was to remain for centuries. (Christopher Hill has suggested that the use of the word 'animal' first gained currency in English in the early seventeenth century because the previously universal 'beast' had become synonymous with the Pope, the Beast of Revelation.)[4] There was nothing subversive about this: if the Catholic Church was the instrument of the devil, then the fight against the quintessential Catholic power, Spain, was lent added urgency – and the victory against the Armada was doubly glorious. Even so, by the reign of James I enthusiasm for the Pope–Antichrist identification had become the sign of a true Protestant, dividing Puritans (that is, Calvinist members of the Church of England and sectarians) from High Anglicans, who were beginning to find the concept crude and embarrassing.

This division was not merely a mark of different degrees of hostility to Rome: underlying it was a growing conviction among Puritans that, although Rome was the seat of Antichrist, the Beast had left his mark on the Church of England, with its Romish hierarchy of bishops, and on the tyrannical government which upheld it. More to the point, this preoccupation with the Antichrist had important implications for the way hard-line Protestants approached the subject of the End. We are confronted yet again by the fact that one cannot invoke the figure of the Antichrist without raising the spectre of the End-time; it is worth bearing in mind that his name in French is Antéchrist, he who appears before the Second Coming of Christ. As early as 1589, the courtier Anthony Marten noted 'the number of prophets that God doth daily send to admonish all people of the latter day, and to give them warning to be in a readiness'.[5] Protestants at every level of society were becoming more and more fascinated by schemes of history which envisaged a millennial drama in the near future. After about 1600, moreover, we begin to encounter that most explosive of ingredients, the predicted date. For the first time and only time in English history, we see something approaching an End-time consensus emerging; not about the exact hour of the Second Coming, but about when, broadly speaking, the final events in human history would be set in motion. And in the years leading up to that designated period we encounter not only an outbreak of millenarianism on an unprecedented scale, but the sudden collapse of the central structures of English society.

Back in the fifteenth century, the prophet Johann Hilten had predicted the End of the World for 1651. As the seventeenth century advanced, eschatological hopes were focussed on its middle decades; many schemes predicted that the beginning of the final drama would take place in the 1650s, though some thought its last act would be delayed until the end of the century. One observer, writing in 1635, noted that many people expected 1657 to be the crucial year; another possibility was 1656, since the Flood was popularly believed to have occurred 1,656 years after the Creation. During the decades leading up to the Civil War there was also an increasing obsession among English Protestants with the fate of the Jews, which is a sure indicator of End-time anxiety, since the return of the Jews to Israel was seen by many to be the penultimate historical event before the Second Coming. (In our own day, no event has contributed to End-time speculation more than the foundation of the State of Israel.)

It would be a gross overstatement to say that millenarian hopes caused the English Civil War. There is no doubt, however, that there was a sharp rise in the eschatological temperature during the 1630s and 1640s. The sense of exaltation and apprehension associated with the approaching End is too often left out of the equation in modern studies of the period. Yet it goes a long way to explaining the disorientating strangeness of the years when the world was 'turned upside down'. The political dimension of apocalypticism, and in particular its tendency to inspire calls for both moderate reform and class hatred, is once again strikingly in evidence. The utopian Puritanism of the 1640s owed much to the conviction that Antichrist was about to fall; and, in the eyes of those Protestants who believed that all tyrannical government was Antichristian, that implied imminent political reformation. John Goodwin, the author of *Anti-Cavalierisme* (1642), argued that, now that the Beast was about to be defeated, it was necessary that God should reveal to his servants 'the just bounds and limits of authority and power, and consequently the just and full extent of the lawful liberties of those that live in subjection'. Others envisaged a more spectacular overturning of the social order: 'The people are brethren and Saints in Christ's Church, but in Antichrist's, parishioners and servants,' cried a radical chaplain in the New Model Army in 1646.[6]

England during the years 1640–60 was saturated with ideas ranging from the mildly apocalyptic to the rabidly millenarian. Christians of every complexion had no doubt that the events of the Civil War corresponded in some way to biblical prophecy. Prophetic timetables, which Charles I's government had quite sensibly censored, began to appear in large numbers, most of them repeating the by now well-established prediction that great events – the return of the Jews, the defeat of the Turk, the fall of Rome – were scheduled for the mid-1650s. The prophetic writer Mary Cary, writing in 1647, expected the conversion of the Jews in 1656 and the Millennium in 1701, but thought that 'before 20 or 10 or 5 years more shall pass' there would be the added bonus of an earthly utopia of the saints. 'Not only men but women shall prophesy,' she predicted. 'Not only superiors but inferiors; not only those that have university learning but those that have it not, even servants and handmaids.'[7]

In fact, Miss Cary's prediction had in many ways already come to pass. We should beware of assuming that prophecy was the exclusive preserve of thin-lipped Puritan preachers. The collapse of rural Catholicism led to many functions of the priest being taken over by the local 'cunning man'. Prophets and astrologers could be found in virtually every village. We have noted before the remarkable mutational qualities of apocalyptic scenarios. These were never more pronounced than in mid-seventeenth-century England, when biblical prophecies became hopelessly intertwined with folk wisdom, astrology and prophecies attributed to Merlin, the Sybil and Nostradamus. William Lilly's *Prophecy of the White King*, supposedly based on a prediction of Merlin, foretold a grisly death for Charles I: it sold 1,800 copies within three days of its publication in 1644.

Apocalyptic ideas even influenced the most remarkable radical movement of the day, the Diggers, whose dreams of 'making the earth a common treasury', together with their rejection of all organised religion, mark them out as perhaps the first secular revolutionaries. The Diggers were not Christians in any accepted sense: their leader Gerrard Winstanley even rejected the word God in favour of Reason. According to Winstanley, Christ was 'the spreading power of light' present in the whole of creation; every man who understood this became Son of God, and no longer looked for an external deity. Yet Winstanley worked within Joachim of Fiore's structure of three ages, believing that the Age of the Spirit was now dawning; he could not resist the notion that history was moving towards its preordained conclusion. And this is true of all the radical sects of the period. As Keith Thomas points out, the fact that the Civil War and the execution of the King had no parallel in English history accounts for the conviction held by so many of the Civil War sects that the period in which they lived was 'somehow the climax of human history, the era for which all previous events had been a mere preparation'.[8]

At one stage during the 1650s, believers in an imminent Christian Millennium came close to seizing control of Parliament. These were the Fifth Monarchy Men, who represented the most literal and fanatical strain of millenarianism among the armed forces, the clergy and the urban poor. Radical but not egalitarian, Fifth Monarchists believed that all human institutions must be stripped away and replaced with biblical models such as the sanhedrin in readiness for the final earthly empire of Daniel's vision. Once this was established under King Jesus, there would be no premature death or famine; tithes would be abolished, the mighty would be humiliated and the righteous would enjoy every outward blessing and creature

comfort. The 'saints', as they called themselves, never numbered more than a few thousand. An opponent described them
as 'Scum, the very raf of Billingsgate', and it is true that most of
the men involved were ill-educated artisans; some of them even
compared themselves to the Münster Anabaptists. But they had
a few powerful supporters, and when the radical Barebones
Parliament met in 1653 the handful of Fifth Monarchist MPs
exercised a disproportionate influence. For the only time in its
history, the House of Commons published a declaration which
was strongly apocalyptic in tone, comparing the age to that
immediately preceding the birth of Christ and looking forward
to his 'glorious coming'. The saints managed to secure places on
most committees, and very nearly achieved their objectives of
abolishing tithes and the court of Chancery. Non-millenarians
felt a shiver run down their spines and made dark references to
Münster in 1535.

In the event, farce rather than tragedy was the order of the
day. Parliament soon tired of the Fifth Monarchists. Cromwell,
who had once flirted with them, moved away from the ideal of
a revolutionary theocracy and acquired the title of Lord
Protector, whereupon the Fifth Monarchists, predictably,
reviled him as Antichrist. A great rally of the saints held at
about this time in Abingdon illustrates both their increasing
disaffection with the state and the comic hopelessness of their
cause. Representatives from all over the country debated the
motion 'whether God's people must be a bloody people' and
passed it overwhelmingly. There was, however, no blood shed
when fifty soldiers appeared and broke up the meeting: as they
were being dragged away, the Fifth Monarchists were reduced
to calling out, 'Lord, appear, now or never for confounding of
these, thine and our enemies!', while their womenfolk shouted,
'Hold on, ye sons of Syon' from the sidelines.[9] In the following
year, 1657, a militant group of London saints led by Thomas
Venner, a cooper who had spent time in America, decided to
implement the Abingdon motion with a national uprising. They
created a secret organisation of cells and printed a manifesto
declaring that the laws of the state would soon be replaced by
biblical laws and rule by the saints. After studying maps of

government forces, about eighty Fifth Monarchists arranged to meet in Mile End Green one evening before moving on to East Anglia to attract recruits. But government troops arrived when the saints were still gathering and marched the leaders off to the Tower. Three years later, Venner led a mob of Fifth Monarchists through the streets of London yelling for 'King Jesus'; confronted by a regiment of Life Guards, it fought with great ferocity and over forty people were killed. Venner was executed, announcing in classic fashion before he died that he was the personification of Christ. And so, bar one or two feeble plots which came to nothing, ended the history of militant English millenarianism.

On the whole the Fifth Monarchists have been ignored by historians, who are generally more interested in the political utopias of the Levellers and Diggers. And it cannot be denied that these most literal-minded of millenarians were essentially a fringe movement. But they are not insignificant: their plans to dismantle the state were seriously debated by a Parliament which, albeit briefly, seemed to share their sense of a fast-approaching End. They are also interesting because, compared to earlier movements, we know quite a lot about them. Two collections of the spiritual autobiographies of millenarian Church members were published in the 1650s; together with other documents of the period, they provide ample evidence of the psychological pressures associated with End-time belief. Bereavement is frequently mentioned: one woman was driven to distraction by the belief that her daughter had committed suicide; another was financially ruined after her husband died; another lost her children to smallpox. Fear of hell and bad dreams figure prominently: a girl of eleven dreamed of fire, a burning lake and saw 'the Devill with his chaines' waiting for her. The horrors of warfare also loom large: one conscript told of his panic under fire, and of a vision which converted him when he was in prison under sentence of death.[10] Of course, these experiences were hardly confined to the mid-seventeenth century: they were part of everyday life for centuries, and have always had the potential to inflame apocalyptic expectations among the psychological and economically vulnerable. But what the history of the years 1640–60 suggests is that, at a time of unique dislocation in English national life, this category could suddenly expand – and, once the crisis was over, just as suddenly contract.

With the Restoration, the Millennium was indefinitely postponed. Apocalyptic hopes, which had begun to fade when the Jews remained unconverted and the Turk undefeated during the key years of the 1650s, could not survive the humiliation of seeing the Merrie Monarch crowned in place of King Jesus. The Antichrist, who had come to represent all the encroachments of the state, shrank back to the manageable dimensions of papal bogeyman. End-time speculation passed out of fashion. 'Take heed of computing,' wrote one dissenter in 1680. 'How woefully have we been mistaken by this.' We have reached a crucial junction in the history of apocalyptic thought. From the late seventeenth century onwards, English interest in the End of the World became polarised. On the one hand, Low Church clergy and scientiests remained fascinated by it; on the other, popular prophets continued to spring up. Neither manifestation had important implications for public life.

In the case of the academics, this reflected a new and sensible mood of caution. The impulse to align man's calendar with God's was as strong as ever. But the attempt to synchronise sacred and natural history – which led a number of intellectuals including Isaac Newton to speculate about a Second Coming in the year 2000 – remained a largely private affair. Apocalyptic authors were aware that the whole area was tainted by association with the English Revolution, and did not generally air their ideas in sermons or in vernacular print. Nor did they often allow themselves the dangerous luxury of interpreting current events in the light of their theories. Indeed, they did not need to, since for most of these authors the Millennium could be brought about only by the gradual and undramatic accumulation of scientific knowledge. Rural prophets, meanwhile, found that they could still occasionally touch a popular nerve, but were no longer taken seriously by the political establishment. In 1694, one John Mason 'announced that the End of the World was at hand, and that only those at Water Stratford would survive; large crowds collected there, but he was not rushed off to prison, as he would have been a century earlier. He was advised to take physic.'[11]

Are we justified, therefore, in writing off the millenarian excitement of the mid-seventeenth century as an aberration which had no lasting impact? The strongest argument against doing so is the persistence of the Puritan millennial vision in New England. But, before looking at that phenomenon, it is worth noting the suggestion of the Marxist historian Christopher Hill that the millenarian ferment of the 1640s and 1650s changed for ever the way the British thought about the world. Its most interesting legacy, says Hill, is that it raised hopes for a *new* utopia on earth. It 'shifted the golden age to the future. Once it had shaken off its apocalyptic associations, it could easily link up with Bacon's scientific optimism to form a theory of progress.'[12] Seen in this light, British economic nationalism of the eighteenth and nineteenth centuries represented a secular form of millenarianism. Indeed, it can be argued that all Western visions of progress incorporate elements of the apocalyptic, drawing unconsciously on Joachim for their dreams of a golden age and on Revelation for their visions of catastrophe. That said, however, there is necessarily a huge gulf between a society which draws explicitly on the Christian millennial tradition and one in which that tradition has become subsumed into an ideology with which it shares a basic structure but little else. This gulf divides the United States from Britain and, to an even greater extent, from Europe. The marginalisation of apocalyptic thought in England was matched by roughly the same process in mainland Europe, both Catholic and Protestant, where, after an intensely apocalyptic sixteenth century, prophecy became the preserve of minority groups and individual eccentrics. To study the continuing influence of the Christian concept of End-time, we must cross the Atlantic.

The American understanding of history was defined by the Pilgrims, whose sole source of inspiration was the English bible. Later waves of immigration merely had the effect of broadening the appeal of the Puritans' New Jerusalem. American Catholics, in their desire to appear as patriotic as their countrymen, unintentionally subscribe to a world-view which is quintessentially Protestant.

For the Pilgrim Fathers, the founding of the American colonies was in itself a sign of the End-time. They had no doubt that their presence in the New World fulfilled the words of Matthew's Gospel: 'And this Gospel of the Kingdom shall be preached in all the world for a witness unto all the nations; and then shall the end come.' Belief in the millennium, wrote one colonist in 1710, 'has ever been received as a Truth in the Churches of New-England'.[13] It continued to exercise the imaginations of New Englanders after the failure of the English millenarian movement, in which they had invested great hopes. After 1660, however, End-time belief became less immediately expectant. New Englanders began to conceive of themselves in terms similar to those once applied to Savonarola's Florence, in which prosperity and international influence were the sign of Elect status. With the collapse of godly rule in England, there was the intriguing prospect that America itself might be the new Israel. 'Look upon [our] towns and fields, look upon [our] habitations and shops and ships, and behold [our] numerous posterity, and great increase in the blessings of land and sea,' said Cotton Mather. God had surely intended 'some great thing' when he planted these American heavens and earth. 'And what should that be, if not a scripture-pattern that shall in due time be accomplished the whole world throughout?'

This vision of the future is so sunny and beguiling that one has to remind oneself that Mather was the author of *Memorable Providences relating to Witchcraft and Possessions* (1685), which did so much to fan the cruel fury of the New Englanders before the Salem witch trials. In fact, Mather's mixture of optimism and paranoia is entirely characteristic of the millennial vision, and the key to understanding it is the End-time. Fear of witches is above all evidence of End-time anxiety, since it was believed that the Last Days would see a terrible loosing of the powers of darkness. But if the New Englanders could keep their 'city on the hill' undefiled by evil, then this could be a sign of the coming of the Millennium. There was room, even among rigorous Calvinists, for both optimistic and pessimistic readings of the bible's complex eschatological passages. They did not believe, of course, that they could earn God's grace through the building of a fortress of prosperity and godly rule; but success in repelling the dark forces, and in commerce and industry, confirmed the efficacy of a scripture-pattern which would transform the world from the province of Satan to that of Christ. If, on the other hand, they did not maintain the purity of their vision, or were forced to yield to the forces of Antichrist – represented by French Catholics and heathen Indians – then this was the sign that they had arrived at the grim tribulation of Matthew's Gospel: a time when nation rises up against nation, when false prophets lead the people astray and men's love grows cold. Admittedly, this tribulation concludes with what might be called a happy ending, when the Son of Man arrives on the clouds of heaven to summon the Elect. But this is only after an era of desperate suffering in which even the most righteous could lose their faith.

As the nation took shape, apparently with God's blessing, this pessimistic reading of the End gradually lost its force. Indeed, the American Revolution was partly produced by a growing sense of confidence in the nation's apocalyptic destiny. Although it has traditionally been interpreted as a secularisation of the Pilgrims' vision, it is increasingly being recognised that explicit millennialism played as important a part in the foundation of the United States as did the theories of the Enlightenment and its classical models. Several of the Founding Fathers believed that the Republic represented the triumph of the godly foretold in Revelation. There was, however, no clear dividing line between those who derived inspiration from the bible and those who looked to the Enlightenment. The latter strain, illustrated by masonic symbolism, was often richly apocalyptic: according to Michael Grosso, the eye enclosed in a triangle which still adorns the dollar bill 'points back to the evolutionary trinity of Joachim's philosophy of history', while the pyramid which the bill depicts is deliberately unfinished, suggesting that the pinnacle of human civilisation lies ahead.[14] But most people would not have read anything sinister into this;

it was merely an alternative way of conveying truths which were also to be found in the bible.

In the decades after the Revolution, the optimistic view of the End threatened to replace entirely the vision of inevitable cataclysm. By now, eschatology had become firmly divided into two schools of thought: premillennialism, in which Christ was expected to appear at the height of Antichrist's terror to initiate the Millennium; and postmillennialism, in which he would not appear until after the thousand-year reign of the saints. The latter school saw victory over the British as perhaps the last great battle against Antichrist. It remained only to defeat evil and tyranny at home; indeed, the prospect of a peaceful Millennium brought about through progress was the most powerful single motivation for social reformers during the first half of the nineteenth century. The campaign against slavery was shot through with postmillennial zeal, though as the century progressed the reformers became less confident that it could be brought about peacefully. There was, indeed, a fragile quality to American millennial optimism: apparently unassailable in the first years of the century, it gradually became clear that the dragon of premillennialism had not been slain. It took only an economic downturn to revive belief in the imminent descent of Christ into a world polluted by sin, and to prepare the ground for the most spectacular and yet undeniably comic outbreak of End-time fever in history: the Millerite fiasco, otherwise known as the Great Disappointment.

William Miller was a farmer from upstate New York, an area where the fires of religious revival spread so quickly and frequently that it became known as the 'burned-over district'. Originally a deist, Miller became obsessed by the eschatology of Daniel and Revelation and by 1822 had fixed on 1843 as the year most likely to witness the Second Coming. His reasoning was exceedingly convoluted: a believer in the 6,000-year theory of history, he challenged the widely accepted calculations of the seventeenth-century divine Archbishop Ussher which pointed to the beginning of the Millennium in 1996, 6,000 years after the creation of the world in 4004 BC. According to Miller, Ussher had made errors in his Old Testament chronology, underestimating the length of reigns and missing out an interregnum, and this had led him to postdate the Creation, and therefore the End, by some 152 years. When Miller first published his conclusions in 1832, their dense and closely argued nature impressed many critics. In the following year he was granted a licence to preach by his local Baptist church; he began to acquire followers, who were greatly struck by the appearance in November 1833 of a meteor which seemed to confirm his arguments.

By the end of the 1830s, the American economy had entered a depression which damaged both economic confidence and postmillennial revivalism; the theme of the Great Tribulation began to reappear in sermons. Against this uncertain background, Miller's calculations began to attract a mass following in Boston and New York City. A newspaper called *Signs of the Times* was founded to promulgate his ideas. Prominent social reformers who had lost their faith in postmillennialism joined the movement. In the absence of any firm prediction from Miller of the hour of the Second Coming, rival camps began to espouse different dates in 1843. Finally, Miller announced that by '1843' he meant the Jewish year running from one vernal equinox to the next; he was therefore 'fully convinced that sometime between March 21st, 1843, and March 21st, 1844 . . . Christ will come and bring all his saints with him'.[15] Inevitably, tension rose during this period; and, when the End did not materialise by the latter date, disillusionment set in. But the drama was not over.

Between March and October 1844 there occurred a sequence of events which sociologists have come to regard as typical of date-setting millenarianism. After the initial disappointment, most of Miller's followers abandoned the movement. For the most committed believers, however, there was only one possible course of action: they must work out why the previous deadline was wrong, and establish the true date of the Second Coming. Curiously, Miller played no part in this process. At a camp meeting of confused and unhappy Millerites in August 1844, one Samuel Snow outlined a new chronology which, rather than predicting that the Second Coming would happen at some stage during the course of a year, pinpointed the very day: 22 October 1844, the 'tenth day of the seventh month of the Jewish sacred year'. The new calculation was eagerly seized upon by the most disappointed of the faithful, who effectively imposed it on Miller himself: he did not endorse it until the beginning of October, announcing that 'if he [Jesus] does not come within 20 or 25 days, I shall feel twice the disappointment I did this spring'. As Stephen O'Leary points out in his study of Millerite rhetoric, there was a new and desperate quality to the justifications for the new deadline: spokesmen 'clutched at arguments that depended not on rational calculation but on God's influence and inspiration within the movement itself'.[16] On the evening of the great day, the Millerites gathered on hillsides to await the Lord. When he did not come, their sense of loss was, as Miller had feared, far greater than before. In the words of one disciple, 'our fondest hopes and expectations were blasted, and such a spirit of weeping came over us as I never experienced before. It seemed that the loss of all earthly friends could have been no comparison. We wept and wept until the day dawned.'[17]

The spectacle of apocalyptic believers on hillsides staring up in disbelief at an empty sky was not easily forgotten. Indeed, one legacy of the second Millerite episode was the comic stereotype of the doomsday prophet; for this was the first time in history that a large-scale apocalyptic movement had been greeted by most of the public as a glorious joke. According to one account, 'the taunts and jeers of the scoffers were well-nigh unbearable. If any of Miller's followers walked abroad, they ran the gauntlet of merciless ridicule. "What! not gone up yet? We thought you'd gone up! Aren't you going up soon? Wife didn't leave you behind to burn, did she?" '[18] Even so, we should not dismiss Millerism as a comic affair involving a few hundred oddballs. The Great Disappointment of October can be seen as a purely sectarian event, but this was certainly not true of the End-time excitement that led up to the earlier deadline. There were around 50,000 Millerites at the beginning of 1844, and perhaps as many as a million people who, while not true believers, were expecting some sort of great spiritual event that year. These people were not the marginalised urban poor: a high proportion were churchgoing members of the middle classes. They cannot be classified as millenarians, but nor were they simply believers in their country's millennial destiny: they occupied the ground in between. Arguably, they represented a sort of near-millenarianism which is characteristic of societies which have experienced rapid but insecure economic growth at a time of crystallising national identity, both of which factors produce a sense of disorientation, albeit a positive one. A parallel might be drawn with parts of the Far East today, where apocalyptic belief verging on the millenarian is characteristic of the hyper-energetic lower-middle classes.

The Great Disappointment did, however, have the effect of completely discrediting date-specific apocalypticism in America for well over a century. Indeed, it marks the moment at which End-time belief in general became the preserve of specific groups rather than a mainstay of the Republic. Postmillennialist optimism was all but wiped out in the Civil War. Liberal Protestants moved away from eschatology and embraced a social gospel rooted in everyday realities. Conservatives, meanwhile, reverted to the premillennialist vision of a world dominated by Satan, to be released from his grip only by the Second Coming. Yet they were determined never again to make fools of themselves by pinning their hopes on a specific date.

In the last decades of the nineteenth century most conservative Protestants were won over by a new model of historical development pioneered by the English evangelical and founder of the Plymouth Brethren, John Nelson Darby. Known as premillennial dispensationalism, it proposed a detailed and ingenious timetable which tried to reconcile the confusing and contradictory references to the End in Daniel, the Gospels, St Paul and Revelation. According to this timetable, God's 'prophetic clock' had stopped at the beginning of the Gospel Age. It would not start up again until the drama of the Last Days had begun, so there was no need for Christians to waste their time attempting to interpret current events in the light of bible prophecy, a favourite occupation of the Millerites. On the other hand, the Last Days might begin at any time, and, once this happened, the blood-soaked prophecies of Revelation would be fulfilled thick and fast. Yet born-again Christians had nothing to fear: although civilisation would be plunged into its death-agonies, they would not suffer, having been lifted bodily out of the earthly arena. Darby based this claim on St Paul's first letter to the Thessalonians, which declares that, when the Last Trump is sounded, Christ will descend, the Christian dead will rise, and then 'we who are left alive shall join them, caught up in the clouds to meet the Lord in the air' (1 Thess. 4: 17). Darby called this upward flight the Rapture, and the name stuck. It remains one of the most powerful pieces of apocalyptic imagery ever devised, removing all Christians from the End-time horrors at a single stroke while allowing them to watch the unsaved perish in the thrilling drama of the Great Tribulation.

With the appearance of premillennial dispensationalism, the history of Christian apocalyptic belief in the West appeared to be over. In the last century, no major biblical End-time theory has emerged to supplant it. In some respects, Darby's timetable is difficult to improve upon: no other system allows millennial expectation to simmer gently for so long, thus maintaining evangelical fervour without allowing it to boil over into full-scale millenarianism. Admittedly, it has never exercised a particularly broad appeal: for most of the twentieth century, it remained the preserve of a conservative and fundamentalist fringe in Middle America, while the rest of the United States embraced a thoroughly secular millennialism. But in the second half of the twentieth century, as we shall see, the gradual and supposedly irreversible marginalisation of apocalyptic belief was in fact reversed. The premillennial dragon began to stir out of his small-town lair; and, with the approach of the year 2000, the ghosts of the Münster Anabaptists, the Fifth Monarchists and even the Millerites have returned to disturb the sleep of governments everywhere.

5

Fin de Siècle

'The people who tell us that a century is merely an arbitrary division of time are poor observers,' wrote the editor of a London magazine in 1901. 'Else would they have noticed a cataclysm of Nature which synchronised with the end of the year 1900. Suddenly, absolutely, the Woman with a Past disappeared from the stage. It is remarkable. We called her *fin-de-siècle*. The century finishes and she no longer exists.'[1]

At which point, it appears, many people throughout Europe and America breathed a sigh of relief. The chattering classes of the 1890s had been obsessed with the phrase *fin de siècle*, which first appeared in France in 1885, and which by 1890 had already inspired a play, a novel and a series of scholarly articles analysing its properties as an adjective and presumptive noun. 'The word has flown from one hemisphere to the other, and found its way into all civilised languages,' noted one observer in 1892. The *Atlantic Monthly* was heartily sick of the phrase by 1891. 'Everywhere we are treated to dissertations on fin-de-siècle literature, fin-de-siècle statesmanship, fin-de-siècle morality,' it grumbled. 'People seem to take it for granted that a moribund century implies, not to say excuses, disenchantment,

103

languor, literary, artistic and political weariness, and that in 1901 the world will make a fresh start.'[2]

It is no accident that the world had to wait until the end of the nineteenth century for the phrase *fin de siècle* to pass into common usage. The notion that the new year witnesses a renewal of time itself is as old as humanity; but the idea that society grows old with the calendar century, and is mysteriously regenerated by its turn, is of far more recent origin. The sense of *fin de siècle* could not evolve until people began to feel that their lives were somehow shaped by the century in which they lived. That could not happen until they had accepted that they were living 'in' a particular century. This is something we take for granted at the end of the twentieth century; but then we also take it for granted that the day is divided into hours and minutes. We forget that both centuries and minutes arrived late on the scene as means of universal orientation. Samuel Pepys's diary, for example, reveals that he almost never made official appointments, but turned up at offices and coffee houses in the hope of running into the right person. For, although he was an important government official, he did not possess a watch, but kept time by listening to church bells. A couple of centuries before him, the abstract framework of uniformly ordered time scarcely existed outside a monastery. It was only with the full flourishing of a monetary economy that, in Lewis Mumford's phrase, time-keeping became time-saving and 'eternity gradually ceased to serve as the measure and focus of human actions'.

This is as true of the wider time-span as it is of daily time-keeping. Until the fifteenth century, most people were only intermittently aware of the Anno Domini calendar; they might know in which year they were born, rather as we today might know which sign we are born under, but the information was not needed for day-to-day orientation. As late as the eighteenth century, only official documents mentioned the AD year; most correspondents dated letters by the year of the king's reign. The universal application of Anno Domini lagged some way behind simple awareness of living in a chronological year. Once adopted, however, Anno Domini had far-reaching implications for the individual's relationship to history and the future. It is significant that the use of the AD calendar should increase at a time when apocalyptic belief was becoming marginalised. The unchangeable forward momentum of Anno Domini tends to work against the assumption that mankind is poised on the brink of apocalypse, except at those times when it is moving towards a year invested with its own apocalyptic significance. The AD calendar creates a precisely measured future which unfolds at an even pace, in contrast to the disorientating acceleration of 'apocalyptic time': the latter precedes the Millennium, which although bounded by the very concrete notion of a thousand years is essentially a preparation for *timeless* eternity.

The growth of popular awareness of the AD year did not mean that the people immediately abandoned the notion of the biblical Millennium. But it certainly contributed to a more sophisticated understanding of history, in which the Second Coming of Christ was merely tacked on to a secular periodisa-tion which extended far into the future. By the eighteenth century, people identified with their own century and could envisage without difficulty the passage of future centuries. This confidence was not far removed from the temperate eschatology of Augustine, which had been ignored by Catholics and reformers alike during the millenarian excitements of the middle ages and the sixteenth century. This sophisticated historical perspective was not as free from apocalyptic influen-ces as it liked to pretend: but its belief in 'progress' was nonetheless close in spirit to the optimism with which the Church had, a whole millennium earlier, attempted to replace crude End-time speculation. Someone who felt a strong sense of belonging to the eighteenth century, and who occasionally daydreamed about what life would be like in the twentieth century, was unlikely to wear out his fingers computing the time of the End. That, after all, was the reasoning which inspired the Church to adopt the AD system in the first place.

The Roman Catholic Church can take much of the credit for the eventual triumph of non-apocalyptic time. Not only did it impose on the West an open-ended chronology, but it played a crucial part in popularising its division into consecutive and distinctive centuries. This might sound like something which is too obvious to need popularising: there is an inevitability about the emergence of a unit of 100 years in cultures which use decimal numbers, particularly when it roughly corresponds to the maximum human lifespan – and, as we have seen, the Etruscans and Romans thought in terms of consecutive *saecu-lae*. But calendar centuries arrived late on the scene. The apocalyptic excitement at the year 1000 was not fuelled by change in the recorded date, as such: the passage of a thousand years was not seen primarily in the context of the AD calendar, and the year 1033 seems to have been regarded as just as much a 'millennium' as the year 1000.

It is not until the end of the thirteenth century that we encounter the first event which can safely be described as a turn-of-the-century celebration. This was the Papal Jubilee of 1300, which offered a plenary indulgence to all pilgrims who visited designated basilicas thirty times during the year. In his bull declaring the jubilee, Pope Boniface VIII referred to an ancient tradition of papal celebrations at the end of the centuries. In fact, there was no such precedent: the 'tradition' was invented by Boniface, who two years later followed it up with another bull, *Unam Sanctam*, which is regarded as the most strenuous assertion of papal temporal and spiritual power in the history of the papacy up to that time. It is interesting that such a triumphalist statement of papal power should follow so soon after the jubilee. No fewer than 200,000 people had flocked to Rome to the celebrations, which may well have concentrated the Pope's mind on the power and status of the papacy. At any rate, it was an inspired public-relations exercise. Modern commentators have tended to assume that Boniface was merely cashing in on the inevitable fascination with the mysterious transition from 1299 to 1300. But, according to the American historian Hillel Schwartz, this misses the essential novelty of the event. 'Regardless of its nod to antiquity, the bull [announcing the jubilee] did not build on custom. It established custom. For the Church: a Jubilee anchored to the '00 of the Anno Domini calendar, exclusive of paschal tables and all other gauges of ritual time. For Christian Europe: an expectation of momentous, once-in-a-lifetime opportunities at century's turn.'[3]

This quotation is taken from Schwartz's 1990 book *Century's End*, a survey of cultural history 'from the 990s through the 1990s' which is the first serious examination of the origins of the *fin de siècle*. Although the early sections of this monumental work vividly describe the turmoil of the 990s, 1090s and 1190s, the author admits that he is 'feeding on coincidence'; any sense of *fin de siècle* in those years is a figment of the modern imagination. According to Schwartz, the barest rudiments of a century's end can be listed as follows: a standard calendar; an additive, arithmetical sense of the passage of time; an especial concern with ages and periods; a habit of looking for historical meaningful conjunctions of events; despair over the decay of institutions and the lapse of moral courage; and prophetic hopes of a new age within history. All these elements were undoubtedly present at the end of the thirteenth century, which was after all the era of Joachim of Fiore and his Age of the Holy Spirit. But they did not add up to much: there was as yet no sense of the passing of the old century, or of the regenerative power of its successor.

If we look at the historical records of the turns of the century between 1300 and 1800, it is extremely difficult to say which anniversary has the best claim to be regarded as the first historical event in its own right. The dawning of the twentieth century was clearly an occasion of all-consuming interest in the West: so much so, in fact, that it has been suggested that the forthcoming end-of-millennium celebrations, however large-scale, are unlikely to exceed its psychological impact. Before the 1900 anniversary, however, the picture is less clear. As one might expect, each end-of-century experience since 1300 is better documented than its predecessor. On the whole, though, it is surprising how long we have to wait before we can make out the familiar Janus-like features of the Turn of the Century, which looks backwards with nostalgia and forwards with bright-eyed anticipation. There are eyewitness accounts of the jubilee of 1300, but none of them ruminates on the end of the thirteenth century or the beginning of the fourteenth. In fact, the very term 'the fourteenth century' would have been an unfamiliar one to the crowds at the jubilee. It does not appear until 1400, when the Florentine humanist Coluccio Salutati embarked on a quest for the writers who best represented the 'quartodecimo seculo'.

It was not until the Reformation that the practice of naming centuries by their ordinal numbers translated into a frame of mind which automatically divided history into centuries. If end-of-century celebrations were pioneered by the papacy, credit for this later development belongs to the Catholic Church's most single-minded opponents, the German Protestant reformers of the sixteenth century. Indeed, it was the very act of chronicling the Roman Church's supposed deviations from Christian truth which helped bring about the division of history into centuries. In 1559 a group of Lutheran scholars in Magdeburg published the first volume of a history of the Church which emphasised the wickedness and corruption of the papacy down the centuries. The series was known as the *Magdeburg Centuries* because it was intended to appear in sixteen volumes, one for each century. Although the project was never completed, its influence was enormous: according to Hillel Schwartz, 'never before in the Christian West had the long span of history been conceived in terms of centuries laid end to end . . . [Without them], we would have neither the English word "century" denoting the period of one hundred years nor the more modern notion of a century's end as the end of a hundred years all their own, from '01 to '00.'[4] The impact of the *Magdeburg Centuries* was even felt in Rome. After reading them, the Vatican librarian Cesare Baronio refashioned his *Annales Ecclesiastici* as a counterblast to them, taking care to emphasise the beginning and end of AD centuries. (He certainly allowed his imagination full rein when he arrived at the end of the tenth century: his description of the monumental panic which gripped Europe at the fateful date is regarded as the origin of the modern Legend of the Year 1000.)

The end of the sixteenth century is an important moment in the development of orientation by measured time. This was an era of movement at both ends of the scale, as it were.

Timepieces accurate to the second began to appear, and the word 'second' passed into common currency. Pope Gregory XIII's reform of the calendar in 1582, the last major reform to date, halted the slow drift of Easter away from spring and towards summer. The occasional reflection on 'our century' crops up in literature of the time: a book by the Italian visionary Tommaso Campanella refers to 'our present century, which has produced more history in a hundred years than the whole world did in the preceding four thousand', an observation which quickly obtained the status of a cliché.[5] Yet apart from the Papal Jubilee of 1600, there was little to mark the actual progression from one century to the next: despite a growing awareness of centuries, few writers in Catholic or Protestant Europe felt the moment itself worthy of comment.

A century later, the picture is very different. During the seventeenth century, the conjunction of time and event was immeasurably strengthened as the population of the West began to use calendars as a means of day-to-day reference. The celebration of birthdays became the norm; and with it came a new sense of identification with one's AD year of birth. The dawn of the eighteenth century was an event in a way that the dawn of the seventeenth was not. The educated classes throughout Europe and America sent each other new century's greetings. In London, one John Jackson, who was to travel to Rome for the Papal Jubilee, wrote to his uncle on 1 January 1700 wishing him a happy new century. Yet perhaps the habit of numbering centuries was not yet fully ingrained, for he managed to get its number wrong. His uncle, none other than Samuel Pepys, pointed out that he had made New Year's Day the first of the seventeenth century. Jackson apologised: ''Twas the 18th century I meant, whatever I might write.'[6] John Dryden composed a masque to celebrate the occasion, which ended with the line ''Tis well and Old Age is out, / And time to begin a New.' In America, Samuel Sewall of Boston paid four trumpeters to sound a fanfare on the Common at daybreak on 1 January to mark the 'entrance of the 18th Century'.

It is worth noting that Sewall's trumpets sounded forth on the first day of 1701, not 1700. If there is one reliable indicator of public interest in century's end, it is the intensity of the debate over whether a new era starts at the beginning of the year '00 or '01. At the beginning of the eighteenth century, we can merely infer that there were two schools of thought. At the beginning of the nineteenth, the debate raged across two continents and the correspondence columns of innumerable newspapers and periodicals. 'It is somewhat singular', commented the editor of a paper in Philadelphia, 'that all those . . . who happen to be *wrong* respecting the termination of the century, invariably set out with declaring the question to be the *plainest* in the world.'[7] The writer was a supporter of the '00 school; but he might as easily have been speaking from the opposing position. According to one supporter of 31 December 1800, the claims of those who believed the century died with the year 1700 were like the 'dreams of a distempered imagination, to support which nothing has hitherto been offered but misconception, noise and fury'.[8] But even supporters of the later date confessed to a certain quickening of the pulse at the numerical change from 1799 to 1800 (though this was the first century's end when people seem to have been greatly struck by the point). As the young Samuel Taylor Coleridge wrote to a friend in January 1800: 'How many Thousand Letter-writers will in the first fortnight of the month write a 7 first, & then transmogrify it into an 8 – in the dates of their Letters!'[9]

In the end, of course, the debate over the end of the century merely reflected the new importance which Europe and America attached to the anniversary. Some contemporaries seem to have felt a personal loss at the passing of 'that good Old Lady known by the name of the EIGHTEENTH CENTURY, who resigned all sublunary cares on Wednesday night last, [and] was buried in the family vault of Eternity'. It is not a big leap from this sort of personification of the century to a full-fledged *fin de siècle*: whether one believed that the year 1800 belonged to the eighteenth or nineteenth century, there was a general assumption that it was an occasion for looking both forwards and backwards. For the first time, there was a distinct feeling of passing from one age to another. To an extent, this was the result of the way people had come to divide history into centuries; but it also reflected the extraordinary circumstances of the age, which had seen a sudden and apparently irrevocable collapse of the European political order at the end of the century. If ever a century came to a climax, it was the eighteenth. The *London Chronicle*, reviewing the year 1799, came close to suggesting that time itself had accelerated: 'Never perhaps did the three quarters of the old world see at once in so short a space of time so many events of every kind succeed one another: never perhaps was the destiny of their inhabitants subjected to so many changes, so many evils, and such vicissitudes.'[10]

The peculiar circumstances of the period inevitably transformed perceptions of the century's end – so much so, in fact, that it is hard to know whether the transition from eighteenth to nineteenth century would have impinged on the popular consciousness to any greater extent than in 1700 if the French Revolution had not happened. This is a question of more than purely hypothetical interest for anyone concerned with apocalyptic belief. In England and America, the end of the eighteenth century witnessed a marked resurgence of prophecy belief. But would there have been this rise in the eschatological temperature if the end of the century had not witnessed such earth-shattering events?

At first glance, the answer to this question appears to be a straightforward no. Most prophecy belief in the 1790s was rooted firmly in interpretations of the French Revolution. In France, the Catholic prophet Suzette Labrousse announced that the Revolution heralded a Millennium beginning in the year 1800. In London, scores of pamphlets described events in France as fulfilment of prophecy. The execution of Louis XIV, like that of Charles I, was welcomed by biblical exegetes not out of republican conviction but because it was a necessary prelude to the End-time. This distinction was of little interest to the British government, which threw the more energetic pamphleteers in jail. In reality, though, the surge in prophetic activity posed very little threat: its leading lights were mostly lonely figures whose support was confined to like-minded eccentrics, servants and labourers. The only exception was

Joanna Southcott, a domestic servant from Exeter who first prophesied in 1792 and ten years later began sealing the 144,000 who were to enjoy the millennial reign with Christ. In the first decade of the nineteenth cntury she had several thousand followers, some of them Church of England clergymen, though her support quickly dispersed after one of the 'elect' was hanged for murder.

Is there any significance in the fact that a prophet such as Joanna, who emerged at a time of raised eschatological awareness caused by events in Europe, should fasten her hopes on the beginning of the century? At the end of the eighteenth century, apocalyptic beliefs could be found 'among Bavarian illuminati, Scandinavian Swedenborgians, Polish and Russian occultists in St Petersburg, Spanish Jesuits, American Shakers, New England Congregationalists, Seneca Indians, Appalachian Methodists, Welsh Baptists, and the more excitable of Freemasons . . .'[11] The existence of this ferment does not in the least alter the fact that, in Europe at least, apocalyptic faith was no longer intellectually fashionable, or the driving force behind mass religious movements. Even so, it is curious that so many prophets envisaged a transformation right at the end of the 1790s. It was as if the new century was exerting a gravitational pull all of its own. Was it possible that the mere fact of a century ending could stir apocalyptic passions?

It has become a commonplace of the 1990s that fears of the End of the World mysteriously shoot up at the end of every century. This assertion often goes hand in hand with extravagant descriptions of panic at the dawn of the year 1000, and, as with that claim, the evidence against seems fairly damning. As we have seen, for centuries people were not aware of the Anno Domini year, and, even if they were, they did not associate it with the structure of their own lives or their own society. Moreover, the adoption of the AD calendar throughout Europe was a precondition for the replacement of apocalyptic belief by secular ideology during the seventeenth and eighteenth centuries.

And yet we cannot entirely rule out the possibility of a

recurring rise in eschatological temperature at the end of centuries. Bizarrely, there is evidence of prophetic activity even at the end of centuries whose passing did not register in the popular consciousness. The drama of the year 1000 is relevant here. The 990s were years of greatly heightened apocalyptic expectations despite the fact that awareness of the 'date' in the modern sense was non-existent. The powerful symbolism of the first Christian millennium lay ultimately in the completion of a 'round number' of years since the birth of Christ. In the same way, though to a lesser extent, other centuries' ends were round numbers which could accommodate all manner of calculations. For example: the year 1200, according to Joachim of Fiore, marked the completion of forty generations since Christ and twenty-two since St Benedict, and was the moment when the Second and Third Ages would begin to overlap. During the millenarian excitement of the seventeenth century, similar reasoning invested the year 1700 – then nearly half a century away – with apocalyptic significance. The Fifth Monarchy Men expected the End-time to begin in the 1650s, but envisaged the start of the Millennium in or around the year 1700. The arithmetic was a little more complicated than Joachim's: the figure 1,700 was arrived at by adding 365, the year when Daniel's prophecy of the 'abomination of desolation' was fulfilled by Julian the Apostate, to 1,290 'days' of a year each and Daniel's forty-five years of tribulation. But the effect was the same: God's designated year turned out to end with two noughts.

In other cases, there is little or no evidence of apocalyptic calculations pointing to the century's end, but a sharp rise nonetheless in eschatological awareness in its last decade. The 1490s are a case in point. The absence of contemporary references to the completion of a millennium-and-a-half since Christ's birth does not mean that it can be ruled out as a factor predisposing Savonarola's audience to heed his message. Florence at the time seems to have experienced a sensation of hovering nervously on the edge of a new age. Although this can be diagnosed as a simple case of apocalyptic foreboding, it is also surprisingly close in spirit to the ambiguous modern response to the dawn of a new century. There is a tantalising reference to the year 1500 in the inscription on Botticelli's famous painting of the Nativity. It reads: 'I Sandro painted this picture at the end of the year 1500 in the troubles of Italy in the half time after the time according to the xith chapter of St John in the second woe of the Apocalypse in the loosing of the devil [that is, the reign of Antichrist] for three and a half years. Then he will be chained . . . and we shall see him trodden down, as in this picture.'[12] The precise End-time scenario which Botticelli is invoking is not the issue: what matters is the lingering impression that the defeat of the Antichrist and the approach of the Joachimite new age are bound up in some mysterious and unspecified way with the passing of 1,500 years since Christ's birth.

There is one case of raised apocalyptic expectation which seems entirely divorced from its end-of-century background. This is the First Crusade, which was launched in 1096 and quickly assumed the dimensions of an apocalyptic struggle. No one has ever suggested that the 1,100th anniversary of the birth of Christ possessed an intrinsic significance, and there was as yet no popular conception of calendar centuries. Even here, however, we may be able to detect the insidious effect of millennial round numbers. As Richard Landes points out, the First Crusade set out precisely a thousand years after the traditional date of the visions of John of Patmos which inspired the Book of Revelation. It is true that we cannot know how, or even whether, this coincidence affected the Crusaders' perceptions of their role. It is, however, a reminder that the millennial undertow beneath Western civilisation is made up of innumerable currents which the modern observer can easily fail to notice. The notion of the recurrence of apocalyptic fears every hundred years is not as far-fetched as it sounds. The First Crusade was a response to the destruction of the Holy Sepulchre by the Fatimid al Hakim, who had cast himself in the role of Mahdi – a Messiah figure who, according to one tradition, would appear every hundred years. It is no accident that the aggressive stance which led to the attack on Jerusalem was adopted in the Islamic year 400 AH. It is not inconceivable that the idea of an apocalyptically charged century's end was transmitted from Islam to the West along with the Arabic numerals which lent such force to the calendar transition. Perhaps it was communicated to medieval Europe via the sophisticated Islamic astrological tradition, whose export produced a new interest in the concept of immovable historical cycles. As Schwartz argues, the cast of mind which could be impressed by astrological conjunctions was similar to the cast of mind which could anticipate the end of each hundred calendar years as inevitably the end of an epoch.

It may even be the case that any society which uses calendars is naturally predisposed to experience a mixture of anticipation and fear at intervals of a fixed number of years. In non-Western societies, this would not reflect a fully formed belief in the clash of good and evil followed by the emergence of a new world; apocalypticism as such seems to have been invented by the Zoroastrians. But there might be a communal experience of calendar change, one which would effectively magnify the emotions associated with the New Year. This seems to have been true of the Aztecs of ancient Mexico, who believed that the end of their fifty-two-year calendar cycle was a time of great danger in which the world might end. According to a sixteenth-century eyewitness, Friar Bernardino Sahagun, the Aztecs would spend the last night of the cycle gazing at the sky, to see if the movement of the heavens would cease; when it did not, 'they were so happy that they yelled, and their yells reached up to heaven, for the world was not coming to an end and they undoubtedly had 52 more years'. Having extinguished every fire in the land, they lit a new fire 'and renewed the pact they had with their idol, that of serving him, and they renewed all the statues of him which they kept in their homes . . .'[13] We have heard something like this before. The Aztec statues are surely the equivalent to Glaber's 'white mantle of churches' which appeared in the aftermath of the year 1000: tokens of the joy and relief which perhaps every society feels when it believes it has turned a corner in time.

We should bear all this in mind when considering the

complicated phenomenon of the modern century's end. It draws on a bewildering variety of influences, from the ancient and instinctive to the highly evolved structures of Christian apocalyptic and secular progress. A great deal hangs on the subtle relationship between these last two concepts, which first became intertwined at the end of the eighteenth century.

The French Revolution certainly produced a fresh spurt of Christian speculation about the End of the World. But this was a period in European history when crude biblical apocalypticism had mostly been supplanted by secular conceptions of time and history. There was no danger of poor Joanna Southcott leading a millenarian crusade; that dream had died with the Commonwealth. Yet it would be wrong to conclude from this that the apocalyptic instinct had entirely disappeared from the intellectual mainstream on either side of the Atlantic. In Europe, especially, that instinct had found new modes of expression. The main legacy of the Enlightenment, according to Nicholas Campion, is that it 'shifted responsibility for the future away from the heavens and into the hands of humanity'.[14] God's plan for history was transformed into theories of human achievement. Although these theories tended to reject the notion of divine preordination, they left much of the apocalyptic structure intact. There was still an assumption that mankind had reached the later stages of the penultimate historical epoch. There was even a faint suggestion of an acceleration of time as history moved to its climax – a millennium of Pure Reason. In America, meanwhile, millennial thought ceased to be the preserve of Christian believers. The image of the nation as the New Israel entered the secular mainstream, where it merged with Enlightenment concepts of progress. The official ideology of the United States became a highly potent compound of religious and secular millennialism in which America effectively assumed the mantle of Last World Empire.

The interaction, and the unexpected compatibility, of religious and secular apocalyptic views of history is the key to understanding end-of-century experiences from the 1790s onwards. The idea of the modern century is bound up with the triumph of a 'secular' view of history – one which has discarded the Christian apocalyptic deadline. Paradoxically, though, the more extravagant the hopes invested in the new century, the more it comes to resemble the Joachimite golden age. Meanwhile, those Christians who await a divine irruption into history subtly tailor their prophecies to the contours of the secular calendar, so that the dawn of the millennial kingdom coincides with the new century. Sometimes, though, this convergence of calendar and religious enthusiasm seems genuinely spontaneous. In the first months of 1801, a religious revival which became known as the Second Great Awakening began to gather pace in the United States. At a camp meeting in Cane Ridge, Kentucky, 25,000 people danced, laughed, shrieked and fell over as the Spirit gripped them. An eyewitness noted that 'saints and sinners of every grade would . . . with a piercing scream, fall like a log on the floor, earth or mud and appear as dead'.[15] The sheer size of the Cane Ridge gathering has led modern commentators to call it the First Woodstock. But a closer analogy is with the 1993 'Toronto Blessing', which caused born-again Christians throughout the world to laugh and cry hysterically as they were 'slain in the Spirit'. Just as the Blessing has been hailed as evidence that the 1990s mark the end of the Gospel Age, so the Second Great Awakening was interpreted as a sign that the nineteenth century would be an era of End-time wonders. The crucial point, however, is that this expectation was reinforced, not contradicted, by prophecies of a nineteenth century of Augustan prosperity and glory. Not for nothing did the newly adopted motto on the seal of the United States read 'NOVUS ORDO SECULORUM': the new order of the ages.

Belief in the *novus ordo* was even stronger at the end of the nineteenth century than it had been at its beginning. It is easy to forget this fact when confronted by innumerable references, both contemporary and modern, to the *fin de siècle*. The phrase goes hand in hand with images of the 1890s as a period of decadence and hopelessness; and it is true that in some circles the era was characterised by a mixture of hedonism and fashionable pessimism. In England, newspapers and magazines were full of articles about the decline of such phenomena as family life, warfare, mental health and religious faith, to say nothing of cricket, bookselling, knowledge of the classics and even canine fidelity. The Jewish-Hungarian author Max Nordau caused a sensation in 1895 with his ferocious attack on *fin de siècle* tendencies. 'The disposition of the times', he wrote, 'is curiously confused, a compound of feverish restlessness and blunted discouragement, of fearful presage and hang-dog renunciation. The prevalent feeling is that of imminent perdition and extinction.'[16]

Most commentators did not view the period with such a jaundiced eye. The British writer Holbrook Jackson argued that what Nordau described as degeneration was actually a sane and healthy expression of a vitality which would have been better named regeneration. The 1890s, he conceded, had produced a 'perverse and finicky glorification of the fine arts', but its effect had been to introduce a new sense of rhythm into art. Far more important, however, was the context in which this 'decadence' arose: a world in which thought-provoking ideas flourished in every sphere, and in which there was a new enthusiasm for social regeneration. The economic depression of the early 1890s produced a new determination to escape the dead hand of the past. 'It was an era of hope and action,' Jackson concluded. 'People thought anything might happen; and for the young, anything happening sufficiently new was good ... Never was there a time when the young were so young or the old so old.'[17]

And never was there a time when people were so conscious of living on the verge of a new era. The decade was marked by acute self-consciousness. The phrase *fin de siècle* was encountered so often that, by the end of the decade, people had become embarrassed to utter it. It was clear to most observers, if not to Max Nordau, that the concept was as much a pose as an event. But it was thought of as a harmless pose which did not take itself seriously. Its pessimism was superficial. There was an exuberance to the whole *fin de siècle* movement which betrayed an underlying optimism about the prospects for the new century. That optimism, which frequently spilled over into utopianism, was not confined to aesthetes or social reformers.

'We *are* on the threshold of a great time, even if our time itself is not great,' wrote the positivist philosopher Frederic Harrison. 'In science, in religion, in social organisation, we all know what things are in the air . . . It is the age of great expectation and unwearied striving after better things.'[18] The stunning pace of technological change and the channelling of organised labour into political parties both held out the promise of a new human era. That era had a name: the twentieth century.

Western Europe and America in the last two decades of the nineteenth century displayed a far greater curiosity about the twentieth century than the 1990s (so far) have about the twenty-first. Hundreds of books and journals included the words 'New Century' in their title. Books on the twentieth century were so numerous, wrote an American reviewer in 1890, 'that the whole subject is in danger of becoming a deadly bore'. There was a fascination with the position of the new century in the dynamic structure of history. Henry Adams, visiting the Paris Great Exposition of 1900, speculated that Western civilisation had begun to gather force during the period 1400 to 1800, and had moved with stupendous acceleration during the nineteenth century. Then, in 1900, the continuity had snapped: the world had been transformed by the appearance of 'the new class of supersensual forces, before which the man of science stood at first as bewildered and helpless, as in the fourth century a priest of Isis before the Cross of Christ'.[19]

Adams's theory made explicit the notion of accelerating time which had been hinted at in the Christian apocalyptic worldview. He was certainly not the only commentator who felt himself being physically pulled towards the year 1900 and wondered whether hidden forces were at work. For the first time, indeed, there was a general curiosity about the whole concept of centuries, and about other end-of-century experiences. Was it possible that the highly charged atmosphere of the 1890s owed something to an undiscovered law of centurial cycles? Max Nordau offered a characteristically sour explanation, involving what he called the Dusk of the Nations, 'in which all suns and all stars are gradually waning and mankind with all its institutions and creations is perishing in the midst of a dying world'. This corresponded in some mysterious way to the old northern doctrine of the Dusk of the Gods, and to traditional (not to say fictional) beliefs in evil destiny at the close of centuries. Holbrook Jackson offered a far more upbeat theory. 'As a matter of fact, the quickening of life during the last years of a century is not without parallel,' he wrote.

> The preceding century closed with the French Revolution, and the sixteenth century closed with the destruction of the Armada and the appearance of Shakespeare ... whilst the close of the fifteenth century saw the Revival of Learning and the discovery of America. One cannot avoid the temptation to speculate on the meaning of such *fin de siècle* occurrences, for we are actually made more conscious of time by the approaching demise of a century, just as we are made more conscious of our age on birthday anniversaries and New Year's Eve. And it is at least thinkable that as we are certainly moved in the latter circumstances to pull ourselves together ... so a similar but racial instinct towards unique activity may come about at so impressive a period as the close of a century.[20]

This cheerful theory was far more in tune with the spirit of the 1890s than gloomy prognostications of the Dusk of Nations. There was more excitement than fear in the air as the new century approached, even if that anticipation was tinged with nervousness. People thought of the era as one of transition. The prevailing optimism affected religious believers as much as anyone, though it had many different expressions. In England, many Christian thinkers embraced a full-blooded socialism. The sacramental theology of the more radical 'slum priests' of the 1890s was inextricably linked to a vision of London as a twentieth-century utopia guided by the spirit of the 'Socialistic Carpenter', Jesus of Nazareth. In America, liberal Protestants did not advocate socialism, but dreamed of a new century in which all the major world religions would be subsumed into a loosely defined, undogmatic brand of Christianity which would preserve the best qualities of their respective traditions. Apocalyptic visions of the End of the World were, generally speaking, at odds with the mood of all the major Christian denominations. In 1889, the Rev. Michael Baxter, editor of the London

Christian Herald, announced in a book called *The End of This Age about the End of This Century* that 1896 would witness the Rapture of 144,000 devout Christians, and that the world would end in 1901.[21] No one took him seriously.

The truth is that there was no appetite for apocalyptic date-setting in England or, more significantly, the United States. Conservative Protestants had still not forgotten the Great Disappointment, subscribing instead to a dispensationalism which taught the need for perpetual readiness for the End while discouraging the application of scriptural prophecy to history. Although most fundamentalists believed that the final era in human history would be one of catastrophic tribulation, this did not rule out the possibility of a sudden and glorious outpouring of the Holy Spirit among the Elect. Furthermore, there was no reason why this outpouring should not coincide with the new century – a century which many fundamentalists, allowing their patriotic enthusiasm to override their theological pessimism, believed would confirm the imperial destiny of the United States.

The coming of the new century fascinated evangelical Protestants in America and Britain. Just as in our own day the year 2000 has become a deadline for international missionary attempts to win the whole world for Christ, so the year 1900 was adopted as a target. When the plan was first mooted in the 1880s, enthusiasm for the 'countdown' was unbounded. In 1889, the Rev. Arthur Pierson, a Presbyterian pastor in Philadelphia, published a book which argued that if 10 million true Protestants worldwide were mobilised, 'it is our solemn and mature conviction that before the close of this century the gospel might be brought into contact with every living soul'. Pierson insisted that his plan was neither impossible nor impracticable: 'It *can* be done; it OUGHT to be done; it MUST be done,' he wrote.[22] But by the 1890s it was clear it could not possibly be done, and the wildly ambitious target figures were revised downwards amid considerable acrimony. Pierson, sensibly, began to talk in rather less specific terms about the new century, which he hoped would be marked by 'an outpouring of the Holy Ghost to which even Pentecost would be simply the first drops of a latter rain'. And, up to a point, this ambition was realised. The desire for a Pentecost beginning with the twentieth century was to lead directly to the emergence of the most vigorous and influential movement in the history of evangelical Christianity.

Modern Pentecostalism, whose adherents experience an ecstatic Spirit baptism often accompanied by speaking in tongues, is the driving force behind the stunning advance of Protestantism in Latin America and the Third World. It has produced one of America's largest denominations, the Assemblies of God, and its influence has been felt in many of the old-established Churches. Many of the most effective, and notorious, televangelists of the 1980s were Pentecostalist, as is the world's largest church, the 700,000-strong Full Gospel Church in Seoul, South Korea. Pentecostal worship first took on the proportions of a mass movement in Los Angeles in 1906, but the movement traces its origins to a single all-night prayer vigil five years earlier at Bethel College, a bible school in Topeka, Kansas. The crucial moment came when a particularly zealous student, Miss Agnes Ozman, suddenly began babbling in unrecognisable tongues – the first authenticated 'Spirit baptism' of modern times. The date: 1 January 1901, the day millions of Americans celebrated as the first of the twentieth century.

Whether Miss Ozman's outburst can be regarded as a *spontaneous* manifestation of the Spirit is a matter of opinion. To the sceptical observer, it seems the ground had been thoroughly prepared by the school authorities: students had been virtually locked away from the outside world and encouraged to fast. But the most important factor was the calendar date. The atmosphere on 1 January was 'at bursting point'. In the words of Agnes Ozman: 'During the first day of 1901 the presence of the Lord was with us in a marked way, stilling our hearts to wait upon Him for greater things. It was nearly eleven o'clock on this first day of January that it came into my heart to ask that hands be laid upon me . . . As hands were laid upon my head the Holy Spirit fell upon me, and I began to speak in tongues, glorifying God. I talked several languages. It was as though rivers of living water were proceeding from my innermost being.'[23]

In the eyes of believers, the twentieth century had produced its first miracle. Perhaps it would turn out to be a century of miracles. The excitement which swelled up inside Miss Ozman on the first day of 1901 was not so very different from that which gripped the crowds at the lavish centurial balls the night before. (The debate between supporters of '00 and '01 had raged with unbelievable fierceness around the civilised world, but the latter camp won the battle as far as festivities were concerned.) Although there was a supernatural dimension to the Pentecostalist vision which was missing from secular dreams of a twentieth-century utopia, both envisaged the glorious transformation of the existing order. They were, however, rather placid and peaceful visions of transformation, of the sort that could be indulged simultaneously by patriotic middle-class churchgoers. For collective hopes of a sudden and total break with the past at the end of the nineteenth century – for classic millenarianism, in other words – one has to look outside Western Europe and North America.

The last years of the nineteenth century witnessed the rise, and fall, of two textbook millenarian movements, one in India and one in Brazil. The former sprang up on the north-west frontier, in a remote and inaccessible area which had not been invaded by foreign troops since the time of Alexander the Great. Then, during the 1890s, British troops poured into previously sacro-sanct tribal areas, followed shortly by roads, bridges, churches and schools. The result was an immediate upsurge in Muslim fanaticism: the unfamiliar word *jihad* began to be heard as Pathan warriors rallied round religious leaders. It took only one attack by tribesmen on a British outpost in the summer of 1897 to trigger a bloody uprising, in which groups of tribesmen formed themselves into war parties. The everyday village mullahs found their authority challenged by charismatic proph-ets who preached about apocalyptic signs and portents. Salvation from the British was at hand, they said, and would lead to an Islamic utopia. A prophet known as the Mad Fakir said the sixty-year reign of the British was over, and that the mouths of their guns would be closed and their bullets turned to water. 'The whole rising has been an astounding business,' wrote one British administrator. 'The people seem to have lost their heads and all view of their own interests in a blind belief that we should be turned out of the country.'[24] The swift defeat of the Pathan rebellion was inevitable: apart from anything else, the wild talk of an Islamic paradise had alarmed the local Indian rulers almost as much as it had the British. It is unlikely that the episode owed something to its end-of-century setting, but not inconceivable: the uprising was, after all, a response to a new British policy which seems to fit exactly Holbrook Jackson's description of a 'racial instinct towards unique activity'.

In the case of the almost simultaneous millenarian outbreak in Brazil, there is no doubt that the approach of the year 1900 played a role. The location was once again remote: the desolate, dried-up backland of the state of Bahia, to which large numbers of peasants fled after the coffee and sugar economy of the north-east went into decline. Here they founded Canudos, a 'New Jerusalem' of tumbledown shacks where they could live undisturbed by the coastal government and practise their religion, a mixture of Catholicism, Indian rites and witchcraft. The spiritual leader of this miserable shanty town was Antonio Conselheiro ('the Counsellor'), a sixty-year-old, half-crazy ascetic who was implacably opposed to Brazil's new republican regime, which he condemned as a masonic conspiracy. In his eyes, the overthrow of the Emperor Pedro II was an act of disobedience to God, a shattering of the patriarchal order so wicked that it must foreshadow the apocalypse. In 1893, Conselheiro had pulled down and burned public notices of republican taxes before retreating to the wilderness. For three years his reputation as a patriarch and saviour grew as disaffected peasants flocked to his 'Zion', which had perhaps 20,000 inhabitants by 1896. In that year, after a scrap between local police and Conselheiro's zealots, the federal government sent 500 soldiers into the backlands. To its astonishment, they were routed disastrously by a group of fanatics armed with blunderbusses, amulets and rosaries.

Amid great public uproar, a new expedition was sent to pacify Canudos. This was a trained force of 1,300 troops accompanied by artillery and led by a celebrated military hero, Colonel Moreira César. But these troops were unprepared for the scorched terrain of the backlands and the very high temperatures. The country was dumbfounded when, in March 1897, the force was all but wiped out and its commander killed. Finally, in October, an army of 10,000 men under five generals surrounded Canudos. Once again, Conselheiro's followers responded with great ferocity, but this time the outcome was not in doubt. 'The fanatics defended their position house by house, foot by foot, displaying a resistance that was not only heroic but fantastic,' writes José Maria Bello. 'Assaulting waves, one after another, were destroyed by the fire of the famished, thirsty and ragged fanatics. On October 5, 1897, the last smoking huts were finally taken. The strange citadel was a shambles. The government troops found no one alive to take prisoner. If any wounded fighters remained alive, they died in the fire that was set by some of the victors, who thought thereby to wipe out the stain of Canudos forever.'[25]

The War of Canudos quickly took on the status of Brazil's major folk epic. Historians are fascinated by its implications. There is broad agreement that the outcome summed up the history of nineteenth-century Brazil: the triumph of the cities and the coastal elite over folk society. The episode represented the past versus the future, progress versus traditionalism and civilisation versus barbarism. The revolt was a protest not against the hierarchy of power, but against the accelerating greed of newly imposed capitalism. All this is no doubt true. The problem is that, in concentrating on the underlying economic realities, historians run the risk of obscuring one simple fact: that many of the followers of Conselheiro expected the End of the World by the year 1900. They were illiterate, and they all died, so we do not have too clear a picture of the world as they saw it. But we do know roughly what 'the Counsellor' told them was going to happen. When he was asked when the world was going to end, he would respond with cryptic prophecies. In 1896 'flocks would flee inland from the sea coast and the sea would turn into the backlands and the backlands into the sea. In 1897 the desert would be covered with grass, shepherds and flocks would intermingle, and from that date on there would be but one single flock and a single shepherd. In 1898, hats would increase in size and heads grow smaller. In 1899 the rivers would turn red and a new planet would circle through space.'[26] Finally, in 1900, 'the sources of light would be extinguished and stars would rain down'.

Why 1900? It is unlikely that Conselheiro or any of his followers could have given a coherent answer. There were no apocalyptic calculations involved; simply a conviction that the End would coincide with a major shift in the calendar. The irony is that the very forces which destroyed Canudos were in their own way equally susceptible to the pull of the century's end. The 'urban elite' of Brazil, like that of many countries, nourished the secret hope that the twentieth century would witness the transformation of their country into the greatest nation state in the world, one in which science and democracy would eradicate all social ills. The War of Canudos was therefore more than the confrontation of past and future: it was a battle between millennial visions. That is why the struggle was fought with what, to the outsider, seemed such incomprehensible bitterness. The very course of history was at stake. And in this respect the smoking ruin of Canudos provided a more revealing glimpse of the coming century than the utopian fantasies of social reformers, dreams of a new Pentecost or the nervous thrill-seeking of the *fin de siècle*.

6

The Apocalyptic Century

In the year 1900 the British writer J. A. Cramb put into words something which millions of Britons felt instinctively: that the British Empire represented the pinnacle of human achievement and (though the phrase had yet to be invented) the End of History. In a series of lectures, Cramb explained that Britain was the fourth of four great world empires, each of which represented an ideal. Egypt possessed mystery; Greece destiny; Rome power. But Britain's quality transcended all these: it was a synthesis of metaphyical speculation and practical skills arising from the Reformation – a world-beating combination.[1] In other words, it was a Last World Empire; or, as tens of millions of people knew it, 'the Empire on which the Sun never sets'. With hindsight, of course, there is a certain pathos in this: though Cramb did not know it, the rapid decline of Britain's imperial power was beginning even as he spoke. As in ancient Rome, pride went before a fall. Within months of Cramb's lectures, the Queen–Empress Victoria was dead, and things were never the same after that. The twentieth century marched to the beat of an entirely different drum.

Or did it? In portraying Britain as the Last World Empire, Cramb was, of course, invoking an ancient archetype; we have charted its progress through the ancient world, and its transformation into an apocalyptic ideal which captured the imaginations of Jewish zealots, early Christian martyrs, medieval millenarians and the Pilgrim Fathers. We should not forget that, in addition to an End-time vision, this structure invariably implies a certain rhythm to history. Usually four- or five-fold, its origins may lie in a neolithic division of time based on the seasons. At any rate, it is extremely persistent and adaptable. Few societies can resist it, and its appeal has not been in the least diminished by the marginalisation of belief in the literal truth of Daniel and Revelation. As Nicholas Campion has demonstrated, the optimists of the Enlightenment and the nineteenth century frequently resorted to four-fold schemes of history. The Abbé de St Pierre cheerfully reversed Hesiod, describing successive ages of iron, bronze, silver and gold. Adam Smith proposed four ages of hunters, shepherds, agriculture and commerce. Hegel, the greatest German philosopher of the early nineteenth century, outlined a pattern of four cultural epochs in which something called the 'World Spirit' drifted from east to west, creating in succession the Oriental, Greek, Roman and German empires, each offering a greater degree of freedom than the last. Meanwhile, the French diplomat and philosopher Count Joseph de Gobineau (1816-82), who is sometimes regarded as the forerunner of Nietzsche, took the four empires of Chaldea, Persia, Greece and Rome and crowned them with the Teutons, who would constitute the fifth and final earthly empire.[2]

Theories of the four- or five-fold rhythm of history seemed to die out in the twentieth century; this is partly because they had been conceived in a spirit of intellectual optimism which had begun to fade before the First World War. Significantly, the only major twentieth-century theory of civilisation which sets out a structure of history divided into four parts is profoundly pessimistic: Oswald Spengler's *Decline of the West*, published in 1922, argues that Europe has reached the winter of its Great Year, in which the birth rate declines, art is replaced by superstition and civilisation collapses.[3] But, although most intellectuals were no longer preoccupied with the old rhythm, the four-fold theories which held sway in the nineteenth century did not lose their force; they merely twisted themselves into new shapes.

From Gobineau, who believed that decline was caused by the mixing of cultures, it is only a short step to the world-view of the Nazis. And Hegel, it is generally agreed, was the greatest single influence on Karl Marx's theory of history. At any rate, both National Socialism and Marxism saw history as the predetermined succession of one civilisation after another. In the former, the division is essentially tripartite, between First, Second and Third Reichs; in the latter, the existence of many contradictory theories makes it difficult to point to a single model, but the consensus is that Marxist history divides into four societies framed at either end by communism. More important than their understanding of the past, however, is the fact that both National Socialism and Marxism were apocalyptic. Their understanding of the present was in some respects that of the first millenarian believers we know about in any detail, the Jewish rebels for whom the Book of Daniel was written. They believed they had arrived at the crucial moment in human history. A new heaven and a new earth was within the grasp of the Elect – so long as they did not yield to the forces of the enemy.

It is a grotesque irony that Nazism should have unconsciously adopted a structure of belief partly developed, though not necessarily invented, by Jews. The Book of Daniel promises a radiant new world if only the chosen people can vanquish their enemies. This world will not be in heaven: it will be an everlasting worldly empire ruled by the just, in which everything that once belonged to the pagans will have passed to the Jewish people. But in terms of bloodshed or sheer malignant hatred of the enemy Daniel and the earliest apocalypses do not begin to rival the Nazis' apocalyptic struggle; for that we must go to the Book of Revelation. There can be little doubt that the thousand-year reign of the saints lies behind the vision of a thousand-year Reich; but a far more important influence on the Nazis was Revelation's portrayal of the Antichrist – an enemy so resilient that he can be defeated only in a cosmic war.

Antichrist is, in fact, pure evil; but he exists in human form, and it is the gift of God's chosen to see behind the mask. Adolf Hitler believed that he had this gift: 'Wherever I went, I began to see Jews,' he wrote, 'and the more I saw, the more deeply they became distinguished in my eyes from the rest of humanity.'[4]

The sheer depth of the Nazis' hatred of the Jews is the best clue we have to the essentially religious nature of their beliefs. It is a cliché to say that they dehumanised the Jews, but that is precisely what they did. The Jews, for Hitler and his most fanatical followers, were a *supernatural* force for evil; and it was this conviction that made the Holocaust possible. National Socialism is usually presented as a monstrously evil but essentially secular creed; at the same time, its appeal is regarded by many commentators as quite incomprehensible. In practice, these attitudes reinforce each other: it is because we insist on portraying Nazism as a secular ideology that we find it so difficult to understand. Yet the millenarian roots of Nazism were exposed forty years ago by Norman Cohn in *The Pursuit of the Millennium*, which placed it in the context of centuries of anti-Semitic violence by millenarian believers inflamed by the vision of Revelation and legends of a new German saviour. Indeed, it was the experience of interviewing SS men as an intelligence officer at the end of the war that led Cohn to write his great study of medieval apocalyptic violence. As he put it in a recent interview, he found himself confronted by a mind-set 'in which one can actually feel it is a *good thing* to shove small children into ovens or to send millions of people to starve and freeze to death'.[5]

This last statement is an obvious reference to Stalin, whose mass slaughter of his own countrymen Cohn believes was also inspired by a form of millenarianism. This was a controversial argument to put forward in the 1950s, when there were still many admirers of the Soviet Union in British universities. Nowadays, of course, the notion of moral equivalence between Hitler and Stalin is widely, if grudgingly, accepted. Even so, there is a marked reluctance to accept any argument which detracts from what is seen as the unique wickedness of National

Socialism. Cohn's point of view is still contentious in some circles, because it suggests that Nazism and Soviet Communism demonised their respective opponents in much the same way, and massacred them for the same underlying reason: they stood in the way of the millennium. And it raises awkward questions about the theoretical framework of Stalin's beliefs, Marxism. If Stalin was an apocalyptic believer, does that make Marxism, like Nazism, an apocalyptic system with its roots in religion rather than science?

In the last decade the voices of those commentators who believe that the answer to this question is an unequivocal yes have become far stronger. The simultaneous discrediting of Marxism as a political system and as social science has greatly strengthened their claim that it was built on a foundation of quasi-religious belief, and ancient belief at that. Both Karl Popper and Mircea Eliade took this view, incidentally, but in the postwar years they were voices crying in the wilderness. Most recently, the argument has been put forward with devastating force by the British historian Nicholas Campion in his book *The Great Year* (1994). His provocative thesis should be required reading in senior common rooms everywhere.

Campion does not shrink from mentioning the Book of Daniel and Marx in the same breath. Daniel envisaged four empires, he says, and Marx four class societies; both saw periodic disorder as part of the seasonal process of the Great Year. 'As soon as we consider the possibility that modern conceptual thought is not a reaction against religion but is derived from it, we must consider the possibility that modern modes of conceptual thought possess religious power,' says Campion.[6] He goes on to suggest that revolutionary Marxism was a modification of Christian millenarianism that stepped into the vacuum left by the latter's decline. But to what degree was it modified? To ram home his point, Campion draws up two parallel lists: one sets out the stages of the Jewish/Christian Great Year, while the other lists the Marxist concepts which correspond to them. And the extent to which they match is indeed extraordinary. The Garden of Eden corresponds to primitive communism; the Fall is the development of private property and the class system; the Last Days are the final stages of unfettered capitalism and imperialism; the Chosen People are the proletariat; the Second Coming (or, in Jewish terms, the Last Battle) is the socialist revolution. Finally, both Christian apocalypticism and Marxism propose a two-stage consummation of history. Revelation's millennium, the earthly kingdom of Christ and his saints, is followed by the new heaven and new earth after the final defeat of Antichrist. In Marxism, meanwhile, the socialist dictatorship of the proletariat merges into true communism as the state withers away and the class war comes to an end. (Absurdly, the Soviet Union under Khrushchev announced at one point that this withering away of the state had been accomplished.) Marxism, in other words, was not even a particularly original apocalyptic system; yet it was potentially much more destructive than other systems because Marx had revived a form of the demonic battle in which it was not individuals who were the enemy, but an entire group of people. Hitler did the same, of course; but, whereas the Nazis selected a traditional enemy for their principal demon, Marx's innovation was to demonise an entire socio-economic class, the bourgeoisie, who had to be destroyed in order for history to progress. 'That is what his followers meant by scientific history,' concludes Campion dryly.[7]

The historical perspective offered by Cohn and Campion is important because it reminds us that, although this has been the century in which active Christians ceased to make up the majority of the West's population, none since the sixteenth has been so affected by apocalypticism. The tens of millions of Jews and Russians who died in its fourth and fifth decades were as much victims of millenarianism as the Jews and merchants cut down during the middle ages; their deaths serve as a reminder that the distinction between secular and religious schemes of history is a fine one, and often meaningless. And this is true not just of totalitarianism, but of modern secular ideologies in general. The familiar rhythm of Daniel can be detected – just – underneath most theories of the rise and fall of civilisations and most political philosophies. At different times both liberal social democracy and free-market capitalism have assumed, with Cramb-like confidence, that they represent the Last World Empire; like Cotton Mather in New England, they have discovered 'a scripture-pattern that shall in due time be accomplished the whole world throughout'.

These competing visions have one thing in common: an optimistic view of the future in which the great convulsions of history – wars, revolutions, man-made disasters – are no longer part of the human experience; this is either because the Last Battle against a racial or class enemy has been won, or, as the postwar West has fervently hoped, because education, economics and technology have triumphed. These are all apocalyptic scenarios, even if they are not recognised as such; and, as with so many visions of future glory, there is something painfully fragile about them. The prospect of an entirely opposite scenario, in which the world slides into chaos, is lurking just around the corner. Many political thinkers of the second half of the twentieth century have found themselves torn between an intellectual belief in accelerating progress and fear that human folly will reduce civilisation to ashes. Unlike, say, the fundamentalist Christians, they have not constructed a scenario in which both glory and disaster can exist side by side; so they have tended to lurch from one to the other. And, in a world whose peace and prosperity have seemed at times to depend on the threat of nuclear holocaust, who can blame them?

The invention of the atom bomb at the end of the Second World War had a galvanising effect on End-time belief. It transformed the concept of worldwide destruction from a traditional End-time image accessible only to believers into a frightening possibility accessible to everyone. It gave birth to a new apocalypticism which was fuelled by an apparently rational fear of total catastrophe; and this offered a grim counterpoint to the optimistic themes of liberals and social democrats whose scripture-pattern was parliamentary democracy and who believed, or tried to believe, in the inevitability of victory in the war against poverty and disease. In the end, the threat of man-made global catastrophe developed a life of its own; it could no more be disinvented than the nuclear bomb. When the prospect of nuclear war faded in the late 1980s, the vacuum was immediately filled by a fears of a disaster which, though more subtle and insidious, was of a similar order of magnitude. The agents of destruction this time were pollution, global warming and the hole in the ozone layer. As with nuclear weapons, the danger may have been real enough; but there were also signs that an ancient dynamic had re-established itself. The Green lobby invariably talked as if the process of decline was accelerating; it divided the world neatly into heroes and villains and effectively presented its audience with the alternatives of the destruction of mankind by an angry planet or the establishment of a post-industrial utopia.

Interestingly, the rhetoric of both the anti-nuclear and Green lobbies was lent extra force by a certain biblical resonance. At times, it was difficult to distinguish the new apocalyptic images from the old; and the confusion was compounded by the fact that traditional Christian apocalypticism was also milking the nuclear threat – and, later, the environmental one – for all it was worth. Hiroshima and Nagasaki fired the imaginations of millions of American fundamentalist Christians as no historical event had for decades; it put flesh on the bones of biblical End-time prophecies of fire from heaven and caused many conservative evangelicals to question the premillennialist prohibition on looking for the fulfilment of scripture in current affairs. The foundation of the State of Israel in 1948 confirmed their suspicions that God's prophetic clock, which had been stopped for almost 2,000 years, was beginning to tick again. It was from this moment that fundamentalists in America began their slow progress from the sidelines of society towards the political and cultural mainstream, a progress which, as we shall see, derived much of its energy from the revival of End-time belief.

Fundamentalists and liberals; Nazis and Communists; Greens and free marketeers: all of these twentieth-century labels carry with them a set of distinctive and usually mutually exclusive beliefs regarding time and the shape of history. Perhaps it is not surprising that this century, above all others, should be one in which people choose to label themselves; for if the adoption of all-embracing beliefs with an apocalyptic sub-text is a response to change and stress, then the twentieth century was bound to be more productive in this regard than any other. The variety of these beliefs, both secular and religious, would have been unthinkable in any previous era; yet they have much in common and many of them have found themselves operating in the same environment. As a result, they have been forced to do battle with each other, borrow from each other and combine in unexpected patterns. And now, as the century draws to an end, they find themselves confronted by a single event over which, in a sense, they have no control, but to which they can react in any way they please. That event is the 2,000th anniversary of the Anno Domini calendar; and, if we want proof of the common apocalyptic heritage of these belief systems, we need only observe the way in which they are all being drawn into the mysterious force-field which already surrounds it.

PART TWO

The New Millennium

7

Thy Kingdom Come

For hundreds of thousands of born-again Christians around the world, 1994 was the year of the Toronto Blessing, a sudden outpouring of the Spirit which caused worshippers to fall over, laugh uncontrollably and even, on occasion, to grunt and bray like farmyard animals. The Blessing was so called because it developed in a church near Toronto airport run by the Vineyard, an international charismatic fellowship which teaches that at the end of the twentieth century the powers of the Holy Spirit (and of Satan) are being manifested as never before. In January 1994, the Airport Vineyard church staged a series of revival services at which large sections of the congregation began to fall over and laugh hysterically. Such behaviour is by no means unknown in the charismatic world, and during 1993 there had been isolated outbreaks of it in a number of churches affiliated to the Vineyard. But the scale and persistence of the Toronto experience was something new.

Night after night, ministers who called down God's blessing found themselves surveying a field of prostrate bodies. News of the phenomenon quickly spread to charismatic evangelical churches in England, where the Vineyard is held in high esteem. English Baptist, Anglican and independent evangelical leaders arrived in Toronto to experience the Blessing, and discovered when they returned home that they could somehow pass it on to their own congregations. By the late summer of 1994, charismatic churches throughout the English-speaking world were in the grip of what they called 'Holy Spirit fever'. They agreed that it was the most exciting thing to happen to them for decades.

The British press, unsurprisingly, found the subject irresistible. Every major newspaper despatched correspondents to churches which were experiencing the Blessing. Andrew Brown of the *Independent*, who visited a fashionable Anglican church in South Kensington, encountered the Blessing at its most flamboyant. 'When the Holy Spirit hit St Paul's Onslow Square, sw7, on Sunday morning, I felt it through the floor,' he reported.

> There were four heavy thuds as congregants fainted and then rapid drummings – like the noise that rabbits make to warn one another – when people began to shake uncontrollably and beat their feet against the floor. Towards the front a woman with short black hair was bouncing like a road mender's drill for about twenty minutes . . . From somewhere came tremendous pantings and gaspings that were not quite sexual. The laughter was really strange. From three or four places in the church you could hear this gut-busting abandoned giggle. It was not an adult sound at all. It was more like the laughter you get by tickling a happy toddler; but it was coming from respectable women in their thirties.[1]

In other places the Blessing seemed to operate at a lower pitch: worshippers would form well-mannered queues, smiling apprehensively as the minister raised his hand over them. Then some of them would fall, or be helped, to the ground. In one church, Ruth Gledhill of *The Times* described those not affected as 'chatting calmly over coffee as if nothing was happening, while bodies were splayed at their feet, bearing beatific smiles and looks of tremendous peace'.[2]

'What in God's name is going on?' asked the *Daily Mail*. The answer, according to some evangelicals, was that the winds of revival were at long last blowing through the decadent nations of the West. 'We could be on the brink of the greatest revival in the history of the Church, the revival that precedes the return of Christ,' suggested one leading Baptist. More detached observers, meanwhile, offered explanations rooted in psychological theory. The psychologist Dr Dorothy Rowe claimed that the Toronto symptoms were due to nothing more than the physical release of adrenalin within a socially contagious atmosphere. Dr Patrick Dixon, a well-known evangelical physician and author, did not rule out a psychological origin. 'My own view is that we are not witnessing brainwashing on a grand scale . . . nor mass hysteria,' he said. 'We are, however, witnessing what happens when a large number of people experience an altered state of consciousness at the same time, as part of a profound spiritual experience.'[3] This altered state might be explained by hyperventilation, euphoria, anxiety or suggestion; but what Dr Dixon could not fully explain was his own reaction to a Toronto service, which left him wheezing with joyful laughter until it hurt.

Many responses to the Blessing pointed out that there were strong historical precedents for hysterical behaviour during times of spiritual excitment. Accounts of revival gatherings by eighteenth-century evangelists were cited as evidence that, as one commentator put it, 'we have been here before'. In 1739, for example, John Wesley attended a prayer meeting in Wapping at which 'some were torn with a kind of convulsive motion in every part of their bodies'. His contemporary Daniel Rowland described unforgettable scenes during a Welsh revival meeting: 'While one is praying, another is laughing; some howl and beat their hands together; others are weeping and groaning; and others are grovelling on the ground in a swoon, making various kinds of antic postures; then they laugh out all at once, and continue laughing for about a quarter of an hour.' Rowland also observed that some believers were 'drunk, and that with the best wine, namely the Holy Spirit'.[4] Apparent drunkenness was also one of the most persistent symptoms of the Toronto Blessing: a number of strait-laced evangelical leaders confessed that after a particularly euphoric prayer session they had to be carried giggling to their cars and driven home by their wives.

Perhaps the most interesting gloss on the Toronto experience was provided by Dr Andrew Walker of King's College, London, the foremost academic authority on the charismatic movement in Britain. He suggested that the Blessing should be seen in the context of evangelical expectations of the year 2000: it was a classic manifestation of 'Pre-Millennial Tension'. Walker's suggestion struck a chord with many observers, both outside and inside the evangelical world. Despite the deliberate humour of the term PMT, the notion of an evangelical community literally suffering from tension made sense. As one leading evangelical put it: 'You only have to attend a meeting of our leaders to see how wound up and exhausted they are.' Furthermore, that tension was certainly linked to expectations of the year 2000, which has become the focus for the most ambitious international and domestic missionary endeavours in the history of Protestantism.

But what precisely are evangelicals expecting to happen when the new millennium dawns? If the press had followed up this point they would have discovered that the Toronto Blessing, although undeniably fascinating, was only one aspect of a far bigger story; one with ramifications extending far beyond the network of suburban churches where middle-class worshippers were hitting the carpet to the accompaniment of Spirit-filled laughter.

For some evangelicals, the year 2000 is a mere date: a focus for activity, perhaps, but absolutely nothing more. For others, albeit a tiny percentage of the total, it is the year in which Christ may return. Between these two extremes lie dozens of different approaches in which ostensibly secular excitement and fears for the new millennium mingle with the symptoms of eschatological fever. Indeed, it is unlikely that any community in the world will be affected more profoundly by the anniversary than born-again Christians. It may even be true to say that the greatest single consequence of the calendar change will be the fresh impetus it will give – and is already giving – to the bewilderingly fast expansion of evangelical faith all over the globe.

The percentage growth of evangelical Christianity probably outstrips that of any religion in the world today, including fundamentalist Islam. We are witnessing the fastest expansion of Christianity in history, far greater than the missionary waves of the past. But, before its impact can be measured, we need to confront certain technical problems. In the first place, there are no reliable independent figures for the numbers of evangelicals. All the statistics are produced by interested parties, and for that reason should be taken with a pinch of salt. Secondly, no one finds it easy to distinguish between different categories of evangelicals. Labels such as born-again Christian, fundamentalist, charismatic evangelical and Pentecostalist all have distinct meanings, yet the categories overlap to an infuriating degree.

So, for example, one often hears about the phenomenal growth of 'charismatic' Christianity throughout the world: a frequently quoted statistic is that of the born-again Church growth expert Peter Wagner, who estimates that the number of charismatic Christians has risen from 90 million to 400 million since 1981. But what is meant by 'charismatic'? In fact, this figure does not relate primarily to the growth of a style of worship. Charismatics, it is true, are so called because they believe that *charismata* – the gifts of the Holy Spirit bestowed on the disciples at Pentecost, such as speaking in tongues – are accessible to modern man. This belief is also held by a minority of Roman Catholics; but they are *not* part of this spectacular growth, which has occurred almost exclusively among the ranks of Protestants, and conservative ones at that. The 400 million are nearly all charismatic evangelicals, some of whom call themselves Pentecostalists. They have far more in common with old-style American fundamentalists (who reject speaking in tongues) than they do with pentecostal Catholics and liberals. Indeed, some sociologists use the term 'neo-fundamentalist' to describe the charismatics whose ecstatic babbling and outstretched arms have been depicted so often in the media recently, and who have been the mainstay of the Toronto Blessing. (To complicate matters further, most evangelicals vigorously reject the fundamentalist label, even if their approach to the bible is painfully literal-minded and they agree with traditional 'fundies' on every point of doctrine except the validity of charismatic gifts. One American psychologist has suggested that this is often a question of class: middle-class evangelicals from the cities do not wish to be associated with Southern rednecks.)[5]

The easiest way through this minefield is to think in terms of 'conservative evangelicals'. This label fits every variety of mainstream Christianity which is growing either in numbers or in influence. References in the media to the fundamentalist/charismatic/evangelical 'explosion' all basically refer to the spread of conservative evangelicalism: that is, a Protestantism in which the bible is both the supreme authority in doctrinal matters and the source of belief in traditional morality. Within this conservative evangelical world, significantly, old barriers are breaking down. Charismatics or Pentecostalists are unquestionably the most dynamic and successful sub-group, but they are a much broader church than they once were. The original charismatic Churches, the working-class Pentecostalist denominations founded early this century (which are mostly responsible for the extraordinary growth of Protestantism in Latin America and the Far East), now work closely with middle-class evangelicals who developed their charismatic style in their independent 'house churches' in the 1960s; and both these groups have forged close links with a new force known as the Third Wave, founded by mainstream fundamentalists who have accepted *charismata* as part of a theology of Spiritual Warfare. But the distinction between charismatics and non-charismatics is also less divisive than it was a few years ago. On both sides of the fence, questions such as the validity of *glossolalia* (speaking in tongues) matter far less than the experience of being born again, common to all evangelicals, and a conservative interpretation of scripture which rules out liberal standpoints on homosexuality and abortion.

The centrality of scripture in the lives of these Christians, who, whatever their cultural background, carry zip-up bibles with them everywhere, has another important consequence.

They are all, to a greater or lesser degree, End-time believers. No one who takes a literal view of the Gospels, St Paul's Epistles or the Book of Revelation can be anything else. The point cannot be made too often that the approaching end of history casts a shadow over the New Testament which the established Churches, naturally fearful of apocalyptic panic, have often professed not to notice. Most conservative evangelicals, in contrast, have always believed that Jesus may conceivably return in their lifetimes, though after the Millerite fiasco very few have indulged in date-setting. As we have seen, this sense of living at the End of Time has become far stronger in the second half of the twentieth century, thanks to the foundation of the State of Israel and the development of nuclear weapons. With the approach of a new millennium, it is stronger than ever, though it takes many different forms and is by no means restricted to a simple belief that the Second Coming is about to take place.

That said, one of the first indications of the effect of the coming anniversary was an outbreak of old-fashioned date-setting. In the 1980s, isolated prophets, mostly elderly American fundamentalists, began to make bold predictions in self-published books and in radio broadcasts of the Rapture of the Church and Christ's return. The prophecy which attracted most attention was that of Edgar Whisenant, a former NASA engineer, in a booklet entitled *88 Reasons Why the Rapture Will Be in 1988*. Whisenant produced dozens of convoluted 'proofs' based on readings of Daniel and Revelation to support his dating. Like so many American fundamentalist prophets who are supposed to regard all occult knowledge as the devil's work, he did not hesitate to invoke astrology, pyramidology and numerology in support of his views. And, in true Millerite style, when his 3 October deadline failed to produce the goods, he claimed his calculations were 'one year off', and that Christ would return in 1989.

In fact, Whisenant was not the only fundamentalist to settle on a 1988 apocalypse. The year had been regarded as special by prophecy students ever since the publication of Hal Lindsey's *Late Great Planet Earth* in 1973. This book, the best-selling work of non-fiction in America during the 1970s, had argued that there would be one generation between the beginning of the End-time drama and Christ's return in glory. God's 'prophetic clock', which had stood still during the Gospel Age, had been touched off by the return of the Jews to the Holy Land in 1948; and, since a biblical generation was forty years, there was a strong possibility that history would come to an end in the late 1980s. Lindsey, a shrewd operator, was not foolish enough to specify a date, but a number of lesser figures decided to take the risk. Hart Armstrong, president of Christian Communications, of Wichita, Kansas, pinpointed the Feast of Trumpets on 29 and 30 September 1988 as 'possible times for his coming' and issued a RAPTURE ALERT in his publications. The Trinity Broadcasting Network, which was expecting a Rapture on 11 to 13 September, cancelled its regular television talk show on those nights and ran videotapes instructing non-believers on what to do if their families suddenly shot into the heavens. Charles Taylor, one of America's most prominent prophecy teachers, organised a tour of Israel to coincide with Whisenant's date, priced $1,850 including 'return if necessary'. His publicity material used the possibility of Rapture from the Holy Land as a sales pitch: 'We stay at the Intercontinental Hotel right on the Mount of Olives where you can get the beautiful view of the Eastern Gate and the Temple Mount. And if this is the year of our Lord's return, as we anticipate, you may even ascend to Glory from within a few feet of His ascension.'[6]

Although each of these predictions of the End offered several parallel 'proofs' pointing to their chosen date, one theory is common to the vast majority of Christian date-setters. This is the theory of the Great Week, which originated in ancient Mesopotamia and continues to exert a hold over modern fundamentalists in precisely the form which the early Church authorities were so keen to suppress: a 6,000-year span of human history leading into the Millennium. Indeed, belief in this theory is one of the marks of true fundamentalists, who have inherited it from their Puritan forebears. Old-style 'fundies' have a great reverence for seventeenth-century English Protantism: for them, the King James bible is the only inspired translation, and many of them also take on board the date for the Creation proposed by Archbishop Ussher of Armagh in 1654, which was inserted into later editions of the Authorised Version as a marginal reference. Ussher's timing for the beginning of Creation, worked out by adding up genealogical lists from the bible, was nine o'clock on the morning of 26 October 4004 BC. Until the nineteenth century, this was accepted without question by most English-speaking Protestants, and it is still taken seriously in fundamentalist circles. Admittedly, many date-setters have minor quibbles with Ussher's figure, subtracting or adding a few years; but the margin of error is usually sufficiently small to ensure that if 6,000 years are added to the Creation date, the start of Christ's thousand-year rule still falls at the end of the twentieth century or the beginning of the twenty-first.

This line of reasoning is far more influential than one might imagine. Although conservative evangelical leaders are at pains to distance themselves from such embarrassing figures as Whisenant and Taylor, they are careful not to attack the theory of the 6,000-year Great Week. To do so would alienate hard-line fundamentalists in the Bible Belt, where every year countless sermons are still preached on the division of history into three periods of 2,000 years each: from Adam to Abraham, from Abraham to Christ, and from Christ to the dawn of the Millennium. But, unlike Whisenant and Taylor, most of these preachers are not prepared to defy the biblical injunction against date-setting. They emphasise that these figures are no more than approximate guidelines, and they will not be drawn into making specific predictions of the Time of the End. Dr James McKeever, editor of the *End Times News Digest*, reckons that the 6,000 years could end 'some time between now and the year 2030'; he thus raises the possibility that the crucial anniversary will be that of Christ's death and resurrection, an idea which flourished in the early eleventh century.

Dr McKeever's assumption that Christ will return within the lifetimes of the current generation is shared by a great many conservative evangelicals, especially those from a traditional American fundamentalist or Pentecostalist background.

Although not all of them think in terms of a 6,000-year timetable, they tend to believe that the completion of 2,000 years of 'the Gospel Age' within a generation of the founding of the State of Israel indicates that the End-time itself is nearing its conclusion. Hal Lindsey, as we have seen, believes this, though he is a rather discredited figure following the non-fulfilment of his prophecies linking the Cold War to Armageddon. More significantly, it is the view of many leaders of the charismatic explosion in Latin America and the Far East.

How many born-again Christians believe the world will end in their lifetime? The sheer difficulty of answering this question tells us much about the fluidity of a world in which the boundaries of fundamentalism merge imperceptibly into the larger evangelical population. The leaders of bodies such as the Evangelical Alliance in Britain tend to soft-pedal the whole question of End-time theology; one gets the strong impression that, in Britain at least, the energetic administrators of the movement are far less susceptible to millennial euphoria than many ordinary believers. But a useful corrective to their measured statements is provided by a visit to almost any conservative evangelical bookshop, whose prophecy sections are invariably stuffed with books speculating on the time of the End.

A good example is the bookshop of Kensington Temple, a spectacularly successful Pentecostal church in West London with strong links to the charismatic Anglican network. Here one can buy tracts identifying the European Community as the ten nations of the Antichrist; videotapes warning against computer technology designed to imprint the Mark of the Beast under the skins of unsuspecting citizens; and a whole shelf of books predicting the return of Christ in the vicinity of the beginning of the third Christian millennium. One of the best known of them, *Armageddon – Appointment with Destiny*, by the Canadian evangelist Grant Jeffrey, argues the case for the year 2000 itself. Jeffrey, an established fundamentalist author whose book carries an endorsement from the President of the National Religious Broadcasters of America, is a great believer in millennial symmetry. He goes to considerable lengths to defend the long-discredited dating of Christ's birth to 1 BC by Dionysius Exiguous. He then slots this into a Great Week beginning in 4000 BC, citing authorities from the early Church and the Reformation in support of a 6,000-year time-frame. They include the Oxford martyr Bishop Hugh Latimer, who wrote in 1552: 'The world was ordained to endure, as all learned men affirm, 6000 years. Now of that number there be passed 5,552 years, so that there is no more left but 448.'[7]

The mere presence of a wide range of End-time books in evangelical bookshops does not, of course, mean that most born-again Christians are firmly committed to one of the many millennial deadlines on offer. But it is an indication of what one might call the free market in apocalyptic theology which operates in the conservative evangelical world. The structured hierarchy of the Churches, and the intensely disciplined lives of their members, can be misleading in this respect. Individual beliefs about the End-time are more varied and idiosyncratic than many pastors realise. This, at any rate, was one of the findings of an extraordinary piece of research by the American psychoanalyst Charles Strozier, who spent five years in the late 1980s and early 1990s interviewing members of evangelical churches in New York City. The institutions Strozier studied were made up of a socially upmarket bible-study group; a declining multicultural Pentecostal church; a dynamic black charismatic church; and a strict fundamentalist Baptist church. This more or less corresponds to the whole conservative evangelical spectrum, both in the United States and in Britain; but Strozier regarded all his congregations as 'fundamentalist', whether or not they were happy to describe themselves as such. As he explained:

> The strict 'fundamentalists' may be the chief carriers of the idea of inerrancy, but it [inerrancy] is a term frequently used in Pentecostal churches, in Bible studies, and by individuals when talking about scripture. It is in the discourse, one might say. Furthermore, what defines the movement psychologically is its unique Christian commitment to the apocalyptic. The ideologues place the greatest emphasis on premillennial dispensationalism, but I found that virtually all my respondents carried

large, if somewhat undigested, parts of the theory with them. Images of the rapture, tribulation, Antichrist, the beast, and Armageddon are quite universal, if by no means always the same, in the minds of fundamentalists.[8]

Strozier discovered that the way in which individual fundamentalists contemplated the future was as much bound up with social class as with theological background. Working-class believers, irrespective of race or gender, tended to believe that history would come to an end during their lifetimes. Some connected this to the approaching end of the millennium: 'I'd be surprised if we reached the year 2000 before he comes back,' was one response. In contrast, the middle-class professionals at the conservative evangelical bible-study centre saw it as 'vulgar, even blasphemous, to even think about a human dating of God's purpose'. They tended to delay the End until after their own deaths; yet they lived 'with a clear sense of the outer limits of the time left for human history. They were loosely but absolutely apocalyptic. They talked about history not lasting past the time of their children or their children's children . . . Two generations, it seemed, was as far as any fundamentalist could see human history lasting.'[9]

Significantly, both groups of believers – those who expected to die a natural death, and those who expected to be raptured before Armageddon – tended to use their own life expectations as an unconscious yardstick. The middle-class bible students envisaged the future as extending for a certain number of years after their own deaths. Working-class fundamentalists, meanwhile, often expected Christ to return at roughly the time when they could expect to die. A thirty-three-year-old black fundamentalist thought mankind would survive for thirty to forty years at the most, while belief in the year 2000 as a deadline was concentrated among older believers. This would explain, incidentally, why so many self-published apocalyptic date-setters are elderly men. There has, though, been more recent research than Strozier's, in the shape of a confidential survey of fundamentalist women in America; this suggests that many believers in their twenties and thirties live in expectation of an End-time drama about five years in the future. So the picture is not entirely clear. What is certain, however, is that evangelical apocalyptic belief is rooted firmly in personal experience: it is formed as much by hopes and aspirations as by premillennial theory – and it is also coloured by the past lives of individual believers, which have often been notably troubled. The notion of a Rapture, in which true Christians are swept up to heaven while billions of 'nominal' Christians and unbelievers remain below to face the agony of the tribulation, is profoundly comforting to people for whom life has been a continual struggle against hardship and temptation. This sense of the wreckage of the past being cleared away by divine intervention also applies to other varieties of apocalyptic belief, including those of the New Age; but it is particularly strong in the conservative evangelical world. Even those born-again Christians who do not believe that they will be raptured in the next few years nevertheless take refuge in a conviction that God's End-time plan is slowly being worked out: for them, a period of intense Spiritual Warfare in the materialist West or unprecedented missionary advances in the Third World may constitute signs of the approaching End; and the fact that they coincide with the bimillennial anniversary of the Saviour's birth is, at the very least, food for thought.

One should not underestimate the intellectual sophistication of the better-educated born-again Christians, particularly in Europe. They are apocalyptic in the original Greek sense of the word: they are filled with excitement at the thought that the hidden is being revealed, a process which cannot be hastened or elucidated by the construction of crude time-frames. But their apocalypticism also bears a strong resemblance to that of the Jews of the first and second centuries BC, who did so much to develop the genre. It is unambiguously tribal in character. It offers collective salvation – though not necessarily an imminent Rapture – to only one group of people: true Christian believers. The rigid distinction between the saved and the unsaved is untouched by complex arguments over whether the world will slide into anarchy or yield to Christian dominion as the End draws near. Yet, unlike the Jews, the tribe is infinitely expandable. Indeed, the saved are under an obligation to win as many souls for Christ as is humanly possible. And what better way of concentrating the mind on this great task than to focus on the fast-approaching horizon of the year 2000?

'And this gospel of the kingdom will be preached throughout the whole world, as a testimony to the nations; *and then the end will come.*' This line from Chapter 24, verse 14 of St Matthew's Gospel, which comes just before a spine-chilling description of the final tribulation, is never far from the lips of conservative evangelical Christians. It places the spread of the gospel squarely within the context of the End. It suggests that by preaching the faith to all nations – as opposed to converting all nations – the born-again Christian is actually *bringing on* the End-time with its terrifying tribulations. And why not? The saved have nothing to fear from these events. Most conservative evangelicals believe that they will rise to meet Christ in the skies just as the tribulation begins. Indeed, it is the ultimate incentive to preach the gospel to the whole world, a task which is known to them as the Great Commission. Born-again believers have been struggling to complete this since the late nineteenth century, when, as we have seen, the year 1900 served as a deadline for their missionary activities. Now, once again, the Great Commission has become linked with the end of a century, although most evangelical leaders are careful not to state that the task will be fulfilled by 2000; for that amounts to saying that they are setting a date for the End of the World. Instead, this tantalising possibility is often left hanging in the air, never acknowledged but sometimes not quite ruled out.

There is no single evangelical push geared to the year 2000. There are dozens of them, involving a host of denominations, only some of which recognise each other's efforts as contributions towards the Great Commission. (It goes without saying that evangelicals are hostile to the dynamic initiatives by groups such as Jehovah's Witnesses, Seventh Day Adventists or Mormons, while those by Catholics and liberal Protestants are regarded as irrelevant to the Great Commission.) Within the conservative evangelical world, the most important initiative is called AD2000, which co-ordinates but does not actually control the missionary endeavours of fundamentalists and charismatics in over one hundred countries. AD2000 has the backing of the big guns of the Pentecostalist movement, which has been responsible for most of the spread of born-again Christianity in the last few decades. But it also enjoys the support of the other strands of charismatic Christianity: the West's independent charismatic Churches and the Third Wave of fundamentalists who have armed themselves with charismatic gifts in readiness for a new period of Spiritual Warfare.

AD2000's official statement of aims is a masterpiece of ambiguity: 'A Church for Every People and the Gospel for Every Person by the Year 2000'. According to Ralph Winter, founder of the US Center for World Mission and one of the grand old men of missionary evangelicalism, this goal has the advantage of being 'eminently measurable'. To the uncommitted observer, however, its most obvious feature is its unmeasurability. What is meant by 'the Gospel for Every Person'? One has to read the small print to find out that it refers primarily to establishing church-planting movements in the middle of 'unreached' ethno-linguistic groups, of which AD2000 reckons there are around 2,500 with populations over 10,000.[10] The vast majority of these can be found within what evangelicals call the '10/40 window', a rectangle running from West Africa to the Far East between 10 and 40 degrees north of the equator. So, although the initiative will increase the total number of born-again Christians in the world, this is not its primary purpose: rather, it defines itself in terms of geographical outreach to countries where Christianity is an alien religion. In other words, 'the gospel of the kingdom will be preached throughout the whole world as a testimony to the nations', a nation here being defined as an ethno-linguistic group.

This nuance is crucial: it is no coincidence that AD2000's stated aim paraphrases a line from the apocalypse of Matthew's Gospel. Yet it does not fall into the trap of equating its efforts with the completion of the Great Commission. 'This Movement does not pretend to suggest when Christ will return,' says Ralph Winter. As for the completion of the Great Commission, 'that, too, is off limits in official AD2000 documents'. But Winter does not wish to deny that there is a link, however dimly perceived, between the initiative and the return of Christ. 'Confusion abounds on this subject,' he admits. 'Some leaders have missed out on the incredible excitement of the AD2000 movement. Why? The reason they have held back is the simple fact that the Return of Christ and the End of History are to them unacceptable subjects of discussion.' But they are mistaken, says Winter. It is one thing to accept that the day of Christ's return will be a surprise to everyone. 'On the other hand, an expectant mother is not completely in the dark about the time of the birth since there are many signs leading up to it.'[11] Making the gospel available to everyone in the world 'on their own linguistic and cultural wavelength' may not be quite the same thing as fulfilling the Great Commission; but it will bring the End closer.

It is worth pausing for a moment to consider the extent to which conservative evangelicalism has already taken root in unpromising soil. Latin America is perhaps the most impressive example of this. In the late 1960s there were around 5 million Protestants in the region; today there are more than 40 million. This is an awesome level of growth, even allowing for the rise in population. In the words of the Chilean sociologist Claudio Veliz: 'Never before since the Reformation have so many Catholics converted to Protestantism in such a brief period of time.'[12] The most dramatic penetration of Protestantism has occurred in Guatemala, where 30 per cent of the population is evangelical, and where the influence of the new faith on public life is disproportionately high. Two recent heads of state have been evangelicals, prompting one leading commentator to write of Protestantism's 'spiritual hegemony' in the country. In Brazil, meanwhile, evangelicals account for around 20 per cent of the population of 150 million. In Chile, the Protestant population is well over a million and accounts for between 15 and 20 per cent of the population. The Jotabeche Cathedral in Santiago, which holds 18,000 worshippers, is among the largest churches in the world; yet even this is dwarfed by the mass rallies of 100,000 or more which are regularly held in sports arenas all over Latin America. In parts of Guatemala, Brazil and Chile, the number of active Protestants outnumbers that of practising Catholics – a fact which is the cause of intense misery and soul-searching among the Catholic hierarchy.

A clear majority of Latin America's Protestants are both charismatic and fundamentalist. The most successful denomination is the Assemblies of God, whose marriage of the techniques of American televangelism with a theology of miracles, spirits and exorcism has enabled it to create super-churches with adherents running into the tens of thousands. This is, in fact, exactly the formula which has worked so well in South Korea, where the Assemblies of God runs the world's largest church. In both Latin America and Korea, and indeed throughout much of the Third World, Pentecostalism has been able to absorb and harness traditions of shamanism common to virtually all developing societies. This is not the good-natured, self-conscious charismatic religion of Catholics and liberal Protestants. It wrestles with the ancient territorial demons which torment millions of people caught up in the disorientating process of modernisation – and with such spectacular results in terms of conversions that many conservative evangelicals in the West, as we shall see, are themselves being drawn towards a theology of evil spirits.

The one thread which runs through the experience of nearly all Latin American evangelicals is what sociologists call the 'conversionist' nature of their faith. The move from Catholicism (often of the nominal variety) to Protestantism involves a conscious rejection of the past, and, in the case of a high proportion of men, of a lifestyle that may have included heavy drinking, sexual immorality or financial dishonesty. The need for such a purgative experience, which tends to be very strong in developing societies, helps explain why the fastest-growing churches in Latin America are Pentecostalist: they offer an overwhelming once-and-for-all drama of conversion coupled with an exceptionally rigid code of morality. But the convert is not alone. This new lifestyle is designed to be experienced within a tight social network which might appear phoney and even sinister to the unbeliever but usually strikes new believers

as warm and genuine. And it is also protective. In a frighteningly unstable society such as Guatemala in the 1980s, where
death squads roamed the streets looking for 'Communists', the
studied apoliticism of the Pentecostals offered a degree of
immunity from political violence which Catholic base communities could never provide. In more peaceful times, too, the
evangelical network offers ready-made friendships to lonely
workers who have moved from the countryside to the cities.
From the point of view of the Churches, of course, the
construction of an airtight social network is highly necessary.
As David Martin argues in his book *Tongues of Fire*, 'the
achievement of radical changes in behaviour and the reversal of
the hierarchies and priorities obtaining in the outside world can
only be achieved in a protected environment'.[13] And this is
every bit as true of West London or Dallas as it is of the tropical
slums of Central America.

The intimacy and sense of being sealed off from the world
which characterise evangelical church life are ideally suited to
the experience of apocalyptic faith. The sharp distinction
between the saved and unsaved is more than a dry doctrine: it is
reinforced by social structures which minimise contact with
unbelievers – those who, if they are still alive when Jesus comes,
will not be raptured and are destined for the fires of hell. As far
as specific End-time beliefs are concerned, conservative evangelicals in Latin America are little different from their spiritual
cousins in the United States. On paper, they are mostly
premillennial dispensationalists, which means that they believe
that the terrible events of Antichrist's reign could materialise at
any moment. In practice, however, many of them are torn
between this and an optimism which verges on postmillennialism, the belief that Christians can capture the world and
exercise dominion over it before Jesus returns. This dichotomy
was also characteristic of America during the 1980s, when
'premils' such as Pat Robertson were so swept up in the success
of the Reagan administration that they seemed to adopt a
radically new eschatology. Significantly, the optimism about the
future – the *national* future – which is found among Pentecostalists in Guatemala is virtually identical to that of apocalyptic

believers in South Korea (where it is rather more grounded in reality). Guatemalan evangelicals are desperate to reproduce both the spiritual and economic miracles of South Korea, where Church and business growth seem to go hand in hand. Not for nothing is Dr David Yonggi Cho a frequent and honoured guest at Pentecostal churches in Guatemala. Dr Cho, who has built up a church of 700,000 members in Seoul, believes that Antichrist is already alive; yet he looks forward to a great future for Korea. He thus exemplifies the way optimistic and pessimistic scenarios have become entangled in the minds of fundamentalists. The reasons for this are complex, but they certainly include the approach of the year 2000. As churches race to sign up as many converts as possible before the new millennium, the prospect of a land peopled by joyous, hard-working believers – and reaping the economic rewards thereof – can easily drive out thoughts of Rapture, the Beast and Armageddon, even though, as the gospel says, once the word has been preached to the whole world the End will come.

Fortunately for those who wish to delay the fulfilment of the final prophecies, it is unlikely that AD2000 will be able to make contact with all its 'unreached' peoples before the end of the century. There is a school of thought which argues that emphasis on the 10/40 window is mistaken, given the resistance of the Islamic world to any form of Christianity: it is simply too tough a nut to crack. And there is continuing confusion over precisely what constitutes an unreached ethno-linguistic group. But disputes over strategy and the deployment of resources cannot disguise the fact that the worldwide picture has never been more encouraging. According to the evangelical Lausanne Statistical Task Force, the number of conversions to bible-believing Christianity *every day* has risen from 70,000 in 1991 to 178,000 in 1994.[14] We should treat this figure with caution, but it certainly reflects a dramatic upward trend. Judged by any criteria other than the purely geographical, AD2000 is destined to succeed: not, perhaps, by opening up vast tracts of North Africa and Central Asia to fundamentalist missionaries (which is what it aims to do) but by firing up existing churches from Santiago to Manila with eschatological fervour.

Churches in already evangelised areas have responded to the movement's call by redoubling their efforts to win over their own districts. To pick a random example, the Faith Community Baptist Church in Singapore is organising believers into cell groups 'similar to military squads'. By 2000 it aims to have one worshipping in every block of flats in the Republic.[15] This pattern, in which cells grow and divide, amoeba-like, is increasingly found wherever conservative evangelicals have put down roots. It positively thrives on targets and deadlines. Ralph Winter may complain that 90 per cent of potential missionaries are in the wrong place to reach unevangelised ethno-linguistic groups; but most of them are in the right place – their own cities – to further the seemingly inexorable growth of conservative evangelicals as a proportion of Christian believers and of the population of the world.

There is, however, one corner of the 10/40 window where AD2000's emphasis on unreached peoples may be triumphantly justified. There is tantalising evidence to suggest that mainland China is on the verge of an evangelical breakthrough which, given time and tolerance on the part of the authorities, could far outstrip that of Korea or Latin America. Already the evangelical community in China is estimated at over 20 million. The house churches of China, to which most evangelicals belong, have been more vigorously persecuted than those of any other Christians. But the experience has only made them tougher, both in physical endurance and in theology. Chinese evangelicals are as fiercely intolerant of moral backsliding as any bible-belt fundamentalist. They are also strong believers in the End-time: according to the Overseas Missionary Fellowship, a recent wave of conversions in Zhejiang province began when two house churches 'felt that the coming of Christ was near. This gave them a great burden for evangelism.'[16] Eventually, churches in the entire region were caught up in a surge of evangelical activity. In less than two months, they had drawn in as many as 10,000 new believers, including a powerful local witch. 'If, as seems likely, the present rate of growth continues over the next decade, by the year 2000 China will probably have the largest evangelical church in the world,' says Tony

Lambert, director of the Fellowship's China Ministries Department. 'We in the West need to take note, and take to heart some spiritual lessons from this vibrant church, which practises the preaching of the word of God and prayer, trusting in God and not man's methods.'[17]

Ten thousand new believers in less than two months! Including a witch! Lambert need not worry that such achievements pass unremarked in conservative evangelical Churches in the West. Reports of mass conversions in far-flung parts of the globe are the life blood of congregations in suburban America and Europe, producing feelings of elation tinged with regret that miracles on such a scale are not taking place on their own doorsteps. There is, however, a determination to learn lessons from Christians in developing countries. In particular, the imagination of conservative evangelicals is gripped by the notion of doing battle with spirits and demons. Judging by the tone of many missionary reports from Africa, Latin America and the Far East, the vanquishing of evil forces is often the key to successful evangelism. If it works in the Third World, the argument goes, why not in the complacent West, where the very existence of evil powers has been denied or played down for centuries?

The preoccupation of conservative evangelicals with demonic powers can be dated back to the early 1980s, when incidents of 'ritual satanic abuse' were reported in towns all over America. The details of the abuse stories could hardly have been more grotesque. Many of them centred round the alleged use of childbearing women as 'brood mares', whose foetuses were sacrificed in rituals organised by an extensive network of devil worshippers. Yet not one single case has been successfully prosecuted either in Britain or in the United States; on the contrary, it was established that time and again children were manipulated by social workers and evangelicals into producing allegations which conformed to the accepted version of the myth. This did not surprise some sociologists, who had insisted from the start that the satanic-abuse scare was a classic 'moral panic' of the sort engineered by earlier generations of evangelical Christians, usually with the purest of motives: an often cited parallel is the furore over the non-existent 'white slave trade' in the years before the First World War.

Whatever the truth of the matter, the scare was evidence of a new mind-set among some evangelical Christians in which Spiritual Warfare against Satan assumed a new prominence. The origins of this, like the origins of the abuse stories, are a matter for speculation. It has been suggested that a rash of Hollywood films about the devil focussed the minds of born-again Christians on the subject of satanic power. But more significant than this, probably, was the emergence of the New Age as a potent cultural force in 1980s America. Evangelical horror at 'channelling' spirits and the occult arts seems to have led, paradoxically, to a new Christian fascination with these areas.

Perhaps the best insight into the frame of mind of many conservative evangelicals in the late 1980s, and indeed today, is provided by the novel *This Present Darkness* by Frank Peretti, which has sold over a million copies and is constantly being reprinted for sale in evangelical bookshops. The plot revolves around a small town in Middle America which is invaded by demons. These creatures are the demons of medieval Christian tradition: foul, scaly creatures with sulphurous breath hovering invisibly around their human agents, who include a New Age professor teaching a course in Goddess Consciousness and a liberal evangelical preacher. The forces of good, meanwhile, are led by a young fundamentalist minister who publicly rebukes adulterers in his congregation; he is protected by giant angels with blond hair and golden wings. *This Present Darkness* has done more than any other book to shape conservative evangelical perceptions of the New Age, to the dismay of moderate evangelicals. Irving Hexham, an evangelical professor of religious studies at the University of Calgary, said in a recent essay:

> What is alarming is the way it has helped to create new social boundaries for many evangelical Christians who escaped from a

restrictive fundamentalism during the 1970s and 1980s. Opposition to the 'New Age movement' and anything which is identified as connected with it, such as ecology, support for nuclear disarmament, or even meditation, has replaced older social taboos like the cinema, makeup and smoking as the criteria used to identify 'true' from 'false' Christians ... As a result this book has unwittingly had a very negative effect on the outlook of numerous evangelicals by labelling many contemporary social movements and institutions as either demonic or potentially evil.[18]

What Hexham is describing is a sort of revived fundamentalism, shorn of some of its old-fashioned trappings and partly defined by its understanding of evil. This is very much the ethos of a new strain of charismatic theology which emerged at around the time the satanic-abuse scare was beginning and which, however 'negative' it appears to critics, has inspired one of the most vigorous religious movements to have appeared in the West since the Second World War.

What has happened, essentially, is that in Britain and America members of non-charismatic churches, including American fundamentalists and Low Church Anglicans, have been won over to a charismatic theology of spiritual warfare. The key figure in this Third Wave, as it is known, is John Wimber, a California-based preacher who founded the Vineyard fellowship in the early 1980s to practise what he called 'power evangelism'. According to Wimber, Christian leaders should prepare to do battle with evil spirits and to act as channels for 'signs and wonders', miraculous workings of the Holy Spirit in which cancer would be cured and the dead would walk again. A worldwide struggle between good and evil was under way, and the future of the world hung in the balance.

None of this was new: the First Wave of charismatics (classic Pentecostalists) and the Second Wave (house-church charismatics) had always been open to dramatic manifestations of the Spirit. But Wimber and his 'power evangelists' had a broader appeal. Middle-class evangelicals in British suburbs were intrigued by Wimber, an easygoing, jolly character who described himself as 'just a fat man trying to get to heaven', but who saw himself as a conduit for supernatural forces of terrifying intensity. His frequent visits to Britain helped solidify an Anglican 'church within a church', a network of Church of England parishes whose ebullient charismatic style reinforced a theology verging on the fundamentalist. One London parish church, Holy Trinity, Brompton, in fashionable South Kensington, acquired a reputation for brilliantly effective recruiting on the cocktail-party circuit. Virtually overnight, it seemed, hundreds of young stockbrokers, estate agents and chalet girls were converted to a Pentecostalist faith which had more in common with the American bible belt than with the Church of England. Services at 'HTB' carried to an extreme the 'happy clappy' style characterised by arm-waving, ecstatic smiles and speaking in tongues. There was a hard edge to the operation which enabled HTB to colonise moribund local churches, raising the necessary funds in record time. New believers were corralled into small groups reminiscent of the cell networks in South Korea or Latin America; one or two critics, including a local vicar, accused the church of exercising a cult-like influence over worshippers' lives, a charge indignantly denied by its ever-growing membership.

The aggressive style of 'Wimberite' Anglican churches such as Holy Trinity, Brompton or St Andrew's, Chorleywood (where it is not unknown for mentally handicapped young people to be warned of the power of the 'evil one')[19] reflects the changing priorities of conservative evangelicals in general. John Wimber's interest in the power of evil, which extends to the medieval concept of 'entry points' for demons, is extremely common in those charismatic churches that see themselves as the cutting edge of evangelism in the West. Graham Kendrick, the composer of many of the rousing choruses heard at rallies in England and America, sets out the prevailing theology in his introduction to his *Make Way Song Book*: 'Satan has the real estate of villages, towns and cities overshadowed by ruling spirits which work untiringly at his command to bring about his malevolent will, fostering fear, violence and deception and successfully ruining lives which God intended for joy, happiness and true worship.'[20]

Kendrick's emphasis on towns, cities and villages is significant. There is a territorial dimension to conservative evangelical theology which arises from their understanding of Spiritual Warfare. Today's New Christians, as they sometimes call themselves, are intent on *winning back* territory from the enemy. Sometimes this involves exorcising their neighbourhoods, street by street. But often it expresses itself in far more practical, even admirable, ways. The emergence of a more tough-minded breed of evangelical can have benefits for the whole community: in many places, a renewed sense of purpose has led to the rediscovery of an evangelical social conscience which had lain dormant for decades. In the South London suburb of Peckham, for example, the independent Ichthus Fellowship runs business courses for 800 unemployed 'clients', roughly 10 per cent of the jobless total for the whole borough. Forty per cent of these clients find real jobs, as opposed to 28 per cent of the unemployed on secular job training schemes.[21]

What has all this to do with the approaching millennium? It goes without saying that these energetic Christian soldiers do not spend their time obsessively drawing up charts marking the completion of 6,000 years (although they are happy enough to sell books by people who do). We noted earlier that, within the conservative evangelical world, barriers have begun to come down, and this particularly applies to the area of eschatology. In Britain and America, evangelicals from premillennial, postmillennial and amillennial backgrounds have all, at times, been swept up in the excitement generated by the Third Wave. The prevailing mood is changeable, but when things are going well reports of 'signs and wonders' are taken as evidence that a great move of God is under way. This could mean that the Second Coming is imminent or, alternatively, that Christians are winning their battle against Satan; but, for the most part, the New Christian footsoldiers are too busy to debate these issues – and, anyway, their understanding of the Last Things is probably every bit as varied and idiosyncratic as Strozier's research suggests.

They are, however, intensely alive to the approach of the year 2000, since most of them belong to churches which have committed themselves to evangelisation targets as a contribution to AD2000. But any sense of a huge task facing them is balanced by an almost ungovernable urge to celebrate their faith. There is a great thirst among these 'neo-fundamentalists' for the immediate thrill provided by rallies, marches and miracles which may reflect a worldwide shift towards experiential religion. On both sides of the Atlantic, Marches for Jesus have become one of the high points of the conservative evangelical year. They are the perfect expression of neo-fundamentalist theology, satisfying the celebratory impulse while reinforcing the conviction that the landscape is in the grip of demonic powers. They also have the advantage of drawing in evangelicals who are uncomfortable about speaking in tongues but who wish to volunteer for Spiritual Warfare.

This is also true of a remarkable new manifestation of revived fundamentalism in America, the Promise Keepers. During 1995, half a million men, mostly baby boomers, met in sports stadia across the country to promise to uphold traditional standards of ethical and sexual purity and to build strong marriages and families. Founded in 1991 by a nationally prominent football coach, the Promise Keepers is a striking example of neo-fundamentalism's ability to harness secular trends for its own ends. In this case, a new consciousness of male identity fostered by such books as Robert Bly's *Iron John* has been used to awaken feelings of guilt at the role men have played in the collapse of family life. The organisation is firmly anti-feminist and anti-gay: the born-again preachers who address its rallies are greeted with huge cheers when they announce that every man is 'mandated to bring his wife to splendour in Jesus Christ'. The men who attend the conferences are mostly 'regular guys' in baseball caps who munch on hot dogs and do the Mexican wave. But during the preaching they reach a state of spiritual exaltation, waving their arms in the air like true charismatics and weeping at the name of the Lord. This is nothing if not experiential religion.

So, of course, is the Toronto Blessing, though not in the same way. The differences between the Promise Keepers and the Blessing are instructive. It is impossible to divorce the former from its American setting. It is a celebration of the ever-increasing vigour and effectiveness of born-again Christians as a lobby in American public life, and of their steady increase in numbers: indeed, the Promise Keepers movement is a brilliant exercise in evangelisation, drawing secular citizens inexorably into the conservative evangelical orbit. It is true that born-again Christians have become caught up in a vicious and dispiriting 'Culture War' with liberal citizens over public morality, but they believe it is a war they can win. The Promise Keepers express a powerful optimism that the tide can be turned in the next few years: the very thought of the year 2000 boosts their morale. The Toronto Blessing, in contrast, has a less celebratory feel to it. Although capable of moving the faithful to new heights of spiritual ecstasy, it has done little to push forward the boundaries of the evangelical constituency.

It is no accident that the country on which the Blessing has made the biggest impact is Britain. In the late 1980s, John Wimber and a group of evangelists called the Kansas City Prophets produced a series of prophecies that a great revival would break out in the British Isles at the beginning of the 1990s. This had the inevitable effect of raising millennial expectations in circles which were already buzzing with the excitement of the Third Wave. But they were very quickly dashed. A rally in Docklands at which the revival was supposed to break out was a dull affair. The prophecies were hastily withdrawn, amid considerable acrimony. A cloud of disappointment settled over the charismatic community which did not lift until the first reports of the Toronto Blessing reached Britain. Was this the prophesied revival, merely delayed by a couple of years? It soon became clear that it was not. For all the excitement it generated, the Blessing had little impact on people who were not already born-again Christians. Indeed, it coincided with a notably unsuccessful nationwide missionary appeal by the Pentecostal Churches, called Jesus in Me, which aimed to win 250,000 new souls for Christ; in the event, only 10 per cent of the target was reached, prompting speculation that in Britain, at least, the market for charismatic evangelical Christianity had become saturated. Several commentators, including

Andrew Walker, suggested that the startling displays of disinhibition associated with the Toronto Blessing were not unconnected to the frustration which had been building up in the charismatic world since the non-appearance of the promised revival.

It is, of course, too early to make a final judgement: as Walker has pointed out, the very experience of the Blessing may be sufficient to reignite the millennial fires.[22] But it is hard to resist the theory that the extraordinary scenes of the summer of 1994 were ultimately an attempt to close the gap between expectation and reality. And, if this is true, then another, rather sobering thought comes to mind: that over the next few years millennial disappointment is just as likely to produce dramatic and unforeseen consequences as the build-up of apocalyptic expectation.

8

The Great Jubilee

There are nearly a billion Roman Catholics in the world, and, although they may not be aware of the fact, every one of them has been given precise instructions about how to prepare for the year 2000. In 1997 they will be asked to focus their minds on Jesus Christ and the mystery of salvation; detailed study of the 600-page Catechism of the Catholic Church is recommended. In 1998 the focus shifts to a 'renewed appreciation of the presence and activity of the Holy Spirit'. In 1999, the third and final year of preparation, the theme will be that of 'a journey to the Father', in recognition of which Catholics will be encouraged to undertake a rigorous self-examination and step up their use of the Sacrament of Penance. Finally, in the year 2000, it will be time to celebrate.

This 'vast' programme of preparation, as the Vatican itself describes it, is outlined in the apostolic letter *Tertio Millennio Adveniente* of Pope John Paul II, published in 1995.[1] Most Catholics are probably only dimly aware of its existence: with the exception of controversial encyclicals, papal letters rarely excite much interest among the ranks of mass-goers, let alone nominal Catholics. But, if the tone of the letter is anything to go by, the Vatican is ready to go to almost any lengths to promulgate its message. These instructions are not meant to be taken lightly. A survey of papal documents since 1979 shows that John Paul II attaches extreme importance to the year 2000: he believes that the entire history of the Church in the past few decades, including the Second Vatican Council, has been a preparation for this 'Great Jubilee'. Indeed, he mentions the subject at the very beginning of his first encyclical letter as pope and has returned to it at regular intervals. But it was not until *Tertio Millennio Adveniente* that the full extent of his fascination with the third Christian millennium was revealed. In it, he states that 'preparing for the year 2000 has become as it were a hermeneutical key of my Pontificate'.[2] He goes some way to explaining why the date holds such importance for him: anniversaries, it appears, are a crucial feature of his understanding of time itself, which is both complex and subtle. At the end of the document, however, the mystery is not entirely dispelled. There is a sense that the Pope is holding something back, something which touches on his understanding of the structure of history and of its inevitable end. But, before entering the realm of speculation, it is worth looking more closely at the text of the letter, which is revealing in itself.

What John Paul II seems to be saying in his letter about the year 2000 is that anniversaries are important because time itself is sacred. Christ is the Lord of Time, in whom human time has reached its fullness, he says; and the fullness of time is, in fact, eternity. 'It is the One who is eternal, God himself. Thus, to enter into "the fullness of time" means to reach the end of time and to transcend its limits, in order to find time's fulfilment in the eternity of God.'[3] The Pope is reminding his readers that the End of Time is a concept inherent in the Christian faith; for 'time' as mankind observes and measures it is a human construct which is destined to pass away. It would be wrong, however, to assume that John Paul II is playing down its significance. One is reminded that this Pope is an admirer of the sociologist of religion Mircea Eliade: he is well aware of, and fascinated by, the intimate connection between all religious belief and the celebration of time. But in his eyes the rituals of the Catholic Church which satisfy the atavistic urge to mark sacred time are profound expressions of the divine will. John Paul believes there is a 'duty to sanctify time', the performance of which in some mysterious way brings man to a closer understanding of God. The example the Pope gives is of the priest at the Easter Vigil liturgy, who proclaims: 'Christ yesterday and today, the beginning and the end, Alpha and Omega, all time belongs to him, and all the ages, to him be glory and power through every age for ever.' As he says these words, the priest inscribes on the paschal candle the numerals of the current year – an action which, though John Paul does not put it this way, amounts to sanctification of the Anno Domini calendar. According to the Pope, the Easter rite emphasises Christ's Lordship of Time: 'He is its beginning and its end; every year, every day and every moment are embraced by his Incarnation and Resurrection, and thus become part of the "fullness of time". For this reason, the Church too lives and celebrates the liturgy in the span of a year. *The solar year is thus permeated by the liturgical year* [his italics], which in a certain way reproduces the whole mystery of the Incarnation and Redemption . . ."[4]

This passage suggests that for the Catholic Church the passage of the solar year is as holy an event as it was for the priests of ancient Mesopotamia or the Hebrews of the Pentateuch. In all the ancient civilisations of the Middle East, the sacredness of the solar year was the central fact from which sprang belief in expanded cycles of time. And one of these cycles, the Hebrew sequence of Jubilee years, is regarded by the Church as divinely inspired. Indeed, the concept of Jubilee is a powerful influence on its understanding of the coming anniversary. In theory at least, the Hebrews observed a sabbatical year every seventh year, during which the earth was left fallow, debts cancelled and slaves freed; and a Jubilee year every fifty years, when the customs of the sabbatical year were broadened with the intention of restoring equality among all the children of Israel. Although John Paul concedes that the Jubilee year was 'more of a hope than an actual fact', he is greatly inspired by the notion of a period of time dedicated to God at the end of a time-cycle. Furthermore, this dedication to God was manifested in ways which, translated to modern times, have the potential to transform human society – by remitting sins and the punishments due for them, and by the restoration of social justice. John Paul is careful to acknowledge the precedent set by his medieval predecessors, whose tradition of Jubilee years sought to reproduce the original Hebrew ethic by granting large numbers of indulgences. He does not point out, as he might have done, that the very concept of the end of centuries was created by this papal tradition; but he does recognise that Jubilee celebrations lend a new authority to the calendars which produce them. And this brings him to the subject of the year 2000.

There are strong reasons to celebrate this event specifically as a Jubilee, according to the Pope. It is a celebration of the life of Jesus, whose life and work bear a Jubilee-like relation to the Old Testament which precedes him. But is it an event whose appeal is limited to Christians? At this stage *Tertio Millennio Adveniente* passes briskly over two difficult areas: the near-certainty that the year 2000 is not the precise bimillennial anniversary of Christ's birth, and its dubious relevance to non-Christians. 'The two thousand years which have passed since the Birth of Christ (prescinding from the question of its precise chronology) represent an extraordinarily great Jubilee,' it says, 'not only for Christians but indirectly for the whole of humanity, given the prominent role played by Christians during these two millennia. It is significant that the circulation of the passing years begins almost everywhere with the year of Christ's coming into the world, which is thus the centre of the calendar most widely used today. Is this not another sign of the unparalleled effect of the Birth of Jesus of Nazareth on the history of mankind?' The impression that the Anno Domini calendar is in itself sacred is confirmed a paragraph later, when it is stated that this Jubilee will be greater than any other. 'For the Church respects the measurements of time: hours, days, years, centuries,' says John Paul, making no distinction between units of time which occur in nature and those devised by man. 'She thus goes forward with every individual, helping everyone to realise how *each of these measurements of time is imbued with the presence of God* and with his saving activity.'[5] There is perhaps a parallel to be drawn here with a view expressed by the Korean Pentecostalist leader David Yonggi Cho. In the 1970s, when he still believed that the Antichrist would appear in the 1990s, Cho predicted that the Beast would sponsor an international attempt to suppress the Anno Domini calendar as the year 2000 approached, so that mankind was not even aware of its proximity and therefore of its spiritual significance. Although Pope John Paul would never endorse such a fanciful idea, the notion that the year 2000 is invested with a spiritual significance which can be grasped only by the believer is one of his many areas of common ground with Christian fundamentalist leaders. This meaning goes deeper than the intrinsic spiritual value of anniversaries. It is clear that it relates in some way to the grand but finite sweep of history. Beyond that, though, we are reduced to searching for clues. On re-reading, there is a teasing edge to the Pope's statement that the year 2000 has become the key to his papacy. He is not so much handing the key to his readers as telling them roughly where it is hidden.

The Pope is at least fairly specific about his hopes for the third millennium. The crucial word, perhaps surprisingly, is 'springtime': this is used in relation to the new century in several documents, including *Tertio Millennio Adveniente*, where John Paul talks about a 'new springtime of Christian life which will be revealed by the Great Jubilee, if Christians are docile to the action of the Holy Spirit'.[6] This sits oddly with the gloomy statements about a spiritual crisis in the West and a crisis of obedience in the Church which have become such a prominent feature of this pontificate. It has been suggested that the Pope's optimism relates to the Catholic Church in the Third World, especially Africa, which he expects to come to the rescue of the disease-ridden West by flooding it with orthodox missionaries. But this is too restricting: recent papal pronouncements, including John Paul's book of personal theological reflections *Crossing the Threshold of Hope* (1994), hold out the possibility of a worldwide spiritual renewal. This regeneration is not limited by geography, and nor is it as purely reactionary in character as one might imagine. In addition to his frequent jeremiads directed at the wickedness of the modern world, John Paul has drawn attention to 'signs of hope' which, he says, are neither properly appreciated nor properly understood. They include: technological advance; a new sense of responsibility for the environment; a desire to restore balance between North and South; promotion of the laity in the Church; the emergence of new Catholic religious communities; and dialogue with other religions.[7] To his liberal critics, it is strange to find Pope John Paul II praising developments with which he has never been particularly associated, and which in some cases they even suspect him of opposing. On the other hand, they can hardly begrudge him his greatest sign of hope, the collapse of Communism, in which, he argues, 'the action of God has become almost visible in the history of our century'. That word 'almost' is very characteristic of John Paul. By talking of the fall of Communism as something in which the hand of God is almost revealed, he introduces an apocalyptic element into his discourse – in the sense that an apocalypse is the revelation of that which is hidden – while retaining a certain distance from it. And this is essentially true of all his 'signs of hope', whose relationship to the glorious springtime is deliberately left obscure. The impression is given that, although the signs will not inevitably lead to the springtime, they may well do so – if mankind makes the right moral choices and if there is a sufficient outpouring of the Holy Spirit.

Is this pious hope or prophecy? The question is an important one, since Pope John Paul frequently gives the impression that he knows more than he is letting on. The growth of materialism and paganism which he perceives in the modern world might seem to contradict his signs of hope; but it makes more sense to think of the two as opposing forces which are growing in influence as time wears on – or, as John Paul would put it, as we approach the third millennium. Shortly before he became pope, Cardinal Karol Wojtyla told an audience in Cracow: 'We find ourselves in the presence of the greatest confrontation in history, the greatest mankind has ever had to confront. We are facing the final confrontation between the Church and the Anti-Church, between the Gospel and the Anti-Gospel.'[8] We can take it that this is more than a reference to the engagement between Marxism and Catholicism. It is an apocalyptic statement about the course of human history. It is difficult to interpret, however, since at no stage in his pontificate has John Paul said how, or when, this confrontation will be resolved, or what he means by describing it as 'final'. The elusive vision of global springtime provides us with one pointer: we can assume that, if it materialises, the battle between the Gospel and Anti-Gospel will have been won by the forces of Christ. But if the final confrontation is over or has at least come to a temporary halt, does this mean that that course of human history has run its course and that Christ is about to return? There is no simple answer to these questions; we must look for more clues. Fortunately these are not hard to find: in *Crossing the Threshold of Hope*, one in particular leaps off the page. This is the Pope's suggestion that the attempt on his life in 1981, when he was shot in St Peter's Square, was linked to an episode which took place more than sixty years earlier: the apparitions of the Virgin Mary at Fatima in Portugal, where in October 1917 a crowd of 50,000 reportedly watched the sun 'dance' and spin like a catherine-wheel while an invisible Mary spoke to three small children.

In the middle of a discussion of the fall of Communism, the Pope asks:

> What are we to say of the three children from Fatima who suddenly, on the eve of the outbreak of the October Revolution, heard [from the Virgin]: 'Russia will convert' and 'In the end, my heart will triumph'. . . ? They could not have invented these predictions . . . And nevertheless it happened just as they had said. Perhaps this is also why the Pope was called from 'a faraway country', perhaps this is why it was necessary for the assassination attempt to be made in St Peter's Square precisely on May 13, 1981, the anniversary of the first apparition at Fatima – so that all could become more transparent and comprehensible, so that the voice of God which speaks in history through the 'signs of the times' could be more easily heard and understood.[9]

Not for the first time, one wonders if the Pope is deliberately tantalising his audience, for his references to Fatima are anything but transparent and comprehensible. Towards the end of the book, he returns to the subject as if it is something he cannot get off his mind. The Pope quotes the dying words of the Polish Cardinal August Hlond: 'The victory, if it comes, will come through Mary.' John Paul adds that, after he was elected pope, he came to have a similar conviction, even though at the time he knew little of the prophecies of Fatima. 'At first, I did not pay attention to the fact that the assassination attempt had occurred on the exact anniversary of the day Mary appeared to the three children at Fatima in Portugal and spoke to them the words that now, at the end of this century, seem to be close to their fulfilment.'[10]

Most reviewers of *Crossing the Threshold of Hope* played down this passage, pointing out that John Paul II's Marian devotion was already well established, and in any case unremarkable in a traditional Polish Catholic. It seemed entirely in character for him to harp on about Fatima. As for the superstitious importance he attached to the attempt on his life on the anniversary of the apparitions – well, that was forgivable, if slightly embarrassing. And, with that, they moved on to the rest of the book, which contained many challenging reflections on the existence of God and the dignity of man, expressed in piercingly lucid prose. But in passing over the Fatima material John Paul's critics may well have missed the whole point of the book. The Pope himself has said that the year 2000 provides the key to his papacy, which by any standards is one of the most remarkable in the annals of the Church; and his understanding of this Great Jubilee is by no means transparent or one-dimensional. It fits into a wider vision of the shape of history which he nowhere reveals in its entirety. But, by invoking the prophecies of the Virgin Mary at Fatima, he has, arguably, given the game away.

It is impossible to understand John Paul II without having some appreciation of the phenomenon of apparitions of the Blessed Virgin Mary. We are not talking here of an essentially static and backward-looking cult. Although one would never guess so from reading the more intellectually reputable Catholic newspapers and journals, belief in the prophetic witness of the Virgin Mary, as revealed in reports of apparitions from around the world, is held more intensely by more Catholics than ever before. It has been developing and gathering pace for decades and, with the papacy of John Paul II and the approach of the new millennium, has moved from the sidelines to the very centre of power and influence in the Church. No study of the year 2000 can afford to neglect it. It is worth looking at in some detail before returning to the subject of the Pope's mysterious vision of the future.

The spring 1995 issue of the Marian newspaper *Queen of Peace* carries a banner headline: 'TIMES OF FULFILMENT'. 'The time has arrived,' announces the lead story.

> After thousands of years of the unfolding of a divine plan, God will now, according to the revelations of the Blessed Virgin Mary, usher the world into new times. Through a series of human, natural and supernatural events, the long awaited 'Era of Peace' predicted at Fatima in 1917 is said to be about to occur.
>
> According to numerous visionaries, in the years remaining before the third millennium, mankind will witness the transformation of the world in an incredible fashion . . . This new era will usher in the greatest period of Christian evangelisation ever undertaken. Indeed, according to the Virgin Mary's messages, God will act decisively, removing all doubt of his existence even from the minds of most atheists . . . The Virgin's words indicate the face of the earth will be transformed. Like the ancient cities of Sodom or Gomorrah, some nations will even vanish. Others, like Russia, are promised to blossom with a new splendour. Peace will rule and the Church will reign, Evil will be paralysed, and like an old well, it will dry up and almost vanish from the face of the earth.[11]

This is a millennial vision that verges on the millenarian: it fits perfectly the textbook formula of vision of a new world, inexhaustibly fertile, harmonious, sanctified and just. Yet it emanates from members of a Church which has always condemned millenarianism. The Pittsburgh Centre for Peace, which produced the newspaper, is run by orthodox, if highly traditionalist, Catholics: they are bound by the Catechism of the Catholic Church, whose 1994 revision associated millenarianism with Satan himself. 'The Antichrist's deception already begins to take shape in the world every time the claim is made to realise within history the messianic hope which can only be realised beyond history through the eschatological judgement,' it says. How, then, can loyal Catholics pin their hopes on what amounts to a suspension of the laws of nature within history, that is, before the Second Coming? The Joachimite idea of a final golden age was prominent in late medieval tradition, but it was never officially sanctioned by the Church and has lain dormant for centuries. Furthermore, traditionalist Catholics have argued for decades that the modern world is witnessing the steady advance of evil. The same issue of *Queen of Peace* argues that society has 'gone morally berserk. There is child abuse. There are countless rapes. There are children killing children. Just in the last three decades crimes of violence have increased 500 per cent and teen suicides have *tripled*.' The contrast between this nightmare and the sense of a new world just around the corner is, of course, typical of apocalyptic belief; but it still seems odd that such potent apocalypticism should be tolerated and even encouraged by a Church which has been anti-apocalyptic since the time of Augustine.

The explanation is that devotion to the Virgin Mary has, throughout Catholic history, represented a route by which apocalyptic belief has entered the Church through the back door, as it were. This is not to play down the importance of the cult of Mary in the Catholic Church, which since the third century has officially sanctioned and encouraged it. But there is a sense in which it has never been fully in control of it. Devotion to the Virgin in her many guises – Queen of Heaven, Mother of Sorrows, Immaculate Conception – remains to this day rooted in popular religion. Although Mary features fairly prominently in the Gospels and the ancient liturgies of the Church, the cult depends heavily on traditions and beliefs which have not been imposed by the Church authorities but which, on the contrary, the faithful have imposed on them. The rosary is one example; another is the phenomenon of apparitions of Mary, which have aroused such pious fervour that the Church authorities (often after a period of initial reluctance) have been forced to declare them 'worthy of credence'. It is worth distinguishing here between visions of Mary, which have occurred throughout Christian history, and the apparition proper: in the latter, Mary is believed to be physically present in a manner which can enable several favoured people to see her at once. It is a phenomenon of extraordinary power. The Church's teaching relating to Mary is in itself subversive of human understanding of time: this is a woman who did not die but was bodily assumed into heaven. Apparitions affirm this timeless quality, enabling Mary to float above human history, gliding in and out of its narrative at will.

Although not unknown before the sixteenth century, apparitions essentially belong to post-Reformation Catholicism. Indeed, they played a crucial part in the development of a sentimental but tough-minded popular spirituality which permeated the Church until the Second Vatican Council. Since the nineteenth century, the apparitions have taken on an especially potent form, in which the visions of small children express the religious and political aspirations of a whole community. At La Salette and Lourdes in France, and subsequently at Fatima in Portugal, the Virgin entrusted messages of great urgency for the whole of humanity to peasant children. According to one school of thought, there is no great mystery about the psychological mechanism at work here: it is the 'white lady syndrome', in which a white-clad woman figure – not necessarily Mary, since the syndrome is not confined to the Christian world – appears to girls at the point when they are becoming conscious of their femininity. The Canadian social scientist Michael Carrol has applied computer analysis to hundreds of apparitions of the Virgin, and discovered a haunting pattern to them. Typically, Mary appears to girls at puberty, and the favoured seer 'usually colludes with the local community before announcing the Virgin's identity'. More remarkably, the seer has often lost a mother or mother figure within the previous eight weeks; and the Virgin imparts secrets and warnings of doom if certain religious formulas are not adhered to.[12] In addition, there is often a strong political dimension to the apparitions, which tend to occur in societies where Catholicism is under threat (such as Portugal in 1917) or where it has become the vehicle for nationalist aspirations (such as present-day Ukraine or the former Yugoslavia). This is not surprising: in a Catholic country, there can be few more effective boosts to the self-esteem of a community, local or national, than a belief that it has been visited by the Mother of God. Such a visitation is a unique sign of God's favour, and is often accompanied by reports of miraculous healings.

The fact that these apparitions often take place against a backdrop of persecution or national unrest may help explain the apocalyptic flavour of the Virgin's messages. We have already noted that stress, either individual or collective, can be a crucial factor in fostering End-time belief; and there is no doubt that in dozens of apparitions and visions the Virgin's warnings are linked to the approaching end of history. They are not crudely millenarian, in the sense of setting specific deadlines for the reformation of human behaviour; in this respect, they operate within the boundaries of apocalyptic belief set by the Catholic Church. But it is hard to avoid the conclusion that the apparitions have quietly pushed forward those boundaries, just as they have had the effect of adding to the beliefs which Catholics are permitted to hold in the quasi-divine powers of the Virgin Mary.

Although the thousands of communications from the Virgin from the 1840s to the present day differ from each other in countless respects, it is possible to identify a core message. This is that mankind must repent of its sins immediately, and show its love for Mary and her Son by saying the rosary. In this way, disaster – war, the spread of Communism, the apostasy of the Church – may be averted or limited through the intercession of Mary. This is the essence of the message. But there is also an apocalyptic sub-text to most of them which suggests that, irrespective of mankind's response to these appeals, the world is destined to experience a time of great trial in which the power of Satan will be unleashed as never before. The final outcome of the conflict between good and evil is not in question; no orthodox Christian can believe that Satan will triumph in the end. But the very urgency of the Virgin's appeals implies that mankind is living in the Last Days. She rarely goes so far as to issue an unambiguous prophecy; for most of this century, however, many messages have hinted at a worst-case scenario, in which mankind rejects the Virgin's appeal and disaster follows, in the shape of the worldwide triumph of Communism or, after 1945, a nuclear war. A message communicated to Sister Agnes Katsuko at Akita, Japan, in 1973, is typical of many. 'If men do not repent,' said the Virgin, 'Father God will inflict a punishment greater than the Deluge . . . Fire will fall from the sky and will wipe out a great part of humanity, sparing neither priests nor the faithful. The survivors will find themselves so desolate that they will envy the dead.'[13] The apparitions at Akita, admittedly, have not been officially recognised; but at the time their dire warnings seemed to confirm widely held pessimistic interpretations of the messages of Fatima, which remains the century's most celebrated series of Marian apparitions.

The Virgin's words at Fatima are nothing if not enigmatic. In one of the most important messages, attributed to 13 July 1917, the Virgin says that if people heed her requests to increase their devotions, 'Russia will be converted and there will be peace. If not, she will spread her errors throughout the world, promoting wars and persecution of the Church, the good will be martyred, the Holy Father will have much to suffer, various nations will be annihilated. In the end my Immaculate Heart will triumph . . . and a certain period of peace will be granted to the world.' John Paul II finds it remarkable that this message should have anticipated the rise of international Communism; sceptics point out that this part of the message was only made public many years after 1917 by the surviving seer Lucia dos Santos (who is still alive at the time of writing). The point to bear in mind, however, is that for many years commentators tended to play down the Virgin's promise of peace, so alarmed were they by the fulfilment of the prophecy of the spread of Russian errors. If that had come true, they reasoned, so would the predictions of persecution and the annihilation of nations. Their fears were compounded by the existence of an unpublished message from Mary known as the 'Third Secret of Fatima', which Lucia entrusted to the Vatican in a sealed envelope with instructions that it was not to be opened until 1950. To this day it remains locked in a drawer; it has been read by Popes John XXIII, Paul VI and John Paul II, all of whom have decided not to publicise it. For many traditionalists, this indicated that its contents were too terrible to reveal, perhaps involving a nuclear Armageddon, and some still suspect this to be the case. In his 1993 book *The Dancing Sun*, the Catholic author Desmond Seward concludes an elegant and mildly sceptical account of a pilgrimage to Marian shrines with the unnerving words: 'I am quite certain that the dancing sun really does mean global disaster, a warning which will surely be confirmed by the Third Secret.'[14]

Such bleak pessimism is, however, increasingly rare in Marian circles. Although the Vatican still refuses to reveal the Secret (on the ground that this would run the risk of 'turning prophecy into sensationalism') there has been recent speculation that it concerns not mass destruction but apostasy in the Catholic hierarchy, in which case no wonder it remains under lock and key. At any rate, fear of global disaster has undoubtedly receded. In its place has arisen the sense of excitement conveyed by the extract from *Queen of Peace*. The prospect of whole nations disappearing is still taken seriously, and there is often the implication that before things get better they will get worse; but the delicate balance between fear and hope has definitely shifted in favour of the latter. Innumerable messages delivered during the 1990s speak of an approaching Era of Peace or of Divine Mercy. Nor is this change of tone confined to apparitions. The Italian priest Fr Stephano Gobbi, who since the 1970s has received dozens of messages from Mary by 'interior locution', claims that she told him in 1990 to expect a Second Pentecost, which would 'come like a river of grace and of mercy which will purify the Church and make her poor and chaste, humble and strong, without a spot or wrinkle . . .'[15]

The most important factor contributing to this new optimism

is undoubtedly the collapse of Communism during the years 1989–91, which traditionalists attribute to the intervention of the Blessed Virgin Mary. Did she not promise that Russia would convert? We should bear in mind that traditionalist Catholics, including the Pope, are well disposed towards Russian Orthodoxy, which they regard as a schismatic branch of the true Church; and the Fatima seer Lucia has said that the promised conversion will initially take the form of a return to its ancient faith. So it is not necessary for Russia suddenly to embrace Roman Catholicism for the Fatima prophecy to be fulfilled. Furthermore, Marian enthusiasts often claim that the fall of the Soviet bloc was predicted in messages received during the early 1980s. This is a rather dubious claim, since at no time did the Virgin forecast a sweeping change in the world political order. But we should not overlook the continuity between the communications of the 1980s and those of today. Although the optimism of the messages becomes much more noticeable after 1989, traces of it are discernible before that date. And, more importantly, the steady increase in the number of apparitions of the Virgin reported around the world certainly dates back several years before 1989. Indeed, one of the reasons for belief in a link between Mary and the fall of Communism is the fact that the latter took place at a time when sightings of the Virgin and related phenomena, such as weeping and bleeding statues, were occurring thick and fast.

A widely held, if sceptical, view is that most of these sightings are indirectly attributable to the excitement surrounding one particular set of apparitions: those at Medjugorje in the former Yugoslavia, which began in June 1981 and show no signs of stopping. Medjugorje follows the pattern of the classic apparitions of Lourdes and Fatima, in that Mary first appeared to peasant children – in this case, six of them, ranging in age from ten to sixteen. She was described by them as a young woman of amazing beauty, dressed in grey and surrounded by a dazzling glow. Within days of the first apparitions, a crowd of 5,000 had gathered to recite prayers on the mountain where the Virgin spoke to the seers. Within a decade, 10 million people had made the journey there. Senior churchmen, including high-ranking cardinals, have spoken up in favour of the authenticity of the apparitions, whose simple and affecting messages call primarily for a return to prayer. Less apocalyptic than those at Fatima, they largely steer clear of the contentious subjects which feature in many contemporary messages. Unlike the messages delivered to a housewife in Conyers, Georgia, USA, they are not preoccupied with abortion. (According to the Conyers Virgin, who cries tears of blood, 'the blood of abortions will fall upon mankind'.)[16] Nor, despite the political turmoil in the region, do they appeal to nationalist or sectarian sentiment: this is in sharp contrast to, say, the apparitions at Hriushaw in the Ukraine, where at the end of the 1980s half a million people were reported to have seen the Virgin hovering in the sky and many heard her promise them an independent state. Even so, Medjugorje is controversial. The apparitions are closely associated with the local Franciscan order, which is not on speaking terms with the Catholic hierarchy. The previous bishop of the area campaigned vigorously against the apparitions, which have not been endorsed by the bishops of former Yugoslavia. Pope John Paul has set up a commission to study the situation and has otherwise kept out of the controversy. But his personal sympathies are thought to lie strongly with the seers and their supporters.

If the worldwide increase in the volume of messages from Mary originated with Medjugorje, does that mean that subsequent reports of apparitions are merely copycat phenomena? This seems too crude an explanation. It may apply to some cases – there were reports in 1995 that another set of children in Herzegovina had seen the Virgin – but it does not take into account the complexity of the situation. Since 1990, new Marian visions have been reported in Syria, Iraq, India and Lebanon. Some of them should certainly be seen in a context of a worldwide increase in religious apparitions, in which Protestants have visions of Jesus and angels, Hindus have visions of their own gods, and so on. Furthermore, the notion that the world faces a time of trial, after which it will be 'purified', is common to many apocalyptic scenarios, including those associated with the New Age movement. In particular, those

Catholics who believe the Virgin is prophesying unprecedented natural calamities before the dawn of the Era of Peace are outlining a sequence of events whose overall structure resembles that proposed by Californian prophets of 'earth changes'. The Marian author Dr Thomas Petrisko, in his 1995 book *Call of the Ages*, insists that since 1989 'floods, fires, hurricanes, earthquakes, rainstorms, droughts and snowstorms have hammered nations around the earth on an unprecedented scale': there is a 'world upheaval both in nature and among men'.[17] Yet Petrisko also believes that Mary is guiding the world towards an Era of Peace which will materialise around the year 2000. The end of the millennium serves as a focal point for his predictions, just as it does for New Age prophets who see natural catastrophes, including the disappearance of vast stretches of American coastline, as a prelude to the establishment of heaven on earth.

There is little doubt that the year 2000 is pulling some Catholics in roughly the same direction as other apocalyptic believers, including New Agers and evangelicals. In her book *The Visions of the Children*, the Medjugorje expert Janice Connell borrows a line from fundamentalist Christians when she notes the symmetry of 2,000 years between the first prophets and Jesus, and between Jesus and the end of the current century. This, she says, 'is an interesting time sequence, which may be significant.'[18] But the excitement in Marian circles at the approach of the year 2000 is not purely an expression of a general apocalyptic mind-set. It contains elements which arise specifically out of Roman Catholic tradition. For example: in December 1983, the Medjugorje seer Mirjana Dragicevic-Soldo received a vision of Satan. She commanded him to leave, and he did – whereupon the Virgin appeared, with an uncharacteristically pointed message. 'Excuse me for this,' she said, 'but you must know that Satan exists. One day, he presented himself before the throne of God and asked permission to try the Church for a period of time. God permitted him to try it during one century. This century is under the power of the devil, but when the secrets which have been confided to you have been fulfilled, his power will be destroyed. Already now he has begun to lose his power, and he has become aggressive: he destroys marriages, stirs up division between priests, brings about obsessions and murders.'[19]

We need not concern ourselves here with the secrets of Medjugorje, which have not been revealed in full and are the source of some confusion among the faithful. Nor is it necessary to debate the source of Mirjana's vision, since the validity of religious apparitions is, by their very nature, more a matter of interpretation and opinion than of empirical judgement. What matters is not so much the nature of the apparition or vision – hallucination, dream, genuine revelation of God – as the contents of the message. And in this case the crucial point is that Mirjana has somehow come into contact with an idea which has been present in Catholic thinking, often at a subliminal level, for decades. Put simply, it is that the twentieth century is under the power of the devil, and that with its passing his influence will be greatly reduced. Although the precise origin of this idea is not known, it can certainly be traced back to the early years of this century, when a story began to circulate in the Vatican that during the 1890s Pope Leo XIII had, like Mirjana, experienced a diabolical vision. According to the conservative Catholic theologian Ralph Martin,

> the story has come down to us through various confidants of the Pope, primarily cardinals who were close to him. While differing in exact details, the main lines are clear. While concluding a liturgical celebration in the last part of the nineteenth century, Leo XIII suddenly stopped and looked transfixed. He later recounted to close collaborators what had happened. He had been allowed by the Lord to overhear a conversation between Satan and the Lord ... Satan declared that if he had enough time and enough power he would be able to destroy the Church. God gave permission to Satan to take the bulk of the twentieth century as a time in which he would be allowed specially to test and tempt the Church, but after that his power would be limited again.[20]

This vision of the diabolical twentieth century is profoundly apocalyptic. The idea that the powers of evil will be allowed a limited time in which to roam the earth, after which order will

be restored, is found in Zoroastrianism, which in the opinion of
a growing number of scholars is the world's first apocalyptic
belief system. In Christianity, its most enduring expression is
the reign of Antichrist, a concept principally upheld by
fundamentalist Christians who believe that this evil incarnation
will appear immediately before the Second Coming. Catholicism, in comparison, is vague on the subject: it has never felt
under an obligation to outline a sequence of events which
conforms in every detail to biblical prophecies. In the late
medieval period, many churchmen believed that the defeat of
Antichrist – an evil prince or Antipope – would mark the
beginning of a long period of earthly peace which was not
necessarily the millennium. The new Catechism of the Catholic
Church, meanwhile, states that before the Second Coming, 'the
Church must pass through a final trial that will shake the belief
of many believers. The persecution that accompanies her
pilgrimage on earth will unveil the "mystery of iniquity" in the
form of a religious deception offering men an apparent solution
to their problems at the price of apostasy from the truth. The
supreme religious deception is that of the Antichrist, a pseudo-
messianism by which man glorifies himself in place of God and
of his Messiah come in the flesh.'[21] The Catechism goes on to
suggest that millenarianism itself can be a manifestation of the
Antichrist, a concept it seems determined not to personify. But,
despite this rather low-key approach to the End-time drama, it
endorses the concept of a period of tribulation before the
Second Coming; and, by identifying the enemy with an abstract
'deception' rather than with an individual, it leaves open the
possibility that Communism and materialism may very well be
the Antichrist, with the turmoil of this century constituting the
time of trial. Such an inference would not commit the faithful to
belief in the imminent end of the world, since Catholics do not
take literally Revelation's references to the seven-year reign of
the Antichrist; and there is a Catholic precedent – Joachimism –
for belief in a golden era on which no time-limit is set but which
is nonetheless the conclusion of human history.

It seems clear that, despite its historic anti-apocalypticism,
Catholic teaching as set out in the new Catechism allows room

for the belief that the Church is now passing through the prophesied tribulation and, by implication, is entering that ill-defined period known as the Last Days. The notion of the diabolical twentieth century is entirely compatible with this belief; furthermore, it helps explain the current optimism of messages from Mary. In the years since Mirjana of Medjugorje predicted Satan's defeat at the end of this century, many other voices have taken up the theme. In 1984, Fr Gobbi was told by Mary that her struggle with the Devil 'was to last throughout the whole century as a proud challenge to God on the part of my Adversary'. At Oliveto Citra in Italy, the Virgin has declared that Satan's final hour 'started a century ago'. Most explicit of all is the anonymous visionary of Cold Spring, Kentucky, who according to Thomas Petrisko was told by the Virgin in 1993 that 'through the grace of the Father, I am permitted to be with you during this time of Great Tribulation on earth. This Tribulation has been present since the beginning of this century, with the start of Satan's 100 year reign, and is escalating at the end of the century. Just as I came to you at Fatima, I continue today to come to you, and with the same messages.'[22] Admittedly, the published Fatima prophecies do not single out the twentieth century. But they do forecast a period of unprecedented strife, at the end of which will come a long-awaited peace. All around the world, Catholics with a special devotion to Mary believe that this peace will arrive with the new millennium; and there are strong grounds for believing that Pope John Paul II is thinking along the same lines.

Is this what he means, then, by saying that the year 2000 is the key to his papacy? His conviction that the prophecies of Fatima are being fulfilled, together with his vision of a 'springtime' revealed by the Great Jubilee, fit so neatly into the scenario of a diabolical twentieth century followed by an Era of Peace that the conclusion is hard to resist.

But it is not easy to guess the innermost thoughts of a pope, especially when the subject is so sensitive: the danger of 'turning prophecy into sensationalism' is so great that even if a pontiff were granted a private revelation of the end of history he would almost certainly feel obliged to keep quiet about it. There is, in fact, a fine thriller by Morris West called *The Clowns of God* about a fictional pope who has just such a revelation. Sitting in the garden of the monastery of Monte Cassino one morning, the newly elected Pope Gregory XVII looks up from his book and finds himself:

> caught up in a fiery whirlwind, hurtled out of every human dimension into the centre of a vast unendurable light. The light was a voice and the voice was a light, and it was as if I were being impregnated with its messages. I was at the end of all, the beginning of all; the omega point of time, the alpha point of eternity . . . In a moment of exquisite agony I understood that I must announce this event, prepare the world for it. I was called to proclaim that the Last Days were very near and that mankind should prepare for the Parousia, the Second Coming of the Lord Jesus.[23]

But, before Gregory can do so, the horrified cardinals force him to abdicate.

No one is suggesting that John Paul has had such a blinding premonition, though a few of his critics have picked up on the apocalypticism of some of his pronouncements. (He is portrayed in the final stages of decrepitude in Peter de Rosa's comic novel *Pope Patrick*, 'his face lime-white, weeping copiously and muttering "Apocalypse, Apocalypse" '.) To unsympathetic liberal commentators, this strain in John Paul's thinking is not something to be taken seriously; it merely joins the long list of wrong-headed views which they ascribe, patronisingly, to his Polishness. But this is unfair on at least two counts. In the first place, it overlooks what might be called the inbuilt apocalypticism of St Peter's chair, which has rubbed off on a good many of its occupants. We should remember that in the late middle ages the popular understanding of the End-time drama often hinged on the figure of the Angelic Pope who would rule over a final glorious era of the Church. In our own day, this myth survives in the form of the Prophecies of St Malachy, a list of 112 popes, identified only by mottoes, which stretches from 1143 until 'the second Peter', the Pope at the End of Time.

Although attributed to Malachy, Archbishop of Armagh from 1132 until 1148, the document was long ago exposed as a sixteenth-century forgery; but this has not affected its popularity, which has increased as the list has begun to show every sign of running out towards the end of the twentieth century or the beginning of the twenty-first.

According to the current interpretation of the list, there will be only two more popes after John Paul II. It goes without saying that no senior Catholic figure, let alone the Pope, will confess to even the mildest interest in Malachy's prophecies. But the list does reinforce a psychological association of the papacy with the end of history to which even the Pontiff may not be immune. Leo XIII was not the only modern pope to experience a terrible vision of the future: Pius X had one, too, during an audience with the General Chapter of the Franciscans in 1909, when he went into trance. According to one report, he emerged from it with a look of horror in his eyes. 'What I have seen was terrible,' he said. 'The Pope will quit Rome, and in fleeing from the Vatican he will have to walk over the dead bodies of his priests.'[24] Perhaps the unique status of the papal office is such that its occupants are naturally susceptible to visions of the End: if a man believes he is God's chief representative on earth, is it surprising that God should choose to entrust him with such information?

The apocalypticism of John Paul II cannot, however, be regarded as something peculiar to his personality or to his office. As we have seen, it reflects a millennial belief in a coming golden age which can increasingly be found wherever traditionalist Catholics uphold the prophetic witness of the Virgin Mary. But how significant is this in terms of the wider Catholic Church? Since Vatican II, the sort of traditionalist who says the rosary every day and looks to Fatima for enlightenment is no longer typical of Catholics as a whole. In Western Europe and America, the full-blown cult of Mary is confined to an elderly minority in parishes or to isolated pockets of resistance to liturgical change. Seen in this light, it scarcely matters if a group of Catholics who belong to an old-fashioned sub-culture are being swept along on a tide of apocalyptic excitement; it does not even affect the situation very much if the Pope shares their view, since it is beyond his power to reverse the trend towards secular liberalism in the Catholic world. No recent figures, from the Pope's beloved Africa or anywhere else, suggest that the decline in church attendance, and therefore in traditional belief, is confined to the degenerate West. Despite the steady growth in the birth rate of nominal Catholics, there are no signs of a Catholic revival to compare to the astonishing spread of conservative Pentecostalism on every continent.

Even so, it would be a mistake to imagine that belief in the imminence of such a revival, to be brought about as much by miraculous intercession as by human effort, is confined to an ultra-traditionalist Marian movement and the lonely figure of Pope John Paul II. There are throughout the world a great many conservative Catholics who, while not especially interested in apparitions of the Virgin, are slowly and perhaps unconsciously working their way towards a semi-apocalyptic understanding of the future of the Church. The Pope's vision of a 'great springtime for Christianity' in the third millennium has undoubtedly boosted the morale of those mainstream conservatives – critics but not opponents of Vatican II – for whom John Paul II is little short of an Angelic Pope, casting out dangerous liberals from their sees and chairs of theology and safeguarding the future by promoting loyal Catholics. It is certainly the case that the Pope's most trusted supporters see themselves as engaged in a battle against the forces of error – and also that they see light at the end of the tunnel. To quote Ralph Martin, a fiercely orthodox Catholic charismatic whose book *The Catholic Church at the End of an Age* has been endorsed by the preacher to the papal household: 'as we approach the end of the century, it appears that the darkness is growing darker and yet the light is shining more brightly'.[25]

We cannot say for certain that John Paul II believes that history is approaching a final climax. Even if this is his view, it is not something he wishes to make accessible to the casual observer; rather, it is something to be perceived with the eye of faith. What we can say, however, is that such a conviction would throw a new light on many aspects of his papacy: the overpowering sense of urgency with which he set about undermining the Communist regimes of Europe; his intolerance of any dissent which, in his view, might weaken the Church in its hour of trial; and, of course, his often expressed desire to live long enough to usher in the Great Jubilee. We must remember that John Paul is an optimist whose heart leaps when he thinks of the year 2000. A sense of accelerating time is common to both apocalyptic believers and old men; and this is one old man for whom it cannot accelerate fast enough.

9

A New Age

As the end of the second Christian millennium approaches, mankind is on the verge of an astonishing transformation, one for which all of human experience until now has been little more than a preparation. Every historical cycle known to man is entering a new phase or about to come to a shuddering halt. We are living in the dying days of the Kali yuga, a period of 6,480 years which Hindus believe is the last and most degenerate stage of a recurring cycle in which mankind slowly descends from light into darkness. We are also in the twilight of what the Greeks called the Age of Iron; a new Age of Gold beckons. The calendar of the ancient Maya, the most mysterious of the civilisations of pre-Columbian America, is about to run out: extending millions of years into the past, it comes to a sudden end on 22 December 2012. Meanwhile, the Age of Pisces, which has dictated the violent content of history for two millennia, is scheduled to give way to the Age of Aquarius, a millennium of wisdom and light, shortly after the year 2000; but in the process the earth may experience such terrible upheavals that the survival of humanity is by no means assured. The warning signs are already there for those with eyes to see:

hurricanes, earthquakes and volcanic eruptions on an unprece-dented scale, with far worse to come. Gaia, the living organism of the earth, may be about to take revenge for the damage inflicted upon her. Man-made disasters such as pollution and overpopulation point to the fulfilment of ancient prophecies of the annihilation of humanity. Plagues of drugs, pornography, and gambling threaten the foundations of civilisation; biblical prophecies of the fall of Babylon have acquired a new and terrible relevance. We may even be heading towards the reign of the Antichrist as we draw near to the year 1999 – a number which, when reversed and turned upside-down, signifies both the Number of the Beast and the divine One. Yet all is not lost. The Elohim, a breed of extra-terrestrial beings who are responsible for planting the first human civilisation on earth, that of Atlantis, may rescue humanity just as they preserved Noah and his family after Atlantis was destroyed in the flood. If mankind heeds the warnings from its scientists and prophets, the forthcoming Apocalypse may be a cleansing experience which marks the evolution of a superior species. Men and women will ascend to something called the Fourth Vibratory Plane, which will be distinguished by a new spiritual under-standing; *homo sapiens* will become *homo spiritualis*. Biblical prophecies of a new heaven and earth will be fulfilled – but only if mankind makes the right choices. And now, as the cosmic drama and time itself gather speed, is the time to decide . . .[1]

The above is neither a parody of New Age beliefs nor an amalgam of the most exotic of them drawn from different sources. It is the outline of a single scenario devised in the early 1990s by the couturier and New Age guru Paco Rabanne in a book called *Has the Countdown Begun?* It is, admittedly, rare to find one theory which draws on so many colourful esoteric traditions at once. But Rabanne is not untypical of that mysterious phenomenon known as the New Age. On the contrary, he merely exhibits its most important features in an unusually concentrated form. He is shamelessly eclectic, bor-rowing indiscriminately from Christian fundamentalism, East-ern religions, the occult and popular science. He is also, of course, a showman and an entrepreneur, and it is tempting to dismiss his writings as the literary equivalent of the Amazons dressed in chain-mail with which he first shocked the world of *haute couture*. But this would be to underestimate the force of his ideas.

The 1990s is a decade bristling with popular theories which combine science fiction, scientific theory and mystical religion. Most, if not all, of them seem heavily influenced by the approach of the year 2000, though they often seem unable to explain why this date is so significant. But this does not deter the public, which is buying books about prophecy and the paranormal in ever greater numbers. Any title which includes the name of the sixteenth-century French seer Nostradamus seems to sell; so does anything with an alien spacecraft on the front cover. The television series *The X-Files*, about a US government conspiracy to hush up a UFO invasion, has been one of the surprise hits of the 1990s. Nor is this trend confined to the marketplace: in America and Europe, the hunger for books and films on esoteric subjects has been matched by a striking increase in reports of near-death experiences and alien abductions. According to some sources, hundreds of thousands of people have been briefly spirited away by extra-terrestrial visitors, and are only now beginning to recover the experiences on the therapist's couch. And all this is bound up, somehow, with radical new approaches to the living organisms of the planet and human body, and an unexpected passion for CDs of chanting monks and American Indians.

It is not easy, however, to fit together the pieces of the jigsaw. Essentially what seems to be happening is that something called the New Age is working its way into the general population – at a time, paradoxically, when the movement of that name is less clearly defined than it was during the 1980s. But what precisely is the New Age? As the public taste for the bizarre and the supernatural becomes more and more pronounced, this question has acquired a new urgency.

Although most people have heard of the New Age, they tend not to know exactly what it stands for. Even academic studies of the subject complain about the difficulty of arriving at a definition of the term, describing it as a 'nebulous' and 'slippery' concept whose boundaries encompass a bewildering variety of activities and beliefs. The term New Age dates back to the late 1960s, when it surfaced among a range of American groups which sought to combine 'Eastern wisdom' with the occult. These, in turn, were descended from certain esoteric religious movements of the nineteenth century: to this day, the overwhelmingly white and middle-class composition of the New Age movement reflects its roots in New England, home of both spiritualism and theosophy. The latter, a late-nineteenth-century attempt to create world harmony by importing to the west Indian doctrines such as reincarnation, has left its fingerprints all over the New Age. It inspired the fashion for Eastern gurus in the 1960s, although the immediate trigger for that enthusiasm was rather more prosaic, namely the ending of the US government's ban on Asian immigration. This should not imply that all New Agers are ex-hippies who spent the Summer of Love rolling joints and listening spellbound to the giggles of the Maharishi. But it is fair to say that the core membership of the movement is dominated by middle-class baby boomers. Although only a minority live together in communities – most of them have ordinary jobs in education, computing, the service industries or the public sector – they tend to share a common background of experimentation with 'alternative' lifestyles. A fair number have moved from left-wing radicalism to esoteric spiritual beliefs; in many cases their belief in the latter has grown out of their disappointment with the former.

The sociologist of religion Robert Ellwood has described the New Age as 'a contemporary manifestation of a western alternative spirituality going back at least to the Greco-Roman world'. This current, he suggests, 'flows like an underground river through the Christian centuries, breaking into high visibility in the Renaissance occultism of the so-called "Rosicrucian Enlightenment", eighteenth-century Freemasonry, and nineteenth-century Spiritualism and Theosophy'.[2] The essence of this tradition, says Ellwood, is a Neoplatonic hierarchical universe governed according to law rather than caprice by a mysterious Absolute. It is a universe in which spirit and matter are completely intertwined, and in which the human and the cosmic are brought together by a panoply of forces and intermediaries, ranging in form from astrology and ley lines to UFO 'spirit brothers' and ascended masters.

This, at any rate, is how the New Age appears to a sympathetic academic. It has to be said, though, that it rarely lives up to this subtle description. Reading the outpourings of, say, a reincarnated Egyptian princess channelled through a Californian housewife, one is not aware of a Neoplatonic intellectual tradition. In practice, the search for common denominators to New Age beliefs is often both daunting and unrewarding: daunting because they never stand still for long, and unrewarding because it seems pointless to analyse beliefs which are adopted and abandoned in such a capricious fashion. The somewhat blurred public perception of the New Age as a mixture of crystals, astrology, corn circles and Shirley MacLaine is not far from the truth: instead of a single corpus of doctrine, the movement provides an arena in which apparently unconnected ideas and fads rub up against each other, often rather uncomfortably. The parameters of this movement can only really be measured by examining the range of material in a New Age bookshop; they are constantly shifting, as one fashion replaces another. Even sympathetic observers recognise a flavour-of-the-month quality to the way in which, for example, the passion for 'channelling' and crystals has recently given way to an obsession with 'Native American' wisdom.

But a common denominator does exist. Put simply, the New Age is apocalyptic: it believes in an End-time. This fact is not always immediately apparent, since the movement tends to concentrate on the process of personal, individual transformation. But there is a sum to these parts, and it is nothing less than the salvation of the entire planet. Most New Agers have experienced some sort of personal transformation in their lives, and believe that if sufficient numbers of people follow their example the face of the earth will be transformed. There is, admittedly, no consensus about how the transformation will come about, or the shape of the world after it happens: vague phrases such a 'shift in consciousness' tend to obscure very different visions of the mechanics of change, which can involve beams of psychic energy, geographical cataclysms, reincarnated masters, extra-terrestrial aliens or, as Rabanne illustrates, all of the above. The crucial point, however, is that this new world, however it is constituted and however long it is supposed to endure, represents the summit of human history.

It is important here to distinguish between what the New Age claims to be, and what it actually is. On the rare occasions when it discusses its own lineage, it stresses the timeless quality of the beliefs it has inherited from the occult and from the cultures of India, China and pre-Columbian America. It can be argued, however, that these borrowings (which tend to be carefully sanitised for modern Western tastes) are irrelevant to the true inspiration for the New Age, which is a belief in the emergence of a perfect world after a time of trial – in other words, the classic apocalypticism which Norman Cohn has dated back to ancient Iran and which entered Western culture with the Book of Daniel. This can take a millenarian form, where the new heaven and the new earth are expected to materialise at any time, and believers are so overcome by this expectation that they reject all social and legal norms. But, as we have seen, there are many less virulent, though still powerful, forms of apocalypticism in which social conventions are respected but the enlightened nonetheless live in the shadow – or the hope – of the end of this world.

New Age beliefs usually embody a 'soft' rather than a 'hard' apocalypticism, in that with a few exceptions their visions do not include scenes of wanton cruelty: there is no question of everlasting punishment for the 'unsaved'. Even so, the classic features of apocalyptic thought are all in place. There is an obsession with prophecy in its many guises, together with a sense of approaching crisis, in which the polarisation of good and evil becomes ever more marked. New Agers tend to view the world to come as being in some sense beyond history, in that mankind will have acquired wisdom which will render obsolete the wars and political struggles that make up history. Furthermore, this new world is often just around the corner;

most believers will live to see it. But, before it can materialise, mankind will experience dramatic upheavals which will have the effect of destroying the old structures of society. Often this carries overtones of the final, titanic struggle. As Professor Cohn points out, 'many New Agers are comfortably situated middle-class people who would be shocked to think that they had exterminatory fantasies. But there is no denying the violence of their ideas, which have unmistakably millenarian features.'[3] Often the violence is concealed by attributing widespread destruction to the workings of nature – especially earthquakes and floods – rather than to an angry God or to the armed forces of the Elect. The effect, however, is much the same. Those that perish may not be evildoers, but they share in the collective guilt of a society which, in many New Age scenarios, is portrayed as terminally sick. And, whatever the criteria for survival, the new world will be inhabited by a generation which is miraculously free of the errors of the past. In the words of the British prophet Benjamin Creme, who regularly announces the impending arrival of a messianic figure, the Maitreya, 'men will quickly end the worst divisions in this divided world; mass poverty and starvation will fade from sight; old wounds will be healed; past wrongs will be forgiven. Thus will the sons of men recommence their journey into their divinity.'[4]

The apocalypticism of the New Age frequently manifests itself in a concern for collective salvation. Indeed, it is often this which places a particular belief within the boundaries of the New Age. For example: the phenomenon of UFO experiences, which dates back to the 1940s, only slowly acquired New Age resonances, as reports of alien abductions increased during the 1980s and the aliens began to deliver messages which foretold disaster for planet earth unless humans mended their ways. Today, there is considerable tension between New Age UFO enthusiasts, for whom the message is more important than the mechanics of the abduction experience, and orthodox 'true believers', for whom details such as the specifications of the spacecraft are of prime importance. In the same way, one can distinguish between traditional spiritualism of the 'Is Anybody

There?' variety, in which the dead communicate with surviving loved ones, and 'channelling', in which they deliver messages of profound importance to humanity, often across a gap of many centuries. Likewise, there is a clear distinction between astrology as a means of personal fortune-telling and belief in an epochal, worldwide transition from the Age of Pisces to that of Aquarius. There is a pattern here. The gnostic and occult currents of Ellwood's underground river are easily detectable in the New Age, but they have become part of the process of apocalyptic transformation.

Astrology is one of the most important of these currents. The imminent shift from the Age of Pisces to that of Aquarius is one of the very few astrological concepts to be grounded in astronomical fact, namely a phenomenon known as the precession of the equinoxes. This term refers to the way in which the axis of the earth's rotation wobbles very slowly in a clockwise direction; so slowly, indeed, that it takes just under 26,000 years to complete a full rotation. During this time the sun, observed when it rises every year at the vernal equinox, will appear to move through the twelve signs of the zodiac, each sign lasting approximately 2,100 years. Although this way of measuring astrological Ages is of comparatively recent origin, the notion of a rotating Great Year is in line with the oldest human understandings of history, such as those of ancient Mesopotamia. For these first historical societies, however, the movement of this Year was cyclical; their concept of history was therefore essentially static. For most New Agers, in contrast, the shift from Pisces to Aquarius is a once-and-for-all apocalyptic event, one which would have been inconceivable until the development of an apocalyptic world-view in the West. For the Age of Aquarius is essentially the longed-for, perfect age, albeit one whose dawn may be attended by terrible cataclysms. There is no danger of history repeating itself because the human race, or the surviving remnant of it, will itself have changed.

When, precisely, will the precession of the equinoxes move the planet from the Age of Pisces to that of Aquarius? There is, in fact, no single answer to this question: it is entirely a matter of opinion. Hence, in part, the popularity of the Pisces/Aquarius scheme. In most versions it is truly a 'soft' apocalypse, in contrast to the 'hard' and frighteningly swift Second Coming of Christ. In a cycle of 26,000 years, it goes without saying that the change of epochs will not occur all at once, and that there should be a useful margin of error of a decade or so. And it is versatile: because it is driven by the least intrusive mechanism imaginable – the movement of the planet – it can be combined with almost any scheme of human or supernatural activity. It therefore provides an ideal framework for the New Age, which is above all eclectic. The precessional shift can be intruded into any theory. It can be used to illuminate the phenomenon of UFO abductions, revealing the aliens as benevolent observers who merely wish to guide mankind through the birth pangs of a new epoch. It can, given sufficiently flexible arithmetic, explain the appearance of Jesus Christ 2,000 years ago and the decline of the Church at the end of the second millennium. (The sign of the early Christians, it is often pointed out, was a fish – the sign of Pisces.) It can offer an explanation for sudden 'break-throughs' in holistic health care which seem to point towards an Aquarian millennium of longevity, if not immortality. Above all, it can be used to explain any convulsive disturbance of the natural, social or political order. The American seer Ruth Montgomery, a former political journalist who turned herself first into a celebrity medium and then into a prophetess of the New Age, paints an unusually grim picture of the 'earth changes' which will attend the transition: earthquakes and tidal waves will devastate California, England, Holland and Japan; and she predicts, with more than a hint of *schadenfreude*, that many of the innumerable casualties will be individuals 'not adequately prepared in spirit'. Those who survive, however, will be transformed into a race of supermen and superwomen. In the Age of Aquarius, an expanded consciousness will enable mankind to tap directly into the minds of others, reading books at a single glance. There will be no need for formal education. Avarice, greed and lust will have passed into history.[5]

Perhaps surprisingly, the single most influential New Age interpretation of the shift from Pisces to Aquarius is one of the few to treat it purely as a metaphor. This is the book *The Aquarian Conspiracy* by Marilyn Ferguson, whose appearance in 1980 set the agenda for the rational and secular end of the New Age Spectrum. Ferguson, the publisher of a journal of alternative medicine called the *Brain/Mind Bulletin*, says in the book that although she knows nothing about astrology she was drawn to 'the symbolic power of the pervasive dream in our popular culture: that after a dark, violent age, the Piscean, we are entering a millennium of love and light – in the words of the popular song *The Age of Aquarius*, the time of "the mind's true liberation".'[6] The agents of this transformation will be members of a leaderless but powerful network which has broken with certain key elements of Western thought and may even have broken continuity with history itself. This network, which is a conspiracy in the literal sense of 'breathing together', seeks power only to disperse it. But its aims are not easily summarised. Ferguson is heavily influenced by the ideas of the unconventional Jesuit thinker Pierre Teilhard de Chardin (1881–1955), who suggested that the human mind is continuing to evolve, and that one day awareness of its own evolution and potential will crystallise as a species-wide enlightenment called the Omega Point. Ferguson's version of this is a 'paradigm shift', in which a traditional framework of understanding (the paradigm) breaks down as the sudden acquisition of new information shatters long-held beliefs; the parallel she cites is Einstein's Special Theory of Relativity, which replaced the 'clockwork paradigm' of Newtonian physics with an 'uncertainty paradigm' which revolutionised man's understanding of the universe. The new Aquarian paradigm, says Ferguson, will emerge as a result of an intuitive leap in a range of disciplines. In medicine, it will shift the focus away from questions of expense and technology, and towards basic questions about the nature of wellness. In education, it will open up a debate about the nature of learning itself. 'For the first time in history,' says Ferguson, 'humankind has come upon the control pattern of change – an understanding of how transformation occurs. We are living in *the change of change*, the time in which we can intentionally align ourselves with nature for rapid remaking of ourselves and our collapsing institutions.'[7]

Seen from a distance of a decade and a half, *The Aquarian Conspiracy* can appear painfully, even comically, naive. There are toe-curling passages in which Ferguson confidently predicts the eradication of world hunger within a few years, together with the destruction of the 'old gods of nationalism and isolationism', which are tumbling 'like the stone deities of Easter Island'.[8] At times, however, the book is genuinely prophetic. Its worldwide paradigm shift may have proved elusive, but its focus on personal development as a key to economic growth foreshadowed, and may even have inspired, the New Age training techniques adopted by some of the fastest-growing industries of the 1980s. The sections on medicine and physics, too, set the tone for a lengthy engagement between esoteric thought and 'new science'. Ferguson's book, it should be said, is engagingly written and nowhere insults the intelligence of the reader; it seemed to many back in 1980 that its synthesis of radical social theory with the latest scientific conjecture could turn the emerging New Age movement into one of the most formidable intellectual forces of the late twentieth century.

That this did not happen is partly due to the millennial undertow of the New Age movement, which has pulled apart the alliance with science and sociology proposed in *The Aquarian Conspiracy*. No one would deny that recent developments in physics have altered our mechanistic view of a universe ruled by cause and effect. But the much heralded interaction of radical science with psychic research has not made much impact on the mainstream scientific community; it is usually regarded as the preserve of maverick academics who have, effectively, become religious believers in the New Age. Likewise, the training techniques which were employed by leading American and British companies during the 1980s proved to be of only limited usefulness, for one simple reason: in the end, they relied upon employees adopting what amounted to religious beliefs, which most of them were understandably reluctant to do.

The truth is that even in the supposedly rational form in which they were presented by Marilyn Ferguson, there is an irreducible spiritual and supernatural component to New Age beliefs. The 'intuitive leap' which will give birth to the paradigm shift is essentially the leap of faith: faith in mankind's ability to transcend physical and psychological limitations which orthodox science regards as intrinsic to the human species. *The Aquarian Conspiracy* suggests that the paradigm shift will enable the human brain to develop new functions and a new consciousness. Although this carries strong echoes of Teilhard de Chardin, it is also not far removed from Paco Rabanne's vision of the sudden evolution of *homo spiritualis*. We might not realise it at first, but we are not far from that borderland of religious belief and science fiction where, for nearly two decades, most members of the New Age movement have made their home. From the early 1980s onwards, Ferguson's metaphor of a conspiracy was taken up not by political thinkers and scientists but by believers in (among other things) astral projection, reincarnated spirits, UFOs and the healing powers of crystals. These people saw more clearly than Ferguson that the much heralded paradigm shift is a purely apocalyptic concept; and, as such, offers a framework for an infinite number of extravagant millennial scenarios.

There were moments during the 1980s when it seemed that a major world religion was emerging. Although the New Age defined itself so loosely that almost any belief could be incorporated into it, the resulting mixture began to take on a distinctive and easily recognisable flavour. Crystals, for example, became a key ingredient. The power of precious stones has been celebrated by the occult throughout its history, but never with such enthusiasm as by the New Age, which employed crystals as a means of tapping into the cosmic powers that bring about personal transformation. Even more significant was channelling, a process by which mediums acted as intermediaries for spirit entities. Channelling was not invented by the New Age: in the late nineteenth century, it was supposedly the means by which Madame Blavatsky, the founder of theosophy, had received the wisdom of a hierarchy of spirit masters. But, for the first half of the twentieth century, communications from the dead received by spiritualists were primarily intended either to reassure relatives or to prove the existence of life after death. From the 1970s onwards, however, mediums began to produce long and portentous communications which in effect outlined new spiritual philosophies for the whole of mankind. The spirit mediums and their chosen intermediaries sometimes made unusual couples: the dead philosopher William James (author of *The Varieties of Religious Experience*) spoke to Jane Roberts, a housewife living quietly in upstate New York; an unnamed entity who hinted that he was the biblical Christ spoke to Helen Schucman, a Jewish, atheist professor of psychology at Columbia University, who published the communications as the best-selling *A Course in Miracles*.

By the 1980s, it seemed that almost everyone connected to the New Age was channelling long texts, often with the most bizarre and unpredictable content. The result, in the caustic view of the American commentator Suzanne Riordan, was 'a bewildering cacophony of cosmic voices [which] babble, gossip and prophesy on every aspect of human and non-human life, offering a myriad of ingenious revisionist (and often mutually contradictory) versions of history, theology and science, and a profusion of clashing – but equally unorthodox – commentaries on current events'.[9] Yet important common themes did emerge from the more successful and reputable 'channels'. Several of these built their philosophy round the doctrine that mankind had become trapped by fear and, in consequence, had lost touch with its power to create its own reality. Salvation, in New Age terms, therefore lay in a process of shrugging off self-loathing and opening the mind to the creative power of the spirit. When this happened, said the angelic spirit channelled through the author Ken Carey, humanity would 'remember to sing the songs that only awakened humans can sing, songs that will bring metals up from the ground, songs that will attract elements, minerals, materials, from across great distances, through the power of their true names'.[10]

This is a friendlier and more democratic universe than that of the fundamentalist Christian. Yet it is unmistakably apocalyptic. Carey, who is a representative New Age figure, proposes two stages of salvation – individual awakening followed by the 'dissolving of the planet into Light' – which correspond roughly to the born-again Christian's conversion and the millennium of the saints. There is no divine punishment; but as the New Age developed it became abundantly clear that the dark side of the apocalyptic equation had not been abolished. The optimism of the channels was often tempered by predictions of worldwide disaster, and towards the end of the 1980s these acquired a new urgency. Although only a minority of New Age prophets made catastrophe the central feature of their teaching, very few ruled it out altogether; in this respect, their prophecies were no different from those of visionaries of all persuasions down the ages, for whom the new heaven and earth would be lent added lustre by the cataclysms which brought it about. The concept of profound, worldwide change is intrinsic to apocalyptic belief. Normally this change will happen suddenly, which naturally entails violent disturbance to the familiar order; but even if the process is gradual, as in the dawning of the Age of Aquarius, it can be punctuated by sudden convulsions such as earthquakes, the natural disaster most favoured by prophets throughout history.

The New Age luminaries who began to issue grim warnings during the 1980s were, in fact, reworking an established tradition of catastrophe prediction by theosophists and psychics. Of these, the most important was Edgar Cayce (1877–1945), an American clairvoyant whose career began at the age of twenty-three when he discovered that he was able to tap into the collective unconscious while he was asleep, speaking lengthy prophecies of which he would remember nothing when awakened. Over a period of forty years, Cayce literally spoke volumes. In the process he built up an alternative history of the world which departed significantly from received opinion. He pictured Atlantis as an advanced civilisation of motor cars, aeroplanes and lasers which was destroyed in the biblical flood, leaving only a handful of survivors who escaped to the classical Mediterranean world and to Central America.

This has proved one of the most durable legends of the twentieth century: Paco Rabanne is one of dozens of New Age authors to dust it down and apply a new gloss to it. But Cayce had visions of the future as well as of the past. He believed that the flood had been caused by a shift of the earth's magnetic pole which would happen again; and, when it did, the map of the earth would have to be drastically redrawn. As a result of these 'earth changes', large areas of America including California and part of the East Coast would disappear under the sea. The world's climates would be shaken up, so that Europe would return to the ice age; this is because, beginning in 1968, the lost continent of Atlantis would rise up from the sea bed, cutting off Europe's 'central heating' from the Gulf Stream. By the year 2000 a new world would have appeared.[11]

Edgar Cayce's prophecies of earth changes have made a powerful impression on the New Age. With their emphasis on the collective fate of mankind, they suited the mood of the 1980s far better than that of the era in which they first appeared. More important than this, however, was the fact that they focussed attention on the last years of the twentieth century. By the early 1980s, the calendar had become a central preoccupation of the New Age. Both the optimistic visions of gradual enlightenment and the doomsday scenarios of Ruth Montgomery and her ilk looked to the end of the second Christian millennium as a period of accelerated change. Of these two groups, however, the latter were by far the more specific in their dating. The psychoanalyst Charles Strozier, whose work on fundamentalist psychology we have already encountered, believes this fits into a pattern. 'In general, both among fundamentalists and New Agers, one consequence of any dating of the end is that it tends to be associated with more violent images of destruction,' he says. 'There is something about naming catastrophe that brings it closer to hand, rather like the difference between those who talk generally about suicide and those who give details of their planned death. As therapists learn from bitter experience, the latter has far more dangerous meanings.'[12]

Certainly, the extra-terrestrial spirits who guide Mrs Montgomery's hands on her word processor have been very specific
about the forthcoming polar shift, which will take place just
before the year 2000. This will happen 'in the twinkling of an
eye', as the earth 'slurps approximately onto its side'. Seasons
will change abruptly, high winds will sweep the planet's
surface, and the oceans will 'slosh about as would a jostled
bowl of water, rushing over adjoining land areas in tidal waves
too massive to escape'. One of the new poles will be in the
Pacific, the other in South America. 'Most of those losing their
lives will be in coastal areas,' say the spirit guides, 'and their
bodies will be swept into the sea, posing no particular health
problems for the survivors of the shift, but others who are
physically extinguished by falling buildings and the like will of
course need to be buried. There will be mass graves, and little
time for public mourning as the survivors look to their own
sustenance during that chaotic time.'[13]

Strangely, though, this will not be a time of sadness or
despair, thanks to 'an enlightenment that will flow to a new
race of people coming in . . . Those who have been lifted off to
safety by extraterrestrial fleets will return to designated areas,
soothing and reassuring them and teaching them new methods
of growing crops more speedily and of erecting dwellings that
require little time or energy.' Some people who are not fit to live
in the New Age will initially survive, say the spirit guides;
fortunately, however, 'they will soon die off'. And all this will
be set in motion before the new millennium, perhaps in June,
September or October 1999.

When discussing earth changes, New Age figures often
manage to describe scenes of incredible destruction in a laid-
back, folksy manner that belies the fact that what they are
talking about is the death of millions. The late Sun Bear, a half-
Chippewa prophet who combined elements of traditional
Indian observance such as the sweat lodge with crystal healing
ceremonies, was convinced that 'some time before the year
2000' life in the world's cities would break down completely as
a result of race riots and natural disasters. He compared the
planet at the time of the earth changes to a big shaggy dog full

of fleas: when he gets sufficiently irritated he shakes himself, sending the creatures flying in all directions. 'The planet will survive, even though perhaps millions of people will perish,' he announced cheerfully. Like a growing number of prophets, Sun Bear dispensed practical advice for living through the catastrophe. He insisted that the only humans to survive would be those who made a conscious decision to change their way of life: they must abandon the coasts and the towns and retreat to the countryside. Furthermore, they should prepare for unusual weather changes by taking sun hats and umbrellas with them; they should stock up on extra layers of clothing and try washing their hair and bathing in five gallons of water heated on a wood stove.[14]

True to Strozier's formula, those prophets who envisaged a peaceful change were the most vague about timing; if they mentioned dates, these simply marked the beginning and end of a slow transformation. Thus a group called the 11:11 Doorway movement claimed that mankind had entered a twenty-year period of opportunity to end the earth's period of conflict between darkness and light. The doorway of opportunity opened on 12 January 1992 and will end on 31 December 2011. According to the group's seer, Solara, the 11:11 symbol was 'pre-encoded within our memory banks long, long ago, prior to our descent into matter, under a time release mechanism, which when activated signified that our time of completion is near'. (This numerical revelation came to Solara, incidentally, while he was staring at a digital clock.)[15]

Although there is no role for the year 2000 in this scheme, it is worth noting that the 'period of opportunity' is roughly centred on it: the period of accelerating change begins as humanity enters the last decade of the millennium. Ruth Montgomery, Sun Bear, the 11:11 group and scores of other prophets were all thinking in these terms by the mid-1980s, at precisely the time that the popularity of crystals and channelling were beginning to create a distinct, if broad-brush, image of the New Age in the public mind. As a result, the movement became inseparably linked with the calendar shift. In the words of the 1992 *Chambers Dictionary of Beliefs and Religions*, the New

Age 'takes seriously the fact that the year 2000 will soon be here, and it seeks to discover and practise new religious paradigms that will be relevant to the new millennium'.[16]

The New Age is not, of course, the only religious movement mesmerised by the prospect of the year 2000. As we have seen, the same is true of the West's only other fast-growing faith, conservative evangelical Christianity. But there, at least as far as their respective adherents are concerned, the similarity between the two movements ends. Born-again Christians and New Agers tend to regard each other with hostility laced with fear and contempt. Indeed, evangelical dislike of the New Age is so extreme that it has had the effect of spreading public awareness of its existence. Evangelical literature is unremitting in its attempts to portray the New Age as the work of Satan, who is seen as engineering a revival of the occult arts as a prelude to the emergence of the Antichrist. Marilyn Ferguson, it is darkly hinted, let the cat out of the bag when she spoke about a conspiracy.

But on closer inspection the relationship between the New Age and renascent fundamentalism is rather more complicated than one of simple mutual antagonism. There are odd similarities between the two, not least in their understanding of time. Consider, for example, the way in which as the 1980s progressed both movements began to produce date-specific prophecies. As we have seen, several fundamentalist date-setters fixed on 1988 as the *annus mirabilis* which would witness the long-awaited Rapture. For some New Agers, too, the year was highly significant; for the author Nada-Yolanda it marked something called the 'sixth-phase rending of the seventh veil', a crucial stage in a worldwide cleansing process lasting from 1960 to 2000.[17] But New Age millennial expectations had in fact reached a peak the year before, on 16 August 1987, when thousands of New Agers had gathered at 'power centres' around the world to celebrate the 'Harmonic Convergence'. According to its spokesman, the author José Arguelles, this event heralded not only 'the return of Quetzalcoatl [the Aztec god–king], but the elimination of Armageddon as well. To some it may even be as another Pentecost and second coming of Christ. Amidst spectacle, celebration and urgency, the old mental house will dissolve, activating the return of long-dormant archetypal memories and impressions . . . [which] will saturate the field and create the impulse towards the new order and lifestyle.'[18]

Born-again Christians inevitably took offence at the equation of the Second Coming with the Harmonic Convergence, an event they regarded as a cheap and sinister stunt. But Arguelles had a point, in so far as the apocalyptic structure of New Age and fundamentalist beliefs do invite comparison. Both movements seem to have been caught in the force-field of the year 2000: hence their almost simultaneous twitches of excitement as the great anniversary hove into view at the end of the 1980s. Furthermore, the similarities between the New Age and the born-again revival, especially in its Pentecostalist form, arguably go deeper than a shared structure of End-time belief. Could it be that in some respects they are essentially the same sort of religion?

For movements which despise each other, the degree of overlap between Pentecostalism and the New Age is remarkable. Both rely heavily on disembodied voices rather than visions: the medium channelling communications from spirit guides and the born-again believers speaking prophecies in tongues resemble each other in method of transmission and sometimes in content of the message (the urgent need for mankind to mend its ways). Both movements stress health and healing: since they regard physical health as a token of spiritual wellbeing, sudden contact with the sacred can result in the miraculous disappearance of 'incurable' diseases and conditions. There is also a stress on material prosperity as a sign of blessing, though the more sophisticated practitioners in both fields tend to soft-pedal this approach. More importantly, both Pentecostalism and the New Age lay huge stress on individual experience of the spiritual leading to complete personal transformation; and this goes hand in hand with a certain 'do it yourself' approach to organisational structure which is common to the strictest biblical literalists and to the most laid-back Californian New Agers.

It is not hard to relate these shared features to developments in Western culture and society over the last few years. The obsession with healing and the replacement of established hierarchies by the authority of personal experience go hand in hand: they reflect the preoccupations of societies in which traditional social and religious structures have been failing or even disappearing. In the West, no institution or authority has remained unquestioned; very few occupations are secure in the way that they were fifty years ago. Yet for some, at least, society offers a range of choices – economic, cultural and spiritual – unthinkable before the 1980s. The populations of North America and Europe are torn between a new materialism and an intense yearning for the sacred; the result has been a significant increase in uncertainty and free-floating anxiety, from which the conversionist dramas of the Pentecostalists and the New Age offer an instant release.

It is not, however, an escape route open to everyone. Apocalyptic belief, even in watered-down form, tends to appeal most strongly to certain personality types, to people on the margins of society, and to 'ordinary' citizens who through a combination of circumstances are momentarily vulnerable. This is as true today as it was at the end of the middle ages, when members of messianic movements were composed not of the fixed bottom rung of the social hierarchy, the peasantry, but of disturbed individuals and members of groups whose place in society had undergone disorientating change. Although there have been times when an apocalyptic world-view has been employed by the establishment for purposes of analysis or propaganda (for example, during the medieval conflict between the Pope and the Emperor), it is generally true to say that apocalyptic belief bears the same relation to orthodox religion as End-time believers do to society at large. It is the religion of the outsider.

Neither the New Age nor revived fundamentalism welcomes this label; but the fact remains that they cannot survive comfortably in the social or intellectual mainstream, as Marilyn Ferguson discovered when her paradigm shift failed to material-ise and as Pat Robertson discovered when he ran for President of the United States. This is partly a function of their opposition to a whole range of orthodoxies, ranging from biblical, historical and archaeological scholarship to the laws of science, to say nothing of their frequent challenges to liberal notions of intellectual freedom. Most fundamentalist Christians and New Agers set themselves up in opposition to received wisdom and are treated accordingly. Admittedly, no religious faith is fully sanctioned by Western society, in the sense of being believed by the majority of people. But a distinction should be made between those creeds which are widely respected, such as mainstream Catholicism, Protestantism, Judaism, Islam, Bud-dhism and so on, together with a range of metaphysical and secular philosophies; and those which are regarded as in some sense beyond the pale – an insult to the intelligence.

The latter category includes almost all forms of apocalypti-cism, and especially those millenarian varieties which expect imminent and total change. This is surely something to do with the fact that apocalypticism refers to the future rather than the past. Belief in miraculous events which are placed far back in history, or in an after-life, is much more easily accommodated by society than belief in a fast-approaching breakdown of the laws of nature. It is one thing to believe that an itinerant preacher in first-century Palestine came back from the dead after his execution; and that he was, in fact, a supreme God whose very flesh is eaten by believers every time bread and wine is consecrated in memory of his death. It is quite another to suggest that most believers now living will not die, but will soon be lifted up bodily to a heavenly city while vast armies destroy the earth. The Real Presence in the Eucharist and the imminent Rapture stand on either side of a line separating doctrines which Western society considers respectable from those it considers invalid, cranky or even dangerous. On the one side lie virtually all religious beliefs hallowed by the elites of the major world religions; on the other lies an equally vast, though infinitely less systematic and coherent, corpus of beliefs that for one reason or another society rejects.

We have already come across the image of an underground river to describe the many currents of belief – occult, Eastern, theosophical and so on – which meet in the New Age. Where this wider category of rejected beliefs is concerned, we should perhaps visualise a huge lake into which rivers and streams flow from many different sources. As they reach this lake, currents from these sources mingle and mix in a thousand different ways, creating unpredictable and ever shifting patterns. There is, in fact, an obscure but very useful sociological term for this metaphorical lake: it is called the cultic milieu. This term usually refers to the range of beliefs associated with the New Age; but it can be argued that, in the end, all beliefs which society rejects ultimately find their way there. And, once there, it becomes impossible for them to keep their distance from one another. Although superficially very different from each other, they are held in a similar contempt by society at large; and perhaps for this reason they tend to appeal to similar types of people.

Although conservative evangelical Christianity as a whole is not as fully immersed in the cultic milieu as the New Age, many less educated fundamentalists feel thoroughly at home in it. The milieu has always provided a breeding ground for those legends known as urban myths, and for decades these have held a strong, if unconscious, appeal for a certain sort of evangelical: it was born-again Christians who were responsible for spreading urban myths about the white slave trade and satanic ritual abuse. It is fascinating to observe the way in which Christian date-setters occasionally succumb to the appeal of theories from other parts of the cultic lake. In 1982, for example, some New Agers became very excited about an alignment of the planets called the Jupiter Effect, which a couple of maverick scientists predicted would slow down the rotation of the planet, leading to an earthquake which would destroy Los Angeles. Leading fundamentalists were not slow to jump on the bandwagon. Hal Lindsey, author of *The Late Great Planet Earth*, wrote that 'what we can expect in 1982 is the largest outbreak of killer quakes ever seen in the history of planet earth along with radical changes in climate'. Not to be outdone, Pat Robertson suggested that the chaos caused by the Jupiter Effect might prove the perfect cover for a Soviet strike against the US. But this prospect did not worry the Southwestern Radio Church: it suggested that the Rapture might occur just before the planetary alignment and that the celestial event might result in 'the earth being righted on its axis and pre-Flood conditions being restored'.[19] Nor was this the first time that fundamentalists had been tempted to explore unfamiliar territory. As the author William Alnor has pointed out, the New Age fascination with pyramids echoes a strange phenomenon called biblical pyramidology which dates back to the nineteenth century. It was Christian pyramidologists who first suggested that the siting of the pyramids corresponds to the configuration of the night sky, and reflects in some way the passage of the sun through the signs of the zodiac – ideas that form the centrepiece of a number of best-selling books of the 1990s. They also believed, however, that the specifications of the pyramids contained coded information about the date of the Second Coming.

All this is evidence of genuine cross-fertilisation within the cultic milieu. In addition to borrowing from others, Christian fundamentalism also serves as a source of myth. Consider, for example, the obsession of many New Age channellers with the figure of the Antichrist. According to Ruth Montgomery in 1986, 'he has already been born and is now an American boy in his early teens'.[20] Paco Rabanne, meanwhile, reveals that in the course of his meditations 'I have seen the face of a young man now living in London, who has surprised important people with his "magic" gifts. He is already extending his psychic undertaking and his personal fortune. Is he no more than a sorcerer with extraordinary powers, or could he be the Antichrist, already in ambush awaiting his hour?'[21]

These New Age borrowings from Christianity pale into insignificance, though, when compared to the extent to which New Agers draw indiscriminately on each other's theories and those of older esoteric traditions. The precession of the equinoxes is almost universal; but not far behind come lost civilisations and life in outer space, usually in tandem. It is an article of faith in the more imaginative New Age circles that the ancient civilisations of Central America and Egypt could not have developed independently, and that their shared features, such as pyramids, must indicate a common origin. One does not have to cast about for long in the cultic milieu to come up with theories to support this: the mythical continent of Atlantis, first described by Plato, has occupied a place in the cultic sub-culture throughout this century, as have extra-terrestrial visi-tors; and the two can be combined with remarkable ease. Indeed, one of the primary functions of the New Age is to provide a forum in which disconnected strands of myth can join up to form elaborate structures. These multiply and fall apart with a rapidity that defies exhaustive analysis. But they have one thing in common: apocalypticism.

A book published in 1995 called *You Are Becoming a Galactic Human* illustrates this point. Its authors, Virginia Essene and Sheldon Nidle, offer a particularly baroque rework-ing of the Atlantis myth. They claim that the ancient civilisation was originally founded by beings from a far-flung solar system, and that it was populated by humans ten feet tall who enjoyed perfect weather created by their own astonishing crystal technology. After the destruction of Atlantis around 10,000 years ago, members of the empire's royal family created rival dynasties in the Middle East and Central America, and it was during the terrible warfare that followed that the crystals failed and the artificial firmament was destroyed – leading to the biblical flood. Fortunately, a few survivors were able to set in motion what we know as human history under the guidance of the ascended masters of other galaxies and the living earth herself (who, we are not surprised to discover, is called Lady Gaia). All these details have been communicated by a galactic presence from Sirius called Washta, who is speaking to them with great urgency. This is because mankind is on the verge of a great physical and spiritual event.[22]

According to Essene and Nidle, we should not be misled by what we can see of the heavens: it is nothing but a hologram. In reality, our solar system is about to enter a vast region of light called the Photon Belt. During the transition, the earth will be plunged into darkness for three days, at the end of which the DNA of the human body will have been altered, giving its cells the means to interact with the soul and rendering it virtually ageless. (Helpful diagrams of new DNA structures are included.) This is clearly apocalyptic territory: the latest date for the transition is the end of 1996. It is, of course, far removed from the plausible theories of Marilyn Ferguson; but, then again, perhaps the distance is not all that great. In *The Aquarian Conspiracy*, Ferguson hints at the emergence of a physically regenerated humanity. And she does suggest that the human brain might be 'a hologram, interpreting a holographic universe', a fact which explains 'the inability of instrumentation to track the apparent energy transfer in telepathy, healing, clairvoyance'.[23]

It is worth looking at one more example of the way New Agers reach out to embrace other outlandish ideas floating in the cultic milieu. In this case, they are not ideas previously associated with the New Age, though they certainly possess the basic qualification of rejection by society at large. In 1995, an investigation by Matthew Kalman and John Murray in the *New Statesman* magazine revealed that two New Age publications, *Nexus* and *Rainbow Ark*, had become vehicles for the anti-Semitic conspiracy theories of the far right; or rather they had dressed them up in New Age clothing, with some very curious results. For example, *Rainbow Ark* had a theory that 'when a person has strong hatred of another race, their higher self often (karmically) makes sure they incarnate in that race to balance them out, thus many of the worst kind of Nazis have already incarnated in Jewish bodies, explaining therefore some of the fireworks which are going on and will go on in Israel'.[24]

According to the *New Statesman*, the influence of the far right is felt 'in an alarmingly large swathe of the growing New Age and green movement'. It cites the example of David Icke, a former television sports commentator whose movement from the Green Party to a New Age philosophy incorporating extra-terrestrials and his own divinity has been a source of great hilarity in the British press. The joke, it seems, has turned sour. Icke has become a firm believer in the danger of a New World Order run by 'bankers' and 'Illuminati' and has championed the authenticity of the infamous *Protocols of the Elders of Zion*, which informed Hitler's notion of a world Jewish conspiracy. Icke believes that many Jews are manipulated by an elite which is 'merciless, sick and diabolical' as well as being controlled by 'the Luciferic Consciousness'. Many Icke supporters are associated with the Battlebridge New Age Centre in King's Cross, London. The centre's organiser, Julie Lowe, was asked about its links with the far right. She replied that she believed in the *Protocols*. 'I met two old Jewish men at Hyde Park Corner one evening who told me they were true,' she said. 'They were saying that if they didn't get their way in the things they wanted, they were able through Philadelphia in America to pull the money out of every city in the world.'[25]

Although many New Agers were shocked to read of this new school of thought, it illustrates perfectly the workings of the cultic milieu. Once someone has taken on board information rejected by the wider culture, whether it refers to UFO landings or to the innate wickedness of Jews, there remain tensions to be resolved: it is necessary to explain why this secret knowledge is dismissed by the world at large, and why possession of it renders the believer so vulnerable to persecution. In the case of fundamentalist Christian doctrine, a highly developed body of apocalyptic teachings closes the gap, as it were; and, where other ideas are concerned, this role is performed by grand conspiracy theories which are often little more than a lightly secularised version of biblical apocalyptic. As we shall see in the chapter on America, the Religious Right has found it especially hard to resist the lure of the notion of an evil world conspiracy. But it should be stressed that this paranoia is not confined to the right: it can be detected throughout the length and breadth of the New Age. Often there is no mention of an evil world order, but the suggestion of conspiracy hangs in the air; one senses it every time an author complains that his or her revolutionary ideas have been swept under the carpet by the scientific establishment. Indeed, it is becoming more noticeable all the time, as the New Age movement prepares to confront the millennium.

The New Age, like many of the theories it embraces, is constantly mutating. It has changed significantly during the 1990s. Those who believed in the late 1980s that a coherent body of New Age doctrine was emerging have been proved wrong. The ideas which once formed the core of the movement, such as the Age of Aquarius and the power of crystals, are still present; but they now have to fight for attention with a range of theories and gimmicks which increases literally every day, as new books arrive on those shelves of bookshops marked 'Mind, Body and Spirit'. But, paradoxically, as the volume of these publications increases, the number of people prepared to describe themselves as New Agers is shrinking.

It may be that in some respects the millennial hopes of the 1980s have already been disappointed. The failure of anything very dramatic to happen after the Harmonic Convergence seems to have weakened the notion of the New Age as a religion *per se*: its apocalyptic ideas have not lost their force, but there is less concern with building a broad-based movement and more with individual marketing exercises. On one level, at least, the New Age seems to be slowly dissolving into the cultic milieu, as the pure vision of the Age of Aquarius disappears behind a pile of books about UFOs, Nostradamus, crop circles and pyramids. This does not mean that the New Age is no longer influential. But it is not what the movement's original prophets had expected or hoped for.

On another level, though, New Age beliefs seem to be held with a new intensity as the year 2000 approaches. In virtually every case of apocalyptic disappointment throughout history, the non-appearance of a new world has led a minority of believers to intensify their hatred of the outside world. This could well be what lies behind the descent of David Icke and friends into the realms of neo-Nazi conspiracy theory; and it also may be a factor in two famously gruesome apocalyptic dramas of the 1990s, involving the Aum Shinrikyo sect in Japan and the Order of the Solar Temple in Switzerland and Canada.

We shall look at Aum in detail in the chapter on millennial belief in Japan. But we should note at this stage that, like the Solar Temple, it dredged the cultic milieu very thoroughly in search of lurid material for its theories. Moreover, in both cases the group's millennial expectations were marked by a degree of frustration and disappointment.

The Order of the Solar Temple, which was based in Francophone Switzerland and Canada, belonged to an occult tradition which has made little impression on the English-speaking world. This is the legend of the Knights Templar, a medieval military and religious order suppressed by the Catholic Church in the fourteenth century amid unproven allegations of witchcraft and homosexuality. In the late eighteenth and early nineteenth centuries, it became fashionable among free-masons and occultists to claim that the Templars had secretly survived, along with their occult secrets. For 200 years, various orders in Europe have based their ceremonies on a combination of these 'secrets' and the occult tradition known as Rosicrucianism, which boasts scientific and alchemical knowledge derived from the (probably fictional) medieval Order of the Rosy Cross. These neo-Templar orders, as they are known, tend to be small groups riven by endless schisms; for most of them, dressing up in fake-medieval robes is the highlight and even the purpose of their existence. The Order of the Solar Temple, which although founded in the 1980s boasted an elaborate neo-Templar lineage, attached great importance to robes and accessories: its initiates wore gaudy hand-sewn cloaks and wielded swords which (ignoring the presence of the manufacturer's label) they believed were a thousand years old.

In other respects, however, the Solar Temple was quite different from its competitors. Its chief theoretician, a charismatic young doctor named Luc Jouret, was fascinated and thrilled by the idea of approaching ecological disaster, which he described in language reminiscent of the Green movement. In a series of semi-public lectures during the 1980s, Jouret spoke in conventional New Age terms of the emergence of a new human archetype, the collapse of materialism and the unification of all world religions. This new dispensation was the Age of Aquarius, he revealed, which was about to begin after 2,000 years of darkness.[26] Interested observers were invited to join one of a number of Archedia Clubs, whose members were attempting to bring about the 'rehabilitation of the world' by changing their personal lives. In 1987 a visitor attending an Archedia outdoor midsummer festival in France reported 'a most convivial atmosphere', as around eighty adults and dozens of young children stood around a pole representing the world's axis. A fire was lit and everyone sang and danced around it; there was a supper of freshly picked organic vegetables.[27] One suspects Ms Ferguson would have felt thoroughly at home.

It was only later, and to a select few, that Jouret unveiled a darker vision. Those Archedia members who showed promise or, more importantly, who were prepared to hand over large sums of money, were introduced to the Order of the Solar Temple. They learned that the coming ecological crisis was the apocalypse of the Book of Revelation; the fire around which everyone had danced gaily would consume the world. But, as with all millenarian belief, there was another side to the coin. The apocalyptic fire would serve to purify the Order's elect, who were in fact the reincarnated Knights Templar. They would then begin a journey across space to the star Sirius, where they would become Christ-like solar beings.

In September 1994 the members of the Order of the Solar Temple lit the last great fire themselves. The drama began in Canada, with the ritual murder by stabbing of a young couple and their three-month-old son. Although the parents, Nikki and Antonio Dutoit, were members of the Order, they had disobeyed one of its leaders, Joseph Di Mambro, by naming their new son Emmanuel; Di Mambro, a sixty-nine-year-old crooked property developer, had insisted that this name should be borne only by his twelve-year-old daughter Emmanuelle, whom he described as a divine incarnation. The Dutoits' baby was declared to be none other than the Antichrist, and two members of the Order were despatched from Switzerland to Canada to kill the family. But, for reasons which are still not clear, this killing was more than a simple execution: it was a prelude to the deaths of the entire inner circle of the Order.

First, the two cult members who had cleaned up after the grisly stabbing of the Dutoits – the murderers had flown back to Europe – took relaxant drugs and set the timer on a petrol bomb which roasted them alive. Four hours later, fire broke out at a farmhouse 4,000 miles away in Chiery, Switzerland. Police arriving at the scene were surprised to discover that the building contained an underground chapel draped with crimson fabric. On the floor lay twenty-two bodies, arranged in a circle round an altar bearing a golden chalice; nineteen of them had been shot in the head, while the others were hooded with black plastic bags. Then, three hours after the Chiery fire, petrol bombs exploded in two ski chalets belonging to the Order in a village 100 miles away. The charred remains of twenty-five cult members were found inside, including those of Jouret and Di Mambro.[28]

It has not proved easy to uncover the real story of the Order of the Solar Temple. Many details have so far defied explanation. How, for example, did the leaders of this exotic cult manage to seduce so many prosperous, and frankly dull, middle-aged professionals? And what was the purpose of the suicide? On the latter point, perhaps the best clue is provided by the sense of anger and disappointment which permeates some of the documents left by the group. One of them, headed 'Transit to the Future', says that:

> although the hidden Hierarchy had planned a more peaceful transition to the future exalted state for the human beings and the earth, the work of dark forces and the persecution of apostates helped by some Governments have forced the Hierarchy to change its plans. The initiates who are evolved enough to understand the Plan will now voluntarily leave this world and reach the Absolute Dimension of the Truth, where they will continue their work, glorious and invisible. The members of the Temple who are not evolved enough will be helped to partake in the Christic fire and share in the benefits of the translation, although unconsciously. They are in fact helped to escape a fate of destruction, now awaiting the whole wicked world in a matter of months, if not weeks.[29]

Reading between the lines, it looks as if the leaders of the Order of the Solar Temple were so frustrated by their lack of success in bringing about the New Age promised by Jouret that they resorted to suicide and murder. If so, their behaviour was roughly in line with that of other millennial groups who have felt the need to bring on their own apocalypse. In such cases, the dividing lines between suicide and murder, expectation and disappointment, become hopelessly blurred in the eyes of believers. Even so, one can only marvel at the readiness of members of the Order – who were not, after all, confronted by vigorous persecution or a state of siege – to submit to the final ritual. It is not possible at this stage to offer an authoritative explanation for the tragedy; but it does illustrate, once again, the ability of disparate elements of the cultic milieu to join forces in new apocalyptic configurations. Between them, the Order of the Solar Temple, the Archedia Clubs and a range of other front organisations run by Jouret covered a vast swathe of New Age territory: astrology, Green issues, the occult, homeopathic medicine, science fiction and even, according to some reports, the far-right conspiracy theories embraced by David Icke. It is possible that, for a vulnerable individual, an interest in any one of these areas could represent an entrance point to the Order's highly charged apocalyptic theology. For the uncommitted observer, such a progression is hard to understand. But, if the Solar Temple episode teaches us anything, it is that the millenarian impulse is unpredictable. In December 1995, long after the media had lost interest in the subject, there were more mysterious deaths. The bodies of sixteen people, three of them children, were discovered in a forest near Grenoble. The bodies were arranged in a star formation; all the adults appear to have been members of the Order of the Solar Temple, bringing the overall tally of deaths to sixty-eight. At the time of writing, there is a theory that two of the dead, who, bizarrely, turned out to be local policemen, had shot the others before committing suicide. But it is unlikely that the mystery of these latest deaths will ever be solved.

The Solar Temple tragedy, together with those involving the

Branch Davidians and Aum Shinrikyo, has had the inevitable effect of highlighting violent manifestations of millenarian belief. In the cases of Aum and the Solar Temple, the violence was very clearly the responsibility of the religious group involved. And both these groups, as it happens, can unhesitatingly be labelled as New Age. They were wildly atypical of the movement as a whole, of course; but the fact remains that they derived much of their apocalypticism from those non-Christian components of the cultic milieu, such as astrology and the occult, which feature most prominently in the New Age. One could hardly ask for more dramatic evidence of the apocalyptic potential of seemingly innocuous material: Aum, for example, attached vast importance to breathing techniques and to the prophecies of Nostradamus, two staples of every New Age bookstore. But what about the millions of people who come into contact with 'alternative' material and feel no inclination to join doomsday sects? We have already noted that the New Age movement of the 1990s is more interested in marketing products – books, videos, seminars, correspondence courses – than in constructing a common theology; yet at the same time most of these products encourage a world-view which is unquestionably apocalyptic, and focussed very sharply on the final years of this millennium.

The most blatant examples of this are the books, films and even board games based on the writings of Michel de Nostradamus (1503–66), a Provençal doctor and mystic whose cryptic verses, or 'quatrains', purport to prophesy important events in the history of the world. Although no two books about Nostradamus agree on the details of his vision of the apocalypse, very few of them explicitly challenge the popular legend that the great seer foresaw the outbreak of Armageddon in the year 1999. What the quatrains actually say is that in 'the year 1999, seventh month, from the sky will come a great King of Terror, to bring back to life the great King of the Moguls, before and after Mars reigns'. Interpretations of this range from vague assertions that 1999 is the turning point in history to firm predictions of the End in July of that year. In contrast, very little is made of the inconvenient fact that Nostradamus himself described his work as 'comprised of prophecies from today to the year 3797': Jean de Fontbrune, a leading authority on the subject, produced a page of impenetrable arithmetic 'proving' that when Nostradamus wrote 3797 he really meant 1999. At any rate, the association of the Seer of Provence with impending disaster seems central to his popularity. Interestingly, one of the few Nostradamus books which has failed to sell in large quantities is a volume called *The Mask of Nostradamus*, by the American magician and psychic investigator James Randi. Not only does Randi expose the shameless distortions of the original quatrains by modern 'experts' in their attempts to make them predict events such as the defeat of Napoleon and the rise of Hitler; he also demonstrates that Nostradamus himself employed every trick in the book to make it appear that he had the power of prophecy. But it would appear that the book-buying public does not appreciate this sort of debunking: while it is presumably not seriously alarmed by suggestions that the world will end in 1999, there is a marked reluctance to accept that there is nothing in the prophecies at all.

The Nostradamus industry, as it has been called, feeds on an openness to suggestion and a willingness to toy with outlandish ideas which has been exploited many times before; one thinks of the best-selling God-is-a-spaceman books of the 1970s. But rarely, if ever, have mainstream publishers taken this market so seriously; and rarely have so many authors managed to intrude an apocalyptic sub-text into works of popular history and science. Consider, for example, a phenomenally successful book called *Fingerprints of the Gods* by the British author Graham Hancock, which went straight to the top of the non-fiction best-seller lists when it was published in 1995. Critical opinion of the book was sharply divided: it was described as 'one of the intellectual landmarks of the decade' by Colin Wilson in the *Literary Review* and as 'nearly 600 pages of witless occult droolings' by David Sexton in the *Guardian*. But it could not be ignored: the *Daily Mail* serialised it every day for a week, and it was the subject of endless radio and television discussions.

Hancock, a former East Africa editor of the *Economist*, believes that all the great monuments of the ancient world, including the Sphinx and the pyramids of Egypt and Central America, were built by a civilisation as advanced as our own which perished 15,000 years ago. This cataclysm happened when the crust of the earth suddenly slipped, burying great cities two miles beneath the South Pole. Before they died out, however, travellers from this civilisation of 'gods' were able to build pyramids in coded configurations which were intended to warn future generations that global disaster would strike again. For reasons that need not detain us, Hancock believes the most likely timing for this is 2012, the end of time in the Mayan calendar.[30] In choosing this date, he is in line with the most fashionable New Age thinkers, who seem mesmerised by an apocalypse which is still more than a decade in the future: another best-selling book of 1995, *The Mayan Prophecies* by Adrian Gilbert and Maurice Cotterell, also warns of terrible upheavals in 2012, though this time the culprit is a cycle of sun spots miraculously anticipated by the Maya.[31] But Hancock is too shrewd to overlook the little matter of the year 2000: he claims that on 5 May of that year Neptune, Uranus, Venus and Mercury will align with the earth on the other side of the sun, 'setting up a sort of cosmic tug-of-war'. This will give rise to 'profound gravitational effects', though Hancock leaves the details to the imagination.

Which is where, of course, the whole phenomenon of New Age history and science originated, and perhaps where it ought to stay. But we should not write it off on the ground that it is driven by marketing. The popularity of books on apocalyptic themes may well reflect a deeper crisis of spirituality in the West, a subject we shall return to later. And we should not underestimate the ability of marketed products to influence and perhaps initiate belief in the supernatural. The last few years have already witnessed an almost incredible demonstration of the ability of popular culture to inculcate quasi-religious beliefs in a section of the public. This is the phenomenon of UFO 'abduction experiences' recalled on the psychotherapist's couch, which has led some enthusiasts to claim that thousands or even millions of people have been abducted by aliens. It appears that in a huge number of cases, serious psychological problems such as Multiple Personality Disorder have been brought to the surface by attempts to revive these 'memories', much as they were in early modern Europe by the witchcraft scare. In the opinion of a growing number of experts, every single one of these abduction reports is ultimately attributable to a UFO craze that has been created and spread by science fiction, newspaper reports, television and the cinema.[32]

It would be foolish, therefore, to dismiss the emergence of a sudden passion for 'alternative science' and 'alternative history' as a meaningless fad. It is too early to measure the full significance of the conjunction of the approaching calendar shift and an increased public appetite for the theories of the cultic milieu. It is obviously not the case that buying a book like Hancock's commits the reader to belief in its predictions of total, universal and irreversible change in the condition of humanity. But people do not buy books which ride roughshod over historical and scientific tradition for no reason: they do so because, at some level, they share the author's lack of faith in the ability of science and history to describe the world in which they live. They find it more rewarding to contemplate apocalyptic change than to celebrate the complex and often slow transformations associated with intellectual orthodoxy. As G. K. Chesterton observed, when people cease to believe in something, they do not believe in nothing: they believe in anything. Whether this suggestible frame of mind has long-term consequences for society is another matter; but it does not point to an easy or uneventful transition from one calendar millennium to the next.

10

Seoul: The Apocalyptic City

In no place on earth is the Second Coming of Christ awaited with such desperate yearning as Seoul, South Korea. Every night the city skyline becomes a litter of red neon crosses, each of them representing a community of born-again Christians. Perhaps a million people in Seoul believe they live in an End-time which will dissolve into eternity soon after the 2,000th anniversary of the birth of Christ. But the crosses are not there to commemorate the earthly Jesus of Nazareth: they are runway lights to guide in the airborne Christ the King who, when the great predestined moment arrives, will appear on clouds of glory to inaugurate the Millennium.

On the face of it, Seoul at the end of the twentieth century is an even more unlikely breeding ground for apocalyptic fantasies than Florence at the end of the fifteenth. If it was hard to imagine the Antichrist skulking behind the columns and statues of the Renaissance, it requires a major imaginative leap to picture him against a backdrop of concrete flyovers and traffic jams. The South Korean capital, which fell to invading armies four times this century, is one of the world's most uncompromisingly modern cities. Japanese and North Korean assaults have almost entirely obliterated the visible symbols of Seoul's past, clearing the way for a random, sprawling development which bears so little resemblance to the old city that visitors returning after a couple of decades have to use the surrounding mountains to find their bearings. The glass skyscrapers in central Seoul are only slightly less imposing than those of Tokyo or Hong Kong, though even the newest of them have the shine taken off them by the abrasive wind which blows in from the Gobi Desert. Outside the centre, the miles of redbrick shops, garages and offices with obligatory neon signs strike a jaunty note: only on the outskirts of town, where row after row of identical numbered apartment blocks cast shadows over the lower slopes of the mountains, is there a sense of rootlessness.

Seoul has sailed through two decades of furious expansion in a spirit of unwavering optimism. Its 12 million inhabitants, more than half of whom were born in rural areas, tend to confront problems such as overcrowding and stifling air pollution with a good humour which only occasionally gives way to displays of the incendiary Korean temper. This is partly because South Koreans are traditionally willing to endure material discomfort until they make enough money to buy their way out of their neighbourhood. But in the case of the city's fundamentalist Christians, whose numbers have grown hugely since the first American missionaries appeared a century ago, this carefree approach reflects an order of priorities which strikes the liberal Westerner as bizarre and even slightly distasteful. Put bluntly, nothing outside the realm of the individual's family life matters very much, because Jesus Is Coming Soon.

The outside world first learned of the Korean fascination with the End in October 1992, when the approach and passing of an apocalyptic deadline produced the inevitable scenes of public humiliation and high comedy. The 20,000 members of a denomination called the Mission for the Coming Days (known as the Tami Church), based in Seoul but with followers all over the world, spent the afternoon of 28 October waiting for the Rapture. They had been promised that, before midnight, they would 'instantly be changed into holy bodies and raised to meet the Lord in the air'. Meanwhile, those 'lukewarm Christians' would remain on earth to perish in a Great Tribulation lasting seven years. Then, in 1999, Jesus would return to earth to initiate the Millennium. The reasoning behind the exact choice of date was complex and confusing, but the calculation of the year of the Rapture would have made perfect sense to a seventeenth-century Calvinist: the 7,000-year Great Week of human history would reach its sabbath in 1999, since there had been 4,000 years from Adam to Jesus, and, if the seven years of the Great Tribulation were subtracted, the Rapture must come in 1992. Some of the Tami faithful had already left their jobs in preparation; one pregnant woman reportedly had an abortion in case she was too heavy to float up. The excitement at the approach of the deadline, and disappointment at its passing, did not appear to be lessened by the fact that a month before the Rapture date the Church's pastor, Lee Jang Rim, was arrested on suspicion of pocketing Church funds and was found to be in possession of bonds which would not mature until 1995.[1]

The débâcle, and the wry amusement with which it was reported in a foreign press which had previously assumed that all Koreans were Buddhists, struck an exceptionally raw nerve among the country's Protestants. Evangelical pastors went to great lengths to distance themselves from the date-setting approach to eschatology, and to portray the Tami Church as a collection of isolated comic misfits. But they were protesting too much. More than 250 churches had flirted with the Tami predictions, and many evangelicals who rejected the deadline nevertheless felt humiliated by the episode, which held up the whole notion of End-time to the ridicule of unbelievers (and Westerners at that).

Apocalyptic belief is an indispensable element in Korean Protestantism. The urgency with which its clergy proclaim the Second Coming is a crucial factor in the phenomenal spread of born-again Christianity during the 1970s and 1980s, which saw the proportion of Christians in the population rise from 15 to 40 per cent. (South Korea's President during the early 1990s, Kim Young-sam, is a born-again Christian, as are around half of the country's army officers.) The most obvious manifestation of the apocalyptic strain in Korean Christianity are the preachers who haunt Seoul's parks and granite-lined under-passes, bellowing their message through hand-held megaphones at knots of giggling students and harassed salarymen. There are, of course, street-corner merchants of doom in all the world's major cities: what distinguishes the Korean variety is their extraordinary profusion, and the fact that they are recruiting for Churches which, on paper at least, belong to the Christian mainstream. (More than fifty denominations in Seoul call themselves Presbyterian, though a European or American Presbyterian would probably not wish to claim kinship with the more fiercely fundamentalist of them.) The first sight which greets visitors from the countryside arriving at Seoul railway station is often a procession of sash-wearing, born-again Christians weaving its way round the forecourt to the accompaniment of insistent, yet oddly melancholy, calls for repentence. At weekends, in particular, there is no escaping the proselytising of apocalyptic groups: foreign tourists who manage to slip past the ranting evangelists at the entrance to major sites are likely to have a tract thrust at them by the little old lady standing behind them in the queue for refreshments.

But the real target of the street evangelists are Koreans, especially those who are visibly among the ranks of the unredeemed. Buddhist monks and nuns are given a particularly hard time by the born-again. An American journalist living in Seoul will never forget the time he ventured into the underground at rush hour in the company of a Korean girlfriend who was spending a few months as a Buddhist nun. Suddenly they found themselves surrounded by a posse of women evangelists, recognisable by their uniform of drab polyester blouses and skirts. 'They bore down on my friend like a flock of angry birds, hurling biblical quotations at her,' he recalls. 'They looked as if they wanted to peck her to death. She told me it happens all the time.' The hostility which most evangelical churches feel towards non-Christian religions extends to many other Christian groups, and especially the Roman Catholic Church. It is fully reciprocated: this, after all, is a country in which Catholics and Protestants even use a different word for God. (They also attach different badges to the boots of their cars, though, being

Koreans, they drive in precisely the same breakneck fashion.) 'There is really no need for us to get on,' says a Catholic missionary. 'Both of us are doing so well in signing up recruits that we don't have to glance sideways. And, in any case, I honestly find the fundamentalist approach quite repugnant. The fact that it works so well doesn't impress me at all.'

Prayers at the Yoido Full Gospel Church begin with a sort of menacing hum, as 30,000 evangelical Christians close their eyes and begin to rock backwards and forwards in their seats. Within seconds the noise swells with a terrific crescendo, as if a goal has just been scored at a football match; but even this yelling is thrown into relief by a series of ear-splitting squawks from women in the congregation who are doing battle with their internal demons. Whole terraces of believers shudder simultaneously, and then resume their rhythmical rocking and chest-beating. Male stewards in white blazers patrol the aisles, occasionally leaning over to clutch the shoulders of a worshipper on the verge of collapse. Then the noise evaporates, as suddenly as a tropical squall, and women in blue and yellow uniforms shoot forward. They push collection boxes under the noses of the still-breathless faithful, and frown impatiently while the worshippers fumble for their purses. Down on the stage, an organ strikes up a sugary French voluntary and everyone rushes for the doors. The ladies' Wednesday afternoon prayer session is over for another week.

The Yoido Full Gospel Church, as the visitor is endlessly reminded, is recorded in the Guinness Book of Records as the world's largest church. Its registered membership stands at 700,000, though only a small proportion of these can fit into the cavernous redbrick auditorium, around the size of London's Festival Hall, which stands next to the National Assembly on the south side of the Han river. The church is conveniently sited for the 15 per cent of Korean members of parliament who belong to it; and it is also very close to the great Yoido Plaza, where at least once a year a million born-again Christians stand with outstretched arms to pray for the conversion of their country. The main speaker on these occasions is invariably Dr

David Yonggi Cho, pastor of the Full Gospel Church, who founded it as a tent ministry in 1958. It was Pastor Cho who devised the structure of home cell groups which, far more than any mass services, hold his vast edifice together. There are around 50,000 ten-member cells in Seoul, meeting once a week to read the bible, listen to a sermon and, most importantly, to pray.

To say that prayer lies at the heart of the Full Gospel phenomenon risks giving the wrong impression. For it is not the contemplative, structured prayer of liberal Western Christianity: it is a string of insistent, pleading requests. The reunification of North and South Korea is invariably high on the agenda, though this demand has something of a ritual quality compared to the shopping list of day-to-day material needs. It is these which lend the prayer sessions their anxious intensity: members of the congregation are asking for blessings – money, health, success in examinations, conversion of family members – which will be delivered only if their faith is strong enough.

The sixty-year-old Dr Cho is a bold and unapologetic exponent of 'health and wealth' Christianity, in which the believer's gaze is directed again and again to the words of St John's Gospel: 'If you abide in me, and my words abide in you, ask whatever you will, and it shall be done for you' (John 15: 7). The fortunes of Dr Cho's own Church are regarded as the ultimate proof of this text. It owns and uses the two high-rise office blocks immediately next to it, one of which has just been purchased at a cost of $40 million. Dr Cho describes this acquisition as 'a greater miracle than the loaves and the fishes'. Jesus came to him in a dream and told him to buy the building, he says: he responded by summoning the businessmen in his congregation and telling them that he would 'drive them out of my Church' if they did not come up with the money. A softly spoken, schoolmasterly figure, Cho summons up a becomingly shy smile when he lists his achievements, which he does incessantly. This is disconcerting until one realises that boasting is a Korean national pastime. Cho's lieutenant, a dapper Korean–American lawyer called Dr Dennis Kim, concedes that his boss has been criticised for stressing the material prosperity which attends rebirth in Jesus Christ. 'But who the hell cares?' he grins. 'If we honour God he blesses us. We have four billion dollars of real estate, *and it's all paid for.*'[2]

The 'health and wealth' message also enables Dr Cho to make a link between the spread of born-again Christianity and the South Korean economic miracle. The mid-1980s, when the economy grew at a dizzying rate of 12 per cent a year, were also years in which Pentecostalism made spectacular advances. The implication is that the more Koreans convert, the better the economy will fare. Dr Cho does not labour the point, however: his focus stays firmly on salvation for the individual and his family. Central to the appeal of his Church is the idea that conversion brings benefits for wives, husbands and children. These include short-term economic benefits, which if enough Koreans convert may translate into a golden era of national prosperity. But, although this is not spelt out at first, it can only be transitory: the new convert soon discovers that the Full Gospel Church does not promise a secure life extending far into the future. On the contrary, it offers families the far greater prize of ringside – and fireproof – seats from which they can safely witness the terrible, and imminent, death-throes of human civilisation.

The blandishments of health and wealth with which the Full Gospel Church attempts to seduce the unredeemed must be seen in the context of its belief that mankind is living in the Last Days. The sense of time running out underlies all its activities, including the publication of its national newspaper (circulation: 1 million), the 2,000 children's heart operations it has funded since 1983, and its missions to forty-eight countries. These are all part of a last great push for Christ before the faithful are raptured at the beginning of the Great Tribulation. To anyone familiar with the beliefs of the Tami Church, this has a familiar ring. The only significant difference between the End-time theology of the much derided Lee Jang Rim and that of Dr David Yonggi Cho, pastor of 'the greatest church in the history of Christianity', as it is sometimes called, is that Dr Cho does not plump for a particular date.

'He's not a great man for date-setting,' says Dr Dennis Kim.

'If we thought the world was about to end we would be dressed in our rapture clothes, not getting ready for further expansion.'[3] But this is disingenuous, to say the least. Dr Cho is in no doubt that the 2,000th anniversary of Christ's birth heralds the final human drama, that of the Antichrist. In his commentary on the Book of Daniel, Cho announces that the 2,000 years of the Gospel Age are about to end. He believes that the world has reached the age corresponding to the feet and toes made of mixed iron and clay of the statue in Daniel's dream, and that these toes are the ten nations of the European Community (which is precisely the conclusion reached by the Tami Church). 'Europe is slowly marching towards unity, and that unity will first be accomplished economically and politically,' says Cho. 'At a certain day and hour in our lifetime, I believe we will hear through the news media that the unity of ten nations of Europe has finally been achieved. Then the drama of the end-times will speed up dramatically.'[4] Cho also suggested a few years ago that during the 1990s the forces of Antichrist would try to replace the Anno Domini dating system, with the aim of concealing from the world the approach of the third Christian millennium.

Dr Cho's vision of the end of history is as bloodthirsty as any prophecy emanating from the American bible belt. In his exegesis, the emergence of Antichrist (whom he is sure is already alive, and may already have begun his career as a politician) will be followed by the Great Tribulation, at which point the whole Church will be swept up to heaven by the Holy Spirit. In the three and a half years that follow, more than half of the world's remaining population will die. A devastating war will ravage the world's cities, a third of the earth's vegetation will wither, and a new American or Russian nuclear weapon called a 'space bus' will plunge into the sea like a burning volcano, killing a third of all sea creatures.[5] All this happens before the battle of Armageddon, in which a Chinese army of 200 million men will meet the army of the Antichrist and do battle until the piles of bodies and weapons are as high as the mountains. But during this battle Jesus will descend: the remains of the two armies will unite to oppose him, but he will annihilate them, bringing the total number of humans slain in the End-times to 300 million. This leaves only the raptured Church, the Jews and a handful of Gentiles to enter the millennial kingdom, during which the earth is populated with saints 'who neither commit sin nor are afflicted by illness'. At the end of the thousand years, the rest of the dead come back to life. Unbelievers already languishing in hell are hauled out, judged again and cast into the lake of fire, while the redeemed process into the new Jerusalem.

Although he never attempts to predict the date of the Second Coming, and therefore makes no specific predictions for the year 2000, everything in Dr Cho's analysis points to a winding up of history in the first years of the twenty-first century. What is less clear is how this affects the daily lives of Church members. To what extent do they live in 'apocalyptic time', in which normal emotions are radically distorted by knowledge of the approaching End? We should bear in mind that membership of the Full Gospel Church is more akin to membership of a rigidly structured sect than of an ordinary church. The vast majority of its members are assigned to a home cell group, where Dr Cho's End-time theories are regularly expounded and updated to take account of changes in the international situation. The cells, each of which is assigned one of the Church's 700 full-time pastors, are also used to correct 'wrong thinking' among the faithful ('After you have seen it in action, you begin to understand the mentality which drives all those party cells in North Korea,' says one disillusioned ex-member). So there is no doubt that the 700,000 Church members are aware of the eschatological time-bomb which is ticking away beneath them. On the other hand, they do not know, and are actively discouraged from trying to work out, when it will explode.

It is this precisely calculated level of uncertainty regarding the timing of the Last Things which makes the Yoido Full Gospel Church one of the most disciplined and energetic apocalyptic groups in the world today. Its End-time beliefs are not extreme by Pentecostal standards: the notion that a 2,000-year dispensation is about to end in the bloody fulfilment of prophecy is held

by millions of American fundamentalists. What distinguishes
the Yoido Church is the intense level at which the belief is
sustained. This is achieved by constant reminders that mankind
is passing over the threshold into the End-time. 'Are the
members of your family all saved?' asks Dr Cho. 'Have you
brought your neighbours to the path of salvation?' Such
questions appeal strongly to the Korean sense of responsibility
to family and community; and they are underpinned by a sense
of accelerating time which, for reasons we shall examine later,
strikes a particular chord in South Korea. Yet there is no
apocalyptic deadline. The faithful are not required to manifest
the full range of histrionic behaviour associated with the classic
doomsday cult: they do not have to burn bridges by leaving
their jobs and selling their possessions. The Full Gospel Church
takes its followers closer to full-scale millenarianism than any
other Pentecostalist group, but, unlike the Tami Church, does
not cross the line.

The psychological effect of this balancing act is to lend a
manic quality to activities which in ordinary Churches are
pursued at a far more leisurely rate. The middle-aged house-
wives who make up around half of the Church membership are
expected to attend three or four long services every week,
including an all-night prayer vigil and a home-cell group
meeting. They might not be required to retreat to the mountain
to await the Rapture, but several times a month they take
themselves off to 'prayer mountain', a hilltop retreat outside the
city where, twenty-four hours a day, relays of preachers
harangue their audience from a podium in a 20,000-seat
auditorium. Women play a vital part in attracting recruits: they
are encouraged to keep notebooks in which they list every
family in their block of flats, which they are told is 'your corner
of the Great Commission'. A Church spokesman cheerfully
admits that these home evangelists call on their unsaved
neighbours at times of trouble. 'We might say "I hear someone
is very ill" and offer to pray for them for a week. If that person
recovers, we find the family usually initiates the offer to visit the
home-cell group. And if they come back three times, they will
usually declare for the Lord.'[6]

Church growth is in itself regarded as a powerful indication of the End-time: Dr Cho teaches that the Holy Spirit will descend 'like a mighty waterfall' before Jesus comes. The evangelisation drive cannot be allowed to falter at such a crucial juncture, either at a domestic or at an international level. The Yoido Full Gospel Church enthusiastically supports the aims of the AD2000 programme. Its worshippers often hear about the '10/40 latitude window' between West Africa and East Asia, in which three-quarters of the world's 'unsaved' people live. In Dr Cho's vision, Korea's destiny is to serve as a launch pad for the evangelisation of China (which is, however, still fated to play an inglorious role at Armageddon). Dr Dennis Kim hopes to be a part of this. 'Back in America, I own many companies. But one day, maybe soon, I will leave all that to become a missionary in China,' he says. But he is vague about when this will happen: he must wait for the opening up of China, an event which will form part of an End-time sequence whose timing depends on the divine will. Much the same applies to North Korea: the Full Gospel Church, in common with most large denominations, has drawn up a detailed blueprint for evangelisation which will be applied with military precision the moment the border comes down. Within days, the North will be saturated with South Korean evangelists attempting to win souls for Christ in advance of rival missionaries. In the meantime, the Full Gospel Church can do little more than watch, hawk-like, for signs of movement.

The vigilance with which the more educated Church members monitor television and the newspapers for the first stirrings of the Antichrist is striking evidence of their apocalyptic belief. Every new international dispute, and every initiative by an international body, is scrutinised with an eye to prophecy. One is reminded at times of the amateur exegetes of the middle ages, for whom terror at the collapse of Christendom in the East was tempered by a thrilling sense of seeing prophecy fulfilled. Yet, for Dr Cho's followers, political events do not have to be dramatic or immediately threatening to possess apocalyptic significance. A minor trade dispute between America and Japan is enough to set their pulses racing; as a junior pastor explains,

'There will be a trade war in the Last Days in which the Antichrist will seize control of world trade.'

Younger Church members seem to have a particularly secure belief in the approaching End. It is hard to imagine more unlikely prophets of doom than Eu-nah Chung and Mi-sup Shim, two sweet-natured girls in their early twenties. But according to Miss Chung, a secretary in a metal company, time is running out. 'We are facing the end of the world,' she says. 'These days even unbelievers think about it. Things are getting worse and worse, with earthquakes in Japan, starvation in Africa, flood in Europe and cholera in Bangladesh. And of course it is also a very wicked world.' Her friend Miss Shim, an English tutor, agrees. 'We are seeing the rise of nation against nation, people against people, that we read about in the bible. We feel that the 2,000th anniversary of the Lord's birth is a very important moment, though of course only God knows what is going to happen.' Both girls believe that Jesus will return in their lifetimes, but probably not before they marry and have children. 'We will get married if we meet the right person, because we cannot tell when the End will come,' says Miss Chung. 'After all, we are very young. The main thing is that we live earnestly. There is still so much work to do.'

The main thing is that we live earnestly. Although Eu-nah Chung was referring specifically to born-again Christians, she could have been speaking for most of her fellow countrymen. The conscious pursuit of excellence is second nature to South Koreans. The transformation from Third World backwater to the world's fastest-growing economy during the 1980s is regarded as a moral as well as an economic triumph. The sense of duty which underlies the drive for self-improvement is one of many elements in the national personality which has been successfully exploited by the purveyors of apocalyptic religion. In a society as target-orientated as South Korea, the evangelicals' relentless focus on growth makes perfect sense. And, by offering the prospect of material success as a reward for spiritual commitment, Churches such as Dr Cho's further sanctify the quest for financial security.

But why should this technique work so well in South Korea and not in the equally success-orientated society of Japan, where Christians still make up less than 1 per cent of the population? The answer lies in the difference between an island nation determined to resist spiritual contamination and a continental people with a history of successive invasions. Korea's fractured history has rendered it particularly vulnerable to the advances of American missionaries. Until well into the nineteenth century, the country was all but invisible to the rest of the world. Known as the Hermit Kingdom, it looked to China for protection and spurned all contact with the West. In the late nineteenth century, it fell apart as a result of infighting and became a helpless pawn in the struggle between China and Japan. In 1910 the Japanese formally annexed the country. By this stage, the first missionaries were on the scene. Mostly fundamentalists, they made crafty use of the principle that contemporary events were re-enactments of biblical episodes. It was common practice for missionaries to tell their audiences that the Korean independence leaders were analogous to Moses, the Korean people to the Israelites and the Japanese (who ruled the country until 1945) to the Egyptians. In this way Christianity could reinforce the sometimes fragile Korean sense of national identity, whereas in Japan it was mostly seen as a purely foreign influence. In the aftermath of the Second World War, of course, this contrast became even more marked. To the Japanese, Christianity was the religion of a victorious enemy, whereas for South Korea it was a faith associated with liberation from both Japanese imperialism and Communism.

But the question remains: why should Protestant fundamentalism, with its apocalyptic time-frame, make significantly greater inroads into Korea than other varieties of Christianity? Its espousal of a 'health and wealth' gospel is only part of the explanation. An equally significant factor is the compatibility of fundamentalism and folk shamanism. Although not organised or codified in scripture, shamanism has a better claim to being the Korean national religion than either Buddhism or Confucianism. It is based on the notion of constant interaction between the real and the spirit world, which are connected through intermediaries, usually female, called *mudang*. Shamanism sets great store by literal belief in evil spirits and demons, as does fundamentalist Christianity. This point was not lost on evangelical translators of the bible, who were careful to choose Korean words which had a specific meaning in folk cosmology. Thus 'unclean spirit' became *sagwi*, the shamanistic 'tramp-spirit' who, having been evicted from his former abode, is condemned to wander the earth. There is also a curious overlap between fundamentalism and shamanism in the prominence both ascribe to dreams. When Dr David Yonggi Cho preaches, he returns frequently to this theme. 'I am a strange person who is given to visions and dreams,' he says, in a tone which suggests that this is his most impressive credential. And so it may well be, in a country where people of all religious persuasions turn their dreams over and over in their minds, often taking momentous decisions on the basis of them, and where one of the first duties of the priest or minister is to interpret the dreams and visions of the faithful.

In the months leading up to October 1992, the Mission for the Coming Days circulated a long and detailed description of the visions of its supporters, many of them Koreans living abroad. It is a curiously powerful document, in which the Tami predictions are reinforced by every sort of apparition. Although some testimonies are obviously confected, others have a hallucinatory quality which brings to mind the reveries of medieval prophets: 'Mrs Hae Sook Chung, a Sunday school teacher from Taegoo, Korea, dreamed one day that the sun and the stars were dyed red, and the stars moved around and at last they fell to the ground. And great volcanoes erupted and all the trees and grasses in sight were burned down, and the whole world turned to ashes and the rivers were frozen and the ashes fell on the ices and everything looked desolate. And at that time she heard a voice, "1992, 1992".' But for some reason it is the cumulative effect of dozens of commonplace visions which makes the greatest impression. A woman dentist sees the numbers 10/28/92 while she is playing golf on a Sunday, after which she 'is no longer the same person as before'. Another woman bends over to wash her face and spots the fateful numbers in the bathroom sink. A young Korean driving on the freeway in California is told the date of Christ's return by that staple of the urban myth, the vanishing hithchiker.[7]

Most Korean commentators concede that the Mission for the Coming Days was merely an extreme manifestation of a wider impulse in South Korean society; and one, furthermore, which is not confined to Christian fundamentalist groups. There is a school of thought which argues that apocalypticism is a consequence of the dysfunctional society produced by the combination of political repression – South Korea was a virtual dictatorship until the 1980s – and unfettered growth. At a time when political debate was heavily restricted, all manner of stresses and strains were transmuted to the safer religious sphere. Professor Yee-Heum Yoon, head of religious studies at Seoul National University, believes that apocalypticism meets a psychological need for what he calls 'a sudden opening' arising from Korea's turbulent history.

'Throughout one and a half centuries of constant turmoil, people have yearned for a dramatic solution,' he says. 'And the only pattern which fits is an eschatological one, offering a fantastic escape from present suffering.'[8] Yoon points to the millennial strain in the 200 or so Korean religions, including the Unification Church (the Moonies), which have emerged since the 1890s. Most of these envisage a heaven on earth centred on Korea which will be sustained by a miraculous fusion of Western technology and Eastern philosophy, an idea which is also typical of Japanese new religions. Often, these religions build on pre-Christian (that is, pre-nineteenth-century) apocalyptic prophecies of a Korean golden age. Ch'ondogyo, a syncretist movement of half a million members founded in the late nineteenth century, reworks an ancient tradition that the centre of the new paradise will be Mount Kyerong. 'In this new world there will be no cold or hot weather, no poor harvest, no flood, no typhoon and no diseases,' it proclaims. 'Man will live as long as he wants at the maximum, till 500 years at medium and till 300 years of age at the minimum . . . There will be no need for money and all transactions will be by barter. The international language will be Korean and its alphabet. At Mt.

Kyerong there will be built a palace of precious stones and a bank of all nations.' But the most important detail is left until last: 'In this new world, there will be no tax.'[9] As Yoon sees it, there is little to choose between this and the ethos of the fundamentalist Christian groups. 'The point is that apocalyptic groups do not care about Korean society or social justice,' he says. 'Their only concern is with divine providence and with the religious experience of the individual. Apocalyptic eschatology always yearns for a new age and society, but it is one which is directly related to the self – to *our* Church or *our* ethnic group, which will form the basis of the next heavenly kingdom.'

The Professor clearly does not approve of this self-centred approach, on the part either of the new religious movements or of Churches such as Dr Cho's, which he feels embrace 'a form of Christianity from which central Christian tenets are missing'. But can one really blame South Koreans for embracing religious philosophies which seek to perpetuate the self by offering salvation for the individual, his family or the Korean ethnic group as a whole? There are many components to apocalyptic belief in the country, but if one had to come up with a single factor which accounts for its spread it would have to be the constant threat to the Koreans' individual and collective sense of identity in the past fifty years. The division of Korea at the 38th parallel after the Second World War has had a far more traumatic effect on the national psyche than centuries of occupation by foreign powers. The stress of artificial division is felt almost as acutely as it was forty years ago. The slow death of the North Korean economy during a period of spectacular growth in the South has done little to defuse the military threat from the North. The garish billboards on the mountains around Seoul serve a double purpose: although ostensibly advertisements for the high-quality consumer goods which have found their way into the most ramshackle South Korean homes since the 1980s, their primary function is to serve as screens for rockets and radar equipment pointing north. As recently as the spring of 1993, during the crisis over the North's decision to quit the Nuclear Non-Proliferation Treaty, the Pyongyang regime warned that 'all-out war' with the South could break out at any moment. The crisis passed, and Kim Il-Sung died soon afterwards; but continuing uncertainty over the succession, together with fears that the North Korean state might suddenly collapse and leave South Korea to pick up the pieces, means that nerves in the South are stretched to breaking point.

This tense situation works to the advantage of fundamentalist churches, as Dr Cho's assistant for foreign affairs, Mrs Lydia Swaine, candidly admits. 'The threat of war always prepares the heart for Jesus. It is a conditioning process for the gospel,' she says.[10] There is surely something more complicated at work here than a simple fear of death. In a city which the dying Kim Il-Sung promised to reduce to 'a sea of fire', there is no denying the potency of a theology which envisages a nuclear strike more terrifying than anything threatened by North Korea: David Yonggi Cho uses the phrase 'sea of flames' to describe the inferno which will consume a third of the world before Armageddon. Part of the success of the Full Gospel Church undoubtedly lies in its ability to conjure up nightmarish visions for an audience which is unusually susceptible to fear of nuclear war – and then to render them as harmless as a horror movie by reminding the faithful that they will have been raptured by the time the first button is pressed.

No less important, however, is the ability of apocalyptic groups to address the sense of disorientation which characterises daily life in South Korea. Behind the freakish economic growth lies a sudden and large-scale uprooting of the rural population which has had traumatic consequences for a society obsessed with familial roots. The scale of the problem is painfully evident every New Year: around 22 million Koreans take to the roads on a wistful pilgrimage to their former home villages, leaving Seoul 'looking like a scene from *The Day After*', in the revealing phrase of one resident. The traditional structure of the extended family, already undermined by the move to the cities, is rapidly receding into the folk memory now that government disincentives to have more than two children are taking effect. The wives of salarymen, in particular, suffer acute feelings of boredom and isolation in their gleaming new apartments; and in these circumstances the evangelist's knock on the door often represents a welcome diversion. Ultimately, what is on offer from apocalyptic groups is a new and highly cohesive extended family in return for unquestioning spiritual commitment: the Yoido Full Gospel Church even assumes responsibility for elderly relatives at its old people's village, the largest such facility in Asia.

As for those of the faithful in full-time employment, there is a subtle correlation between the pace of life in South Korea and the contours of apocalyptic eschatology. The constant setting of targets should be seen in the context of a national preoccupation with speed. 'We built as much in twenty years as other countries did in a hundred,' says a retired politician. 'Quick, quick, quick, that is Korea.' But it is not only speed that matters: for decades, South Koreans have aimed at constant acceleration. Indeed, so entrenched is belief in the national ability to break records year after year that many South Koreans still dream that their country (GDP per head: $8,500) will overtake Japan ($37,500) by the end of the century. Obviously, no one involved in running the economy thinks along these lines; but one does not have to go much below the level of senior management to find the belief in economic triumph over Japan *by the end of the century* held with religious fervour.

It is no accident that the middle-ranking executives or factory managers who hold most firmly to this belief are far more likely to be fundamentalist Protestants than their social superiors or inferiors. These are people who, perhaps more than any other section of the population, worked themselves to the point of physical collapse during the 1970s and 1980s to bring about the leap from poverty to affluence in one generation. For them, the year 2000 is the moment at which their sacrifices will bear fruit in the form of an irreversible shift of economic power from the West, and Japan, to the Korean peninsula. (As we shall see, very similar attitudes prevail in Japan, where the end of the century is seen as coinciding with the triumph of the countries of the Pacific Rim.) What could be more natural, then, than the adoption of religious beliefs in which the transfer of economic power to Korea is matched by an equivalent move of the Holy

Spirit? Interestingly, Dr Cho has a theory of history not unlike that of Hegel, who envisaged the spirit of civilisation moving gradually westwards around the globe. Cho thinks of history in terms of a circumnavigation of the globe by the Holy Spirit, which moved from the Middle East in biblical times to Rome, then to Protestant Northern Europe, then to America. Now it is moving to Asia, bringing the Great Year to its conclusion by closing the circle.

The danger, though, is that Dr Cho and his fellow fundamentalist leaders are creating a mood of breathless expectation which will be impossible to sustain. For years, the unspoken assumption of Korean Pentecostal theology has been that the End-time Church is being swept towards the mysterious year 2000 by a tide of signs and wonders, and that the motion will accelerate. This vision closely resembles the way many Koreans thought about the economy – and it is proving similarly unrealistic. In the past few years, the rate of Church growth has slowed significantly along with that of the economy, and perhaps for the same underlying reason: namely, that the younger generation of Koreans is more attracted by the lifestyle of its laid-back Western and Japanese counterparts than by that of their hard-working parents.

Yet in many respects the outlook for South Korea has never been brighter. A recent survey of South Korea by the *Economist* newspaper concluded that the country 'is at that glorious stage of development when it is brimming with ideas but has not yet become complacent'.[11] The democratically elected government is reversing many of the authoritarian policies of previous decades. The ethos of rapid growth through discipline and sacrifice is being replaced by a long-overdue emphasis on deregulation and foreign investment. The key word in government circles is 'globalisation', a concept which one might expect fundamentalist Christians to oppose, detecting in it sinister overtones of the Antichrist. On the contrary: Dr Cho's Church is all in favour of globalisation, which it correctly assumes will make it easier to run foreign missionary programmes. Senior Church officials talk disparagingly about the traditions of the Hermit Kingdom and speak with great enthusiasm of South Korea's forthcoming integration into the world economy.

Indeed, one of the most unexpected, and puzzling, features of Christian apocalyptic belief in South Korea is its faith in the future. Although at times the fundamentalist Churches seem positively thrilled by the prospect of Armageddon, at other times they exude a spirit of optimism which transcends the smugness of the Elect. They can be shockingly manipulative, preying on financial insecurity and fear of nuclear holocaust; but they are also quick-thinking and adaptable. It is hard to escape the conclusion that in addition to reflecting the dynamism of South Korea they also contribute to it. The Full Gospel Church, in particular, is a formidable piece of human engineering: its End-time theology and cell-like structure combine to produce a degree of commitment which inevitably spills over into the secular life of the believer. For many years this process has been facilitated by the approach of the year 2000, which has created a degree of excitement about the Second Coming perhaps unmatched in any other country. But Dr Cho and his colleagues know exactly how to harness and redirect this enthusiasm, and they have already drawn up plans for the future which extend well beyond the millennial anniversary. In theory, of course, they long for the End, when they will be plucked into the air to watch their valuable real estate disappear in the fires of Armageddon – but, in the words of St Augustine, not yet.

11

'A Doom Is Nearing the Land of the Rising Sun'

On the evening of 27 June 1994, Yoshiyuki Kouno, a salesman living in the town of Matsumoto, Japan, heard a suspicious noise outside his front door. On opening it, he was confronted by the sight of his two dogs, a setter bitch and her puppy, lying on the ground, shaken by convulsions and foaming at the mouth. Then they died. Rushing back inside the house, Kouno found his wife on the living-room floor, her body racked by violent spasms. He ran to phone the ambulance, and then found himself losing consciousness as his vision broke into brightly coloured fragments. Inside the ambulance he vomited uncontrollably. 'We ate Thai rice pilaf for dinner,' he managed to splutter to the medics; but the rice was not the culprit. The truth was that clouds of sarin, a poison gas many times deadlier than cyanide, were floating through the narrow alleyways of Matsumoto. The gas hung close to the ground, just as it was intended to by the Nazi scientists who developed it during the Second World War: though never used at the time, it was designed specifically to wipe out huge numbers of allied troops on the battlefield. As Kouno made his telephone call, seven of his neighbours were dying in agony.

The next morning, the streets of Matsumoto were littered

with the bodies of dogs, cats and birds. The Japanese police, public and media were shocked and completely mystified. At first, police detained Kouno, suspecting that he had inadvertently produced sarin while making a homemade herbicide in his back garden; but it soon became clear that the attack was premeditated, and that Kouno could not have had access to the necessary chemicals. There was furious speculation about international terrorists and extremists of the left and right. One wild theory suggested that Japan's wartime biological warfare unit, which killed over 3,000 people in experiments in Manchuria, had somehow come back to life. Three months after the attack, newspapers reported that the authorities still had no idea who created the gas, how they did it, or for what purpose.

It was not until the end of the year that the authorities began to take seriously one of the more colourful theories about the poisoning: that it was the work of an 'Armageddon cult' named Aum Shinrikyo which had bought land near Matsumoto several years earlier. Aum, whose doctrines were a mixture of Buddhism and yoga heavily flavoured with Western apocalypticism, claimed to have attracted tens of thousands of followers since its foundation in 1987. In a country in which hundreds of new religious movements are created every year, this was not in itself unusual; but even by Japanese standards Aum followers were exotic, attaching wires to their heads which were supposed to synchronise their brainwaves with those of the sect's founder, a bearded, half-blind guru called Shoko Asahara. Furthermore, unlike most new religious movements, Aum had acquired a genuinely sinister reputation. For one thing, it was suspiciously wealthy. Asahara had built a small business empire of computer shops, noodle restaurants and fitness clubs, on the back of a law granting protection and tax breaks to religious corporations. But it was rumoured that much of the money had been extorted from followers. Aum was widely suspected of being behind the disappearance in 1989 of a civil rights lawyer, his wife and their baby son; the lawyer, Tsutsumi Sakamoto, had represented around twenty former Aum followers, including one who had been tricked into paying 1 million yen (around £6,500) for a vial of Asahara's blood. Like many controversial new religions, Aum was both the object and the initiator of a great deal of legal action. At the time of the Matsumoto incident, it was being sued by a landowner who claimed that it had bought a site from him under false pretences. The verdict was expected in June 1994, but was postponed because the three presiding judges were too ill to attend. On 27 June, it turned out, they had been staying in a dormitory less than 100 metres from where the sarin emission occurred. Were they the real targets of the attack?

On 1 January 1995, the Japanese newspaper *Yomiuri* reported that traces of a phosphorous compound that could have been produced by sarin had been found in Kamikuishiki, a village in the shadow of Mount Fuji which for the past four years had been home to Aum Shinrikyo. More than a thousand members were rumoured to live in and around a ramshackle compound of factory-style buildings which Aum had built there despite anguished opposition from local people. The newspaper, wary of Aum's trigger-happy legal department, did not even mention the sect; but by this stage it did not need to. The article jogged villagers' memories of acrid smells emanating from the cult's compound, of sudden attacks of nausea when passing the area, and of Aum followers in their strange headgear lying apparently senseless by the roadside.

If the Japanese media was generally reluctant to point the finger at Aum, at least one Western publication threw caution to the winds. *Esquire* magazine published an astonishingly bold and, as it turned out, prescient article by Andrew Marshall headed 'The Nazi nerve gas mystery' which stated that 'if anyone can solve the sarin mystery, His Holiness the Master Shoko Asahara can'.[1] After all, it pointed out, he had already answered some of the universe's most vexing questions, such as where UFOs come from (answer: the Heaven of Degenerated Consciousness, of which Asahara had been king 'a number of times') and who designed the pyramids (Asahara again, in his previous incarnation as the Egyptian architect Imhotep). Marshall had been to Kamikuishiki to talk to disgruntled local people. They told him that Aum had littered the village with empty chemical containers; that it played endless mantras through loudspeakers late at night; and that on one occasion 300 sect members had marched down the street, looking like the Ku Klux Klan and 'scaring the hell out of the children'. After learning about the possible sarin outbreak in the village, local people were anxiously trying to work out what Aum was planning. One local resident directed Marshall's attention to a windowless white structure further up the slope of Mount Fuji. 'That's where we reckon the mass suicide will take place in 1997,' he said. 'Everyone's really worried that Kamikuishiki will turn into another Waco.'

These words had acquired a terrible new resonance by the time the *Esquire* article appeared on the newsstands. Shortly after eight o'clock on the morning of Monday, 20 March, rush-hour travellers on the Tokyo subway started coughing, choking and vomiting. It was immediately obvious that strong-smelling gas was leaking from punctured plastic bags wrapped in newspapers, but subway workers who tried to remove them collapsed one after another. At no fewer than sixteen stations, desperately ill commuters had to be loaded on to stretchers; by the end of the day, 5,500 people had been treated in hospital and twelve eventually died. Chemical warfare experts spent days searching the trains, tunnels and stations; they concluded that whoever had released the gas had intended train-loads of dying commuters to converge simultaneously on Kasumigaseki station, which lies underneath a network of government agencies in the heart of Tokyo. So this was not a random act of terrorism: it was a carefully planned attack on the Japanese state itself.

Although only a handful of people died, the gas attack frightened Japan far more than the Kobe earthquake a couple of months earlier, in which 6,000 people were killed. The nightmarish sight of police in gas masks combing the subway was like a glimpse of the final crisis of civilisation: a postmodern Armageddon in which the familiar spectre of a nuclear blast had been replaced by invisible agents of destruction which creep up without warning. To the Japanese media and public, it made sense that the attack should be the work of a doomsday cult; and, given the likely connection between the

Kamikuishiki and Matsumoto sarin outbreaks, Aum Shinrikyo was the obvious culprit. Writings of Asahara were produced which predicted the imminent breakdown of Japanese society and its destruction in a nuclear war with America. Lists of Aum members were published which showed an alarming preponderance of highly educated graduates, some of them with specialist knowledge in biochemistry and nuclear physics. It was revealed that Kyle Olson, vice-president of America's Chemical and Biological Arms Control Institute, who had studied the Matsumoto incident and suspected that Aum was behind it, warned the authorities at the time that it could be a prelude to a major terrorist attack in Tokyo: indeed, he was quoted to this effect in the *Esquire* article. But this evidence that the attack could have been prevented served only to increase public rage against Aum Shinrikyo.

Within the week, Japanese police had carried out raids on twenty-five Aum centres throughout Japan. These raids had, in fact, been planned before the subway attack as part of an investigation into the disappearance of a prominent Aum critic, Tokyo notary Kiyoshi Kariya, and there were suggestions later that advance warning of them had actually precipitated the gas incident. At any rate, the purpose of the raids had inevitably changed: the aim was now to find evidence that Aum had produced the sarin, and police did not have far to look. Investigators carrying canaries to detect toxic gas confiscated truckloads of more than 400 types of chemicals from different sites, including forty bottles of solvent that could be used to make sarin. These were found in the Kamikuishiki headquarters, which turned out to be every bit as bizarre a place as local people had suspected. A crude sculpture of Buddha overlooked a makeshift laboratory full of huge vats of foul-smelling chemicals. Members of the sect lived in damp, shoddy dormitories, and at the time of the raid several of them were comatose; tests showed traces of dangerous drugs including pentobarbital, an anaesthetic no longer used by doctors because it can cause mental disorders, convulsions and even death. There was, however, no sign of Asahara, who issued a series of press releases denying any involvement in the subway attack. 'We are

Buddhists!' he said. 'We do not kill living beings – even insects.'
While admitting that large quantities of chemicals had been
found, Asahara insisted that they were used for industry,
housing, art and medicine. As for sarin, far from producing it,
his own community had been poisoned by it: together with
several other noxious substances, it had been sprayed over them
by US Air Force jets. 'Although antibiotics are helping to
sustain our lives, we are in a very critical condition,' said
Asahara. 'For this reason I appeared in public only a few times
after May 1994.'[2] And now he had vanished. It took another
police raid on Kamikuishiki on 16 May to uncover his hiding
place: a secret chamber, little bigger than a coffin, sandwiched
between two floors. The portly guru was carried out, dressed in
a purple robe (like the Roman emperors, he reserved this colour
for himself), and was served with an arrest warrant for murder
and attempted murder.

In the spring and summer of 1995, public fury over Aum
Shinrikyo reached such levels that a few commentators found
themselves wondering whether the sect was not being made to
bear responsibility for crimes it had not committed. Amid
continuing confusion over how and why the sarin had been
manufactured, the British *Sunday Times* magazine ran a piece
by James Dalrymple attacking what it called 'almost hilarious'
stories in the Western press, and in particular reports of a 'Fu
Manchu-style plot' by Aum to overthrow the Japanese government with nerve gas and weapons supplied by the Russian
mafia. The piece also pooh-poohed reports that Aum had tested
sarin on sheep in the Australian outback; Asahara, it claimed,
was 'more interested in noodles than sarin gas'.[3] A few
academics specialising in new religious movements sympathised
with this view: they suspected that, as in the case of Waco two
years earlier, anti-cult spokesmen were determined to make
Aum Shinrikyo appear more malevolent and dangerous than it
really was.

Yet the truth, as it emerged from the confessions of members
during late 1995, was that Aum had indeed planned to wage
war on society at large, using any weapons it could get its hands
on. The Fu Manchu-style plot was not an invention of Western

journalists. Aum almost certainly intended to use its foothold in Russia (where it claimed 30,000 adherents, three times the number in Japan) to secure nuclear weapons, and had successfully infiltrated the Kurchatov Institute, a leading Russian nuclear physics laboratory. The former Soviet Union figured prominently in the group's plans: it had already bought a Mil-17 helicopter, was making enquiries about a second-hand Russian tank, and was organising 'military training tours' in Russia for its followers. There seemed no limit to Aum's resourcefulness: by the time the trial of Asahara and his lieutenants finally began in 1996, there was evidence that it was developing biological weapons, trying to secure uranium, assembling guns and rifles, manufacturing LSD and using truth serum on its followers. Far from representing the climax of its criminal activities, it seemed that the Tokyo gas attack had been intended as the opening shot in a terrorist war. Even after most of its leaders had been arrested, Aum nearly succeeded in perpetrating an even more spectacular outrage. On 5 May 1995, in the middle of Japan's Golden Week holidays, lethal chemicals were discovered in two vinyl bags left side by side in a public lavatory in Tokyo's Shinjuku station. One contained sodium cyanide, the other diluted sulphuric acid. When found by a passer-by, the first bag was on fire. Had the flames spread to the other bag and the two chemicals mixed, enough hydrocyanic gas would have been unleashed to kill an estimated 10,000 people.[4] Aum Shinrikyo, it appeared, had no compunction at all about murdering people: it had developed a theology of death in which the act of taking life could earn spiritual grace for both killer and victim. No one knows exactly how many Aum followers died as a result of drug experiments or executions; some authorities believe that more than a dozen bodies were burned in the sect's microwave ovens.

Japan has not found it easy to come to terms with Aum Shinrikyo. Intellectuals and media analysts have written hundreds of articles and books attempting to explain why such a violent group, run by an almost ludicrously sinister guru, should have attracted up to 10,000 Japanese followers, most of them in their twenties and thirties and many with university degrees. The focus of most of these articles has been on the stress caused by Japan's mercilessly judgemental education system, and by the freakish economic boom of the 1980s: the consensus is that the combination of the two placed intolerable pressure on young people who did not measure up to expectations, and induced feelings of disgust in bright students who did not subscribe to the materialistic ethos of the 'bubble economy'.

These are important points we will return to later; but they do not explain why Aum Shinrikyo attempted to slaughter thousands of early-morning commuters. As far as one school of thought was concerned, Asahara was simply a psychopath who brainwashed his followers; it was pointless to search for method or logic in his actions. For other commentators, mere mention of the fact that Aum was a 'doomsday sect' was explanation enough: the implication was that people who are crazy enough to believe that nuclear war is about to break out between America and Japan, as Aum often suggested, have lost touch with reality so totally that they are capable of anything. But this still left unanswered the question of how Aum Shinrikyo became a doomsday sect in the first place. Originally a peace-loving and idealistic Buddhist yoga circle, it had been transformed within the space of a decade into an organisation of murderous fanatics dedicated to spreading human suffering through mass poisoning and nuclear blackmail. The answer presumably lay in the way Aum's theology had changed; but in the confused atmosphere of 1995 most Japanese were only too happy to put this question to the back of their minds and concentrate on the more urgent business of bringing Asahara and his followers to justice.

Any attempt to analyse Aum Shinrikyo's theology requires the skills of a detective. Its official statements of belief are unreliable guides, since their chief function was to win recruits or to polish Aum's media image: from the very beginning, Asahara set great store by the oxygen of publicity and was always issuing self-congratulatory press releases. Lying and dissimulation were part of the fabric of life in the group's communes, which may help explain why no two ex-members seem able to agree on exactly what they were taught. Even so, it is now more or less possible to chart the shifts in theology which led Aum in the direction of apocalyptic violence.

This was, of course, a path followed by millenarian believers many times before. But Aum moved down it with astonishing speed and determination, and ended up in territory rarely, if ever, explored by a purely religious movement. Instead of believing passively in the imminent end of civilisation, Asahara dreamed of actually bringing it about; and unlike, say, the Bohemian Adamites or the Anabaptists of Münster, who entertained similar fantasies, he had access to weapons of mass destruction. We should not underestimate the threat posed by Aum Shinrikyo: given a few more months to perfect its production of sarin and botulism – which according to some ex-members it intended to spray on the population from helicopters – it could have precipitated the worst civil defence crisis ever experienced by a developed nation. It is true that, at the time of writing, no document has been produced which explicitly links Asahara with the Tokyo subway attack or with plans to acquire nuclear and biological weapons; but then nor is there any documentary evidence to link Adolf Hitler with the Holocaust. People who conceive such plans are usually careful not to commit them to paper.

The comparison between Asahara and Hitler holds up surprisingly well. We should keep in mind Norman Cohn's theory about the atrocities associated with twentieth-century totalitarianism: that they were the product of a millenarian mind-set 'in which one can actually feel it is a *good thing* to shove small children into ovens or to send millions of people to starve and freeze to death'. The same applies to releasing poison gas on the underground: it is the act of someone for whom accepted notions of good and evil have been twisted and inverted by apocalyptic faith. But the similarities between Asahara and Hitler are not confined to the structure of their belief systems. Comparing their early lives, one is struck by the way in which the development of these beliefs was informed by the experience of humiliation and disappointment. Admittedly,

Aum's ideology, unlike Hitler's, was not always malevolent; it gradually took on sinister aspects. But even as a child Asahara exhibited megalomaniac tendencies, and from the moment of Aum Shinrikyo's foundation exercised a degree of control over his followers unusual even in new religious movements. His leadership was reinforced by a bureaucracy which parodied the structure of a government, complete with ministries and spokesmen; in this respect Aum was closer to the Nazi party of the 1930s than to most 'cults'.

Shoko Asahara was born in 1955 as Chizuo Matsumoto, the fourth son of a weaver of tatami mats on the southern Japanese island of Kyushu. Half blind as a result of glaucoma, he was educated at special schools where his teachers remember him as a 'total fantasist' with a gift for storytelling. As a teenager he was fascinated by the mysteries of Chinese medicine and at the age of fifteen was already wearing the white robes of a guru. But he had not abandoned conventional ambitions; after leaving school he sat the entrance exams to Tokyo University, which roughly corresponds to Oxford and Cambridge in terms of prestige and easily outclasses them in its monopoly of the leaders of government and industry. His failure in the examination was, by his own admission, a terrible humiliation – but also a turning point. 'For the first time I stopped and thought, "What am I living for? What must I do to overcome this sense of emptiness?" ' he wrote in 1986. 'The desire to seek after the ultimate, the unchanging, awoke within me, and I began groping for an answer. That meant that I had to discard everything.'[5] Asahara started a business in Chinese herbal medicines and joined Agonshu, a new religious movement which teaches that the key to life is the removal of bad karma through esoteric Buddhism and yoga. Many of Agonshu's ideas were to surface in Aum: an emphasis on meditation and bodily discipline; a belief that science can produce psychic powers; and the importance of magical rituals in ridding the body of bad karma.

In 1984 Asahara left Agonshu and founded his own yoga circle; this was when he adopted the name Shoko Asahara, using Chinese characters that add up to a lucky number. In the following year he took on the mantle of a great charismatic leader. According to his own account, the moment of transformation occurred while he was performing the role of a homeless monk and prostrating himself on a Japanese beach. Suddenly the figure of Shiva, the Hindu god of opposites – creation and destruction, life and death – materialised in front of him. Shiva told Asahara that he had been chosen to recreate the Kingdom of Shambhala, a mythical hidden valley in Tibetan Buddhist tradition whose last king will defeat the Muslim infidels in a final war and establish the reign of Buddhism. Asahara would be this messianic figure, and it was consciousness of this which led him to the Himalayas in 1986 to perfect his ascetic practices.

It is interesting that Asahara had seized on one of the relatively few Buddhist traditions which is unquestionably apocalyptic. For the most part, Buddhism is not an apocalyptic religion: its beliefs in degenerative change within fixed cycles and in the individual withdrawal into nirvana are not easily compatible with a vision of an imminent, once-and-for-all moment of collective salvation and damnation. On the other hand, Buddhism is quite flexible enough to accommodate apocalyptic belief on its fringes. This is especially true in Japan, where different Buddhist philosophies have been in acrimonious competition with each other for centuries, and where there is a tradition of spiritual improvisation and rivalry. Many of the country's new religions offer a sort of benign apocalyptic Buddhism: they claim that the performance of their spiritual exercises will produce such glorious material benefits for the initiate that in the long run everyone will adopt them and a new age will dawn. Asahara encountered this sort of religion in Agonshu, and he took on board some elements of it, such as the emphasis on collective salvation. When he founded Aum Shinrikyo, which means 'the religion of supreme truth', he made it clear that the movement's practice of yoga was the key to mankind's future; once mastered, it would release mysterious bodily energies known as *kundalini* which would establish new standards of human purity and wisdom. There was at this stage little mention of Shambhala or the inevitability of war.

But in at least one respect Asahara's group was unlike many new religions in Japan's spiritual marketplace. It did not promise to raise the believer to new heights of material prosperity. On the contrary, it taught that intense suffering was essential for personal growth, and that, once wisdom had been acquired, money and success would become meaningless. This message of withdrawal from the world might not strike the Western observer as original; but it was an unusual approach for a new religious movement in the Japan of the 1980s, a society which, it is sometimes claimed, amassed the greatest concentration of wealth in the history of the world. Asahara's world-renouncing doctrines undoubtedly struck a chord with students who were weary of the bubble economy; they bought his books in large numbers. And, for some of them, they were a revelation.

Asahara's homilies were not devoid of subtlety: in their insistence that rebirth must be preceded by a spiritual dead-end and a sense of 'meaninglessness', they were tailor-made for young people who had experienced personal failure or felt lost and disorientated despite success. One former Aum member, a young concert pianist, recalls that she was tormented by the feeling that her life lacked purpose; her technique stagnated and she started feeling tired and weak. After reading a book on meditation and breathing by Asahara, she joined Aum; after practising exercises which involved sitting in the lotus position for hours at a time, she felt a sudden surge of energy and her playing improved spectacularly. Eventually she sold her possessions and moved to an Aum commune. Another member, Shinnosuko Sakamoto, was educated at Tokyo University and after an unhappy career with a major trading firm drifted into graduate research. By this time he was already reading Asahara's books and practising breathing techniques; but it was not until he made a pilgrimage to Kamikuishiki that he was fully converted. On the first day he was put into a small, dark chamber and told to meditate for twelve hours. At first his visions were colourful and happy; then he felt fear and pain and realised that his academic ambitions were the source. He had a vision of his research papers tossed into the air and scattered.

He was overjoyed. 'I felt as if I had ascended to a higher plane,' he said. 'A bright light fell from above and entered me.'[6]

Such stories indicate that Aum Shinrikyo attached great importance to control of its own environment. Those who came into contact with the sect through training sessions and by joining its communes found their freedom severely circumscribed. This is not unusual in new religious movements, of course; but few have subjected new members to such a range of ordeals. It should be borne in mind that some of the ancient yogic practices followed by Asahara are themselves rather fearsome: in that known as *gaja karani*, for example, large quantities of water are consumed and then vomited in order to clear the alimentary canal. But Aum soon developed even more rigorous exercises of its own. Its programmes of meditation turned into periods of enforced sleep- and light-deprivation, the mind-altering effect of which was often reinforced by the use of psychedelic drugs. For those followers who welcomed such a regime – and, inevitably, many did not and left Aum – the effects were predictable: during the late 1980s visitors began to report encounters with members who conformed in every respect to the stereotype of the zombie-like cult follower, with the electrical headgear providing a final grotesque touch. But Asahara's ambitions went well beyond simple manipulation of his own followers: his attempts to remould their personalities were only one aspect of the ungovernable creative urge of the megalomaniac.

Back in 1986, when the first Aum commune was set up at Kamikuishiki, few observers felt any cause for concern. At the opening ceremony in August of that year, Asahara spoke of the need to create a safe and tranquil place for his followers. More than a thousand of the faithful were present; they responded with a thundering ovation. The commune was described as a 'Lotus Village', which would provide everything from food, clothing and housing to places for religious practice, education, employment, medical treatment, weddings and funerals. Only later was it announced that Aum would also establish facilities for 'creative research in medicine, science and agriculture'. Professor Susumu Shimazono of Tokyo University, Japan's foremost authority on Aum, has described the 1986 opening ceremony as a scene familiar to any observer of Japanese new religions. The faithful gather to express their hopes of establishing a holy place which will be a model of heaven on earth; the figure of the founder smiles benignly as he feels their enthusiasm and urges them on. All this is unremarkable, says Shimazono; it is typical of the optimism of new movements.[7] Yet within three or four years Asahara was preaching a highly distinctive apocalyptic message with undertones of violence and despair. What lay behind the transformation?

Part of the answer is that the Lotus Village was a sham: far from being warm and tranquil, it was a place where disturbed young people submitted themselves to self-destructive rituals. And it was never intended as an end in itself: it belonged in the wider context of its founder's messianic mission. During the late 1980s, with his membership growing, a confident Asahara began to talk publicly about this sensitive area. In 1988 Aum published a pamphlet which revealed for the first time a plan to develop Japan into Shambhala. 'This plan, unequalled in scope, will extend Aum's sacred sphere throughout the nation and foster the development of multitudes of holy people, making Japan the base for saving the entire world,' it announced. Significantly, Aum chose to justify this grandiosity by drawing attention to what it described as a 'very dangerous' situation in Japan and the world at large. 'Master Asahara's prophecies – worsening trade relations, increased defence spending, abnormalities in the Fuji volcanic region and the Pacific Plate, etc. – have already been proved true,' it said. Whether Asahara had actually predicted these things is not clear; until this point his statements had mostly been optimistic, even utopian, in content. What matters is that by 1988 he had cast himself in the role, by no means unfamiliar in Japan, of the doomsday prophet. Moreover, like many such prophets, he insisted that only he could save the world from apocalyptic destruction.

From 1988 onwards, Asahara's message seemed to become gloomier and more lurid with every passing month. His overall scheme retained some Buddhist elements, such as the belief (not apocalyptic in itself) that the world has reached a final degenerative stage known as the *Mappo* in which faith is weak and society falls apart. Increasingly, though, he reached out towards Western apocalyptic tradition, both Christian and occult. In early 1989 he published an interpretation of the Book of Revelation which predicted Armageddon within a few years. But, as Shimazono points out, its sense of crisis was still relatively vague. Although it suggested that the American President elected in 1996 would lead the world into war, it did not foresee the collapse of the Soviet Union until 2004 and the nuclear destruction of China until around 2005. Later in 1989, however, Asahara published a book called *From Destruction to Emptiness* which is written with a far greater sense of urgency, and reveals that only those who have received spiritual tuition from Aum can expect to survive the coming holocaust. With hindsight, of course, this has an extremely sinister ring to it; but it is not actually very different in flavour from the doomsday scenarios of New Age writers such as Ruth Montgomery and Sun Bear, for whom survival was essentially a question of spiritual correctness. 'It will be possible to limit the destruction if Aum works to produce large numbers of people who have reached *gedatsu* [a state of ultimate happiness],' says Asahara. 'The number of those who die at Armageddon will then be no more than a quarter of the world's population . . . At present, though, my plan for salvation is behind schedule and the percentage of those who will survive is getting lower and lower. It is already impossible to limit the victims to less than one-fourth.'[8]

However desperate this situation might appear, Aum Shinri-kyo was still convinced at this stage that it could engineer the survival of a large proportion of humanity. Within a year or two, however, it had abandoned any hope of saving those outside the group. During the early 1990s Aum members retreated into their communes as Asahara's apocalyptic vision took on ever darker hues. This was a period in which the physical and theological retreat from the outside world closely coincided; yet it was also a time, paradoxically, in which Asahara became far more eclectic in his approach. In a sense, this was inevitable, since the Eastern traditions on which he had hitherto relied could not provide the theological underpinning for paranoia offered by Western apocalypticism. Buddhism has no equivalent of an all-powerful devil who gradually increases his sway over mankind, an idea which appealed strongly to Asahara. And, although images of religious war are not foreign to Buddhism, only apocalypticism can transform the hopes and fears of a small group of embattled believers by assuring them that they, *and only they*, will survive the destruction of the world.

But, as the saying goes, just because you are paranoid it doesn't mean that they aren't out to get you; and it does seem that the changes in Aum Shinrikyo's theology were partly a reaction to growing hostility to its activities. Although Aum was officially recognised as a religious body by the Japanese authorities in 1989, the year also witnessed a number of high-profile protests from relatives of members. A popular magazine ran a series of articles headed 'Aum Shinrikyo's Insanity' which focussed attention on the enormous sums of money signed over by new recruits. Then, in February 1990, Aum ran twenty-five candidates for the Lower House of Parliament. It was convinced that they would all romp home; instead, they were heavily defeated. Asahara, who stood in a Tokyo constituency, received a miserable 1,783 votes.[9] For a man who had always found disappointment hard to handle, such a public humiliation was perhaps the last straw: many observers believe that it was chiefly responsible for the transformation of Aum into a closed sect which, far from trying to save the world, was effectively at war with it. Soon after the defeat, a strange gathering of more than 12,000 people took place on the remote Japanese island of Ishigaki. Ostensibly organised by Aum to celebrate the approach of Austin's Comet, it was also the moment at which many of Asahara's followers committed themselves to living in communes.

There can be little doubt that life in those communities was lived in the shadow of the apocalypse. There was a brief attempt to improve Aum's public image with public performances of elaborate 'dance operettas' illustrating the group's doctrines; there were also efforts to win the sympathy of various academics by stressing the contrast between the crude materialism of some new religions and Aum's sophisticated reworkings of Buddhist thought. In reality, though, Asahara's message was by this stage both crude and sensationalised. In a series of lectures in 1992 he predicted that Armageddon would occur by the year 2000 and that atomic, biological and chemical weapons would destroy 90 per cent of the world's urban population. He also claimed that Aum's spiritual practices, and in particular breathing exercises progressively reducing the intake of oxygen, would make the believer resistant to such weapons. This is an important detail: belief in invulnerability to weapons is one of the most persistent features of extreme apocalyptic belief, from the People's Crusades to millenarian uprisings in twentieth-century Africa. It is difficult to say whether Asahara was cynically invoking this tradition in an attempt to attract followers, or whether he genuinely believed in these miraculous powers. Either way, it is interesting to note how a quintessentially Eastern concept such as the transcendental breathing exercise was slotted neatly into a highly coloured End-time scenario heavily dependent on Western tradition.

By 1993, a sense of inevitable doom permeated all Aum Shinrikyo's activities. Indeed, such was the extent of Asahara's control of the environment that his followers found it difficult to think about anything else. The site of his Kamikuishiki headquarters may well have been chosen with this in mind. The immediate surroundings of the compound are strangely unsettling: a gentle landscape of golf clubs and dairy farms is completely overshadowed by the vast profile of Mount Fuji, which for believers of many different faiths is the spiritual epicentre of Japan. Mountains possess a religious significance for every culture which encounters them, and this has always been exploited by End-time prophets. In the Far East, indigenous traditions of mystics retreating to the mountains have provided a foothold for the Western-influenced apocalyptic beliefs of both Korean Pentecostal Christians and Japanese new religions. Asahara, just like the Taborites of Bohemia in 1420, and invoking the same biblical texts, taught that in the Last

Days the Elect of God would flee to the mountains, where they would survive Armageddon. He explained that this was why the faithful should live next to Mount Fuji. Every time they looked up to the skyline, they would be reminded of the approaching End.

Not that they needed much reminding. The term 'virtual reality' is over-used, but it is an irresistible description of life inside Aum Shinrikyo's compounds. On the one hand they were as enclosed as any medieval monastery, and did, in fact, employ quasi-medieval imagery in their depiction of the punishment awaiting backsliders: the living quarters were festooned with pictures of hellfire, another non-Buddhist concept eagerly appropriated by Asahara. On the other hand, Aum Shinrikyo was obsessed with state-of-the-art technology, especially that of destruction, and with the propaganda potential of new media and popular culture. It understood a crucial feature of the new channels of information opening up in the 1990s: that, despite their cross-cultural appeal, they make it easier, not more difficult, to control a closed environment, and thus to manipulate believers. Aum's compounds were awash with electronically generated images of Master Asahara and Armageddon. Like the American far right, Aum used computer bulletin boards to keep tabs on its opponents; but members also spent a good deal of time playing officially sanctioned computer games. Aum took entertainment seriously, producing a stream of videos and comics in the fashionable 'Manga' style to drum home the message of salvation and apocalypse to initiates and potential converts, most of whom were under thirty years old.

At first glance, Aum's fascination with popular culture might appear to sit oddly with its apocalyptic teachings. In fact, the two complemented each other: youth culture in the past few decades has often been drawn to images of destruction, and, as we shall see later, this is particularly true of Japan. Furthermore, Aum's attempts to reach this audience may partly account for its lurch towards Armageddon theology in the 1990s. Professor Shimazono has a theory that Asahara resorted to extreme, almost comic-book, doomsday prophecies in a desperate attempt to win recruits at a time when members were drifting away. But there are several other possible factors, and the weight that should be attached to each of them remains a subject of intense debate in academic circles. The Gulf War, for example, seems to have made a deep impression on Asahara and his lieutenants, not only by raising expectations of Armageddon but by introducing them to the thrilling subject of chemical weapons. Then there is the question of Asahara's eyesight and general health, both of which declined in the early 1990s. Did this push him to the brink? And we should not neglect the time factor – the ticking of the millennial clock as calendar dates approached which Asahara had long predicted would witness the opening stages of the final conflict.

It should be stressed that Asahara never produced a simple timetable for Armageddon and beyond: right up until the subway attack he continued to make predictions of a Third World War, but its dates were constantly changing. At the beginning of 1995 Aum produced a book called *A Doom Is Nearing the Land of the Rising Sun*, which consists of transcripts of conversations between Asahara and his leading disciples on Aum's own radio station. This book, which in its English version never got beyond an unedited proof, is perhaps the most useful evidence we have of Asahara's state of mind at the time. He suggests in one place that the final war could break out at any moment, and in another that it might not take place until the 2040s; for the most part, however, he concentrates on the last years of the 1990s. Something unusual will happen in 1995 or 1996, he says; 'intense and fearful' phenomena will occur until the year 2000. He has a vision of Tokyo being 'gulped down by the sea' as the Japanese archipelago sinks; but he also sees Japan reduced to 'burned earth' after a nuclear attack by the US and the UN between 1996 and January 1998.[10] One gets the strong impression that these visions do not particularly distress Asahara. Japan, which decisively rejected salvation in the 1990 elections, fully deserves its miserable fate.

Significantly, despite all the contradictory dates, there is no real sense of apocalypse postponed. Other Japanese new religions which prophesied catastrophic events for the end of the 1990s have become less specific in their predictions as the new millennium has drawn closer. Aum Shinrikyo was still talking of an imminent conflagration, albeit in a rather confused fashion, as late as the beginning of 1995. The introduction to *A Doom Is Nearing the Land of the Rising Sun*, which was clearly written after the Kobe earthquake in January, is headed 'A War Has Already Begun'. Signed by 'Aum Press editorial staff', it claims that on 1 January that year Asahara had predicted a major earthquake in the Kobe region, and suggests that the quake itself was artificially produced by a secret technology known as 'earthquake weapons'. It does not identify the culprit, but hints that the weapons were developed in the US with the knowledge of American and Japanese seismologists. 'Will you be able to survive by choosing wise actions?' it asks. 'Or are you going to be simply tossed by the current of the drastically changing end of the century, and to die for nothing? At any rate, a warning has already been made.'[11]

This last statement, issued a matter of weeks before the Tokyo sarin attack, cannot be dismissed as typical Aum hyperbole. In the transcripts of discussions between Asahara and his disciples, most of whom describe themselves as scientists, there is much talk of the uses and effects of chemical and biological weapons, including sarin. Despite assurances from one 'expert' that breathing techniques can protect against radiation, the conversation returns several times to the pressing need for fallout shelters in the coming conflict. There is much head-shaking over Japan's failure to prepare for the emergency and, in particular, to build underground railway stations which are deep enough to double as shelters. But there is apparently one exception: Kasumigaseki, in front of the Diet building in central Tokyo. This station is mentioned by speakers more than once, and with benefit of hindsight one cannot help wondering whether it was on their minds for some other reason; it was, of course, the main target of the infamous sarin attack.

The attack itself remains something of a mystery. It may well have been a bizarre diversionary tactic: a few days earlier, Aum Shinrikyo was tipped off about forthcoming police raids by an informer, perhaps via a computer bulletin board. But it was also probably a test-run for a much more ambitious terrorist campaign. A notebook later seized from a senior Aum official contained a scribbled reference to 'a war in November 1995', and the testimony of former members suggests that Aum entertained fantasies of a national coup. Asahara seems to have believed that the Japanese state was too fragile to withstand any crisis: he may have been thinking of its response to the Kobe earthquake, which struck many commentators as shockingly disorganised. But the precise moment at which Asahara decided to declare war on society cannot be pinpointed. The whole episode serves as a reminder that, however much we know about apocalyptic belief systems, the day-to-day workings of the millenarian mind usually resist rational analysis; if they possess an internal logic, it is often completely incomprehensible to the outsider – especially if, as seems likely in this case, mind-altering drugs are involved.

Yet Aum Shinrikyo does not defy categorisation. It has features in common with other groups which have resorted to violence in their pursuit of the millennium. The most important of these is the guru himself: nearly every case of millennial bloodshed involves an authoritarian leader with messianic pretensions. In the case of Aum, the sheer extravagance of the guru worship almost beggars belief. Recruits were forced to watch videos of Asahara's talks for up to twenty hours at a time in solitary confinement; they also drank his bathwater and brews consisting of his boiled hair.[12] Furthermore, it has long been recognised that cults which attack the outside world tend to be those which physically harm their own members. The most dangerous groups, inevitably, are those which actually kill members of the group; the crime is then typically justified with theological arguments which overturn accepted notions of guilt and death. Aum Shinrikyo belongs in this category. In the early 1990s Asahara promulgated a set of secret teachings based on Tantric Buddhism. He discovered a concept known as *poa*, in which the spirits of the dead are transferred to a higher status by secret rites based on the magical power of the guru. As Shimazono argues, 'the absolutization of this power can give rise to the perverted logic that if a person of low spiritual status is murdered by one with *gedatsu* then the former person's karma improves, making the murder a good deed'.[13] Finally, an enclosed and controlled environment appears to be a precondition for millennial violence, irrespective of its target. To cite a famous example from the 1970s, the mass suicide and murder of the Rev. Jim Jones's followers was confined to his jungle compound at Jonestown; members of the People's Temple in the United States did not even contemplate killing themselves. Aum Shinrikyo used every conceivable method of control over its members: solitary confinement, sleep-deprivation, drugs and, more subtly, a theology of relentless self-transformation which limited contact between the faithful, thus further strengthening Asahara's authority. It is small wonder that commune residents lost their grip on reality.

Aum Shinrikyo fits the description of a violent millennial cult as well as any group in history. Seen from most angles, it clearly belongs in the company of the Adamites, the Anabaptists of Münster, the People's Temple and the followers of Charles Manson. No one can predict when and where such groups will arise; they are like a deadly but mercifully rare poisonous plant which can spring up overnight from any soil. Yet this explanation does not quite suffice in the case of Aum. One of the reasons Japan was so traumatised by the subway incident is that Aum was in some respects so typically Japanese. When news of the attack broke, the international reaction was one of astonishment that such a nightmarish drama should be played out in Tokyo, of all places, at the nerve centre of the world's best-managed economy and most cohesive society. Many Japanese shared this feeling; but others felt that perhaps they should have seen it coming. For the truth is that once the incident is placed in the wider context of Japan at the end of the twentieth century it is difficult to imagine it happening anywhere else.

Japan is not a religious nation in the Western sense of the word. Most Japanese do not claim exclusive allegiance to one faith: they are more than happy to accept a mixed religious heritage in which an aesthetically refined Buddhism coexists with the legends and superstitions of Shinto. In theory, the gulf between Buddhism and Shinto is vast: the one is bound by precise formulations of abstract thought; the other consists almost entirely of earthy folklore and has no conception of dogma. In practice, the Japanese simply choose whichever system best suits a particular occasion. Buddhism, not surprisingly, is felt to be ideal for funerals; Shinto is for weddings. Perhaps the crucial fact about Japanese religion is that, in contrast to the West, there is no unbroken tradition of state-sponsored observance. At different times over the last millennium, the governing power has imposed a succession of different brands of Buddhism, sometimes combined with Confucianism, and more recently State Shinto (emperor-worship, not to be confused with popular Shinto).

The consequences of this are far-reaching. In the first place, Japan's most ancient and primitive religious traditions have never disappeared: they are the basis of popular Shinto. Most Japanese are brought up with stories of territorial spirits known as *kami*, some of whom are good, many of whom are evil, but all of whom are capricious. This animist belief has been virtually untouched by Japan's transformation into an economic superpower. No Japanese company would dream of building a factory without first holding a *jichinsai*, or Shinto ground-breaking ceremony. Indeed, Shinto is in some ways well suited to the modern world. The unpredictability of economic cycles actually reinforces popular fatalism; however well things are going, the Japanese never rule out the possibility of sudden disasters inspired by malicious spirits. The other great consequence of Japan's fragmented religious past is a national genius for spiritual improvisation and appropriation. The Japanese are entirely open to the religious ideas of foreign cultures, but there is no question of buying them wholesale: they insist on adapting them or extracting elements from them which can be combined with native Japanese traditions. This is why Pentecostal Christianity has made so little headway in Japan as opposed to South Korea. As it happens, animist beliefs similar to Japan's also flourish in Korea, where fundamentalist missionaries have cleverly exploited them by pointing to the many references to evil spirits in the New Testament. But this approach has never worked in Japan, an island nation whose self-image is far less fragile than that of its mainland neighbour, and where the notion of basing a religion entirely on a foreign text such as the bible is unthinkable. On the other hand, Japanese religious leaders have no compunction whatsoever about borrowing from Christianity; many of them cheerfully appropriate the sayings of Jesus, while others incorporate large chunks of Christian apocalyptic belief into their philosophies.

This willingness to innovate, together with the persistence and respectability of ancient superstition, explains the most remarkable feature of religious life in Japan today: its new religions. The proliferation of these is mind-boggling. According to the government's Cultural Affairs Agency, there are 183,470 groups registered as religious corporations; of these, 5,888 cannot be described as entirely Buddhist, Shinto or Christian.[14] There are, in short, thousands of home-made new religions in Japan, most of which would be ridiculed as 'cults' in the West; in Japan, however, there is no stigma attached to joining them. Sociologists of religion divide the creation of these new religions into four 'waves'. Significantly, each wave roughly coincides to a period of rapid change in Japan. The first growth period occurred just after the Meiji Restoration in 1868, when after centuries of isolation Japan began a rapid process of industrialisation. The second occurred during the 1920s, when Japan was experiencing severe social problems in the wake of the devastating Tokyo earthquake. The third religious boom began amid the intense suffering that followed the Second World War; its major beneficiary was Sokagakkai, the powerful Nichiren Buddhist lay organisation whose millions of members believe that the act of chanting *namu myoho rengekyo* ('adoration to the exquisite law of the Lotus Sutra') prepares the way for the creation of a new world.

The fourth religious boom began around 1978 as a period of unlimited economic growth came to an end.[15] In many ways it was quite unlike its forerunners. Many of the so-called 'new new religions' which sprang up during the late 1970s and early 1980s appealed directly to belief in evil spirits, miracles and the occult. There is no doubt that Japanese interest in the supernatural grew substantially during these years, particularly among young people. A widely reported 1984 survey of respondents in their twenties and seventies found that 57 per cent of the young people believed in UFOs as opposed to only 6 per cent of the old people, which may not be surprising; but when they were asked if they were interested in fortune telling the margin was roughly the same: 54 per cent to 8 per cent. As for evil spirits, 66 per cent of young people believed in them, as opposed to 46 per cent of old people.[16] These findings puzzled a lot of commentators at the time; they make sense, however, if we bear in mind that this fascination with the occult and evil spirits did not mark a simple return to traditional animist beliefs, but rather reflected powerful influences from the West.

The new ingredients in this spirituality have been derived from American popular culture, the Western occult tradition and the New Age. The 'new new religions' are as interested in the 'underground river' described by Robert Ellwood as they are in Buddhism and Shinto. In fact, they have become thoroughly immersed in the cultic milieu, the vast lake in which all information rejected or not taken seriously by society at large – conspiracy theories, astrology, reports of miracles and UFOs – seems to gather and mix. As we saw in the chapter on the New Age, the cultic milieu is the perfect breeding ground for apocalyptic beliefs: there is something about the nature of rejection which leads inevitably to questions about why certain information is accessible only to a privileged few. (Answer: because only they have been chosen to survive the coming changes, whatever they might be.) So perhaps it is not surprising that the fourth Japanese religious boom, the only one heavily influenced by the cultic milieu, should also be the most explicitly millennial in its approach.

We noted earlier that Aum Shinrikyo took a very different line from most of its rivals on the subject of the Japanese economic miracle. But in many ways it was typical of the most recent wave of new religions. Although it started out as a yoga circle, it soon began to take on board information from every region of the cultic milieu; and, as it did so, its teachings became more conventionally, if crudely, apocalyptic in the Western tradition. By the beginning of 1995, when it produced *A Doom Is Nearing the Land of the Rising Sun*, the range of obscure cultic theories at its disposal was truly awe-inspiring. In the course of the rambling discourses of Asahara and his 'scientists', there are inevitable references to Nostradamus (known in Japan as Nosutorodamusu), to the occult traditions of English freemasonry and to a bizarre theory, current in some outposts of the American far right, which places the British royal family at the centre of an international conspiracy. There are interminably long discussions about astrology and aspects of the New Age in the West: Asahara refers approvingly to the Scottish prophet Benjamin Creme, who has been predicting for years that a world saviour called Lord Maitreya is about to emerge from the Pakistani community in the East End of London.[17] Finally, and most unexpectedly, we find Asahara delving into Roman Catholic folklore. He quotes the Prophecies of St Malachy – correctly – to the effect that there are only two popes left after John Paul II, 'so it will be approximately twenty years at most to the end of the last pope'; but unlike other interpreters of the prophecies he takes this as a signal that Christianity is about to be replaced by the supreme truth of Aum Shinrikyo.[18]

Aum is not alone in its ingenious borrowing from popular Western apocalypticism: as we shall see, its deadliest rival, an extraordinary outfit called Kofuku-no-Kagaku (the Institute for Research into Human Happiness), displays an equally impressive eclecticism, citing the prophecies of Fatima in support of its predictions of catastrophe.[19] But we should not assume that the apocalypticism of Japan's newest new religions is constructed entirely from imported materials. These groups could not have flourished so spectacularly if doomsday scenarios did not somehow match the mood and expectations of many Japanese. The appeal of these scenarios obviously goes beyond a simple appetite for Western ideas: as with all apocalyptic belief, stress and change play vital roles. Few societies in the world have experienced such consistently high levels of stress as twentieth-century Japan. Although it has been industrialised far longer than its Far Eastern neighbours, every decade of this century has been marked by rapid economic change; furthermore, this has been accompanied by the traumatic experience of defeat, the complete redesign of the nation's official ideology, a disorientating economic boom, the looming challenge of a post-industrial society; and, always at the forefront of the national consciousness, the thrilling but still elusive prospect of becoming the greatest economic power of the twenty-first century.

The importance of this last ambition can hardly be overestimated. For all of this century Japan has been acutely conscious of the Anno Domini calendar, even if it still resists using it for every purpose. At the same time Japanese intellectuals have maintained a keen interest in Western theories of the rise and fall of civilisations: to this day, Sokagakkai reveres the memory of Arnold Toynbee, using his writings to justify a vision of a great civilisation rising in the East. Indeed, the Japanese are understandably keen on the idea, first mooted by Hegel but essentially an adaptation of the Four Empires of Daniel, that the spirit of civilisation moves around the world from east to west. (The Pentecostal Koreans, as we have seen, embrace a version of this in which the Holy Spirit moves westwards in a sort of Great Year which will culminate in a great End-time revival in Asia.) At any rate, the combined effect of these two factors – belief that the West is 'falling' while the East is 'rising', together with increasing orientation by the AD calendar – has led to a widespread assumption that the end of the second Christian millennium is the moment at which the torch of civilisation will be passed to the Far East – dominated, of course, by Japan. But, in typically Japanese fashion, these hopes have always been clouded by worry that things will not go to plan; and, as in other countries of East Asia, fear of natural disasters is deeply ingrained in the national psyche. But this serves only to enhance the credibility of apocalyptic scenarios in which great changes in society are accompanied by equally great disruptions of the natural order.

In a sense, of course, Shoko Asahara did his best to subvert the vision of a triumphant Japan entering into its rightful inheritance at the turn of the millennium. He predicted, and hoped, that it would be reduced to ashes in the Battle of Armageddon. But the society that would be destroyed was the old, corrupt Japan that had rejected its saviour; in the aftermath of the conflict, a new Japan ruled by the Master was to become the centre of the Millennium Kingdom. And the time-scale was essentially unchanged: the new world would take shape in the early years of the AD calendar millennium. In any case, Asahara was not the first Japanese prophet to build his scenario around an end-of-century Armageddon. He was well aware of, and admired, the writings of the prewar thinker Katsutoki Sakai, who claimed to have received a vision of the future from God. According to Asahara, the content of this vision was that 'Armageddon will occur at the end of this century. Only a race of compassionate sages will survive. Their leader will come from Japan.'[20]

Although most new religions do not feature Armageddon in their teachings, there is an ambiguous quality to their pronouncements about the end of the twentieth century. The period of transition is rarely described as peaceful. Interestingly, the translation of Nostradamus into Japanese during the 1970s made a deep impression on the new generation of gurus: they were particularly struck by his references to a great war in 1999 and to an unnamed power which will 'grow above all the other powers of the Orient'.[21] In the years following the publication of the quatrains, the Seer of Provence became part of Japanese popular culture. He even cropped up in children's television cartoon shows, one of which was all about a spaceship unable to return to earth after Nostradamus' prediction of the End of the World in 1999 unfortunately came true. But for the majority of new religious movements which take an interest in the subject, including Aum, the cataclysms envisaged by Nostradamus are not the End: they are a prelude to a new civilisation on earth.

If asked to justify this view, most Japanese gurus would refer to the text of the celebrated quatrains. For one leader, however, there is a higher authority: Nostradamus himself, with whom he claims to have personally discussed the fate of civilisation at great length. The guru in question is Ryuho Okawa, founder of

Kofuku-no-Kagaku and, with the exception of Asahara, the most famous of all the religious leaders to emerge from the so-called fourth wave. In 1985 Okawa was a thirty-year-old financial trader working for a Japanese firm on Wall Street. He resigned his job after a Great Revelation in which he learned that he was the reincarnation of Buddha and was given the power to communicate with hundreds of spirits, including those of Jesus Christ, Moses, Confucius and Nostradamus. (Critics have pointed out unkindly that this Nostradamus perpetuates errors in the translation of the quatrains found in the first popular Japanese edition of the work.)[22]

When Kofuku-no-Kagaku was founded in 1986, it had just four members; its aim was to teach self-improvement through constant study of the Buddhist principles of love, wisdom, reflection and development. Over the next four years it was transformed from a small study group into a formidable organisation offering mass lectures and publishing hundreds of titles a year. By 1990 Okawa claimed to have 50,000 followers; in the ensuing year he stood before an audience of 40,000 at his Birthday Festival and announced his real identity. He was El Cantare, the 'supreme grand spirit of the terrestrial group' who had previously been incarnated as Sakyamuni Buddha and as Hermes. 'It is I who have all authority from the beginning of the earth until the end,' said Okawa. 'For I am not human, but am the Law itself.'[23] In December of that year Okawa, dressed in a gold robe and an alarmingly wobbly crown, addressed another mass rally. He announced that membership (always a loosely defined concept) had risen to 5 million. In 1994, after three years of inexorably rising 'membership', the leader announced that the 'age of true teaching' had begun; this went hand in hand with a series of extremely virulent campaigns against Okawa's opponents in the press and other new religions. Kofuku-no-Kagaku developed a particular loathing of Aum Shinrikyo: on Saturday 18 March 1995, it organised a rally of 5,000 people in Tokyo to protest against the kidnapping of Kiyoshi Kariya; two days later, of course, the sarin gas attack took place.

A full description of Okawa's theology would take many

pages. He has developed a hierarchical cosmology of the spirit world of staggering complexity, in which hundreds of historical figures are assigned positions in different dimensions (Einstein and the Archangel Gabriel are in the eighth dimension, Chopin is in the realm just below it, while Mozart and Henry Ford are in the relatively lowly seventh dimension).[24] He has also outlined a history of the creation of the world which makes *You Are Becoming a Galactic Human*, by Virginia Essene and Sheldon Nidle, read like a work of cautious scholarship. According to Okawa, Venus was once populated by a highly intelligent life form, a cross between animal and vegetable. Its upper half looked like a lily, and its lower half had legs with foliage on the back of them to facilitate photosynthesis.[25]

But these colourful details are mere embellishments: they do not account for Okawa's success. No one takes seriously his claim to have a following of 10 million, or 10 per cent of the Japanese population; but Kofuku-no-Kagaku can certainly boost an active membership of 300,000, which is an astonishing total less than ten years after the initial vision of the founder. How could this happen? Despite the lectures and publicity stunts, Okawa relies mainly on books to spread his message; he has sold around 60 million of them. These are not sacred texts distributed free of charge to the faithful, but mass-marketed volumes which compete with thousands of other titles in ordinary bookshops. This seems to prove that, in Japan at least, secular marketing can play a role in drawing members of the public into a religious movement. But more important than this is the message itself, which is one of self-transformation in an environment of apocalyptic change. Kofuku-no-Kagaku teaches that early in the next century Japan will become the centre of a great East Asian civilisation; in the meantime, 'countless disasters' may take place. In fact, Okawa has warned that if Kofuku-no-Kagaku does not continue to grow, then there may be another earthquake as big as the Tokyo quake of 1923 (in which 91,000 died) or Mount Fuji itself may erupt.[26]

Okawa's critics complain that when he talks like this he sounds just like his arch-enemy Shoko Asahara, and there are indeed obvious resemblances: both are highly eclectic, unashamedly apocalyptic and focus the attentions of their followers squarely on the person of the leader. Yet Aum and Kofuku-no-Kagaku never found themselves competing for members. Asahara appealed to disappointed students or to leftists who rejected the bubble economy and all it stood for. Okawa reaches out to ambitious young men and women who want to perform even better in the workplace. While fearful that everything may be thrown off course by natural disaster or international conspiracies, they are confident that, in their leader's words, 'as the Sun of God's Truth gradually rises, a great light will glow from a corner of the earth. That very corner is the chosen land, Japan.'[27] In other words, there is little danger of former Aum members drifting into the still vibrant Kofuku-no-Kagaku. Whether that is in any way reassuring is another matter; for what it indicates is that radical apocalyptic preachers who deal in fantastic myths and blood-curdling warnings of catastrophe have managed to carve out two entirely separate constituencies among Japanese young people. Naturally, one would not wish to equate Okawa with the murderous Asahara; but with the latter safely behind bars and Aum disbanded we should perhaps ask which, in the long run, is likely to prove more significant: the grotesque sarin incident, or the fact that in one of the world's most advanced societies a bizarre new religious sect can sign up hundreds of thousands of believers in less than ten years.

It is not surprising that Japan should remain preoccupied with Aum Shinrikyo; after all, it seems clear that the attack could have been prevented if the Matsumoto poisoning incident had been properly investigated. But that outrage, in contrast, could not possibly have been foreseen. We must not assume that among the lessons the world can learn from the Aum Shinrikyo affair is the secret of anticipating millennial violence: the apocalyptic mind-set is so complex and volatile, and there are so many groups in existence, that no state can offer its citizens blanket protection from physically threatening apocalyptic sects. On the other hand, such groups will never form more than a tiny minority of End-time believers. In most cases, the violence – the terrible wars, volcanic eruptions and earthquakes – will be confined to the realm of the prophetic imagination.

Yet, if there is a lesson to be learned from the wider Japanese experience, it is that apocalyptic faith will loom large in the religious landscape of the twenty-first century, at least in the Far East. Japan may be more vulnerable in this respect than other countries; but the experience of South Korea and the first signs of Pentecostal growth in China indicate that all the societies of East Asia are susceptible to the appeal of apocalyp-ticism. For although they are at different stages of development they have much in common. Japan is a society at the peak of its creative powers; South Korea is still flexing its muscles; China, as Napoleon predicted, is finally waking up. What unites these countries is a capacity to withstand, and even develop an appetite for, the most far-reaching change. At the same time, each of them has preserved its heritage of capricious local spirits, gods and demons – and in practice this is easily combined with the crudest exports of the West's cultic milieu. All this undoubtedly adds up to a recipe for new apocalyptic belief systems; we can only speculate about the shapes and colours they will take on. The possibilities are endless.

12

Waco and the Culture Wars

In July 1995, a front-page story in the *New York Times* reported the mysterious cancellation of an event called the Conference of the States. The conference, scheduled for Philadelphia in October, was intended to provide a new forum in which leaders of state government could discuss their relationship with Washington: an event, in other words, which would probably have been as exciting and controversial as a meeting of the Association of County Councils in Britain. But then, to the astonishment of the organisers, one state after another pulled out of the conference, until only fourteen out of fifty were left. The explanation, according to the *Times*, was that the states had given in to a campaign by 'right-wing extremists', who saw the conference as a clandestine constitutional convention that could nullify basic states' rights – perhaps as part of a sinister plot to impose a totalitarian One World Government.

The report continued: 'Conspiracy theories, the ancient art of the suspicious, have been especially widespread since the April 19 bombing of the federal building in Oklahoma City. But even before that, whispers about evil plots were growing so loud around the country that they started to penetrate mainstream

278

politics and government, and in some cases, influence their actions.'[1] One of the most prevalent theories – the impending takeover of America by foreign forces loyal to the United Nations – had actually forced the Indiana transportation department to change its road signs. According to local protestors, numbers written on the back of the signs were actually secret signals intended for the invading army. 'People were calling, saying that we were part of the UN takeover plan,' said a spokeswoman for the transportation department. 'And then they were painting over the signs. It got so we couldn't ignore it.' So the road signs had been officially replaced, in order to 'reassure those in the motoring public who had these suspicions'.

The *New York Times* reported all this in the mystified and indignant tones which the liberal media reserves for the activities of conservative Middle America – precisely the tone, in fact, which it employed in the 1980s to chronicle the rise of the Religious Right. 'Conspiracy Theories Penetrating Mainstream Politics,' ran the headline to the story, which was peppered throughout with disapproving references to 'the far right wing'. Yet, despite the slightly hysterical tone of the piece, there was nothing tendentious about its claim that there was a new dimension to many Americans' traditional mistrust of the federal government. Writing at about the same time in the *New York Review of Books*, the historian Garry Wills – one of the few heavyweight pundits with a real appreciation of the fundamentalist mentality – insisted that there was something new about the groups emerging after the Oklahoma bombing. As he put it: 'However these groups differ among themselves – some espousing violence, some not; some religious, some secular; some millennial, some pragmatic – they all agree in their intense fear of the government, and they have framed a complex analysis of the machinery of governmental repression, one that even non-extremists share on this point or that.'[2]

As for the suggestion that fear of the government was penetrating the mainstream, that, too, appeared incontrovertible. In the previous year, the *Times* pointed out, fifteen states had passed resolutions affirming the Tenth Amendment, which reserves to the states all rights not prohibited to them or delegated to the United States by the Constitution. 'This serves as a Notice and Demand to the federal government [note the lower-case letters], as our agent, to cease and desist, effective immediately, mandates that are beyond the scope of its constitutionally delegated powers,' thundered the House of Representatives of Colorado. So far, however, only one state has voiced explicit fears of global conspiracy, passing a resolution in 1994 which ordered the United States Congress 'to cease any support for the establishment of a "new world order" or to any form of global government'. The state, by a strange irony, was Oklahoma.

This fear of a New World Order may not be shared by the mainstream American media, but it frequently cites it as evidence that the United States has entered a new Age of Anxiety. In the summer of 1995 John Weir, a writer for the street-smart New York magazine *Details*, followed the trail of Timothy McVeigh from Arizona to Oklahoma. After being warned by dozens of nednecks about the creeping presence of the Beast of Revelation, as represented by President Clinton, the FBI, the United Nations and the Jews, he concluded that 'there is indeed a fight going on for the soul of the country, a fight as messy and exhilarating as it looks, and the paranoiacs are winning'.[3]

The conflict Weir referred to is often expressed in geographical images: an urban coastal elite pitted against the rural occupants of a Middle America which has always been there but suddenly seems larger and more threatening than before. The Oklahoma bombing, the militias, the rediscovered passion for states' rights and the triumph of the Christian Right in the 1994 mid-term elections all fit into this landscape, although it is not easy to define the precise relationship between these phenomena. But one landmark is clearly visible from every inch of this territory, despite the fact that it was bulldozed by federal forces in 1993: the wooden compound known as Mount Carmel outside Waco, Texas, built by a little-known fundamentalist sect called the Branch Davidians. On 28 February 1993, Mount Carmel was raided by armed federal agents looking for illegal arms. Four of them were killed. A fifty-one-day siege followed, which ended abruptly when the government lost patience and sent in tanks and CS gas. A mysterious fire swept through the building and within minutes eighty apocalyptic believers were dead.

There is broad agreement that, if Waco had not happened, any conflict would be taking place on a far smaller scale. The tragedy did not create the new mood, but it served to harden the attitudes of rural conservatives who already felt threatened and who went on to discover the perfect vehicle for their agression in part-time militas. (Although reliable figures are hard to come by, it is likely that most of the 80,000 or so militia members enlisted in the two years between Waco and Oklahoma.) And, just as significantly, Waco planted half-formed suspicions in the minds of millions of normally unexcitable citizens whose distrust of the government had been growing steadily during the years of recession. Waco conspiracy theories, based on genuinely unanswered questions, found as ready an audience in the suburbs as they did in the right-wing separatist communities in the Pacific North-west.

But public disquiet following Waco was more complex, and more profound, than it first appeared. Its chief feature was a vastly increased hostility to the federal authorities which was partly a reaction to their gross mishandling of the affair, but was also fed by currents of anxiety familiar to any student of American history. It was noticeable that attitudes to the victims of Waco went beyond mere sympathy for victims of federal persecution. The government line that the Davidians were child-abusing cultists who committed mass suicide, Jonestown-style, encountered a degree of resistance which could not be explained simply in terms of a blanket refusal to believe anything put out by the authorities. For whatever reason, public opinion was more sensitive to historical nuances than the government: it recognised that the Mount Carmel community was less exotic and more typically American than the authorities and their advisers in the 'anti-cult' movement would have it believe. And not the least typically American feature of the Davidians was their belief in the approaching End of the World.

*

The sheer weirdness of Mount Carmel's guitar-playing 'Messiah', Vernon Howell (a.k.a. David Koresh) has tended to obscure the fact that his followers stood squarely in a centuries-old American tradition of apocalyptic believers who isolate themselves in expectation of the End. The Davidian Community at Mount Carmel, which had been in Waco since the 1930s, possessed a contorted theological lineage which stretched back via the Seventh Day Adventist Church to the Millerite Great Disappointment and the apocalyptic theology of the Pilgrim communities. To adapt the group's own image, the Branch Davidians were a small and stunted outgrowth of a tree with roots deep in American soil. The larger branches are the flourishing millenarian sects of the United States, such as the Mormons, Jehovah's Witnesses and mainstream Seventh Day Adventists; further down the trunk, however, are dozens of tiny dead branches which were once small millennial communities.

A century or so ago the map of the United States was dotted with these groups. Their flavour was brilliantly captured in the 1870s by Charles Nordhoff, a veteran newspaper reporter who visited virtually every communitarian society in existence, from New England to Oregon. His book *The Communistic Societies of America* contains long essays on two celebrated groups who might be thought to represent polar opposites: the Shakers, austere spiritualists who completely forswore sexual relations, and the Oneida Perfectionists of John Humphrey Noyes, who believed that 'in a holy community, there is no more reason why sexual intercourse should be restrained by law than why eating or drinking should be'. In terms of day-to-day life, however, the Shakers, the Oneida Perfectionists and the dozen or so other communities Nordhoff visited had far more in common with each other than they had with the outside world.

Whether advocates of celibacy, free love or simple continence, these groups, like so many apocalyptic believers before them, were united by an earnest preoccupation with the control of sexual behaviour: the Perfectionists discouraged violent sexual emotion and insisted on a form of *coitus interruptus* which must have been almost as hard to maintain as full-scale celibacy. There was generally a strong interest in a correct diet:

many communities avoided meat, and there was a particular abhorrence of pork. There was an almost uniform drabness to the buildings, which often housed many families and which, according to Nordhoff, 'had the appearance of factories or human hives'. And, despite their very different origins and theology, the groups tended to experience similar anxieties: fear of falling numbers, ageing membership and unsuitable recruits who might divide the community. In his chapter on the Harmony Society, a collection of high-minded German celibates who lived in the immaculately neat village of Economy, Pennsylvania, Nordhoff relates the story of an adventurer styling himself Count Maximilian de Leon. Having secured a lodging at Economy, the Count 'began to announce strange new doctrines, marriage, a livelier life, and other temptations to worldliness; and he finally succeeded in effecting a serious division, which, if it had not been prudently managed, might have destroyed the community'.[4] The Count eventually departed with over $100,000 of the community's money and around 250 new followers; but an attempt to found a new community failed, and he absconded in a boat to Alexandria on the Red River, where he died of cholera.

The Harmony Society illustrates the most important feature these tiny sovereign states had in common, their unshakeable millennialism. In some cases this was implicit: 'communistic' groups tended to see themselves as pioneers of a perfect social structure whose gradual adoption by society would mark the dawn of a golden age. Sometimes it was explicit, and the community saw itself as the remnant which would survive the coming apocalypse. More often, the line between these two conceptions was blurred. Both the Oneida Perfectionists and the Shakers believed that their discovery of the perfect lifestyle heralded the End of Time. Members of the Harmony Society, meanwhile, had been assured by their founder 'Father' George Rapp that Christ would soon appear in the heavens and the whole world would be renewed. (Rapp had hoped this would happen in his lifetime. Lying gravely ill at the age of ninety, he cried out: 'If I did not know that the dear Lord meant I should

present you all to him, I should think my last moment come.'
They were his last words.)[5]

Apocalyptic beliefs aside, it is worth noting how many
features of life in nineteenth-century millennial communities
were also present at Mount Carmel. For most of its history,
until Koresh rebuilt it, the compound was more like a 'human
hive' than a fortress. There was constant fussing over a healthy
diet, as befitted a group whose Seventh Day Adventist forebears
had pioneered Kellogg's cornflakes. And over the years there
were a number of power struggles and rows involving unsuitable recruits, one of whom, a stone-crazy bicycling hippie called
Jesus Amen, presented himself at the door of Mount Carmel
during the FBI siege. As for sexual morality, there is a familiar
feel to the complex theological arguments which prescribed free
love for David Koresh and strict celibacy for everyone else: they
may appear preposterous to the outsider, but no more so than
Noyes's institution of 'complex marriage', which forced young
girls to sleep with old men, or Brigham Young's defences of his
own polygamy. A more intriguing analogy, however, is with
Cyrus Teed (1839–1908), a mysterious figure who, after serving
in the Union Army and claiming to have discovered the secret of
alchemy, announced that he was the seventh Messiah, Jesus
being the sixth. Teed, who sometimes used the Hebrew version
of his first name, Koresh, saw himself as a 'man of sin' who was
nevertheless a final saviour figure before the apocalypse.
Accused by jealous husbands of seducing female recruits, he
made great play of the fact that his followers were enjoined to
celibacy. He founded a small utopian community in Florida
which dwindled after he died in 1908 and failed to rise from the
grave.

The unorthodox sexual practices at Mount Carmel belonged,
in any case, to the Koresh era. From the 1930s until the point
Vernon Howell took it over, nothing much distinguished the
Davidian community in Waco from dozens of eccentric, and
not very successful, groups whose apocalyptic beliefs were the
only remotely colourful thing about them. Although these
communities tended to die out naturally, a minority faced the
threat of violence from neighbours or police authorities who

found their beliefs incomprehensible. This is what happened to one of the few unqualified successes among the millennial groups, the Latter-Day Saints, who were driven westwards from one sanctuary to another and whose founder was killed by an Illinois frontier mob in 1844. A few of the first Quakers were hanged by Puritans, and the early Shakers were, according to Nordhoff, 'violently opposed and in some cases attacked by bigoted or knavish persons'.[6] On the whole, though, it is surprising how few of these sects were harassed by their neighbours or other authorities. Many of the groups Nordhoff visited came from northern Europe, where they had been vigorously persecuted by the police: in America, they were left alone.

In the aftermath of Waco, several commentators suggested that a similar drama could easily have been played out in the colonies at Salem, or in the new Republic during the nineteenth century. This is a fair argument, in so far as it recognises the continuity between Mount Carmel and a succession of enclosed millennial groups who gazed across their ramparts at an outside world ruled by the forces of darkness. But the point is that all these earlier groups survived or died of natural causes. The apocalyptic radicals of seventeenth-century New England found sanctuary and statehood in Rhode Island; the Mormons – whose beliefs and practices were far more exotic than the Davidians' – found them in Utah; and the Shakers were left in peace to experience the slow apocalypse of groups which practise voluntary celibacy. Koresh's followers practised celibacy, too, though whether it was voluntary is another question; but we will never know whether, in the long run, the increasingly grotesque demands made on them by Koresh would have torn apart the community.

The almost total destruction of a religious community by federal forces is without precedent in American history. Supporters of the government's handling of the siege concede this point, but argue that the threat posed by the Davidians was also without precedent, at least on American soil. They maintain that the FBI assault on the compound on 19 April 1993 must be seen in the light of truly unique circumstances.

Koresh, in their view, was so convinced of the inevitability of apocalyptic slaughter that any standoff was bound to end in tragedy. However inoffensive the original community might have been, it had fallen under the sway of a madman whose eschatology actually *required* the destruction of Mount Carmel by fire. Critics of the FBI, on the other hand, have consistently maintained that no one need have died if the authorities had paid sufficient attention to the theological views which governed life at Mount Carmel. Either way, the dispute is as much about the real nature of the Waco community as about the government's tactics. There is a belated recognition that the key to the episode lies in the strange – and, to the authorities, thoroughly unfamiliar – world of End-time theology.

At the beginning of 1993, Mount Carmel's residents included 'British and Australian subjects, Caribbean islanders, Hawaiian and mainland Americans, one millionaire, several paupers, people of Asian, African, Native American and European descent, former barflies and former teetotallers, an Argentine-Israeli Jew and a set of adult twins'.[7] Though they had little else in common, all but seven of the seventy-two adults had some connection with the Seventh Day Adventist Church, a denomination of 8 million members whose biblical fundamentalism is overlaid with a series of highly idiosyncratic beliefs about the role of Christ and the shape of history. This has much to do with the origins of Adventism, which was born during the night of the Great Disappointment, 22–23 October 1844, when the resurrected Christ failed to appear to William Miller's disciples. One of them, a farmer called Hiram Edson, left the vigil to pray in a barn, where he was given a vision which explained why the Lord had not returned: a great event had indeed taken place, not on earth but in heaven, where Jesus had begun 'the Investigative Judgement of the dead' in preparation for his return to judge the living.

Edson's vision was developed and popularised by the unlikely figure of Ellen G. White, a stern-faced housewife who had been a sickly teenager at the time of the Disappointment. 'Sister White' fused the Investigative Judgement with the unorthodox sabbatarianism of a Boston sea captain, Joseph Bates, who taught that Christians should observe the Jewish sabbath. To this mixture she added a vast body of new teachings, many of them concerned with diet and health: Mrs White regarded meat-eating with horror and battled heroically against her own addiction to Southern fried chicken. She was also passionately opposed to masturbation. By the time she died, at the age of eighty-eight, she had experienced 300 visions and published more writings than any woman in history. As a result, Seventh Day Adventism acquired a *magisterium* of labyrinthine complexity, little of which, thankfully, is relevant to the story of Waco.

But two ideas are of prime importance. The first of them inculcated a profound distrust of civil authority which was inherited by everyone at Mount Carmel. Ellen White taught that the millennium would not take place on American soil, because the nation was in league with the devil. True sabbath-keepers could expect nothing but persecution from a government which would force them to choose between the laws of God and the laws of man. Once, during a trance, Mrs White foresaw that 'in time of trouble, we all fled from the cities and villages, but were pursued by the wicked, who entered the houses of the saints with a sword. They raised the sword to kill us, but it broke, and fell as powerless as a straw.'[8] During the Waco siege, Koresh's followers believed this prophecy was about to be fulfilled. (To this day, incidentally, millions of mainstream Adventists try to minimise their contacts with civil authorities: they do not regard them as exclusively satanic, as do their distant cousins the Jehovah's Witnesses, but their distrust of politics is sufficiently great to keep them out of the Religious Right coalition.) The second doctrine relevant to the Waco episode is that of a gradual revelation of God's purpose throughout history. In Adventism, the teachings of Jesus are in no sense the last word: they are clarified and even superseded by the pronouncements of subsequent prophets such as William Miller and Ellen White. But this evolution of doctrines is matched by the degeneration of the world, whose inhabitants become progressively more debased as they yield to Satan.

In retrospect, it is not difficult to find the germ of many of David Koresh's ideas in these teachings. Adventism adds a new twist to the traditional mistrust of government by declaring that it is in the nature of all governments to persecute believers. And its concept of a prophetic chain extending 'from eternity in the future' leaves room for future prophets, whose task will be to evolve doctrine further by deciphering parts of the bible whose true meaning has remained obscure. This is precisely what David Koresh sought to do with the opening of the seals in the Book of Revelation. He did so as a self-proclaimed 'sinful messiah', whose own failings set him apart from previous prophets; but this sinfulness was entirely appropriate, because it coincided with the falling trajectory of human morality first observed by Ellen White. It would be unfair, however, to lay any of the blame for Waco at the door of the Seventh Day Adventist Church. Although Koresh and his followers regarded themselves as authentic Adventists – to the extent of constantly pestering members of the local mainstream congregation to recognise the truth of their claims – they belonged to a tradition which the Church leadership had condemned as heretical more than fifty years earlier.

Mount Carmel was founded by Victor Houteff, a Bulgarian-born washing-machine salesman who had joined the Seventh Day Adventists in 1918, attracted by their clean-living habits and literal interpretation of the bible. He became a teacher at an SDA school in Los Angeles, where he began to meditate on the End-time. Houteff believed that much of scripture was written in a secret code which only he could decipher. He was also obsessed by the horrors of the apocalypse and the imminent return of Christ, themes which he came to believe were not sufficiently stressed by the Adventist leadership. By 1930 he had drawn up his own statement of belief; he demanded changes in SDA doctrine and was forcibly ejected from Church meetings. Convinced that the end would come within a year or two, he left California in 1935 with a dozen families who settled on land he had bought near Waco, Texas. He named it Mount Carmel, in honour of the place where

Elijah fought with Baal, and settled down to wait for the apocalypse.

The sect did not exactly prosper, but it managed well enough: a visitor in 1937 wrote that 'one of the most remarkable things about this place is the cheerful attitude of practically all, both young and old, toward the inconveniences which go with pioneering . . . It should ever be kept in mind that the very name, "Mt. Carmel", indicates a place where we are being severely tested as to whether we will serve God or Baal.'[9] Like generations of millenarian believers before him, Houteff was thrilled by the prospect of the Jews returning to Palestine. In 1942, convinced that King David's regal dominion was about to be restored, he renamed his group the Davidians in preparation for the ingathering of the 144,000 faithful and the Second Coming. Houteff did not set a firm apocalyptic deadline but tried to keep his followers in a state of perpetual readiness for the End: a clock in the main building at Mount Carmel was permanently set to eleven o'clock as a reminder that time was nearing its conclusion and that the Davidians were to be instrumental in inaugurating the last stages of history.

The history of the Davidians from Houteff's death in 1955 until Vernon Howell seized control in the late 1980s is of one of decline punctuated, but not arrested, by occasional power struggles. In 1957 the hard-up Davidians were forced to move to another site, the one made famous by the siege, and it was here, on 22 April 1959, that hundreds of Davidians and apocalyptic believers gathered to await the fulfilment of a prophecy issued by Houteff's widow Florence. According to Mrs Houteff, this was the day on which the faithful would be slaughtered, resurrected and carried up to heaven. Her prediction was broadcast around the United States, and a large crowd gathered outside Mount Carmel, some of them pitching tents. When the appointed hour passed, according to a journalist, 'it was a bit pitiful to view the massive, collective disappointment. Of the thousands there, more or less, only one person was relieved. Me.'[10]

The next few years saw a series of court cases brought by former Davidians claiming land and money accumulated by the group, and the establishment of splinter groups. The most significant of these was led by Ben Roden, who called his following the Branch Davidians. Although Roden took control of Mount Carmel his real interest was in leading Davidians back to the Holy Land; a few families were even despatched there, and he had some success in attracting disaffected Adventists from around the world to Mount Carmel. After his death in 1978 leadership passed to his widow Lois, who added a twist of her own to the sect's doctrine: the Holy Spirit, she announced, was the female component of the Trinity. Following her death in 1986, the leadership briefly passed to her son George, a shambling, disturbed individual with few admirers. But by this stage there was a far more powerful figure on the scene: Vernon Howell, a semi-literate rock guitarist with a fantastically detailed knowledge of the bible and an overwhelming urge to uncover its secrets.

Vernon Howell, it has been suggested, 'put oxygen – or maybe ammonia – into the nose of an asphyxiating sect'.[11] He was, by any standards, a highly unusual personality. The description 'charismatic', employed by many commentators, somehow misses the point: he had an ability to preach extempore for hours at a time, but in a slangy, conversational style not normally associated with self-styled messiahs. Visitors to Mount Carmel expecting a wild-eyed prophet were often surprised by his casual manner. A sign over the dining hall read: 'This is not a restaurant. If you don't like the food, f.u.', a message which seemed to sum up Howell's contemptuous attitude towards many of his disciples. Rising hours later than everyone else, he would drag everyone into the lecture hall to listen to a homily lasting until the small hours; as he spoke, he might munch an ice-cream bar or some other snack forbidden to the faithful, who were forced to follow a vegetarian regime whose rules about food combination changed frequently. Yet they did not seem to mind. Some of Howell's laid-back approach clearly rubbed off on his followers: interviewing survivors for his book *The Ashes of Waco*, the Texas journalist Dick Reavis was surprised to find that they were 'not Bible-beaters or street-corner preachers, either. They did not tell me to snuff my cigarettes, nor urge me "to accept Jesus Christ as your Lord and Saviour". When I asked why they didn't make such appeals, one of them told me, "Well, because what we believe is not so simple that we can explain it in fifteen minutes." '[12]

That is something of an understatement. By the time Vernon Howell had become David Koresh, he had mapped out an apocalyptic theology so intricate that it is unlikely that anyone, himself included, could have given an entirely coherent statement of it. He was still in the process of developing it when he died. Its rambling complexity is partly a function of his personality: it is the work of a suburban redneck with a phenomenal knowledge of scripture and a talent for making the most radical reinterpretation of it sound plausible, at least to his highly suggestible audience. But there is an important element of continuity with the convoluted theology of Ellen White and Koresh's Davidian predecessors. For example: during the siege, Koresh told FBI negotiators that on a trip to Israel in 1985 he had been taken up into the heavens by angelic beings in a sort of celestial flying saucer, a 'spaceship' that 'travels by light, the refraction of light'. To the FBI, this must have been confirmation that they were dealing with a madman who incorporated his own UFO fantasies into his theology. In fact, as Dick Reavis has pointed out, Koresh's vision, however bizarre, was in line with Davidian tradition: both Victor Houteff and Ben Roden had stated their belief in flying saucers, basing their arguments on Old Testament accounts of the movement of angels around the heavens. Roden's widow Lois had discovered that there was precedent for this belief in Hebrew folklore: a succession of ancient Jewish visionaries had believed themselves carried up to heaven and back in a Throne-chariot attended by warrior angels called a Merkabeh. Koresh knew of this tradition, and was trying to explain to the FBI men that he, too, had been swept up by the Merkabeh. And having embarked, perhaps reluctantly, on the story, Koresh felt compelled to finish it. 'I was taken past Orion,' he told the FBI man. 'I went up and found that God was actually [the creator of] an ancient civilisation that was before the world.'[13] This smacks of the cultic milieu, but it also reveals yet again Koresh's debt to Ellen White, whose visions involved her in a great deal of space travel, and who declared that when the Holy City finally descended it would do so through 'the open space in Orion'.

These points are of minor importance, however, compared to another doctrine which David Koresh shared with his predecessors. This was a belief not only that prophecy was being fulfilled in modern times – that was taken for granted – but that the events described in the bible would be re-enacted with contemporary players. The doctrine, which labels the biblical characters as the 'type' and their present-day counterparts as the 'antitype', is by no means confined to Adventists and the Davidians: something very similar lay behind the Pilgrim Fathers' conviction that they were the New Israel. The basis of the Davidians' belief in their chosen status was a passage in the Book of Malachi which, after a description of the Last Day full of the imagery of fire ('the day cometh, that shall burn as an oven'), stated that the Messiah could not arrive until Elijah returned from the dead. Jesus implies in the Gospels that John the Baptist is the resurrected or antitypical Elijah; Victor Houteff believed he was the antitypical Elijah of the Second Coming.

What exactly did David Koresh believe about the End of Time? Unlike White, Houteff and the Rodens, he wrote no books or pamphlets. He was fairly good at persuading Adventists from around the world to come and live at Mount Carmel, but at least until the final showdown he exhibited no great urge to preach his message to the masses. So we have to judge his ideas from one or two documents and the reports of witnesses. From these, there is little doubt that Koresh inherited many of his ideas from his predecessors; even the novel concept of the 'sinful messiah' owes something to Adventist notions about the shape of history. But, despite this continuity, it cannot be denied that life at Mount Carmel after Koresh seized control was significantly different from life before it.

It goes without saying that the community lived in the shadow of the End: it had done so at every stage of its existence.

But Koresh intensified and radicalised this sense of living on the frontiers of time. His understanding of his own role was closer to that of messiah than prophet. He taught that what he called the Christ spirit had appeared at various times – as Melchizedek, then Jesus of Nazareth, and now, finally, as himself. But he enjoyed playing several antitypical roles at once: he took the name 'David' to suggest renewal of the Israelite kingdom, and 'Koresh' to suggest that his role would be that of Cyrus, the Persian king who defeated the Babylonians and allowed the Jews to return to their homeland. (The original Cyrus, incidentally, provided a grant for the rebuilding of the temple – a project which is close to the heart of many Christian End-time believers.)

Above all, David Koresh focussed the attention of the Davidians more clearly than ever before on the inevitability of a titanic apocalyptic struggle between the forces of good and evil. Koresh believed that the prophecy of the 'seven seals' which are opened one after the other in the Book of Revelation was now being fulfilled. The breaking of the first seal brings forth a rider on a white horse carrying a bow, who is given a crown and goes out to conquer: this figure is usually taken to represent Jesus Christ, but Koresh believed it prophesied his own ministry. The second, third and fourth seals bring forth respectively a rider on a red horse who 'takes peace from the earth', a rider on a black horse, and a pale horse ridden by Death. We cannot be sure how seals two to four were interpreted by Koresh, but we do know that by 1992 he was talking in terms of the imminent opening of the fifth seal, which depicts the 'souls of those who had been slain for the word of God' crying out for vengeance. They are told to wait a little longer (a 'little season', in the King James version) until the deaths of fellow brethren who will be killed in the same way. This text was to prove of crucial importance during the siege.

Koresh's understanding of the forces of darkness depicted in Revelation and other biblical texts was far more specific than that of previous Davidian leaders. The idea that the faithful would face a life-and-death choice between obeying the will of God or man was a built-in feature of life at Mount Carmel; but it was not until Koresh's day that it was seen exclusively in terms of violent conflict with the federal government. The question of what lay behind this identification of the government with the forces of destruction is an interesting one. It goes beyond Adventist theology, which despite its demonisation of earthly powers teaches conscientious objection to all warfare; it is far closer in spirit to the right-wing 'survivalist' mentality which had emerged in rural America during the 1970s and 1980s. We shall examine the phenomenon of survivalism later: for the moment, it is sufficient to note that, although it exists in many varieties, all of them draw on a mythology in which 'true believers' – in the bible or the American Way – are pitted against a society which has been hijacked by the evil forces. This mythology would have been familiar to any Texas redneck who, like Koresh, regularly visited gun shows. One wonders at times whether it was the influence of paranoid gun enthusiasts, rather than this own reading of the bible, which led Koresh to rebuild Mount Carmel during the late 1980s as an armed camp. It is never easy to work out Koresh's intentions, not least because he possessed a sense of humour and a gift for self-parody. Was he seriously expecting an armed assault by federal forces? And, if so, is that why he amassed the material for turning large numbers of rifles into machine guns – the act which precipitated the initial raid by the Bureau of Alcohol, Tobacco and Firearms (ATF)?

No one, to date, has provided a completely satisfactory answer to this question; but a clue may lie in the grand-jury testimony of Graeme Craddock, a disciple of Koresh who was summoned to Waco from Australia by a telephone call from Koresh's lieutenant Steve Schneider in March 1992. Schneider told him that the End-time was about to begin and that he should pack his bags for Mount Carmel immediately.[14] Although Craddock obeyed, he was surprised by the news: it contradicted a specific timetable issued by Koresh in 1985, according to which the End-time would begin exactly ten years after his 'coronation' as head of the Davidians that year – in 1995. Why the sudden telescoping of the scenario? 'We were under the understanding that we were about to be investigated by welfare workers,' Craddock told the grand jury, 'and our understanding of the biblical prophecies is that we would undergo a long siege.' In other words, the occupants of Mount Carmel had been prepared for some sort of siege, but not until 1995. But so great was their suspicion of the authorities that it took only the first hint of investigation by welfare workers for them to revise their timetable for the apocalypse.

Even so, it is not safe to assume that a violent showdown was inevitable. The stockpiling of weapons parts at Mount Carmel is not as straightforward a piece of evidence as it first appears. Koresh may have been intending to convert rifles to automatic fire (an illegal activity, since he lacked the necessary permit), or he may have intended simply to undercut local gun dealers by assembling the rifles himself (which would not necessarily have been illegal). Either way, the records of Koresh's extensive dealings with local gun enthusiasts suggest that before 1992 his overriding motive was to make a profit. This does not mean, of course, that Koresh ruled out the possibility of using some of these weapons in an armed conflict with the government which he certainly expected to take place at some stage in the future. But a theological belief in the inevitability of such a conflict is not the same thing as a determination to precipitate one. And the fact remains that, although Koresh and his followers would have sorely tried the patience of any state, the Waco siege began with an armed intervention on the part of the federal authorities, not the Davidians.

It is little wonder that both federal agents and Davidians died during the ATF raid on Mount Carmel on 28 February 1993. In the weeks before the raid, the ATF's clumsy strategy of billeting agents near the compound disguised as highly unconvincing 'students' had given Koresh ample warning that a raid was being planned. And on the morning of the raid itself Mount Carmel had accidentally discovered what was afoot; the agents knew this, but went ahead regardless. Their action, which cost the lives of four of their colleagues, was disastrously ill conceived. It was based on faulty intelligence about the accessibility of weapons in the compound; it lacked the vital element of surprise; and it was of dubious legality, since the search warrant issued for the raid did not authorise forcible entry.

The underlying reason for the bloodshed, however, is that the violent assault on the compound conformed precisely to the Davidians' End-time scenario. This fact explains, if it does not excuse, the use of violence by the Davidians, who believed they were entitled to use any force in resisting the enemy. (The question of who fired the first shot has, however, never been resolved.) It accounts for their absolute determination not to leave Carmel during the fifty-one-day siege. The Davidians' millenarian beliefs are the most important single factor in the drama of Waco; and the authorities' ignorance of these beliefs, which bordered on a determination to ignore them, explains why so many lives were lost.

The history of conflict between embattled millenarian groups and the state is complex, but it teaches one simple lesson: that dramatic demonstrations of force by the authorities provoke instead of intimidate. The point was spelt out in an angry essay written immediately after the siege by Professor Michael Barkun, a world-renowned authority on millenarian belief. He wrote:

> The government's actions almost certainly increased the resolve of those in the compound, subdued the doubters and raised Koresh's stature by in effect validating his predictions. Attempts after the February 28 assault to 'increase the pressure' through such tactics as floodlights and sound bombardment now seem as pathetic as they were counterproductive. They reflect the flawed premise that the Branch Davidians were more interested in calculating costs and benefits than in taking deeply held beliefs to their logical conclusions. Since the government's own actions seemed to support Koresh's teachings, his followers had little incentive to question them.[15]

Barkun, of course, was writing after the event. But the extent of the government's misjudgement was obvious to a number of informed commentators even during the siege. On 11 March 1993, James Dunn of the Baptist Joint Committee and Dean Kelley of the National Council of Churches wrote to President

Clinton begging him to demilitarise the conflict in Waco. 'Threats of vengeance and the mustering of troops and tanks are but proof to the "faithful" that the powers of the world are arrayed against them, evidence of their importance in the cosmic struggle – confirmation of their worst fears and validation of their fondest prophecies,' said the letter. 'Their level of commitment to their faith is higher than most people give to anything and is therefore very threatening to others. To invade a centre of energy of that kind is like sticking a finger in a dynamo. *Whether it explodes or implodes, the result will be tragic for all* [my italics].'[16]

The FBI's failure to heed this warning is compounded by its failure to follow through an initiative by two academics who, after studying the opening of the seals in the Book of Revelation, put forward a plan for ending the siege peacefully. Dr James Tabor, a professor at the University of North Carolina, and Dr J. Phillip Arnold, a former professor at Houston Graduate School of Theology, argued that the siege would end only if the Davidians were persuaded that it was the will of God. Knowing of Koresh's obsession with the seals of the Book of Revelation, they became convinced that the key to the affair lay in the fifth seal, in which the slain martyrs are told 'that they should rest yet for a little season, until their fellow servants also and their brethren, that should be killed as they were, should be fulfilled'.

According to Tabor and Arnold, the ATF raid on 28 February was hailed by the Davidians as the killing of the first martyrs; the rest of the seal would be fulfilled in their eyes only when the remaining faithful at Mount Carmel were killed, after which God would intervene in apocalyptic fury. But if Koresh could be persuaded that God intended the 'little season' to last until after the end of the siege, giving him time to stand trial and then resume a worldwide ministry, then the standoff would end peacefully. After listening to an audiotape of Tabor and Arnold offering their new interpretation of the fifth seal, David Koresh signed a document promising to leave Mount Carmel when he had finished a lengthy written exposition of the seven seals.[17] The existence of this promise is not well known: if the authorities mention it at all, it is usually to dismiss it as worthless in view of Koresh's tendency to alter his negotiating position, and even the theological arguments on which it was based, from one day to the next. Yet we know that Koresh did begin work on his exposition of the seals, and had reached the end of the first seal by the time the government lost patience and sent in the tanks.

The government's decision to attack the compound on 19 April seems to have been partly a response to (still unproven) allegations of child abuse which were being put about during the crisis by the 'anti-cult' movement. Michael Barkun, for one, is convinced that this network of 'cult experts', which is largely made up of apostates from religious groups and members' relatives, bears much of the responsibility for the Waco tragedy. Their 'questionable and highly partisan expertise', he has written, was attractive to the FBI because their hostility to the Davidians mirrored the authorities' own anger and frustration.[18] But another factor may have been even more significant: after weeks of round-the-clock negotiations, the FBI was simply running out of staff qualified to keep up the dialogue. As it was, the negotiators found that talking to bible-quoting fundamentalists was exceptionally stressful. Many of them came from a Catholic background which ill equipped them for on-the-spot exegesis. And they were unfamiliar with religion's ability to drive human behaviour to the point of sacrificing all other loyalties. They reacted by treating the Branch Davidians as they would hijackers and hostage-takers. Hence the sudden, and catastrophic, assault on the compound.

The question of how the blaze started is unlikely ever to be settled. We should remember, though, that not everyone who died was killed by the fire: some two dozen, including Koresh, died from gunshot wounds. Others were crushed to death by debris. The bodies of six women were found dead from smoke inhalation, within feet of an underground escape route which had been blocked by a tank. As for the fire, there is nothing farfetched about the theory that the FBI started it accidentally: the CS gas canisters they shot into Mount Carmel contained a chemical, methylene chloride, which produces flammable vapour–air mixtures in large volumes and is a recognised explosion hazard in a confined space. On the other hand, it is possible to put together a convincing case, based on the Davidians' theology, that David Koresh started it himself. Fire loomed large in the community's images of the Last Battle, as indeed it does in virtually every apocalyptic narrative in the history of mankind. Some authorities maintain that Koresh could not have started the fire because scripture indicates that it will be ignited by heavenly beings, not a human being. But J. Philip Arnold argues that Koresh saw himself in more than human terms: by the end, he identified himself not only as King David and Cyrus, but as the angel of the Book of Revelation.[19] In Chaper 8, verse 5, the text states: 'And the angel took the censer, and filled it with fire of the altar, and cast it into the earth; and there were voices, and thunderings, and lightnings, and an earthquake.' Perhaps, says Arnold, Koresh considered this passage as a prophecy that his last act on earth would be to start an eschatological fire. He may even have had in mind the last words of the first David in the Book of Samuel, which conclude with the phrase 'and they shall be utterly burned with fire in the same place'.

There is a sense in which the origin of the fire is immaterial. Even if Koresh started it, the authorities are not absolved from responsibility for the tragedy. The possibility of Mount Carmel going up in flames was one of many subjects the negotiators discussed with the Davidians during the siege. It sends an authentic shiver up the spine to read the transcripts in which Steve Schneider advises the FBI that if they want to get rid of the bullet holes in the front door which, he claimed, proved that the ATF fired the first shots on 28 February, they should 'burn the place down, kill all the people'. Later, he suggests that if they wanted to end the siege they should 'throw a match to the building, people will have to come out . . . Sometime when you have the chance, read Isaiah 33 about people living in fire and walking through it and coming out surviving.'[20]

There seems little doubt that the Davidians envisaged an end to the drama in which they would either pass through the flames or be consumed by them. They would certainly have been familiar with the story of the Jewish resistance fighters at Masada in AD 72, who set fire to their compound before undergoing a self-inflicted martyrdom. It seems incredible that the authorities were not aware of the appeal of such martyrdom for millenarian believers, nor of the extent to which the violent intervention of 19 April would conform to their eschatological script. As it was, the FBI consulted its own experts – the people who draw up psychological profiles of murderers – who advised them that the risk of self-destruction was slight. For all we know, they were right: most of the deaths may have been accidental. But it is hard to think of a single detail which reveals more about the authorities' attitude to the Davidians than the fact that, when it came to the crunch, they turned to experts not on apocalyptic faith, but on serial killers.

The scale of the Waco tragedy, unprecedented in United States history, placed the Davidians in a different league from the American millennialist communities which in many respects they resembled so closely. Instead, it invited analogies with medieval and sixteenth-century groups whose expectations of bloody conflict turned into a self-fulfilling prophecy as the vastly superior forces of the state bore down on them. One thinks of the Apostolic Brethren in their Alpine valley, waiting for the Last Emperor to slaughter the carnal Church and being drawn into a fatal battle with the authorities at Monte Rebello. One thinks of the siege of Münster in 1535, when militant Anabaptists under a 'king' with messianic delusions were slaughtered by imperial troops. Taborites, Adamites, the peasant followers of Thomas Müntzer – history is full of examples of millenarians who have died by the sword. There is a legend that the earliest Christian millenarian sect, the second-century Montanists of Phrygia, reacted to an imperial decree banning them by shutting themselves in their churches and burning them down.

Inevitably, some analogies with Waco work better than others. But, in most cases where apocalyptic believers perished in a showdown with the authorities, it is fair to assume that they greeted the conflict as an eschatological event: a cleansing ordeal which, whether they survived it physically or not, would ensure their salvation. In this respect, Waco in 1993 is no different from Münster in 1535. And there is undoubtedly something about the figure of David Koresh which suggests these parallels. Although in so many ways a creature of his environment – bible-believing, gun-toting east Texas – there are times when Koresh resembles one of the more earnest millenarian visionaries of the middle ages. His conviction that the unfolding End-time drama corresponded to the opening of the seals of the Book of Revelation may have baffled his FBI interviewers; but it would have been instantly understood by the twelfth-century mystic Anselm of Havelberg, for whom the seals were the basis for the division of the ages of history.[21] At other times, however, rather more sinister parallels come to mind. It is difficult to contemplate the steady inflation of Koresh's spiritual claims during the Waco crisis without being reminded of the way earlier messiah figures lost their grip on reality. Perhaps there is something about the state of being under siege which brings on such *folie de grandeur*. Koresh, who before the ATF raid had merely claimed to represent the 'Christ spirit', said in an interview after the raid that he had been the one who spoke to the woman at the well 2,000 years earlier. He also became the angel of Revelation and, remarkably, signed two of his last letters 'Yahweh Koresh'.[22] All this is sadly reminiscent of Jan Bockelson, the leader of the besieged Anabaptist city of Münster, who on becoming its 'king' declared himself the Messiah of the Last Days with power over all the nations of the earth.

But in attempting to place Waco in the context of state-sanctioned violence against millennial groups we must bear in mind that in many instances the millenarians have brought it on themselves. The experience of living in the Last Days can have the effect of removing all constraints on behaviour: what Richard Landes has called 'the breathtaking violence of the apocalyptic imagination' finds expression, through the medium of antinomian theology, in acts of spectacular cruelty. The millenarians described in *The Pursuit of the Millennium* mostly posed a serious threat to the established order, which destroyed them without compunction or regret.

In contrast, the nature of the threat posed by the Davidians was never clear. They may have been guilty of serious offences, such as the abuse of minors and the manufacture of illegal weapons; then again, they may not. The manner of their deaths seems to have combined elements of mass suicide, punishment by the state and a grotesque accident. There was, and still is, no hint of a consensus of American public opinion about the tragedy. This lack of agreement went far deeper than simple disputes about the burden of responsibility for the tragedy. It produced reactions in ordinary people which, one suspects, were of an entirely different order to those of earlier generations confronted by the violent deaths of millenarian believers. Millions of Americans who could not have identified a single doctrine they held in common with the Davidians found themselves, to their surprise, asking the question: whose side am I on?

Three decades ago the historian Richard Hofstadter delivered a lecture at Oxford on an aspect of American political tradition which previous generations of scholars, if they were aware of it at all, had glossed over in embarrassment. He described 'an old and recurrent mode of expression in our public life which has frequently been linked with movements of suspicious discontent and whose content remains much the same even when it is adopted by men of distinctly different purposes . . . while it comes in waves of different intensity, it appears to be all but ineradicable'.[23] He called this phenomenon 'the paranoid style in American politics'. The characteristics of this style, he said, were similar to the symptoms of clinical paranoia. Both the paranoiac and the spokesman for the paranoid style tended to be aggressive, suspicious, grandiose and apocalyptic in expression. The difference was that the paranoiac felt that a hostile and conspiratorial world was directed specifically against him, while the spokesman found it directed against 'a nation, a culture, a way of life whose fate affects not himself alone but millions of others'.[24]

Hofstadter described a succession of conspiracy theories, whose villains were respectively the secret society of the

Illuminati in the 1790s, freemasons in the 1820s and 1830s, Catholics in the middle decades of the nineteenth century and 'international gold gamblers' in the 1890s. All of these enjoyed the support of folk movements of considerable power and, in one case, a political party. In the words of a Populist manifesto of 1895: 'Every device of treachery, every resource of statecraft, and every artifice known to the secret cabals of the international gold ring are being made use of to deal a blow to the prosperity of the people and the financial and commercial independence of the country.' For 'international gold ring', one could just as easily read freemasonry, the Vatican or, indeed, the Kremlin. One of the chief purposes of Hofstadter's lecture was to demonstrate that the populist anti-Communists of his own generation, from Joe McCarthy to Barry Goldwater, could be best understood in the context of the paranoid tradition. But they, too, reflected the anxieties of 'a small but vocal segment of the public'. The lecture quotes from a story in the *New York Times* of 21 June 1963, giving a sample of current conspiracy theories. They included claims that:

> 35,000 Communist Chinese troops bearing arms and wearing deceptively dyed powder-blue uniforms are poised on the Mexican border, about to invade San Diego; the United States has turned over – or will at any moment – its Army, Navy and Air Force to the command of a Russian colonel in the United Nations; almost every well-known American or free world leader is, in reality, a top Communist agent; a United States Army guerilla-warfare exercise in Georgia, called Water Moccasin III, is in actuality a United Nations operation preparatory to taking over our country.

These are precisely the sort of conspiracy theories to which the *Times* also drew attention in 1995. Indeed, some of them have survived unchanged. A good example is the story about UN troops disguised as US soldiers on exercise, which on the face of it expresses a quintessentially 1990s fear of a post-Communist New World Order; it is interesting to find it circulating, fully formed, at the height of the Cold War. Are we, then, simply witnessing one of the successive waves of paranoia to which Hofstadfer drew attention in 1963? There does not appear to be any significant qualitative difference between the theories of the 1990s and their precursors. They all regard a vast international conspiracy as the motive force in historical events; their currency is 'the birth and death of whole worlds, whole political orders, whole systems of human values'. They present the enemy – whoever it might be – as an 'amoral superman', a master of manipulation whose techniques of seduction rarely fail. And they are apocalyptic: mankind is always at a turning point; time is for ever running out.

It is one thing, however, to demonstrate that America is witnessing a recrudescence of ancient fears; it is quite another to persuade people that therefore nothing unusual or alarming is taking place. It is not just liberals who feel that the paranoid style is penetrating mainstream politics: conservative commentators agree that mistrust of the federal government is running at unprecedented levels. And the question is no longer one of purely academic or psephological interest. It was hatred of the government which inspired the worst act of terrorism in American history: the bombing of the Alfred P. Murrah building in Oklahoma City on 19 April 1995, the second anniversary of the Waco fire, in which over 200 people died. The fact that, as it quickly emerged, the perpetrators of the outrage were isolated figures did little to allay suspicions that a new and terrible strain of ultra-conservative fanaticism had been identified. For it was the Oklahoma bombing which alerted the public to the existence of armed militias in no fewer than thirty-eight states. These groups all invoked the Second Amendment to the Constitution, which states: 'A well regulated Militia being necessary to the security of a free State, the right of the people to keep and bear Arms, shall not be infringed.' But, despite their appeal to this venerable document, none of them dated back more than a couple of years.

Furthermore, although the militias might not have laid the Oklahoma bomb, they subscribed to the bombers' conspiratorial fantasies; so they were guilty by association. The mixture of fear and disgust which the newly discovered militias aroused in the cosmopolitan inhabitants of New York and Washington was reflected in the coverage of the subject in the main East Coast broadsheets, the television networks and, especially, the foreign media. The London *Daily Telegraph* printed a full-page profile of 'The American Fundamentalist', complete with a drawing of an ape-like figure clutching a bazooka. 'He is frustrated and embittered, probably armed and potentially very dangerous,' it read. 'He believes central government to be inherently corrupt, its agents state-sponsored terrorists. He owes no loyalty to his government because he believes in higher ideals and universal truths. He would consider himself deeply religious, yet he may be virulently racist and anti-Semitic . . . He is anti-social and mixes only with his own sort, for he loathes the decadent world he inhabits. He is the modern American fundamentalist.'[25]

It was not long, admittedly, before this caricature was challenged. The militia movement turned out to be far from homogeneous. Many groups had no connection with white supremacists or neo-Nazis. The commander of the 3rd Brigade of the Oklahoma Militia, which covers Oklahoma City, is of Pakistani ancestry. According to Bob Fletcher, spokesman for the Montana Militia, 'if a guy's in a trench shooting, if he's black, Jewish or whatever, if he's shooting the right way then he's on our side.'[26] Some militias, in the words of one respected commentator, were no more than 'defensive clusters of ordinary people seeking to protect constitutional rights against what they see as an abuse of power by Washington'.[27] But it was difficult to draw a line between these legitimate groups and clandestine organisations whose ethos was undoubtedly racist. And it could be argued that even the most law-abiding militia members had, by the very act of signing up for weekend exercises, effectively issued a declaration of war. The anti-racist Mr Fletcher, interviewed in a rock-music magazine in 1995, displayed a loathing of the federal government which put his fellow right-wingers' hatred of other races in the shade. 'Let the enemy be warned,' he announced. 'We have cooperation at every level of the Army, Navy, Marines, at every level up to Admiral . . . We want to know this: Why is the US army creating civilian prison camps within the US bases? . . . In

Michigan they're already going down in the sewers and putting sensors down there in anticipation that the patriots might hide in them.'[28] Fletcher said he had been thinking along these lines for the past ten years. Yet the militia phenomenon itself is of astonishingly recent origin. Groups calling themselves citizens' militias – as opposed to small groups of armed right-wingers, which had been around for many years – do not seem to have existed before 19 April 1993.

The Waco tragedy was clearly an event of immense significance for the militias and their supporters. Its symbolic power derived from many different aspects of the drama: the agonising manner of the victims' deaths; the unforgettable visual impact of the burning compound; the mystery of how the blaze started; and, above all, the almost inexplicable stupidity of the government's handling of the crisis, which positively invited the attentions of conspiracy theorists. Indeed, the latter were already on their guard before Waco as a result of a shocking incident which cast the authorities in a similar light. In 1992, US marshals had shot and killed the wife and son of Randy Weaver, a far-right activist who had withdrawn to his cabin in Ruby Ridge, Idaho after failing to appear in court to answer a charge of selling an illegal sawn-off shotgun. The parallels with Waco were obvious: apocalyptic believers had shut themselves away in the expectation of a fatal assault by the forces of law and order, who had promptly obliged.

But Ruby Ridge and Waco were only catalysts. They inspired the creation of the militias by magnifying fears and confirming suspicions which had been developing for a long time. In the eyes of liberal America, the militias are only the latest addition to a ghastly menagerie of anti-abortion militants, right-wing talk-show hosts and frighteningly effective local activists from the Christian Coalition. Taken as a whole, they present a more insidious threat to liberal notions of tolerance and diversity than either the conservative administrations or the televangelists of the 1980s. As Gary Wills points out, the suspicion that government has become the enemy of freedom crosses ideological lines. The New Revolutionaries, as he calls them, have taken full advantage of this – and the federal authorities have played into their hands, not least in their handling of Waco. In the final analysis, however, the elevation of Hofstadter's paranoid style into something dangerously close to a national mood cannot be explained simply in terms of skilful opportunism or governmental blunders. There are a number of long-term factors to be taken into account which, when considered together, lend powerful support to theories that America is entering a new era of anxiety – but one that is partly based on a rediscovery of its roots.

The first of these factors is the movement of fundamentalist Christians over the last twenty years or so towards the mainstream of American life. The most dramatic evidence of this so far has been the success of the Religious Right in the political arena; but it is by no means the only manifestation of renewed vigour in conservative evangelical circles. The capture of the Southern Baptist convention by biblical inerrantists, the purchase of significant chunks of the entertainment media by born-again Christians and the worldwide spread of American Pentecostalism are part of the same phenomenon.

In the process, apocalyptic belief has also moved closer to the American mainstream than would have seemed possible a couple of decades ago. For the most important characteristic of fundamentalism – that which really sets it apart from other brands of Christianity – is its apocalypticism. Although conservative evangelicals often disagree about the order of the acts in the End-time drama, they are wonderfully secure in their belief that the Second Coming is fast approaching. This conviction is the source of the tremendous vitality of many evangelical churches; and, because the Second Coming will be preceded by the reign of the Antichrist, it also explains their sense of paranoia. Richard Hofstadter was right to emphasise the startling affinities between the paranoid style and apocalyptic belief – the demonisation of opponents, the sense of time running out, and so on. But he stopped short of making a more direct connection between the two. He did not consider the possibility that the paranoia he identified actually derived from apocalyptic belief; that the people who spread scare stories about Catholics, masons, Illuminati and Communists were End-time believers for whom the conspiracy in question formed part of the eschatological drama. The persistence of such belief in the United States rather than Europe surely explains why the paranoid style seems so quintessentially American. (It is much less common in Canada, for example, where apocalyptic Protestantism, the faith of the Pilgrim Fathers, has never been the dominant religious ideology).

Perhaps the reason Hofstadter failed to make the connection is that, at the time he was writing, fundamentalist Christianity, the main repository of End-time belief in the United States, appeared to be a spent force. For most of this century, fundamentalism has operated, partly by choice, on the margins of American culture. Traditionally apolitical and anti-intellectual, its adherents have not shrunk from identifying themselves as 'outsiders' engaged in spiritual warfare with an all-powerful and malevolent enemy.

This changed during the 1970s and 1980, when fundamentalism sprang to life again. It not only entered the political arena but largely abandoned its anti-intellectual stance: the emphasis was on fighting liberal culture on its own terms, by running its own universities, schools, newspapers and television stations. But as Walter Capps has argued in his book *The New Religious Right*, fundamentalism remains in crucial respects a counterculture.[29] Indeed, it learned valuable lessons from the experience of watching its great adversary, the 1960s counterculture, move from the periphery towards the centre of national life and back again. 'Fundies' and hippies even had a certain amount in common: they both took advantage of a disillusion induced by Vietnam, and as a result tended to embrace conspiracy theories which cast the government in the role of villain. And, despite the very different belief systems which originally inspired them, the distinction between the two countercultures has occasinally become blurred. These days not all fundamentalist Christians wear blazers and crewcuts. In his travels round Texas and Oklahoma, a bemused John Weir noted that 'die-hard redneck bigots now look like the long-haired biker hippies killed by die-hard redneck bigots in movies like *Easy Rider*'.[30] Obvious refugees from the 1960s who played in rock bands turned out to be believers in the Beast. This cultural miscegenation, which is typical of the cultic milieu, is clearly relevant to someone like David Koresh, and also to the right-wing survivalist communities which live alongside genuine hippies in places like Idaho and Washington state.

Even mainstream fundamentalism, for all its successes, continues to identify with the 'outsider'. Conservative evangelicals have woken up to the fact that they operate most effectively by exploiting individual grievances at a local level. They have learned from the failure of their attempt to capture the centre – the presidential campaign of Pat Robertson in 1988 – and have been painstakingly assembling a new power-base at the level of city councils, school boards and state government. This bottom-up strategy means that the standard-bearers of the Religious Right have become a far more disparate group than during the televangelist era. Hence the penetration of mainstream politics – albeit only at state level and below – by conspiracy theorists such as Colorado state senator Charles Duke, who believes the government had 'the motive, the means and the opportunity' to plant the Oklahoma bomb.[31] Duke's opinions, it should be said, are extreme even by the standards of the Religious Right; but we should not underestimate the degree of tolerance which is afforded to these views in respectable fundamentalist circles.

The mythology of the God-fearing outsider, an 'authentic' American who inhabits the wilderness, is afforded huge respect by suburban born-again Christians. Many of them are enthusiastic supporters of the gun lobby. This support derives, in part unconsciously, from their theology. Millions of fundamentalist Christians believe that the final confrontation between the forces of God and Satan will begin in their lifetimes; and, although most of them hope they will be plucked up to heaven before the battle starts, they are still unhappy at the prospect of Christians being disarmed by a government which may well be under the control of the enemy. This line of thinking explains the fundamentalists' strong support for the militia movement, which in their eyes served the dual purpose of reconnecting

Americans with their historic roots while also preparing them for the apocalyptic battle to come. It also explains why millions of bible-believing Christians identified so strongly with the Davidians, whose theology was far removed from fundamentalist orthodoxy but whose determination to fight to the last against an all-powerful enemy appealed to their deepest instincts.

The second long-term factor which has contributed to the new mood is the collapse of Communism and, in particular, the way the Religious Right has reacted to it. In the opinion of some commentators, the fall of the Soviet Union has brought on a national crisis of identity. 'The image of the Soviet Union as monolithic evil held in place the image of the United States as monolithic virtue,' writes the columnist Lewis Lapham. 'Break the circuit of energy transferred between negative and positive poles, and the two empires dissolve into the waving of sectional or nationalist flags. Lacking the reassurance of a foreign demon, we search our own neighbourhoods for fiends of convincing malevolence and size.'[32] The fundamentalist is likely to be at the forefront of this search; but he still scans the horizon for a truly global conspiracy. The huge canvases of the Books of Daniel and Revelation compel prophecy believers to think in terms of a drama involving whole nations. For decades, the existence of a Communist bloc engaged in a manichean struggle with the free world made this task ridiculously easy. Its collapse has forced fundamentalists to adopt less straightforward models, in which America's position in the vanguard of the forces of righteousness, and its ability to resist the wiles of the Antichrist, can no longer be taken for granted. The old notion of a takeover of the United States by the agents of a New World Order has been dusted down and given new specifications. This process was accelerated by the fact that President Bush, in an ill-advised moment, actually used the phrase 'new world order', thereby wiping out in a matter of seconds any advantage which he had gained from years of patently insincere cultivation of the born-again constituency. It was a slip Ronald Reagan would not have made.

The early 1990s were awkward years for American fundamentalists. It has not proved easy to find an adequate
replacement for an End-time theology which invested the fight
against Communism with prophetic significance. The problem
is well illustrated by the figure of Pat Robertson, who, although
the architect of the dynamic new strategy of building local
power-bases, must also take some of the responsibility for the
reversion to old-fashioned paranoia. Robertson's book of post-
Communist eschatology, called, inevitably, *The New World
Order*, thrashes about wildly in search of satisfactory villains
and ends up with a variation on an ancient theme. 'Can it be
that the phrase *the new world order* means something entirely
different to the inner circle of a secret society than it does to the
ordinary person?' asks Robertson. 'Indeed, it may be that men
of goodwill like Woodrow Wilson, Jimmy Carter, and George
Bush, who sincerely want a larger community of nations living
at peace in our world, are in reality unknowingly and
unwittingly carrying out the mission and mouthing the phrases
of a tightly knit cabal whose goal is nothing less than a new
order for the human race under the domination of Lucifer and
his followers.'[33] For over 200 years, it turns out, this cabal, its
successors and their converts, have worked ceaselessly to bring
about this new world. But who are the members of this cabal?
Robertson replies by leading his readers on a grand tour of
American conspiracy theories which takes in every bogeyman
mentioned by Hofstadter bar the Jesuits. It begins with 'a small
secret society called the Order of the Illuminati' who, says
Robertson, first gained control of the freemasons and then
proceeded, through the agency of bankers who just happened to
be Jews, to set in motion both the French and Russian
revolutions. He goes on to suggest (without quite committing
himself) that the Cold War, the collapse of Communism and
the Gulf War could all have been engineered in order to
promote globalism and to make money for 'monopoly bankers'
and their masters, the Illuminati.

In an article in the *New York Review of Books* in 1994, the
conservative writer Michael Lind argued that the views
expressed in *The New World Order* had little to do with

ordinary evangelical Protestant theology. 'They are rooted, rather, in the underground literature of far-right populism that purports to interpret world history as dominated by Jews, Freemasons and "international bankers",' he said.[34] Maybe so: but that is the direction in which the Religious Right is moving. Indeed, Lind reluctantly acknowledged as much. 'Not since Father Coughlin', he wrote, 'has a prominent white American so boldly and unapologetically blamed the disasters of modern world history on the machinations of international high finance in general and on a few influential Jews in particular. And not since Huey Long, with his Share Our Wealth movement, has there been a radical populist movement as powerful in American politics as Robertson's Christian Coalition.'

Like Coughlin and Long, the Coalition has appeared on the scene at a time of huge upheaval and uncertainty in the domestic life of the nation. The crisis is less severe than in the 1930s, but we should not underestimate the intensity of the anxiety felt by the American workforce, especially in those industries which are hastily restructuring themselves in the light of the competition from the Far East and the Third World. The erosion of economic security is the third long-term trend which has contributed to the paranoid and apocalyptic quality of America's mood in the 1990s. But it cannot be considered in isolation: it coincides with other trends such as high immigration and family breakdown, which reinforce the sense of economic disintegration. The result is a growing fear that America is 'balkanising into antagonistic ethnic and economic enclaves', as the *Los Angeles Times* recently put it. No section of society is more vulnerable to this process than the working-class and lower-middle-class white-collar workers who now make up around half of those Americans who permanently lose their jobs. They are also, incidentally, the people most likely to be fundamentalist Christians. This is suggestive, for no section of society is better equipped, psychologically, to deal with this process of balkanisation than fundamentalist Christianity. It is, after all, a world which has always thought of itself as an enclave, even if it calls that enclave 'the true America'. The slow unravelling of the economic and social ties which bind together the outside world – the province of the Beast – causes it no distress whatsoever; and even the hardship endured by the faithful can have the sting taken out of it by shifting the blame to the agents of Satan. And if those agents include the federal authorities responsible for managing the economy, then so much the better.

The new technology which has caused this disorientating economic change is in itself a powerful factor contributing to the paranoid mood. We saw in the last chapter how Aum Shinrikyo used every available medium – video films, computer games, electronic bulletin boards – to create an apocalyptic 'virtual reality' for its members. Something rather similar is happening in America, though the prophecy believers and conspiracy theorists are of course free to assemble the constituent elements themselves. As in Japan, readily accessible information, if sifted and arranged in the right order, makes it easier for the apocalyptic believer to construct a paranoid world-view. It is important to realise that the American far right is made up not of know-nothings but, on the contrary, of information junkies. They spend much of their time combing through newspapers, magazines, legal textbooks and, of course, the bible, for nuggets of information that can be inserted into their chosen scenario; and this activity has become far more productive – and much more fun – since the arrival of the Internet.

It is hard to overestimate the impact of the Internet on the world of prophecy belief and conspiracy theory. The news groups relating to prophecy are among the busiest on the Internet: they receive communications every day from both evangelical Christians and New Agers and, inevitably, have witnessed some bloody engagements between representatives of the two camps. But if there is one activity for which the Internet and computer bulletin boards could have been tailor made it is the circulation of rumours. The instantaneous distribution of material, the facility for exchanging information and, above all, the impossibility of policing the network, all offer an unrivalled opportunity to purveyors of conspiracy theories. They have been quick to seize it: an astonishing number of far-right sympathisers are plugged into the network; and those who are not 'on line' make use of the next best thing, the American Patriot fax network. Dr Stephen O'Leary, a communications professor at the University of Southern California who specialises in apocalyptic rhetoric, believes most of the militias are connected to the Internet. He keeps a daily watch on their postings. 'It is fascinating to observe the organic process which begins when a catchphrase like "New World Order" is tossed about on the Internet,' he says. 'It is like a seed which quickly sprouts into elaborate and detailed scenarios of a dictatorial government of the future.'

O'Leary sees a close analogy between the first computer networks and the first generation of mass printing presses. In both cases, the sudden appearance of a new medium, entirely independent of state control, proved a godsend to those producing material which the state might wish to suppress. In the early sixteenth century, this was bound to take the form of challenges to religious orthodoxy or the political order; extreme apocalyptic beliefs, such as those of the Anabaptists, fitted the bill to perfection because they challenged both. By the late twentieth century, in contrast, one might imagine that the range of 'unacceptable' material would be so great that Christian apocalyptic polemic would form only an insignificant proportion of it. On the contrary: in America, at least, nothing worries the authorities more than communications from millenarians urging fellow believers to take the law into their own hands. It would be an over-simplification, however, to assume that the threat to political order arises directly from apocalyptic belief. In present-day America the equation is often inverted. A nagging grievance against the government can develop – perhaps through the medium of the Internet – into fear of a New World Order, a concept which contains the seed of scenarios in which the End of the World is at hand. The Internet has highlighted a quality of apocalypticism which was already evident in the early Christian era: its ability to take root and flourish in the most unpromising environment.

The final long-term factor that must be taken into account in analysing America's new mood is perhaps the most intriguing and the most difficult to evaluate. It is the effect of the coming millennial anniversary on the national psyche and, especially, on End-time believers. We have already examined the theological significance of the year 2000 for fundamentalist Christians and the New Age movement. Sheer weight of numbers means that the effect of the anniversary within these two groups is likely to be more pronounced in the United States than anywhere else. But we also need to consider to what extent expectations of the new millennium will affect, or are already affecting, American society as a whole. Can one argue, for example, that all the manifestations of violence and paranoia described in this chapter ultimately reflect the approach of the year 2000?

In the aftermath of Waco, many commentators suggested that the authorities should prepare themselves for similar confrontations with millennial believers as the end of the century approached. In some cases, this view appeared to be based purely on the familiar confusion between the theological and calendar millennia – that is, the thousand-year reign of the saints and the thousand years which will end with the twentieth century. The assumption was that nothing excites millenarians like the dawn of a millennium; therefore, there will be other Wacos in the next decade. In fact, not one piece of evidence suggests that the Davidians were drawn to the millennial anniversary of the year 2000: until the ATF moved in, they worked on the assumption that the End-time would begin in 1995, after the tenth anniversary of David Koresh's 'coronation'. This does not mean, however, that there is no danger of violent conflict between armed millenarians and the government occurring in the next few years. The Ruby Ridge and Waco tragedies indicate a new willingness on the part of the authorities to take drastic action against apocalyptic believers who run foul of the law, especially in the sensitive areas of firearms and the treatment of children; and, given that such intervention invariably conforms to a millenarian script, violence is always a possibility. This is especially true of groups known as 'posttribulationists' which believe that they will not be removed from the earth in the Rapture, but must fight their way through the Great Tribulation. And if matters come to a head during the next few years, then the millennial anniversary is very likely to be a factor. As the time draws nearer, the dawn of the third Christian millennium will inevitably feature in apocalyptic scenarios; if the Waco confrontation had occurred five years later, the ever-resourceful Koresh would almost certainly have incorporated it in his highly flexible theology. Any group which expects the End of Time in the near future will find it hard to resist the symbolism of the figure 2000, even if it had not previously shown any interest in millennial arithmetic.

There are already indications that various 'posttribulationist' groups, commonly known as survivalists, are falling under the spell of the coming anniversary. Most of them operate in the wilds of the Pacific North-west, which since the 1970s has provided a refuge for isolated clusters of far-right activists. These break down into three schools of thought. There are a few, mostly elderly, neo-Nazis, admirers of the Third Reich. There are Christian Patriots, who invoke the bible and the Constitution. And there are perhaps 20,000 members of the Christian Identity movement, whose ideology lies somewhere between the Nazis and the Patriots: they believe that white Aryans are the direct descendants of the tribes of Israel, while Jews are the spawn of Satan. The roots of the Christian Patriots and Identity are very different. While the Patriots are essentially fundamentalists, Identity grew out of an eccentric late-nineteenth-century movement called British Israelism, which, as its name suggests, taught that the British were the true Israelites; during the course of this century, it crossed the Atlantic, assumed an American identity and developed a powerful hatred of the Jews. In practice, however, it is not easy to distinguish between Patriots and Identity members. Ideological rigour is not a qualification for joining the scattered communities in the North-west: what matters is a shared sense of the imminence of the Last Days and fear that the world is about to fall into the hands of primal evil. Both the Patriots and Identity are survivalists. Michael Barkun, in his 1994 book about Identity, *Religion and the Racist Right*, has drawn attention to the complex tension between withdrawal and engagement which is created when survivalists withdraw into the wilderness. They go there to escape the world, but also in readiness for a final assault by the forces of evil. And the more completely they withdraw, the more tempted they are to ignore and break the laws governing the world beyond the ramparts, with predictable consequences.[35]

The delicate balance which allows most survivalists to live undisturbed in their rural fastness has never seemed more precarious as the millennial anniversary draws closer. The newest presence in the survivalist world is Lieutenant Colonel James 'Bo' Gritz, a retired Green Beret commander who was cited sixty-two times for valour and was reputedly the model for Rambo. Gritz is selling plots of land in Idaho to survivalists who wish to form a 'covenant community' to stand firm against persecution by a tyrannical government. 'I believe by 1996 we're going to see the noose tightened around people's necks,' he says. The Colonel was briefly associated with ex-Klansman David Duke's 1988 presidential bid and has publicly praised the Christian Identity movement. But, like so many figures on the far right, he is difficult to pigeonhole. He is not, by survivalist standards, especially racist, and has fathered a number of children by a Vietnamese woman. To Gritz, the real enemy is not the Jews but a government under the control of the Antichrist: he is a firm believer in scare stories about new technology which will imprint citizens with the Mark of the Beast. He expects Armageddon soon, but in the Middle East, not America. His newsletter says: 'I highly recommend you secure a place; a refuge in a time of Lot, an ark in a time of Noah. If none of these signs are true, the Bible is false and God is dead; we are still left with a magnificent home in a secure environment to enjoy the days of our lives. Call Jerry . . . for details, plot maps and information.'[36]

The novelist William Vollmann, who interviewed Gritz in 1994, found him more impressive than he had expected. 'He was a soldier,' wrote Vollmann. 'He was a slablike man with big hairy arms and a white mustache, with a twinkle in his eyes like Reagan's. Bo Gritz had the courage to accuse his own government of lies, murder, and racketeering, and because he used to work for that government, because he had something to lose by making those accusations, I respect him for it.'[37] For most of the press, however, the story was a rather simple one, encapsulated by the headlines: 'Rambo gets ready for the End of the World'; 'Bo Gritz sees Armageddon in Idaho'. What seemed to excite the media more than anything was the idea – not actually spelt out by Gritz – that his fears were somehow bound up with the end of the calendar millennium. Just as there would be 'more Wacos' as the year 2000 approached, there would be more figures like Bo Gritz, holed up in their mountain retreats waiting for the end of the world. It was all wonderful material for feature articles about a disturbing, yet faintly comic, aspect of life in the *fin de siècle*. Then the Oklahoma bomb exploded and America discovered its militias.

Just as discussions about Waco often intrude a reference to end-of-millennium fears, so no analysis of the polarisation of American society is complete without the phrase *fin de siècle*. It is as if the mere mention of this mysterious calendrical event is a sufficient explanation for the otherwise incomprehensible paranoia which is gripping the country. The truth, as we have seen, is more complex. There are many reasons for the new mood. The coming anniversary is a factor, especially for the sort of fundamentalist who expects an assault by the government in the next three or four years. It is also a profoundly important theological event for Christian believers and some New Agers, though paranoia is far from being the main emotion it evokes in those circles. In any case, nearly all the unsettling developments we have discussed can be traced back to a period when the third Christian millennium was no more than a distant prospect.

There is, however, an overarching thesis which does appear to tie together all these developments. It was first outlined in 1991 by Professor James Davison Hunter of the University of Virginia in a book called *Culture Wars: The Struggle to Define America*. This charts the emergence, over the course of a century, of a division which runs right through public life in the United States, fracturing political parties, the professions and religious institutions. Across this line are fought the 'Culture Wars' for control of American secular culture. On one side can be found Christian fundamentalists, traditionalist Catholics, Orthodox Jews and conservative Republicans and Democrats; on the other, progressive Protestants, Catholics, Jews and the 'liberal establishment' of politics, the law and academia. Hunter argues that the conceptions of moral authority to be found on either side of the orthodox/progressive breach have more in common with one another than with those of liberals and progressives who technically belong to the same community; that a liberal Jew may have more in common with a civic humanist than with an orthodox Jew, and that a fundamentalist Baptist may feel more comfortable in the company of a conservative Catholic such as Patrick Buchanan than with a liberal Baptist such as Bill Clinton.[38]

It has not taken long for the term 'Culture Wars' to work its way into public discourse. It is an extremely useful concept. Not only does it provide a framework for analysing battles over abortion, the family, education and the law, it also sheds light on the sense of anxiety which has overcome so many Americans in recent years. That anxiety does not arise from a lack of vision; it arises from the fact that there are, broadly speaking, two visions of a future America, liberal and traditional, and precious little common ground between them. On the contrary, both sides are attempting to force their fellow citizens to adopt new patterns of behaviour, through single-issue legal battles over abortion or gays in the military or all-embracing codes such as political correctness. For those millions of Americans who do not identify with either side, the threat of being caught in the crossfire is a constant source of worry.

The tireless energy which both sides in the Culture Wars display in fighting for these causes derives from their hatred and, above all, ignorance of their opponents. Liberals and conservatives (to use one of many possible sets of labels for the antagonists) regard each other's mental landscapes as enemy territory which exists only to be conquered and destroyed. The cruder the caricature of their opponent, the better for the morale of the troops. The problem, though, is that, on those rare occasions when liberals and conservatives are trying to avoid trouble, they are saddled with these caricatures. Waco is a classic illustration of this. The Davidians and the federal authorities are perhaps unlikely representatives of conservatism and liberalism, but they belong on opposing sides of a Culture War between the traditional and the secular. The ignorance of apocalyptic belief displayed by everyone on the government side from Janet Reno downwards is entirely characteristic of the American liberal establishment. It may well have cost the Davidians their lives. (It is hard not to agree with Eldridge Cleaver, who wrote after the siege that 'the clamouring chorus of civil libertarians, whose shrieks and screams would have been audible clear up on Mars had this event happened under Reagan/Bush, has been strangely quiet. This can only be explained by their pro-Clinton bias and their fawning over Janet Reno, The First Female Attorney General.')[39]

Ruby Ridge, Waco and Oklahoma can be seen as skirmishes in a long-drawn-out conflict, or as earthquakes on a fault line running through the nation. The metaphor is immaterial: what matters is that they are viewed in the context of a widening gulf between conflicting philosophies. In no other nation is this division so clear-cut; but then no other nation owes its very existence to an apocalyptic world-view. The American millennial tradition, which is underpinned by the notion of manichean struggle, sustains and rejuvenates the huge fundamentalist constituency which largely sets the agenda for the 'conservative' side in the Culture Wars. But fundamentalists are not its sole inheritors: despite its distaste for Christian apocalyptic belief, the left has a sense of being engaged in a life-and-death struggle for 'American values' which surely owes something to a millennial inheritance.

There remains the question of the role the dawn of the new millennium will play in this drama. We can predict with confidence that it will galvanise the conservative forces, partly because fundamentalists have such powerful, if ill-defined, expectations of the 2,000th anniversary of Christ's birth. There will be elements in the Religious Right who, expecting the end of the 2,000-year Gospel Age at any moment, will redouble their efforts to bring salvation to the whole nation through the medium of public policy. But the approach of the anniversary will also serve as a reminder to Americans on both sides of the Culture Wars that the 'battle to define America' has so far proved bloody but inconclusive. There is likely to be a terrific struggle to gain the upper hand by the year 2000; there is, after all, a presidential election that year. The psychological effect of the calendar shift is, as ever, a potent and unpredictable factor. All the signs are, however, that the stakes will be raised; and that even non-believers will behave as if winning their particular battle in the Culture Wars will unlock the gates to the thousand-year paradise awaited by the Pilgrim Fathers.

13

The End of Time?

Do whole societies suffer from anxiety at the end of historical eras? The German Protestant theologian Paul Tillich (1886–1965) believed that anxiety rises as civilisations decline. In a series of lectures at Yale in 1952 entitled *The Courage to Be* he argued that there have been three major periods of society-wide anxiety in world history: at the end of the ancient world, at the end of the medieval world, and in his own day, which he placed towards the end of the modern world. At each of these times, said Tillich, mass anxiety took on a distinctive quality. In ancient times it was primarily 'the anxiety of fate and death'. From Alexander until the fall of Rome, men felt so threatened by the prospect of extinction that they searched desperately for a heroic courage that could overcome it. At the end of the medieval period, in contrast, anxiety centred on guilt and condemnation. Symbolised as the 'wrath of God' and intensified by the image of hell, it drove people to try various means of assuaging it, including pilgrimages, devotion to relics and exaggerated participation in masses and penance. But its root causes were sociological: the middle ages were disintegrating as the authority of the state replaced the old rural hierarchy and feudalism gave way to early capitalism. Finally, Tillich saw the immediate postwar years as a period of great anxiety, produced not so much by the experience of war as by victory and peace. Its causes were 'the breakdown of absolutism, the development of liberalism and democracy, the rise of a technical civilization and its own beginning disintegration'; these resulted in what he called 'the anxiety of emptiness and meaninglessness'.[1]

One of Tillich's major concerns was the relationship of individual to collective anxiety. The former is potentially present in every individual, he insisted: it becomes general 'if the accustomed structures of meaning, power, belief and order disintegrate'. This is, of course, nearly identical to what historians and sociologists say about apocalyptic and millenarian belief: that they flourish when social or intellectual structures break down and people become disorientated. They are responses to change and the rate of change; and, since the end of a historical era is essentially a period of accelerated change, it should not be difficult to construct a unified theory of change, anxiety and apocalyptic belief. But in practice, as we noted before, history is not so accommodating. Disorientation is a necessary but not a sufficient condition for the spread of apocalyptic belief: few collective experiences have been as disorientating as the Second World War and the Holocaust, yet no significant millenarian movements were created by them. Belief in the End of the World does not follow the apparently random contours of political and social history, and nor does it possess a clearly identifiable periodicity of its own. If we stare hard enough at the history of the last thousand years, we can perhaps identify traces of unusual activity at the ends of centuries; but we will find ourselves in very deep waters indeed if we try to argue that this is due to anything more than the psychological effect of a calendar change.

There is, in any case, no straightforward link between calendars and belief in the End of Time. To listen to many commentators, one could be forgiven for assuming that the link is clear and simple. People were scared out of their wits at the end of 999; from then on, every century's end has produced collective feelings of anxiety, and these will inevitably surface again, only on a much larger scale, at the end of 1999. But this view of history, which has become alarmingly fashionable in the last few years, does not stand up to close analysis. It goes without saying, of course, that calendars have a profound effect on the psyche. Calendars are among the first human creations; they satisfy a basic human need to measure time which has become progressively more complicated as the calendars themselves have increased in scope and sophistication. But beyond the single year their units of time are necessarily artificial: the decade and the century have no origin in the natural world, other than the ten digits of the human hands. So perhaps we should not be surprised that the phenomenon of human anxiety which gives rise to apocalyptic belief does not respond in a simple mechanistic way to the ends of centuries.

The calendar millennium is admittedly a different proposition: it may be artificial, but it goes back much further in the tribal memory than the century, and its approaching end is a major factor in the current flowering of apocalypticism in the West. But we should not become so distracted by the figure of a thousand, or indeed by the decimal system, that we ignore the powerful influence on our understanding of time of the natural world of the sky and the seasons. It is difficult to grasp the full significance of the millennium unless we put it in the context of common human assumptions about the shape of history; and that shape almost always places the present moment towards the end of a Great Year of three, four or five seasons. As we have seen, this simple rhythm was present throughout the ancient world, and is it detectable in most secular theories of history. It is compelling evidence that most historical schemes have a common origin in the human psyche – and this is as true of Paul Tillich's three periods of anxiety as it is of Daniel's four empires, Joachim's Ages of the Father, Son and Holy Spirit or Marx's four class societies. In the final analysis, Tillich's proposition that peaks of anxiety in Western history coincide with the transition from one era to another is a little too neat to be entirely convincing; more to the point, it leans heavily on a tripartite breakdown of history into ancient, medieval and modern which is just as much a creation of the human imagination as any other scheme.

The sense of humanity's nearness to the end of a Great Year or cycle is not, of course, quite the same thing as apocalyptic belief: it is far older than the notion of a heaven on earth just around the corner. It seems to represent a deep-seated human urge to escape from time which, in the earliest societies, was usually met by dreams of a return to a golden past. Apocalypticism offered a radical change of direction, a move *forward* into a world ruled by the saints in which the enemy had been vanquished. It was therefore rather more specific in its appeal than older systems: it reached out to people experiencing certain kinds of stress, for whom the images of battle with an enemy, punishment of the wicked and eternal reward of the just were irresistible because they gave shape and meaning to their inner conflicts. But we must remember that apocalypticism grew out of earlier systems and, like them, addresses fundamental human concerns. Although in its purest manifestations it is the refuge of an embattled minority, it is not always sharply distinguished from what we regard as the mainstream of Western thought. Its own division of the world into the saved and the unsaved is not matched in practice by a hard and fast distinction between apocalyptic and non-apocalyptic belief.

Modern secular thinkers may be trapped in the Great Year, as it were, by a prehistoric desire to situate mankind towards the end rather than the beginning of time; but they also respond unconsciously to the structures which apocalypticism has built on this foundation. We see this in the way their visions of the future oscillate between Revelation's New Jerusalem and the anarchy and violence of the reign of Antichrist. The contrast between optimistic and pessimistic scenarios is one of the central characteristics of apocalyptic thought; it plays a hugely important role in the history of the twentieth century, though it has not usually taken the form of two schools of thought slugging it out simultaneously. Instead, we have witnessed a lurch from optimism to pessimism: from the utopias of Communism and liberal democracy – often regarded as opposites but united in a belief that they could render war and poverty obsolete – to a sense of impotence and impending doom.

Seen from a distance, the apocalyptic roots of Communism and the more naive formulations of liberal democracy are plainly visible. We wince when we encounter books from the late 1960s such as *The Coming of the Golden Age: a view of the end of progress*, by the once fashionable American social commentator Professor Gunther Stent, which argued that 'the age-old struggle against nature to vanquish poverty is nearly over. It has been a hard fight, won thanks to man's indomitable fighting spirit and the closing of the ranks between the knights of science and technology.'[2] Twenty years later, Francis Fukuyama's celebrated essay *The End of History* was less crudely optimistic but struck an equally confident note of finality. Published in 1989 as Communism in Eastern Europe tottered and fell, it declared that 'as mankind approaches the end of the millennium, the twin crises of authoritarianism and socialist central planning have left only one competitor standing in the ring as an ideology of potentially universal validity: liberal democracy, the doctrine of individual freedom and popular sovereignty'.[3] Although less than a decade has elapsed since Fukuyama wrote these words, it is hard to escape the conclusion that he has already met the fate of all intellectuals who conjure up the End-time in one form or another: he has been overtaken by events.

But what are we to make of the new pessimism of recent books and articles with titles such as *The New Middle Ages, The Great Reckoning* and *The Coming Anarchy*? If they make us feel uncomfortable, it is because their terrifying prognoses have not yet been overtaken by events; indeed, a sense of living on the edge of chaos has become an intellectual orthodoxy of the 1990s. The metaphor of the New Middle Ages, which was invented by the French intellectual Alain Minc, is now employed by specialists in a number of fields (including computer enthusiasts who believe that the emergence of an impregnable 'virtual community' will enable them to shut themselves off from the chaos outside like medieval monks). Minc, like Fukuyama, suggests that civilisation is reaching a state of equilibrium after centuries of progress; but it is one of near anarchy. He argues that during the 1990s parts of the West's cities have become 'grey zones' in which there are no longer any policemen, social workers or even schoolchildren and the only authority is provided by the drug economy.[4] An almost identical point is made by Norman Stone, Professor of Modern History at Oxford University, who believes that the conditions of the fifteenth century, with its robber barons and 'competing leagues of parasites', are being reproduced throughout Europe as nationality gives way to tribalism.[5] Add to this the best-selling books which suggest that the world is about to become as defenceless against mutating viruses as medieval Europe was against the plague, and a nightmarish scenario emerges, 'apocalyptic' in the sense that popular culture understands the term.

But if it is truly an apocalyptic vision – that is, a projection of ancient fears and therefore essentially a product of the imagination – then need we be too alarmed? Some aspects of the nightmare, such as the coming plague, are as tendentious as the frantic prophecies of the Green lobby in the 1980s; apart from anything else, the mantra-like use of the phrase 'as we approach the millennium' suggests that some commentators have themselves succumbed to their favourite condition, Pre-Millennial Tension. Moreover, this is not the first time that intellectuals have predicted a return to the barbarian status quo. Oswald Spengler described 'a new Vikingism' which takes over after 'high history . . . lays itself down weary to sleep. Man becomes a plant again, adhering to the soil, dumb and enduring. The timeless village and the "eternal" peasant reappear, begetting children and burying seed in Mother Earth . . . In the midst of the land lie the old world-cities, empty receptacles of an extinguished soul, in which a historyless mankind slowly nests itself.'[6]

It is, of course, reassuring that such pessimistic visions are not entirely self-sufficient: they are easier to confront if we recognise their debt to apocalypticism and the Great Year. But by doing so we do not entirely rob them of their power to alarm us; for that, we have to see them proved wrong, and the fact that their authors are unconsciously fastening on ancient archetypes is no guarantee that this will happen. As we noted in the case of Aum Shinrikyo, even paranoids have enemies; by the same token, the existence of conspiracy theories does not mean that people do not hatch plots; and fears which are influenced by apocalypticism can be grounded in reality. Consider, for example, a long essay by Robert D. Kaplan which appeared in the *Atlantic Monthly* magazine in 1994. Entitled 'The Coming Anarchy', it paints a picture of the twenty-first century which is almost too terrible to contemplate. It uses the image of an air-conditioned 'stretch limo' in which the educated middle class of the future will travel through the devastated landscape in which most of the world's population lives. It will not be safe to get out of the car. Outside will be 'a rundown, crowded planet of skinhead Cossacks and *juju* warriors, influenced by the worst refuse of Western pop culture and ancient tribal hatreds, and battling over scraps of overused earth in guerrilla conflicts that ripple across continents and intersect in no discernible pattern'.[7] After reading Kaplan's essay, which draws on the author's extensive experience of the Middle East and West Africa, it is hard not to share his conviction that a paradigm is breaking down – the paradigm of the nation state, conceived in the West over a number of centuries and now collapsing in areas of the world as different as central China and Sierra Leone. Its place is being taken not by one set of loyalties but by a whole range of them – cultural, religious, ethnic and tribal. As a result, the nature of war as well as of peace is changing. Kaplan quotes the military historian Martin van Creveld, author of *The Transformation of War*, to the effect that warfare is reverting to a pattern which preceded state conflict. The threefold division of society into government, army and people no longer applies, as the Bosnian conflict illustrates; and, perhaps more significantly, the distinction between war and crime is becoming increasingly blurred.

Whether all this constitutes what Tillich called 'the end of an era' is a matter of opinion; but what is abundantly clear is that the conditions described by Kaplan are conducive to the spread of mass anxiety. As he points out, urban poverty is more destructive of morale than rural poverty; furthermore, even in the most desolate corners of this new landscape contact between, and awareness of, different cultures has sharply increased, making conflict more likely than in the past. Meanwhile, life inside the stretch limo is neither relaxing nor secure. The disorientating effects of sudden prosperity have already made themselves felt in the Far East; and in all developed nations the computer age is destroying the livelihood and self-esteem of the blue-collar worker, to say nothing of the unemployable underclass. A sense of anxiety and dislocation is likely to become almost universal in the next century – unless new structures emerge which are capable of absorbing and harnessing these feelings.

And those structures are indeed emerging; but they are not, for the most part, the harmonious local communities dreamt of by political philosophers. The structures are held together by shared religious allegiance, and inspired more by revealed truth than by reason. They range in size from tiny communities of two or three believers to state-wide theocracies. The most successful of them are robust enough to hold together fragile societies or to overturn the political order: militant Islam is the classic example, though the spread of Hindu and Buddhist religious nationalism throughout the Third World is producing others. As for fundamentalist Christianity, its political ambitions are less far-reaching than those of Islam, but its functions are similar: it provides a conversion experience and a tight framework of belief and daily living for people who might otherwise find themselves overwhelmed by social and economic change. Indeed, both Islam and born-again Christianity benefit enormously from the social fragmentation which is undermining liberal democracy. They are, after all, hostile to the liberal order; not because they feel threatened by it, but because their stark division of the world into the saved and unsaved is incompatible with liberal notions of tolerance and diversity. It is, however, compatible with the dynamics of apocalyptic faith. This is not to say that End-time belief is the sole driving force behind the worldwide advance of fundamentalism; that would be a gross over-simplification. But both militant Islam and conservative evangelicalism can do something which political ideology has lost the power to do: they can persuade people that the world may yet be miraculously transformed.

As we have seen, apocalyptic belief tends to flourish at times and in places where the familiar order is threatened. This can be the order of society, fragmented by an earthquake or a depression, or the order of an individual's life, destroyed by the death of a loved one or failure in an examination: it cannot be stressed too strongly that there is no simple formula by which the appeal of End-time belief can be measured and predicted. Nor is there a single point in any belief system – Evangelical, Catholic, Marxist, Islamic, New Age – at which conventional belief becomes apocalyptic. That said, however, classic millenarians – people who live in daily expectation of doomsday or a new age – clearly occupy one end of a spectrum. Their faith is totally absorbing: it completely reshapes their sense of time and their relationship to the rest of humanity; it often effects a dramatic personality change; and in most cases it must be experienced in a highly controlled environment. So it is hardly surprising that only a tiny minority of people join doomsday cults. Although, in theory, almost anyone can be turned into a wild-eyed millenarian by a combination of circumstances, they tend to be highly unusual circumstances.

There are, however, many less extreme varieties of End-time belief which are accessible to large numbers of people; indeed, their appeal seems to be growing. And there are larger issues at stake than the approach of a calendar millennium, important though that has been as a catalyst. The simultaneous growth of evangelical Christianity and the New Age has occurred at a time of irreversible cultural, social and economic change, in which ancient spiritual monopolies have been broken for ever while computer technology is destroying patterns of employment and community dating back to the industrial revolution. No secular ideology is capable of restoring the status quo or of guaranteeing stable growth; even the laws of physics are no longer immutable. Never before have people been confronted by such choices or such uncertainty; never before have the uneducated been at such a disadvantage. Yet the technology which has unravelled the social fabric is, paradoxically, enabling many people to take refuge in apocalyptic fantasies. The remarkable versatility of End-time faith, which we have noted many times, has never been more apparent than in its alliance with computer technology. Thanks to bulletin boards and the Internet, it is only too easy to trawl the cultic milieu and to experience the artificial intimacy which is so important for the maintenance of apocalyptic belief.

We must not, however, become so distracted by the ways in which End-time believers withdraw from the world, or turn violently against it, that we ignore their often vigorous contribution to society. Many successful apocalyptic groups manage to achieve a precarious balance between withdrawal and engagement, and between the conflicting impulses to shun believers and to win converts. At the same time they try to steer a course between conventional ideals of peace and charity which have popular appeal but have lost their power to shock, and doctrines of the End which are thrillingly dramatic but too fantastic to be easily assimilated. Fundamentalist Christianity is particularly good at negotiating these straits. Much of its energy is devoted to closing the credibility gap associated with such exotic ideas as the Rapture and Armageddon. It does so in many different ways: by investing unlimited authority in a highly partial reading of the bible, by surrounding the convert with fellow believers, and also – though this is not immediately apparent – by allowing the faithful to view the prophecies of the Last Days through the prism of their own personal expectations. (Remember that the fundamentalists interviewed by Charles Strozier tailored their eschatological beliefs to their own life expectancy.) And this last point is in many ways the secret of its success, and that of all large-scale apocalyptic belief systems.

End-time belief addresses not only the anxieties of everyday life, but the human condition itself. There is a powerful confluence between apocalyptic belief and the universal human experience, and as a result it often fits easily into the personal horizon of the individual. The sense of time accelerating, which surfaces again and again in eschatology, corresponds to the perceptions of most human beings as they get older; we feel that time really does speed up, though we realise that this acceleration is purely subjective. Furthermore, when we look back at this century we are struck by what looks like an increase in the rate of change in societies everywhere; and this observation, which we believe to be objective, breaks down our resistance to theories which suggest that we are moving inexorably towards a crisis. The development of nuclear weapons and the Third World's slide into anarchy have lent a new credibility to the apocalyptic nightmare; and, in a contrast worthy of the Book of Revelation, hundreds of millions of people are enjoying a level of material comfort which is without precedent in history. Yet almost no one feels confident about the future. On the contrary, it seems that individual anxiety has becomes collective, just as Tillich said it would at the end of an era – which is precisely where we feel we stand.

But which comes first: anxiety or the sense of an approaching end? The answer is that this is a false dichotomy, as Tillich well understood. He defined anxiety as a universal awareness of mortality which can be dealt with in many ways, not least by transmuting it into fear, a more manageable emotion which attaches itself to specific objects or situations. But it can never be conquered: it can no more be argued away than death itself. And it is this which ultimately explains the persistence of apocalyptic belief. Its prophecies of the End resonate with the human consciousness of death. It feeds on this anxiety; it even alleviates it by conjuring up horrifying but convenient objects of fear. And it has grasped a crucial point about the human understanding of time, which is that it is always distorted by the prospect of death. The belief that mankind has reached the crucial moment in its history reflects an unwillingness to come to terms with the transience of human life and achievements. Our urge to celebrate the passing of time fails to conceal an even deeper urge to escape from it. This is why our celebrations of the year 2000 will have a slightly desperate and bittersweet quality to them; as Sigmund Freud said in 1900, the only thing we know for certain about the new century is that we shall die in it. If apocalyptic groups have prospered during the 1990s, it is partly because they can smell the anxiety that lies behind our confused feelings about the millennium. The chances are that the hopes and fears associated with the great anniversary will subside remarkably quickly after the event; but belief in collective death and rebirth will survive for as long as human beings face the inevitability of their own personal apocalypse.

Epilogue

Just before Easter 1997, a comet appeared in the night sky. Like the comet of the year 1000, it was interpreted by some people as a thrilling portent of the Last Days. But, unlike the monks of Lotharingia, members of the San Diego-based UFO cult Heaven's Gate did not contemplate the End in silent prayer. Instead, thirty-nine of them calmly killed themselves, convinced that in so doing they had not only ascended to a higher level of existence in another galaxy but had escaped a terrifying apocalypse in which the whole earth would be 'spaded under'.

The Heaven's Gate mass suicide is one of the most peculiar episodes in American history. No Hollywood scriptwriter could have devised anything more tragic or more tacky. On March 26, police were called out to the cult's spacious villa in Rancho Santa Fe, one of California's wealthiest residential enclaves. They found the bodies of eighteen men and twenty-one women, all but two laid out on bunk beds and covered by a purple shroud – an interesting detail, since it was the beginning of Holy Week, when images in Catholic churches are draped in penitential purple. Underneath the shrouds, both men and women wore flowing black shirts, black trousers and new Nike trainers. Each body bore identification papers to assist the police; their bags were packed with clothes, and their pockets were filled with five-dollar bills and rolls of quarters. There were even videotaped messages in which cult members explained happily why they were killing themselves: a better world awaited in another galaxy to which they would be transported by a spaceship. But the most gruesome discovery came with the post-mortem, when it emerged that six of the men had been castrated long before their deaths. They included the leader of the group, sixty-five-year-old Marshall Herff Applewhite, a former music teacher who had been involved in a homosexual scandal as a young man and who ever since had regarded the control of sexual urges as the key to enlightenment. Hence the androgynous clothes and the castrations.

Applewhite, it turned out, was very much a veteran of America's New Age fringe: for twenty-five years he had been travelling around the country inviting 'lost sheep' to join him on an intergalactic voyage to a Higher Plane. For thirteen years he had done so in the company of his close companion Bonnie Lu Nettles, a former nurse with a passion for astrology. The two called themselves by toe-curling nicknames such as Tiddly and Wink, Bo and Peep, Nincom and Poop, and, most recently, Do and Ti. These last names survived Nettles' death from cancer in 1985: 'Do' insisted that 'Ti' had merely left her human vehicle and that she would continue to direct the activities of the group from the next level.

In the days following the suicides, a remarkably detailed picture of the group emerged. No millennial group in history has left behind such an exhaustive record of its beliefs and activities. Most of its members were Internet buffs; many designed Web sites for private clients, and since the early days of the network they had been bombarding it with promotional material setting out their fantastic cosmology. After 1995 the material took on a darker and more urgent tone, though it is doubtful whether anyone noticed among the thousands of sci-fi pages on the Internet. Paranoid conspiracy theories began to appear; continuing public indifference was cited as 'the signal to us to begin our preparations to return home'. Finally, the appearance of the Hale-Bopp comet, together with reports that there was a UFO four times the size of earth trailing behind it, was welcomed as a sign that it was time to shed 'earthly containers' and go to the level above, 'what humans call dead'. In the chirpy words of one videotaped disciple, 'I look very, very forward to this next major step of ours, shedding these creatures . . . moving on to the next evolutionary level'.

The crucial question, of course, is how thirty-nine people could be so convinced of their destiny that they could kill themselves in such a premeditated and apparently cheerful fashion, eating apple sauce laced with phenobarbital and then, in some cases, allowing themselves to be finished off with plastic bags over the head. The history of End-time belief provides us with a few parallels, though we should be wary of trying to force them all into the same category: apocalyptic suicides do not follow a simple pattern. At Jonestown, Guyana, in 1978, more than 900 members of the People's Temple died by drinking poisoned Kool-Aid on the orders of Jim Jones; of these a great many were clearly murdered, and the tragedy bears the marks of a last-minute panic brought about by the approach of congressional investigators. At Waco, the Davidians' willingness to undergo death by fire grew out of their understanding of Revelation; on the other hand, none of them would have died if a jittery federal government had not obligingly furnished them with the prophesied onslaught by the forces of evil.

In both Jonestown and Waco, the imagery of Christian martyrdom loomed large. Heaven's Gate had a more original and disturbing understanding of death. Suicide was a treat in store, a great privilege which would enable the cult members to ascend to the Heavenly Kingdom in the sky. By far the closest parallel here is with the Solar Temple, who saw death as the moment of regeneration as 'solar beings' in another dimension beyond Sirius. Interestingly, at about the time that members of Heaven's Gate were making the last preparations for their departure, a small cottage in the French Canadian village of St Casimir burst into flames; inside were five disciples of the Solar Temple. The similarities between the two groups are striking, and seem to point to the emergence of a new strain of apocalypticism, in which UFOs assume a sinister new significance. Could it be that belief in the accessibility of other worlds robs death of its terror, and that, in future, security forces and sociologists of religion should regard the presence of spaceships in apocalyptic cosmology as a possible signpost to mass suicide?

On the other hand, almost nothing in Heaven's Gate's theology was original. On the contrary, it was distinguished by a manic eclecticism which surpassed even that of Aum Shinrikyo. The group's core belief was that the creator spirits of the Heavenly Kingdom had taken over their bodies, which were no more than temporary vessels which would soon be discarded. As Kenneth Woodward argued in *Newsweek* magazine the week after the tragedy, this is strongly reminiscent of Gnosticism, with its radical dualism of body and soul, in which the soul descends from above and takes on the body as a necessary but unworthy container. Moreover, Do's notion of implanted souls is very close to the Mormon doctrine that all human beings begin life as 'spirit children' of heavenly parents; and his science fiction universe often looks suspiciously like that of the Church of Scientology.

As for the coming apocalypse, Do fitted it into a time-frame that borrowed heavily both from Buddhism and from traditions of astrology and theosophy. In one videotape, Do apologises for sounding like a typical New Ager, which indeed he does. His insistence that every two thousand years earth is visited by heavenly 'representatives' at the End of the Age, the last visitor being Jesus Christ, is standard New Age fare. The same could be said of the 'spading under', which Do describes as a 'weeding out of the garden' which will be carried out by the original gardeners, the Kingdom of God. As with Sun Bear and his image of the shaggy dog shaking himself, Do's folksy metaphor should not conceal the fact that he envisages the slaughter of millions. 'The only ones who will survive the recycling', he says, 'are those who have found a teacher who can give them the information they need to leave' the planet.

But the question remains: how could this man persuade thirty-eight of his followers to kill themselves? The answer may lie as much in personalities and circumstances as in do-it-yourself theology. Do's disciples were not, as the media first reported, bright-eyed computer geniuses straight out of college. They were mostly disturbed and lonely middle-aged individuals, a remarkable number of whom had first fallen under Applewhite's sway in the 1970s. Many had drifted in and out of his group; nearly all had cut off relations with their families. Do himself was quick-thinking, witty and autocratic – the sort of charismatic leader who is present whenever millennial groups are inspired to acts of violence or self-destruction. This sort of personality also tends to react with extreme bitterness when he is criticised by the outside world. It is worth noting that both Shoko Asahara and Do stepped up the apocalyptic content of their preaching soon after various publicity stunts backfired; in Do's case, the stunt was a full-page ad in *USA Today* which was vigorously mocked by columnists everywhere. Furthermore, the regime at Rancho Santa Fe was designed to produce the sense of disorientation which is every cult leader's most powerful weapon. At one stage, the group drank nothing but 'master cleanser', a mixture of lemonade, cayenne pepper and maple syrup. Criticism, sensuality, inappropriate curiosity and 'exaggerating vehicular symptoms' were all banned, along with smoking, drinking and (of course) sex. The community rose at four every morning to stare at the heavens where, light years away, their new home awaited.

Yet in other respects the members of Heaven's Gate were as devoted as any teenager to the junk culture surrounding them. As we have noted, all millenarians have to strike a difficult balance in their relations with the outside world. But no group ever has gone about this in such a curious fashion; as one commentator put it, 'they died of kitsch'. In the days before the suicide, Heaven's Gate organised outings to *Star Wars,* San Diego Wild Animal Park and Sea World; after recording their final messages, they all went out for a pizza and watched Mike Leigh's *Secrets and Lies.* Finally, on the last full day of their lives, they visited their favourite restaurant and ate chicken pie and cheesecake. All this might seem perverse behaviour for cultists on the verge of death. What it proves, however, is that 'apocalyptic time' can be created and sustained in the middle of an entertainment-driven popular culture, which instead of intruding reality into the lives of cult members actually furnishes them with the core elements of millenarian belief. Heaven's Gate looked to feature films and television for inspiration rather than for diversion. 'We watch a lot of *Star Trek,* a lot of *Star Wars,*' says one video testimony. 'To us, it's just like . . . training on a holodeck. It's time to put into practice what we have learned.' The implication is clear: for the group's members, and indeed for countless thousands of others from California to Japan, the mysteries of science fiction – alien abductions, UFOs, extraterrestrial spies – provide a machinery for apocalyptic transformation which can no longer be found in established religion. (David Koresh, for all his mastery of biblical exegesis, was obsessed with a 1992 sci-fi film called *The Lawnmower Man,* in which a mentally retarded gardener becomes a genius after his brain is fed with computer software; Koresh believed this was more or less what had happened to him, and he preached interminable sermons about it.)

This fascination with popular culture may also illuminate another aspect of the Heaven's Gate drama, namely its relationship to the calendar. The deaths occurred just as the force-field of the year 2000 was beginning to exert an influence on daily life in the West, yet before any sort of consensus had been reached as to its true meaning. At the time of this writing, attempts by mainstream churches to reclaim the millennium seem doomed to failure by the sheer lack of imagination shown by their leaders; meanwhile, businessmen and politicians have invested heavily in the concept, but the public is not keen to see it take on the cheap neon aura of a marketing device. In such a confused situation, the success of conspiracy-orientated television shows such as *The X-Files* and *Dark Skies* – both Heaven's Gate favourites – has lent new plausibility to the theory of premillennial angst, in which the most important function of the coming anniversary is seen as its capacity to instil fear, both in the general population and among apocalyptic believers.

The disturbingly theatrical tragedy of Rancho Santa Fe fits all too neatly into this view; coming after Waco, the Solar Temple and Aum Shinrikyo, it suggests that we can expect several more of these awful events before the end of the century. But before we shake our heads in disbelief at the infinite gullibility of End-timers, we should perhaps ask who bears the responsibility for this state of affairs. Not the least unsettling aspect of the San Diego suicides is the suspicion that they were somehow a response to prophecies of 'Pre-Millennial Tension' which have been shaped by Hollywood and circulated by the news media. In a society in which so few people know what to make of the year 2000 and yet so many are open to suggestion, film and television supply an audience of millions for apocalyptic dramas whose script they have helped to write. Watching Do's spaced-out disciples smile one last time for the camera, it is difficult to banish the thought that they died not just for their beliefs, but for our amusement.

Notes

Introduction
1. *Byrthferth's Manual*, quoted in Hillel Schwartz, *Century's End: A Cultural History of the Fin de Siècle from the 990s through the 1990s*, Doubleday, 1990, pp. 35–6
2. Richard Landes, *Whilst God Tarried: Disappointed Millennialism and the Genealogy of the Modern West*, Basic Books, NY, pre-publication draft.
3. Hillel Schwartz, 'Millenarianism: an overview', in Eliade (ed.), *The Encyclopaedia of Religion*, vol. 9, New York and London, 1987

1: The Roots of Apocalypse
1. Mircea Eliade, *The Myth of the Eternal Return*, Princeton University Press, 1971, pp. 53–4
2. Chinua Achebe, *Arrow of God*, Heinemann, 1964
3. Nicholas Campion, *The Great Year*, Penguin Arkana, 1994, p. 105
4. ibid., p. 101
5. ibid., p. 99
6. Richard Heinberg, *Memories & Visions of Paradise*, Aquarian Press, 1990, p. 42
7. ibid., p. 47
8. ibid.
9. Campion, op. cit., p. 318
10. Norman Cohn, *Cosmos, Chaos and the World to Come*, Yale, 1993, pp. 98–9
11. ibid., pp. 95–6
12. Eliade, op. cit., p. 134
13. David E. Aune, *Prophecy in Early Christianity and the Ancient Mediterranean World*, Eerdman's, Michigan, 1991, p. 127

14. Campion, op. cit., p. 303
15. David Miller, 'Chiliasm' in *Facing Apocalypse*, Andrews, Bosnak and Goodwin (eds), Spring Publications, Dallas, 1987, p. 13
16. E. J. Bickerman, *Chronology of the Ancient World*, Thames & Hudson, 1980, p. 63
17. Schwartz, *Century's End*, p. 19
18. G. C. Brauer, *The Age of the Soldier Emperors*, Noyes Press, NJ, 1975, p. 4
19. ibid., p. 3
20. ibid., p. 29
21. Richard Landes, 'Lest the Millennium Be Fulfilled: Apocalyptic Expectations and the Pattern of Western Chronography 100–800 CE', in *The Use and Abuse of Eschatology*, V. Werbecke et al. (eds), Leuven University Press, 1988, p. 141
22. Augustine, Letter 199, *Writings of St Augustine*, vol. 12, Fathers of the Church Inc, NY, 1955, p. 387
23. Augustine, quoted in Landes, *Whilst God Tarried*
24. Landes, 'Lest the Millennium', p. 147
25. ibid., p. 183
26. ibid., p. 176
27. ibid., p. 191
28. ibid., p. 192
29. ibid., p. 202

2: The Mystery of the Year 1000

1. Ralph Glaber, *Histories*, Book III, Ch. 3, quoted in Henri Focillon, *The Year 1000*, London, 1970, p. 66. (For the full text of the *Histories*, see *Rodulfus Glaber Opera*, J. France (ed.), Oxford University Press, 1989.)
2. Charles Mackay, *Memoirs of Extraordinary Popular Delusions and the Madness of Crowds*, London, 1852, pp. 257–8
3. Charles Berlitz, *Doomsday 1999 AD*, New York, 1981, pp. 9–12
4. Jules Michelet, *History of France*, Whittaker & Co., 1844, pp. 143–4
5. Ferdinand Lot, 'Le mythe des Terreurs de l'an Mille', *Mercure de France*, 1947, p. 300
6. Abbo, *Liber apologeticus*, quoted in Focillon, op. cit., p. 54
7. Stephen Skinner, *Millennium Prophecies*, Virgin, 1994, p. 69
8. Guy Bois, *The Transformation of the Year One Thousand*, Manchester University Press, 1992, p. 1
9. Felipe Fernández-Armesto, *Millennium: A History of Our Last Thousand Years*, Bantam, 1995, p. 47
10. Christopher Brooke, *Europe in the Central Middle Ages*,

Longman, 1987, p. 8
11. Richard Landes, 'Giant with Feet of Clay: The Arguments against an Apocalyptic Year 1000', Boston University pre-publication draft
12. Glaber, op. cit., Book II, p. 12
13. Conference on the Second Coming organised by Time Ministries at High Leigh, Herts, attended by the author, November 1994
14. Landes, 'Giant with Feet of Clay'
15. Focillon, op. cit., p. 63
16. Glaber, op. cit., Book V, p. 1
17. ibid., Book II, p. 12
18. ibid., Book III, p. 13
19. ibid., Book IV, p. 5
20. ibid., Book IV, pp. 4–6
21. Landes, 'Giant with Feet of Clay'
22. ibid.
23. In Thomas Head and Richard Landes (eds), *The Peace of God: Social Violence and Religious Response in France around the year 1000*, Ithaca and London, 1992
24. ibid.
25. Landes, 'Popular Participation in the Limousin Peace of God', in Head and Landes, op. cit., p. 190
26. Glaber, op. cit., Book IV, p. 5
27. Quoted in H. Daniel-Rops, *The Church in the Dark Ages*, J. M. Dent, 1959, p. 544
28. Thietmar of Merseburg, quoted in Brooke, op. cit., p. 226
29. Schwartz, *Century's End*, p. 28

3: Pursuing the Millennium

1. Bernard McGinn, *Visions of the End: Apocalyptic Traditions in the Middle Ages*, Columbia University Press, 1979, p. 92
2. ibid., p. 35
3. ibid., p. 115
4. Marjorie Reeves, *Joachim of Fiore and the Prophetic Future*, SPCK, 1976, p. 10
5. McGinn, op. cit., p. 208
6. Norman Cohn, *The Pursuit of the Millennium: Revolutionary Millenarians and Mystical Anarchists of the Middle Ages*, Pimlico, 1993, p. 129
7. McGinn, op. cit., p. 152
8. Robert E. Lerner, 'Medieval Prophecy and Religious Dissent', *Past and Present* No. 72, p. 18
9. McGinn, op. cit., p. 173

10. ibid. pp. 174–5
11. ibid. p. 267
12. Reeves, op. cit., p. 85
13. ibid. pp. 88–9
14. ibid. p. 91

4: A New Jerusalem
1. Cohn, *The Pursuit of the Millennium*, p. 270
2. Arise Evans, quoted in Christopher Hill, *The World Turned Upside Down: Radical Ideas During the English Revolution*, Penguin, 1991, p. 93
3. Ruth Bloch, *Visionary Republic: Millennial Themes in American Thought, 1756–1800*, Cambridge University Press, 1985, p. 6
4. See Christopher Hill, *Antichrist in Seventeenth-Century England*, Verso, 1990
5. Keith Thomas, *Religion and the Decline of Magic*, Penguin, 1991, p. 167
6. Hill, *The World Turned Upside Down*, pp. 103–4
7. ibid., p. 322
8. Thomas, op. cit., p. 170
9. B. S. Capp, *The Fifth Monarchy Men*, Faber & Faber, 1972, p. 116
10. ibid., p. 95
11. Christopher Hill, *Some Intellectual Consequences of the English Revolution*, University of Wisconsin Press, 1980, p. 58
12. ibid., p. 59
13. Cotton Mather, *Magnalia Christi Americana*, quoted in Garry Wills, *Under God: Religion and American Politics*, Simon & Schuster, 1990, p. 208
14. Michael Grosso, *The Millennium Myth: Love and Death at the End of Time*, Quest Books, 1995, p. 130
15. Stephen D. O'Leary, *Arguing the Apocalypse: A Theory of Millennial Rhetoric*, Oxford University Press, 1994, p. 105
16. ibid., p. 107
17. ibid., p. 108
18. William H. Alnor, *Soothsayers of the Second Advent*, Fleming H. Revell Co., NJ, 1989, p. 58

5: Fin de Siècle
1. *Fun* magazine, January 1901, p. 22
2. *Atlantic Monthly*, 67, 1891, p. 859
3. Schwartz, *Century's End*, p. 58
4. ibid., p. 93

5. ibid., p. 104
6. ibid., p. 114
7. ibid., p. 141
8. ibid.
9. ibid., p. 143
10. ibid., p. 149
11. ibid., p. 135
12. Reeves, op. cit., p. 93
13. Adrian Gilbert and Maurice Cotterell, *The Mayan Prophecies*, Element, 1995, p. 130
14. Campion, op. cit., p. 425
15. Harold Bloom, *The American Religion*, Simon & Schuster, 1992, p. 61
16. Holbrook Jackson, *The Eighteen Nineties*, Pelican edition, 1939, p. 16
17. ibid., p. 27
18. Karl Beckson, *London in the 1890s: A Cultural History*, W. W. Norton, 1992, p. ix
19. Schwartz, *Century's End*, p. 169
20. Jackson, op. cit., p. 16
21. Beckson, op. cit., p. ix
22. Todd M. Johnson, *Countdown to 1900, AD 2000*, Birmingham, Alabama, 1988, p. 32
23. Nils Bloch-Hoell, *The Pentecostal Movement*, Allen & Unwin, 1964, p. 23
24. Akbar S. Ahmed, *Millennium and Charisma among the Pathans*, London, 1976, p. 109
25. José Maria Bello, *A History of Modern Brazil*, Stamford, 1966, p. 155
26. Mario Vargas Llosa, *The War at the End of the World*, Faber & Faber, 1985, p. 5

6: The Apocalyptic Century

1. J. A. Cramb, *The Origins and Destiny of Imperial Britain*, quoted in Campion, op. cit., p. 437
2. ibid., p. 437
3. Oswald Spengler, *The Decline of the West*, Allen & Unwin, 1934, vol. 2, p. 311
4. Adolf Hitler, *Mein Kampf*, Pimlico, 1992, p. 52
5. Interview with the author, *Sunday Telegraph*, 7 January 1995
6. Campion, op. cit., p. 449
7. ibid., p. 451

7: Thy Kingdom Come

1. The *Independent*, 21 June 1994
2. *The Times*, 2 July 1994
3. Patrick Dixon, *Signs of Revival*, Kingsway, 1994, pp. 258–9
4. Letter from Daniel Rowland to George Whitefield, quoted in Guy Chevreau, *Catch the Fire: The Toronto Blessing*, Marshall Pickering, 1994, p. 209
5. Charles B. Strozier, *Apocalypse: On the Psychology of Fundamentalism in America*, Beacon Press, Boston, 1994, p. 6
6. Alnor, op. cit. p. 29
7. Grant R. Jeffrey, *Armageddon: Appointment with Destiny*, Frontier Research Publications, Toronto, 1988, p. 178
8. Strozier, op. cit., pp. 10–11
9. ibid., p. 117
10. *Mission Frontiers* bulletin of the US Center for World Mission, Pasenda, Ca, May/June 1995
11. ibid., March/April 1995
12. Richard Gott, 'The Latin Conversion', the *Guardian*, 10 June 1995
13. David Martin, *Tongues of Fire: The Explosion of Protestantism in Latin America*, Blackwell, 1990, p. 285
14. Nigel Scotland, *Charismatics and the Next Millennium*, Hodder & Stoughton, 1995, p. 1
15. Roger Forster and John Richard (eds), *Churches That Obey: Taking the Great Commission Seriously*, M Publishing, Carlisle, 1995, p. 104
16. ibid., p. 68
17. ibid., p. 69
18. Irving Hexham, 'The Evangelical Response to the New Age', in James R. Lewis and J. Gordon Melton (eds), *Perspectives on the New Age*, State University of New York Press, 1992, p. 156
19. This disturbing sight was witnessed by the author on a visit to the church in 1991.
20. Graham Kendrick, *Make Way Song Book*, quoted in Scotland, op. cit., p. 121
21. Ian Cotton, *The Hallelujah Revolution: The Rise of the New Christians*, Little, Brown, 1995, p. 85
22. Tom Smail, Andrew Walker and Nigel Wright, *Charismatic Renewal*, SPCK, 1995, p. 162

8: The Great Jubilee

1. Apostolic Letter *Tertio Millennio Adveniente* of His Holiness

Pope John Paul II to the Bishops, Clergy and Lay Faithful on Preparation for the Jubilee of the Year 2000, 1995, IV, pp. 40–55
2. ibid. III, p. 23
3. ibid. II, p. 9
4. ibid. II, p. 10
5. ibid. II, p. 16
6. ibid. III, p. 18
7. ibid. IV, p. 46
8. Thomas W. Petrisko, *Call of the Ages*, Queenship, Santa Barbara, Ca, 1995, p. xxi
9. John Paul II, *Crossing the Threshold of Hope*, Jonathan Cape, 1994, p. 131
10. ibid., p. 221
11. *Queen of Peace*, Pittsburgh Centre for Peace, Spring 1995
12. John Cornwell, *Powers of Darkness, Powers of Light: Travels in Search of the Miraculous and the Demonic*, Viking, 1991, p. 184
13. Petrisko, op. cit., p. 375
14. Desmond Seward, *The Dancing Sun: Journeys to the Miracle Shrines*, Fount, 1994, p. 201
15. Petrisko, op. cit., p. 442
16. Ann Marie Hancock, *Wake Up America!: The Inspirational Story of Marian Apparitions, Healing and Faith in Conyers, Georgia*, Hampton Roads, 1993, p. 76
17. Petrisko, op. cit., p. xxi
18. Janice T. Connell, *The Visions of the Children*, St Martin's Press, NY, 1992, p. 17
19. Petrisko, op. cit., p. 121
20. Ralph Martin, *The Catholic Church at the End of an Age*, Ignatius Press, San Francisco, 1994, p. 31
21. *The Catechism of the Catholic Church*, Geoffrey Chapman, 1994, par. 675, p. 155
22. Petrisko, op. cit., p. 122
23. Morris West, *The Clowns of God*, Coronet Books, 1982, p. 25
24. Skinner, op. cit., p. 75
25. Martin, op. cit., p. 300

9: A New Age

1. Paco Rabanne, *Has the Countdown Begun?*, Souvenir Press, 1994
2. Robert Ellwood, 'How New is the New Age?', in Lewis and Melton, op. cit., p. 59
3. Interview with the author, October 1995
4. Message channelled through Benjamin Creme, *Share International*, June 1995

5. Ruth Montgomery with Joanne Garland, *Ruth Montgomery, Herald of the New Age*, Fawcett Books, NY, pp. 250–74
6. Marilyn Ferguson, *The Aquarian Conspiracy: Personal and Social Transformation in Our Times*, Paladin, 1982, p. 19
7. ibid., p. 30
8. ibid., p. 442
9. Suzanne Riordan, 'Channeling: A New Revelation?', in Lewis and Melton, op. cit., p. 107
10. ibid., p. 123
11. Gilbert and Cotterell, op. cit., pp. 173–7
12. Strozier, op. cit., p. 230
13. Montgomery and Garland, op. cit., p. 267
14. Strozier, op. cit., p. 233
15. ibid., p. 231
16. 'New age religion' in Rosemary Goring (ed.), *Chambers Dictionary of Beliefs and Religions*, 1992, p. 367
17. Strozier, op. cit., p. 230
18. Lewis and Melton, op. cit., p. 205
19. Alnor, op. cit., p. 68
20. Montgomery and Garland, op. cit., p. 264
21. Rabanne, op. cit., p. 181
22. Virginia Essene and Sheldon Nidle, *You Are Becoming a Galactic Human*, S.E.E. Publishing, Santa Clara, Ca, 1994
23. Ferguson, op. cit., pp. 198–9
24. Matthew Kalman and John Murray, 'New-age Nazism', *New Statesman & Society*, 23 June 1995
25. Kalman and Murray, 'The Icke Man Cometh', *New Moon*, November 1995
26. Jean-François Mayer, *The Templars for the Age of Aquarius*, research paper produced for the Centre for Studies on New Religions (CESNUR), Turin
27. ibid.
28. Russell Miller, 'Bonfire of Insanity', *Sunday Times Magazine*, 1 January 1995
29. Document headed 'Transit to the Future', obtained by CESNUR
30. Graham Hancock, *Fingerprints of the Gods*, Heinemann, 1995, p. 492
31. Gilbert and Cotterell, op. cit., p. 211
32. See Jim Schnabel, *Dark White: Aliens, Abductions and the UFO Obsession*, Penguin, 1994, pp. 282–301

10: Seoul: The Apocalyptic City

1. Peter Hillmore, 'Apocalypse Now', the *Observer Magazine*, 25

October 1992
2. Interview with the author, Seoul, May 1995
3. ibid.
4. David Yonggi Cho, *Daniel: Insight on the Life and Dreams of the Prophet from Babylon*, Word Publishing (UK), 1990, p. 31
5. Cho, *Revolution: Visions of Our Ultimate Victory in Christ*, Word, 1991, p. 94
6. Introductory talk for visitors to the Full Gospel Church, May 1995
7. Documents in the files of INFORM (Information on Religious Movements), London School of Economics
8. Interview with the author, Seoul National University, May 1995
9. George D. Chryssides, *The Advent of Sun Myung Moon: The Origins, Beliefs and Practices of the Unification Church*, Macmillan, 1991, p. 90
10. Introductory talk, see footnote 6
11. Survey of South Korea, *The Economist*, 3 June 1995

11: 'A Doom Is Nearing the Land of the Rising Sun'
1. Andrew Marshall, 'The Nazi Nerve Gas Mystery', *Esquire*, April 1995
2. Aum press release, INFORM
3. James Dalrymple, 'The Day Mighty Japan Lost its Nerve', *Sunday Times Magazine*, 13 August 1995
4. 'Terror in the Heart of Japan', *Japan Times* Special Report, July 1995
5. Susumu Shimazono, 'In the Wake of Aum: The Formation and Transformation of a Universe of Belief', *Japanese Journal of Religious Studies*, Spring 1996, p. 395
6. 'Terror in the Heart of Japan'
7. Shimazono, op. cit., p. 397
8. ibid.
9. 'Terror in the Heart of Japan'
10. Shoko Asahara, *A Doom is Nearing the Land of the Rising Sun*, unpublished proof, 1995, p. 71
11. ibid., Introduction
12. Shimazono, op. cit., p. 405
13. ibid., p. 406
14. Sadao Asami, 'New Religions in Japan Today', briefing paper for Foreign Press Centre, Tokyo, April 1995
15. Mark R. Mullins, 'Japan's New Age and Neo-New Religions', in Lewis and Melton, op. cit., p. 236
16. Asami, op. cit.

17. Asahara, op. cit., p. 19
18. ibid., pp. 32–3
19. Ryuko Okawa, *Buddha Speaks: Discourses with the Buddha Incarnate*, IRH Press, Tokyo, 1995, p. 89
20. Shimazono, op. cit., p. 395
21. Erika Cheetham, *The Final Prophecies of Nostradamus*, Futura, 1989, p. 533
22. Trevor Astley, 'The Transformation of a Recent Japanese New Religion: Okawa Ryuho and Kofuku no Kagaku', in *Japanese Journal of Religious Studies*, Spring 1996, p. 377
23. ibid., p. 360
24. ibid., p. 366
25. Ryuho Okawa, *The Laws of the Sun: The Spiritual Laws & History Governing Past, Present & Future*, Element, 1996, p. 16
26. Okawa, *Buddha Speaks*, p. 95
27. Astley, op. cit., p. 363

12: Waco and the Culture Wars

1. *The New York Times*, 6 July 1995
2. Garry Wills, 'The New Revolutionaries', *The New York Review of Books*, 10 August 1995
3. John Weir, 'God, Guns and Country', *Details*, August 1995
4. Charles Nordhoff, *The Communistic Societies of the United States*, Dover, 1996, p. 79
5. ibid., p. 86
6. ibid., p. 132
7. Dick J. Reavis, *The Ashes of Waco: An Investigation*, Simon & Schuster, 1995, p. 49
8. ibid., p. 56
9. ibid., p. 60
10. ibid., p. 62
11. ibid., p. 83
12. ibid., p. 15
13. ibid., p. 96
14. ibid., p. 184
15. Michael Barkun, 'Reflections after Waco: Millennialists and the State', in *From the Ashes*, James Lewis (ed.), Rowman & Littlefield, 1994, p. 44
16. Letter from James Dunn and Dean M. Kelley to President Clinton, in *From the Ashes*, p. 237
17. J. Phillip Arnold, 'The Davidian Dilemma: To Obey God or Man?', *From the Ashes*, p. 23
18. Barkun, op. cit., p. 43

19. Arnold, op. cit., pp. 28–9
20. Reavis, op. cit., p. 271
21. Anselm of Havelburg, *Dialogues*, quoted in McGinn, op. cit., pp. 114–16
22. Arnold, op. cit., p. 29
23. Richard Hofstadter, *The Paranoid Style in American Politics and Other Essays*, University of Chicago Press, 1979, p. 6
24. ibid., p. 4
25. Stephen Robinson, 'The American Fundamentalist', *Daily Telegraph*, 24 April 1995
26. William T. Vollmann, 'Inside the Militia Movement', *Spin*, September 1995
27. Ambrose Evans-Pritchard, 'A Holy War', *Sunday Telegraph*, 23 April 1995
28. Vollmann, op. cit.
29. Walter H. Capps, *The New Religious Right: Piety, Patriotism and Politics*, University of South Carolina Press, 1990, p. 10
30. Weir, op. cit.
31. *The New York Times*, 6 July 1995
32. Lewis Lapham, *Hotel America: Scenes in the Lobby of the Fin-de-Siècle*, Verso, 1995, p. 137
33. Pat Robertson, *The New World Order*, Word Publishing (UK), 1992, p. 37
34. Michael Lind, 'Rev. Robertson's Grand International Conspiracy Theory', *The New York Review of Books*, 2 February 1994
35. Michael Barkun, *Religion and the Racist Right: The Origins of the Christian Identity Movement*, University of North Carolina Press, 1994, pp. 251–2
36. Vollmann, op. cit.
37. ibid.
38. James Davison Hunter, *Culture Wars: The Struggle to Define America*, Basic Books, 1991, pp. 46–7
39. Eldridge Cleaver, 'Waco: Bill Clinton's Bay of Pigs', in *From the Ashes*, p. 236

13: The End of Time?

1. Paul Tillich, *The Courage to Be*, James Nisbet & Co., 1952, pp. 53–9
2. Gunther S. Stent, *The Coming of the Golden Age: a view of the end of progress*, Natural History Press, 1970, p. 127
3. Francis Fukuyama, *The End of History and the Last Man*, The Free Press, 1992, p. 42

Notes

4. Interview for 'The New Middle Ages', BBC2 *Late Show* special report, 1994
5. ibid.
6. Spengler, op. cit., vol 2, p. 435
7. Robert D. Kaplan, 'The Coming Anarchy', *The Atlantic Monthly*, February 1994

Index

American Patriot fax network 314
American Revolution 97
AM I *era mundi* 31, 43, 46
AM II *era mundi* 31, 32, 33, 43
Anabaptism 85, 86, 92, 102, 254, 300, 314
anarchism 68
Anglicans *see* Church of England
animism 268
Annales Ecclesiastici (Baronio) 108
Annales Hildesheimenses 48
Anno Domini calendar *see under* calendar(s)
annual cycle
  and religion 5–6
  and the supernatural 4
Anselm of Havelberg 62–3, 301
Anti-Cavalierisme (Goodwin) 90
anti-nuclear lobby 134
anti-Semitism 130, 215, 305
Antichrist 21–2, 31, 38, 42, 44, 47, 53, 57, 58, 60–6, 72, 78, 79, 80, 83, 88, 90, 92, 94, 97, 98, 114, 129–30, 132, 148, 149, 156, 157, 171, 176, 185, 192, 208, 213, 219, 226, 233, 236, 307, 310, 317, 325
Antiochus Epiphanes, Seleucid King of Syria 16, 17
apocalypse
  biblical 57
  as a cleansing experience 192
  'hard' 199
  medieval 56
  'soft' 199
  timing 224
apocalyptic literature 13–14
apocalypticism
  and AM II 34
  assaults on the social order 72
  Aum Shinrikyo and 221–2, 247, 271
  and Buddhism 256
  and the calendar millennium 324
  and calls for both moderate reform and class hatred 89
  Church authorities' mistrust of 29
  complex role in European history 66
  and concepts of time and history 116
  date-specific 101
  and a dysfunctional society 240
  feeding on uncertainty and disorientation 61
  as a form of rhetoric 72, 74

and fundamentalism 307
as a 'genre born out of crisis' 14
and the Great Week 29
Internet and 314
and invention of the atom bomb 133
Jews and 61, 151
John Paul II and 187, 188
juxtaposition of terror and bliss 58
maintains that mankind is nearing the End of the World xiv
medieval 57, 61
and millenarians xiv
New Age and 196, 197, 203, 209, 221–2
offering a radical change of direction 325
Order of the Solar Temple and 221–2
and political reconstruction 65
and progress 72
supplanting of cyclical theories 78
versatility of 61
volatility 74–5
and Zoroastrianism 15
Apostolic Brethren 67–70, 300
Appalachian Methodists 112
Aquarius Conspiracy, The (Ferguson) 199–202, 215
Aquitaine 48, 49
Archedia Clubs 219, 221
Arguelles, José 208, 209
ark of the covenant 31
Armada 88, 120
Armageddon 21, 148, 150, 157, 180, 209, 222, 233, 236, 242, 245, 249, 260, 262, 263, 264, 273, 317, 318, 331
Armageddon - Appointment with Destiny (Jeffrey) 148–9
Armstrong, Hart 146
Arnold, Dr J. Phillip 297, 299
Arrow of God (Achebe) 4–5
Aryans 316
Asahara, Shoko (Chizuo Matsumoto) 247, 248, 250–4, 255–67, 271–6
ascended masters 195
Ashes of Waco, The (Reavis) 290–1
Assemblies of God 122, 155
Assyria/Assyrians 5, 6
astral projection 202
astrology 90, 91, 145, 271
  and the Great Year 8
  Islamic 115
  New Age and 195, 198, 221, 222

Index

Papal Jubilees 106, 109
papal letters 167
paradigm shift 200, 201, 202, 210
paradise
 nearly universal belief in 9–10
 oldest surviving description 10
Paris Great Exposition (1900) 119
Pathans 123
Patmos 21
Paul, St 20, 21, 23, 57, 101, 102, 144
Paul VI, Pope 180
Peace of God movement 40, 48, 49, 50, 59
Peasants' Revolt (1525) 84
Peckham, London 163
Pedro II, Emperor of Brazil 124
Pentecost 121, 122, 126, 143, 208
Pentecostalism *see under* Christianity
pentobarbital 250
People's Crusade 59, 262
People's Temple 267
Pepys, Samuel 104, 109
Peretti, Frank 160
Persian Empire/Persians 15, 16, 128
Peter, St 30
Petrarch 78
Petrisko, Dr Thomas 183, 186
Philip, Emperor of Rome 27, 28
Philistines 13
Photon Belt 215
Phrygia 28
physics 201
Pierson, Rev. Arthur 121
Pikarts 77
Pilgrim Fathers 95, 96, 97, 128, 282, 292, 308, 321
Pittsburgh Centre for Peace 175–6
Pius X, Pope 188
plague, as an outbreak of erogtism 49–50
Plato 8, 12, 214
Plymouth Brethren 101
poa 266–7
Polish occultists 112
pollution 192
Polybius 25
polygamy 85
Pompeii 19
Pope Patrick (de Rosa) 187
Pope, the
 as the Antichrist 83, 88
 Apostolic Brethren and 67–8
 Taborites and 75

versus the Holy Roman Emperor 72, 73, 210
Popper, Karl 131
pornography 192
Portugal 178
postmillennialism 38, 98, 99, 101, 156, 163
'posttribulationists' 315, 316
'power centres' 208
power evangelism 161
Prague 75, 76
'Pre-Millennial Tension' xi 142, 327
premillennial dispensationalism 101, 102, 149, 156
premillennialism 38, 98, 101, 63
Presbyterians 229
priesthood, and the art of timing 4–5
printing press 87, 314
Proletariat, Dictatorship of 60
Promise Keepers 164–5
Prophecies of St Malachy 187–8, 271
prophecy
 of the Antichrist 79
 deadlines 70, 145
 End-time 57–8, 62
 Gamaleon 73–4
 Hussite reform and 75
 New Age and 196
 'political' 73, 74
 as the preserve of minority groups and individual eccentrics 95
Prophecy of the White King (Lilly) 91
prophetic clock 101, 134, 146
prophetic timetables 90
Protestantism 83, 87, 122, 142, 144, 146, 211, 228
Protestants
 conservative 101, 121, 143
 and Creation date 147
 English millenarian 66
 evangelical 121
 in Latin America 122, 124, 154–7
 liberal 101, 120, 152, 155
 and millennial drama 88–9
 and a New Jerusalem 86
 reformers invoke End-time 74
 and religious apparitions 182
 and a social gospel 101
 in South Korea 229–30, 243
 and tyrannical government 90
Protocols of the Elders of Zion 216

UNIVERSITY PRESS OF NEW ENGLAND
publishes books under its own imprint and is the publisher for
Brandeis University Press, Dartmouth College, Middlebury
College Press, University of New Hampshire, Tufts
University, and Wesleyan University Press.

Library of Congress Cataloging-in-Publication Data

Thompson, Damian, 1962–
    The end of time : faith and fear in the shadow
of the millennium / Damian Thompson.
        p.   cm.
    Includes bibliographical references and index.
    ISBN 0–87451–849–0 (cl.). ISBN 0–87451–880–6 (pa.).
    1. Millennialism—History of doctrines—20th
century. I. Title.
    BT891.T46   1997
    291.2'3 — dc21   97-21661
    ⊗